THE INTERTEXTURE OF
APOCALYPTIC DISCOURSE
IN THE NEW TESTAMENT

Society of Biblical Literature

Symposium Series

Christopher R. Matthews,
Editor

Number 14

The Intertexture of
Apocalyptic Discourse
in the New Testament

THE INTERTEXTURE OF
APOCALYPTIC DISCOURSE
IN THE NEW TESTAMENT

Edited by
Duane F. Watson

Society of Biblical Literature
Atlanta

THE INTERTEXTURE OF
APOCALYPTIC DISCOURSE
IN THE NEW TESTAMENT

Library of Congress Cataloging-in-Publication Data

The intertexture of apocalyptic discourse in the New Testament / edited by Duane F. Watson.
    p. cm. — (Society of Biblical Literature symposium series ; no. 14)
    Includes bibliographical references and indexes.
    ISBN 1-58983-041-5 (alk. paper)
    1. Apocalyptic literature—History and criticism. 2. Bible. N.T.—Criticism, interpretation, etc. 3. Bible. N.T.—Relation to the Old Testament. 4. Bible—Socio-rhetorical criticism. 5. Eschatology—Biblical teaching. I. Watson, Duane Frederick. II. Symposium series (Society of Biblical Literature) ; no. 14.
    BS646 .I58 2002b
    225'.046—dc21   2002011758

10 09 08 07 06 05 04 03 02   5 4 3 2 1

Printed in the United States of America
on acid-free paper

CONTENTS

CONTRIBUTORS

L. Gregory Bloomquist
Associate Professor, Faculty of Theology
Saint Paul University

David A. deSilva
Professor of New Testament and Greek
Ashland Theological Seminary

James Hester
Professor of Religion, Emeritus
University of Redlands

Edith Humphrey
Associate Professor of New Testament
Pittsburgh Theological Seminary

B. J. Oropeza
Most recently of George Fox University
Ph.D., University of Durham

Vernon K. Robbins
Winship Distinguished Research Professor of New Testament and
Comparative Sacred Texts in the Humanities
Emory University and University of Stellenbosch, South Africa

Russell B. Sisson
Associate Professor of Religion and Philosophy
Union College (Barbourville, Kentucky)

Wesley H. Wachob
Senior Minister, Glenn Memorial United Methodist Church, and
Adjunct Associate Professor of New Testament and Ministry,
Candler School of Theology, Emory University, Atlanta, Georgia

Duane F. Watson
Professor of New Testament Studies
Malone College

ABBREVIATIONS

Primary Sources

Ant.	Josephus, *Jewish Antiquities*
Apoc. El. (C)	Coptic *Apcalypse of Elijah*
Apoc. Pet.	*Apocalypse of Peter*
Ascen. Isa.	*Mart. Ascen. Isa.* 6—11
As. Mos.	*Assumption of Moses*
2 Bar.	*2 Baruch (Syriac Apocalypse)*
b. Sanh.	Babylonian Talmud tractate *Sanhedrin*
CD	Cairo Genizah copy of the *Damascus Document*
1 Clem.	*1 Clement*
2 Clem.	*2 Clement*
1 En.	*1 Enoch (Ethiopic Apocalypse)*
2 En.	*2 Enoch (Slavonic Apocalypse)*
Eth. nic.	Aristotle, *Ethica nichomachea*
Exod. Rab.	*Exodus Rabbah*
Gos. Thom.	*Gospel of Thomas*
Herm. *Mand.*	Shepherd of Hermas, *Mandates*
Herm. *Vis.*	Shepherd of Hermas, *Visions*
Hist.	Herodotus, *Historiae*
Hist. eccl.	Eusebius, *Historia ecclesiastica*
Inv.	Cicero, *De inventione rhetorica*
Jub.	*Jubiliees*
L.A.B.	*Liber antiquitatum biblicarum* (Pseudo-Philo)
Lev. Rab.	*Leviticus Rabbah*
Mek.	*Mekilta*
Midr. Pss.	*Midrash Psalms*
Midr. Rab.	*Midrash Rabbah*
m. Sanh.	Mishnah tractate Sanhedrin
Mos.	Philo, *De vita Mosis*
Pol. *Phil.*	Polycarp, *To the Philippians*
Post.	Philo, *De posteritate Caini*
Pss. Sol.	*Psalms of Solomon*
1QH	*Thanksgiving Hymns*
1QM	*War Scroll*
11QMelch	*Melchizedek*
1QpHab	*Pesher Habakkuk*

1QS	*Rule of the Community*
Rhet.	Aristotle, *Rhetorica*
Rhet. Alex.	Anaximenes of Lampsacus, *Rhetorica ad Alexandrum*
Rhet. Her.	*Rhetorica ad Herennium*
Sib. Or.	*Sibylline Oracles*
T. Ab.	*Testament of Abraham*
T. Ash.	*Testament of Asher*
T. Benj.	*Testament of Benjamin*
T. Dan	*Testament of Daniel*
T. Issa.	*Testament of Issachar*
T. Jos.	*Testament of Joseph*
T. Jud.	*Testament of Judah*
T. Levi	*Testament of Levi*
T. Mos.	*Testament of Moses*
T. Napht.	*Testament of Naphtali*
T. Sim.	*Testament of Simeon*
T. Zeb.	*Testament of Zebulun*
Tg. Neof.	*Targum Neofiti*
Tg. Ps.-J.	*Targum Pseudo-Jonathan*
War	Josephus, *Jewish War*
y. Sanh.	Jerusalem Talmud tractate *Sanhedrin*
y. Ta'an	Jerusalem Talmud tractate *Ta'anit*

Secondary Sources

AB	Anchor Bible
ABD	*Anchor Bible Dictionary*. Edited by D. N. Freedman. 6 vols. New York: Doubleday, 1992.
AnBib	Analecta biblica
ANRW	*Aufstieg und Niedergang der römischen Welt*. Edited by H. Temporini and W. Haase. Berlin: de Gruyter, 1972–. Part 2. Principat, 25.6. Edited by Wolfgang Haase. New York: de Gruyter, 1988.
AUSS	*Andrews University Seminary Studies*
BBR	*Bulletin for Biblical Research*
BETL	Bibliotheca ephemeridum theologicarum lovaniensium
Bib	*Biblica*
BibInt	Biblical Interpretation
BibS(N)	Biblische Studien (Neukirchen-Vluyn, 1951–)
BKAT	Biblischer Kommentar, Altes Testament
BR	*Biblical Research*
BT	*The Bible Translator*
BTB	*Biblical Theology Bulletin*
BZ	*Biblische Zeitschrift*

CBQ	*Catholic Biblical Quarterly*
CBQMS	Catholic Biblical Quarterly Monograph Series
ConBNT	Coniectanea biblica, New Testament
CurBS	*Currents in Research: Biblical Studies*
EDNT	*Exegetical Dictionary of the New Testament.* Edited by H. Balz and G. Schneider. 3 vols. Grand Rapids: Eerdmans, 1990–93.
ETL	*Ephemerides theologicae lovanienses*
EvQ	*Evangelical Quarterly*
EvT	*Evangelische Theologie*
ExpTim	*Expository Times*
FAT	Forschungen zum Alten Testament
FB	Forschung zur Bibel
ForTLing	Forum Theologiae Linguisticae
FRLANT	Forschungen zur Religion und Literatur des Alten und Neuen Testaments
GBS	Guides to Biblical Scholarship
HBD	*HarperCollins Bible Dictionary.* Edited by P. J. Achtemeier et al. 2d ed. San Francisco: HarperSanFrancisco, 1996.
HNTC	Harper's New Testament Commentaries
HTR	*Harvard Theological Review*
HUT	Hermeneutische Untersuchungen zur Theologie
IBC	Interpretation: A Bible Commentary for Teaching and Preaching
ICC	International Critical Commentary
IDBSup	*Interpreter's Dictionary of the Bible: Supplementary Volume.* Edited by K. Crim. Nashville: Abingdon, 1976.
Int	*Interpretation*
JBL	*Journal of Biblical Literature*
JSJSup	Supplements to the Journal for the Study of Judaism
JSNT	*Journal for the Study of the New Testament*
JSNTSup	Journal for the Study of the New Testament Supplement Series
JSOTSup	Journal for the Study of the Old Testament Supplement Series
JSPSup	Journal for the Study of the Pseudepigrapha Supplement Series
JSS	*Journal of Semitic Studies*
JTC	*Journal for Theology and the Church*
KEK	Kritisch-exegetischer Kommentar über das Neue Testament
LCL	Loeb Classical Library
LEC	Library of Early Christianity
Neot	*Neotestamentica*

NIB	*The New Interpreter's Bible*
NICNT	New International Commentary on the New Testament
NIGTC	New International Greek Testament Commentary
NovT	*Novum Testamentum*
NovTSup	Supplements to Novum Testamentum
NRT	*La nouvelle revue théologique*
NTS	*New Testament Studies*
OTL	Old Testament Library
OTP	*Old Testament Pseudepigrapha.* Edited by James H. Charlesworth. 2 vols. Garden City, N.Y.: Doubleday, 1983–85.
QJS	*Quarterly Journal of Speech*
RB	*Revue biblique*
RHPR	*Revue d'histoire et de philosophie religieuses*
RTP	*Revue de théologie et de philosophie*
SANT	Studien zum Alten und Neuen Testaments
SB	Sources bibliques
SBL	Society of Biblical Literature
SBLDS	Society of Biblical Literature Dissertation Series
SBLSP	Society of Biblical Literature Seminar Papers
SE	*Studia Evangelica*
Sem	*Semitica*
Semeia	*Semeia*
SHR	Studies in the History of Religions (Supplements to *Numen*)
SNTSMS	Society for New Testament Studies Monograph Series
SSEJC	Studies in Scripture in Early Judaism and Christianity
ST	*Studia theologica*
SWJT	*Southwestern Journal of Theology*
TDNT	*Theological Dictionary of the New Testament.* Edited by G. Kittel and G. Friedrich. Translated by G. W. Bromiley. 10 vols. Grand Rapids: Eerdmans. 1964–76.
TGl	*Theologie und Glaube*
TLZ	*Theologische Literaturzeitung*
TJ	*Trinity Journal*
TS	*Theological Studies*
TynBul	*Tyndale Bulletin*
TZ	*Theologische Zeitschrift*
VT	*Vetus Testamentum*
WBC	Word Biblical Commentary
WMANT	Wissenschaftliche Monographien zum alten und Neuen Testament
WUNT	Wissenschaftliche Untersuchungen zum Neuen Testament
ZNW	*Zeitschrift für die neutestamentliche Wissenschaft*
ZTK	*Zeitschrift für Theologie und Kirche*

All quotations from the Old Testament Apocrypha are from the NRSV. All quotations from the Old Testament Pseudepigrapha are from the *Old Testament Pseudepigrapha* edited by James Charlesworth. All quotations from ancient writers are from the Loeb Classical Library editions.

Introduction

Duane F. Watson

The contributions to this volume were presented in a panel discussion on the topic of "The Intertexture of Apocalyptic Discourse in the New Testament." The panel was part of the program of the Rhetoric and the New Testament Section of the Society of Biblical Literature at the Annual Meeting in Boston in 1999. The steering committee of this section chose the following definition of apocalyptic discourse that was used by all the panelists to guide the discussion and the writing and rewriting of these contributions: "Apocalyptic discourse reconfigures our perception of all regions of time and space, in the world and in the body, in light of the conviction that God will intervene to judge at some time in the future." In addition, another helpful way to define further the nature and components of apocalyptic discourse was used by several contributors:

> *Apocalyptic discourse* refers to the constellation of apocalyptic topics as they function in larger early Jewish and Christian literary and social contexts. Thus, apocalyptic discourse should be treated as a flexible set of resources that early Jews and Christians could employ for a variety of persuasive tasks. Whenever early Jews and Christians appealed to such topics as visions and revelations, heavenly journeys, final catastrophes, and the like, they were using apocalyptic discourse.[1]

Using these definitions, contributors identified apocalyptic discourse and *topoi* in their assigned portions of the New Testament. They then proceeded to identify the intertexture of the apocalyptic discourse. Intertexture involves the use of tradition and texts in a new text and the relationship between the old and the new as meaning is created. It also explores how social and cultural systems provide the meaning in textual composition.[2] In its initial ventures into intertextuality, biblical studies has

---

[1] Greg Carey and L. Gregory Bloomquist, eds., *Vision and Persuasion: Rhetorical Dimensions of Apocalyptic Discourse* (St. Louis: Chalice, 1999), 10.

[2] Resources on intertextuality include Jay Clayton and Eric Rothstein, eds., *Influence and Intertextuality in Literary History* (Madison: University of Wisconsin Press, 1991); John Hollander, *The Figure of Echo: A Mode of Allusion in Milton and After*

concerned itself with borrowing among literary texts, especially the use of the Old Testament in the New Testament. Recently there has been a shift to investigate how tradition is interpreted and reinterpreted by later generations and their texts. The movement is away from prophecy-fulfillment and historical construction to the interaction between traditions and texts as later generations reinterpreted previous texts and traditions in the texts they created.[3] To this is added a growing interest in the influence of the social and cultural world upon the text's creation and how it provides the text meaning.[4]

Many contributors to this volume worked with the understanding that intertexture is "a text's representation of, reference to, and use of phenomena in the 'world' outside the text being interpreted. In other words, the interaction of the language in the text with 'outside' material and physical 'objects,' historical events, texts, customs, values, roles, institutions, and systems."[5] Intertexture is, in other words, those points of intersection within a text with other textual (oral or scribal), social, cultural, or historical worlds that are not the immediate world that is created by the text itself. Intertexture is the intersection of the inner world of the text, which is created by literary and narrative means, with the outer world within which the text developed.[6] Intertextual analysis tries to determine the way the text configures and reconfigures phenomena from the world outside the text.

There are four kinds of intertexture: oral-scribal, cultural, social, and historical. *Oral-scribal intertexture* pertains to oral or written sources, canonical and noncanonical, utilized by a discourse. It also involves *how* these sources were utilized, whether by recitation, recontextualization,

---

(Berkeley and Los Angeles: University of California Press, 1981); Michael Worton and Judith Still, eds., *Intertextuality: Theories and Practices* (Manchester: Manchester University Press, 1990).

[3] Michael Fishbane, *Biblical Interpretation in Ancient Israel* (Oxford: Clarendon, 1985); idem, "Inner Biblical Exegesis: Types and Strategies of Interpretation in Ancient Israel," in *Midrash and Literature* (ed. G. H. Hartmann and S. Budick; New Haven: Yale University Press, 1986), 19–37.

[4] For an overview of intertextuality and biblical studies, see Gail O'Day, "Intertextuality," in *Dictionary of Biblical Interpretation* (ed. John H. Hayes; 2 vols.; Nashville: Abingdon, 1999), 546–48. See also George Aichele and Gary A. Phillips, eds., *Intertextuality and the Bible, Semeia* 69/70 (1995); Craig A. Evans and James A. Sanders, eds., *Paul and the Scriptures of Israel* (JSNTSup 83; SSEJC 1; Sheffield: Sheffield Academic Press, 1993).

[5] Vernon K. Robbins, *Exploring the Texture of Texts: A Guide to Socio-Rhetorical Interpretation* (Valley Forge, Pa.: Trinity Press International), 40.

[6] Ibid.

reconfiguration, narrative amplification, or thematic elaboration.[7] *Cultural intertexture* is a text's interaction with culture through direct reference or allusion and echo, to word and concept patterns, values and codes, and myths.[8] Examination of this interaction with culture helps to determine the self-understanding and stance toward culture reflected in the text, whether affirming, challenging, or reconfiguring. It seeks to delineate how the text interacts with culture and positions itself toward it. *Social intertexture* concerns social knowledge. "Social knowledge is commonly held by all persons of a region, no matter what their particular 'cultural location' may be.... In other words, social knowledge is readily accessible to all people through general interaction, in contrast to cultural knowledge, which must be taught with careful use of language and transmission of specific traditions."[9] Social knowledge includes social roles, social institutions, social codes, and social relationships.[10] The meanings of these are investigated by texts, inscriptions, archaeological data, and the like. *Historical intertexture* concerns events that have occurred at specific times and locations. Knowledge of the social, cultural, and ideological phenomena within an event is needed to interpret the event.[11]

Most of the contributors to this volume have focused on the oral-scribal and cultural intertextures of the apocalyptic discourse in the books of the New Testament that they have examined. As would be expected, oral-scribal intertexture is found with all portions of the Old Testament, either Hebrew or Greek versions, especially the Prophets and Psalms; a plethora of extrabiblical Second Temple Jewish texts; and early Christian materials, particularly from the oral tradition as reflected in the Gospels and Q. Cultural intertexture is found with Jewish tradition familiar to those of Jewish background and Gentiles familiar with that tradition from specific instruction. Cultural intertexture is found also with emerging early Christian tradition as reflected in preaching and teaching. Some secondary ancient Near Eastern cultural intertexture is found as it came through Judaism. Cultural intertexture with Greco-Roman culture is also evident.

Vernon Robbins investigates the interaction between the oral-scribal and cultural intertexture of apocalyptic discourse in the Gospel of Mark,

---

[7] Ibid., 40–58; idem, *The Tapestry of Early Christian Discourse: Rhetoric, Society and Ideology* (London: Routledge, 1996), 97–108.

[8] Robbins, *Exploring the Texture of Texts*, 58–62; idem, *Tapestry of Early Christian Discourse*, 108–15.

[9] Robbins, *Exploring the Texture of Texts*, 62.

[10] Ibid., 62–63; Robbins, *Tapestry of Early Christian Discourse*, 115–18.

[11] Robbins, *Exploring the Texture of Texts*, 63–68; idem, *Tapestry of Early Christian Discourse*, 118–20.

approaching it through Mark's use of *topoi* and enthymematic argumentation. He finds prophetic discourse to be the overall discourse of this Gospel, into which apocalyptic, miracle, wisdom, and suffering-death discourse are interwoven. In 1:1–20 there is oral-scribal intertexture with prophetic literature of the Old Testament, to which is interwoven apocalyptic *topoi* evoking the recognition of apocalyptic patterns of God's activity at the end time and its fulfillment. Mark 1:21–8:26 is dominated by prophetic-miracle discourse with apocalyptic and wisdom *topoi* embedded in it. *Topoi* of wisdom discourse are used to present a public challenge characteristic of prophetic discourse, supported by apocalyptic *topoi* intertwined with miracle discourse. There is cultural intertexture with contemporary *topoi* of apocalyptic discourse used enthymematically, but not oral-scribal intertexture with apocalyptic literature. In 8:27–12:44 suffering-death discourse functions as the centripetal mode within the overall prophetic discourse and is fundamental to Jesus' public argumentation leading to his crucifixion and death. In the apocalyptic discourse of Mark 13 the discourse continues to return to wisdom, miracle, prophetic, and suffering-death *topoi* uncharacteristic of fully apocalyptic discourse. Mark 14–16 is dominated by suffering-death discourse. Apocalyptic *topoi* appear in argumentative narration in Jesus' trial before the Sanhedrin.

Gregory Bloomquist identifies all the places in Luke-Acts that contain apocalyptic discourse and then maps out the intertextural resources used. In the Gospel of Luke the apocalyptic discourse is focused on the journey to Jerusalem (9:51–19:44) as it culminates in the apocalyptic discourse of chapter 21. In Acts, apocalyptic discourse reemerges in the context of the mission to the Gentiles as part of the redemptive plan of God.

Regarding Luke's Gospel, Bloomquist finds oral-scribal intertexture with early Christian materials, the Old Testament text as found in Hebrew or Greek, and Second Temple Jewish texts not found in the Old Testament. Early Christian texts include Mark, Q, and the material also known as L, with the bulk of material used in apocalyptic discourse being from Q, with L a close second. When borrowing from Mark, Luke used few sections employing apocalyptic discourse, but when he does he heightens the existing apocalyptic expectation in Mark with intertexture of Old Testament oral-scribal and cultural materials. In Acts, Luke's use of oral-scribal early Christian material is nearly impossible to trace. When using the Old Testament, Lukan apocalyptic discourse borrows marginally from Genesis and Deuteronomy in the Torah, heavily from Isaiah and Ezekiel in the Prophets, and the Psalms most heavily in the Writings. Second Temple Jewish sources appear as cultural echoes from the *Psalms of Solomon* rather than from oral-scribal intertexture. There is no evidence of oral-scribal intertexture with Greco-Roman texts in Lukan apocalyptic discourse.

As for the selection of oral-scribal intertextural materials and the invention of argumentation, Luke uses the Old Testament to heighten the apocalyptic themes of God's grace and deliverance as well as revenge upon the enemies of God's people. Argumentative strategies in Lukan apocalyptic discourse are deductive enthymematic and inductive paradigmatic argumentation characteristic of Greco-Roman argumentation, but with distinctive patterns drawn from the intertextural resources. The warrants for Luke's argumentation are drawn from shared prophetic literature and expectations that give them their persuasive force. Lukan apocalyptic argumentation is also composed of chreia elaboration by Jesus or by apostles in speeches about events concerning Jesus. Jesus' thesis within the chreiai have no oral-scribal intertexture, indicating that Jesus' authority to interpret Scripture rather than the authority of Scripture itself is the focus. Understanding Lukan apocalyptic discourse as midrash is thus misguided.

James Hester uses Fantasy Theme Analysis to analyze apocalyptic discourse in 1 Thessalonians. Paul gave the Thessalonians a dramatizing message that formed the basis of group fantasy sharing. Fantasies are interpretations of events that fulfill rhetorical needs to make sense out of the group's experience and anticipate its future. From the fantasies the group constructs a rhetorical vision that provides a broader view of the world and a shared value system that motivates their ethical stance. This process raises and sustains group consciousness.

Apocalyptic discourse encompasses Paul's dramatizing message of resurrection and the *parousia*. Apocalyptic discourse gives specific content to the community's fantasies and shared rhetorical vision of eschatological hope. It forms and sustains the Thessalonians' group consciousness as "insiders," the holy, chosen community that will escape the coming wrath of God. It provides a moral imperative that stems from shared values developed from the shared vision of how to behave toward those inside and outside the community.

Paul faces the problem that some within the community have elaborated his dramatizing, apocalyptic message into fantasies that do not properly derive from it. The original rhetorical vision had failed to account for the death of a member of the community prior to the *parousia*. Paul has to use the original vision and modify and create new fantasies concerning the ultimate fate of the community. He has to make his rhetorical vision theirs. He explains what these shared interpretations of reality say about the community's future and what is expected of its members in light of that future. Righteousness is the pragmatic, ethical expression of apocalypticism.

Hester concludes by comparing the similarities between symbolic convergence theory and Vernon Robbins's sociorhetorical criticism, particularly oral-scribal intertexture and its subdivisions of recitation, recontextualization, and reconfiguration. These types of intertexture can be used to mold previous themes, types, and traditions that may or may not have been part of apocalyptic discourse in the past in order to create and revise fantasies within the community. Apocalyptic topics can function outside the context of apocalyptic sources per se. Paul uses topics typical of apocalypses, but not limited to apocalyptic texts, to create apocalyptic discourse suited to his exigence.

Russell Sisson argues that Q contains apocalyptic discourse in Q 17:20–37 that evokes a spatial and temporal dualism typical of apocalyptic discourse. Other apocalyptic *topoi* are scattered throughout Q and indicate that an apocalyptic worldview characterized the Q community. However, apocalyptic discourse is found surrounded by material that reflects a nonapocalyptic worldview and overall Q is nonapocalyptic or sapential in tenor.

Rather than isolate apocalyptic and sapiential discourse in order to construct a consistent eschatology, Sisson argues that we should study how they interact. Q's apocalyptic discourse does not need to be understood as arising out of an apocalyptic situation. Unlike the wisdom tradition, Q locates wisdom outside rather than inside cities in the agricultural area. This reflects the hatred of urban society by the agrarian Galilean society from which Q emerged. The message is that divine intervention in the world against the current, corrupt social and political order in urban society is imminent, but the continued search for wisdom outside that order is necessary. Apocalyptic discourse functions primarily to motivate the Q community in its prophetic mission and to sanction their pronouncements against those in the city who reject their prophets and their message. The Q community created the apocalyptic discourse as a modification of wisdom discourse, and the former is not a later addition in Q's compositional history.

Edith Humphrey examines the oral-scribal, cultural, and social intertexture of representative portions of apocalyptic discourse in 2 Corinthians, including portions that are midrashic (2:14–4:18), exhortative (6:1–7:4), and polemical (12:1–12). Paul reconfigured apocalyptic discourse in light of his affirmation that the future judgment and salvation have already intervened in Jesus Christ, continue to be disclosed through the Holy Spirit, and will eventually be fulfilled.

Regarding oral-scribal intertexture, in 2:14–4:18 Paul retells the story of Moses, especially in Exod 32–34 and Deut 9–10. The glory of the new covenant in Christ is shown to outshine the glory of Moses, a glory working to reconcile Paul and the Corinthians and to provide a new perspective on the Christian life. Paul and the Corinthians work to reflect that glory more and more. Cultural intertexture includes reference to a Jewish mystical tradition of Moses as one who was transformed by contact with the divine, a transformation that Paul also experienced through ecstasy and one that the church is promised. Social intertextuality tinges the "everyday" with the glory of the sacred. In 6:1–7:4 Paul establishes that in light of salvation as "now," holy living, especially in the form of working together, is the appropriate mode of conduct. He describes himself in terms of the Isaianic figure of the servant of God calling God's people and others to God, a ministry to which he invites the Corinthians as part of their working together. In 12:1–12 Paul uses his visionary experience to garner authority, but his reticence to give details and focus instead upon his thorn in the flesh teaches the Corinthians that weakness is what glorifies the Lord.

B. J. Oropeza argues that the Corinthians had adopted an overrealized eschatology that led to immorality and divisive conduct. Paul presents two strategies from an apocalyptic framework in which the culmination of God's present blessings is future. First, he appeals to Isaiah and reconfigures three major motifs: (1) the new exodus motif with its topics of re-creation/restoration in the desert by water/Spirit, monotheism/theodicy, and the appearance of God's servant/deliverer; (2) polemic against the wise and proud; and (3) monotheism and idolatry. Second, Paul presents an argument from utopia to humility. While this age is an age of the spirit, it is also an age of the cross. While Christians are free from slavery to sin, they are on a new exodus through the wilderness on their way to the promised rest. This is a cause for humility, not elation. He uses the Isaianic utopian traditions to reverse expectations. He redirects the Corinthians' utopian assumptions with the topics of the cross of Christ teaching humility rather than boasting, true wisdom versus the wisdom of this age, the resurrection of the body, and divine judgment. With both strategies Paul encourages the Corinthians to avoid factionalism, worldly wisdom, idolatry, and any behavior that will be judged by God.

While the Epistle of James cannot be classified as apocalyptic, Wesley Wachob examines several topics in James that are also frequently found in apocalyptic literature to see how they function in James's deliberative rhetoric. These topics include trials of faith, justice, judgment, the kingdom of God, the rich and the poor, and the *parousia* of the Lord. James's choice of these topics is an important part of his inventional strategy. From a subcultural position of Jewish-Christianity within Jewish culture, the rhetoric of James uses the values of Jewish culture counterculturally against the values uniting the dominant Hellenistic-Roman culture. James's rhetoric is subcultural to Jewish tradition because it is a Christian version of a Jewish value system. James appropriates the Torah through the teachings of Jesus about the fulfillment of the Torah in the love commandment. Loving the neighbor as self is to fulfill the Torah. James configures apocalyptic topics to support his argumentation and to appeal that his countercultural community live as Jesus lived. The eschatological future determines present behavior, and the faith community should live like Christ in light of that future.

In my contribution on Jude and 2 Peter, I argue that Jude's use of inter-texture is colored by his apocalyptic outlook and influenced by his rhetorical approach. He uses various forms of oral-scribal and cultural inter-texture in his *logos* or argumentation to create proofs that the false teachers of his community are ungodly and subject to the approaching judgment of the *parousia*. These forms of intertexture include uses of oral-scribal recita-tion, recontextualization, and reconfiguration, as well as cultural references and allusions—all to the Old Testament, Jewish extrabiblical texts and tra-ditions, and early Christian traditions.

Jude's use of intertexture is also guided by the needs of *ethos* and *pathos*. The intertextural material is primarily prophetic. Jude's confident application of these prophecies to the false teachers indicates that he is a prophet of the community. The negative emotions associated with the intertextural connections help Jude elicit negative emotions from his com-munity that can be directed to the false teachers and their program.

Jude's use of written sources places the letter within Palestine among Jewish-Christian circles whose outlook was highly apocalyptic. Jewish apocalyptic texts are interpreted in light of Jesus inaugurating the last days. These texts and traditions are understood as eschatological typology and apocalyptic prophecy, and used to create argumentation to prove that the false teachers in the churches are the fulfillment of prophecy about the *parousia* and subject to its judgment.

In the apocalyptic discourse of 2 Peter, the author utilizes a variety of oral-scribal and cultural intertextural connections to mold Jewish and early Christian traditions and texts to create argumentation or *logos* to refute an attack upon the veracity of the proclamation of the *parousia*. He uses recitation, reconfiguration, and cultural allusion. He uses early Christian tradition that incorporates Old Testament messianic texts pertaining to the day of the Lord and its judgment and applies these to Jesus as ruler of the nations and as judge at the *parousia*. Our author relies heavily upon early Christian tradition for his apocalyptic discourse, but unlike Jude, the dom-inant vehicle expressing faith in Jesus is not apocalyptic. Apocalyptic materials are used as a resource to reaffirm the *parousia* in light of escha-tological skepticism.

Like Jude, our author's use of intertexture is guided by the need to increase the *ethos* of his argumentation and generate *pathos*. The authority of these sources lend authority to his argumentation. However, ultimately our author relies upon the *ethos* of the apostle Peter through the use of pseudonymity. Whereas Jude uses prophetic intertexture to present him-self as a prophet, the author of 2 Peter relies more upon the prophetic nature of the testament genre to present Peter as a prophet. The author vil-ifies his opponents as subjects of the fulfillment of early Christian prophecy of apostates and endtime scoffers and generates negative *pathos*.

David deSilva examines the oral-scribal and cultural intertexture of Rev 14:14–16:21. He explores connections and associations with Jewish Scriptures and intertestamental literature and Greco-Roman literature, focusing on the rhetorical contributions of intertexture in this pericope. John has an overall deliberative rhetorical strategy supported by epideictic rhetoric. His is a narrative demonstration tracing out courses of action, their incentives and disincentives, and their consequences. The effectiveness of the narrative demonstration depends upon how plausible the audience finds John's depiction of the future. John uses oral-scribal and cultural intertexture to create that plausibility and lend the narrative *ethos* and power. John weaves in their language rather than cite these sources and draw authority away from his own apocalyptic vision. Historical precedents and examples remind the audience of the premises that guide the unfolding of history and provide a basis for foretelling its future, and align the audience with values and courses of action appropriate to that future.

The Intertexture of Apocalyptic Discourse in the Gospel of Mark

Vernon K. Robbins

This essay addresses interaction between the oral-scribal and cultural intertexture of apocalyptic discourse in the Gospel of Mark by paying special attention to *topoi* and enthymematic argumentation.[1] Under the influence of rhetorical interpretation, distinctions recently have been drawn among "apocalypse," "apocalyptic eschatology," "apocalypticism," "apocalyptic," and "apocalyptic discourse."[2] The current essay focuses on "apocalyptic discourse," which has received the following definition in rhetorical discussion:

> *Apocalyptic discourse* refers to the constellation of apocalyptic topics as they function in larger early Jewish and Christian literary and social contexts. Thus, apocalyptic discourse should be treated as a flexible set of resources that early Jews and Christians could employ for a variety of persuasive tasks. Whenever early Jews and Christians appealed to such topics as visions and revelations, heavenly journeys, final catastrophes, and the like, they were using apocalyptic discourse.[3]

In order to tap the full resources of rhetorical interpretation, it is important to modify the first sentence to read: "Apocalyptic discourse refers to the constellation of apocalyptic *topoi* as they function in early Jewish and Christian descriptive, explanatory, and argumentative discourse." *Topoi* received considerable attention in New Testament interpretation during the last part of the twentieth century.[4] The current essay builds on Wilhelm H.

---

[1] Vernon K. Robbins, *The Tapestry of Early Christian Discourse: Rhetoric, Society and Ideology* (London: Routledge, 1996), 96–115, 121–24, 129–43; idem, *Exploring the Texture of Texts: A Guide to Socio-Rhetorical Interpretation* (Valley Forge, Pa.: Trinity Press International, 1996), 40–62.

[2] Gregory Carey, "Introduction: Apocalyptic Discourse, Apocalyptic Rhetoric," in *Vision and Persuasion: Rhetorical Dimensions of Apocalyptic Discourse* (ed. Gregory Carey and L. Gregory Bloomquist; St. Louis: Chalice, 1999), 8–10.

[3] Carey, "Introduction," 10.

[4] Abraham J. Malherbe, "Hellenistic Moralists and the New Testament," *ANRW* 26.1:320–25 (originally completed in 1972); Wilhelm H. Wuellner, "Toposforschung

11

Wuellner's awareness that *topoi* have a twofold function: (1) argumentative-enthymematic and (2) amplificatory-descriptive.[5] Abraham J. Malherbe and his associates have made extensive investigations of the amplificatory-descriptive function of *topoi* of the Hellenistic moralists in New Testament literature.[6] Their focus on these *topoi* reveals that early Christians participated actively in first-century Mediterranean wisdom discourse. In addition, members of the Context Group have identified the presence of common social and cultural topics and values in all the writings in the New Testament.[7] A major task for New Testament interpreters now is to produce rhetorical analysis and interpretation both of the amplificatory-descriptive function and the argumentative-enthymematic function of the *topoi* and values in all six major kinds of New Testament discourse: wisdom, miracle, prophetic, suffering-death, apocalyptic, and precreation.[8]

A beginning point for merging Wuellner's insight about the twofold nature of *topoi* with the rich investigations by Malherbe and his associates and the Context Group is the understanding that "specific (*idioi*) *topoi*" attain the status of "common (*koinoi*) *topoi*" in regional, ethnic, and even

---

und Torahinterpretation bei Paulus und Jesus," *NTS* 24 (1978): 463–83; Johan C. Thom, "'The Mind Is Its Own Place': Towards a Definition of Topos," in *Early Christianity and Classical Culture: Essays in Honor of Abraham J. Malherbe* (ed. John T. Fitzgerald et al.; Valley Forge, Pa.: Trinity Press International, forthcoming).

[5] Wuellner, "Toposforshung," 467: "eine zweifache Funktion: eine argumentativ-enthymematische und eine amplifikatorisch-darstellerische Funktion." Cf. Walter J. Ong, *Orality and Literacy: The Technologizing of the Word* (New York: Routledge, 1982), 110–11.

[6] Malherbe, "Hellenistic Moralists," 320–25; idem, *Moral Exhortation, A Greco-Roman Sourcebook* (LEC; Philadelphia: Westminster, 1986), 144–61; idem, "The Christianization of a Topos (Luke 12:13–34)," *NovT* 38 (1996): 123–35.

[7] For the basic range of these topics, see Bruce J. Malina, *The New Testament World: Insights from Cultural Anthropology* (rev. ed.; Atlanta: John, 1993); John H. Elliott, *What Is Social-Scientific Criticism?* (Minneapolis: Fortress, 1993); John J. Pilch and Bruce J. Malina, eds., *Biblical Social Values and Their Meaning: A Handbook* (Peabody, Mass.: Hendrickson, 1993); John J. Pilch, *The Cultural Dictionary of the Bible* (Collegeville, Minn.; Liturgical Press, 1999); cf. Robbins, *Tapestry of Early Christian Discourse,* 159–66; idem, *Exploring the Texture of Texts,* 75–86. For publications of the Context Group, see http://www.serv.net/~oakmande/index.html.

[8] Vernon K. Robbins, "Argumentative Textures in Socio-Rhetorical Interpretation," in *Rhetorical Argumentation in Biblical Texts* (ed. Anders Eriksson et al.; Emory Studies in Early Christianity; Harrisburg, Pa.: Trinity Press International, 2002, 27–65); cf. idem, "The Dialectical Nature of Early Christian Discourse," *Scriptura* 59 (1996): 353–62. (http://www.emory.edu/COLLEGE/RELIGION/faculty/robbins/dialect/dialect353.html).

imperial social and cultural-rhetorical environments. The *topoi* Malherbe and his associates analyze are specific *topoi* that became common *topoi* in the writings of the Hellenistic moralists. Participants in the Context Group, in contrast, focus on *topoi* characteristic of ancient, preindustrial society and culture. For rhetorical analysis and interpretation, it is important to understand that: "Once a topical pattern has developed into common use, it will be used over and over in various manifestations and will be effective by virtue of its recognizability."[9] This recognizability sometimes is distinctive of a particular kind of culture in a particular region of the world.

Another important point is an understanding of the expanding enthymematic-argumentative nature of *topoi*. Aristotle's insight that enthymemes are the "substance" of persuasion itself[10] has been expanded in modern times to an awareness that a "cultural system can be envisioned as a set of major premises—similar to a philosophical, theological, or legal system—from which its more specific minor premises can be derived."[11] The rhetoric of people "lead[s] staircase fashion from opinion ... to further opinion.... [I]ts syllogistic motion *generates* all the possible arguments in relation to a given case. At each point, the possibilities are not reduced or eliminated, as in dialectic, but multiplied.... [T]he end is an ambidextrous wealth of arguments."[12] The "background conventions" supporting the "provisional judgments" in enthymemes "are not simply private intuitions but 'social knowledge' that spills over into the common experience of many people. What is referenced by publicly articulated enthymemes is the mosaic of commonplaces, conventions, traditions, and provisional interests making up the *doxa* of [their] rhetorical culture."[13] Early Christians interwove biblical, Jewish, and Mediterranean *topoi* and values together into argumentative-enthymematic and amplificatory-

---

[9] Barbara Warnick, "Two Systems of Invention: The Topics in *Rhetoric* and *The New Rhetoric*," in *Rereading Aristotle's Rhetoric* (ed. Alan G. Gross and Arthur E. Walzer; Carbondale and Edwardsville: Southern Illinois University Press, 2000), 110; cf. Ong, *Orality and Literacy,* 110–11.

[10] Thomas B. Farrell, "Aristotle's Enthymeme As Tacit Reference," in Gross and Walzer, *Rereading Aristotle's Rhetoric,* 94.

[11] James L. Peacock, *The Anthropological Lens: Harsh Light, Soft Focus* (Cambridge: Cambridge University Press, 1986), 35; cf. Vernon K. Robbins, "The Present and Future of Rhetorical Analysis," in *The Rhetorical Analysis of Scripture: Essays from the 1995 London Conference* (ed. Stanley E. Porter and Thomas H. Olbricht; JSNTSSup 146; Sheffield: Sheffield Academic Press, 1997), 33–35.

[12] Margaret D. Zulick, "Generative Rhetoric and Public Argument: A Classical Approach," *Argument and Advocacy* 33 (1997): 113.

[13] Farrell, "Aristotle's Enthymeme As Tacit Reference," 99.

descriptive discourse that functioned as persuasive discourse in late Mediterranean antiquity.

In sociorhetorical terms, the twofold function of *topoi* in early Christian discourse produced multiple "rhetorolects," because *topoi* emerge from a variety of conceptual locations with a "richness and connectedness of knowledge available for recombination" and function as "a source of patterns and relationships" within "the habits of thought, value hierarchies, forms of knowledge, and cultural conventions of the host society."[14] Enthymematic argumentation functions as an important means of persuasion in this context, since it moves from probable premises to a probable conclusion, regularly "start[ing] with the conclusion (or 'question') and . . . searching for an argument to warrant thinking the subject and the predicate terms, or to warrant dissociating them if what one needs is a negative answer."[15] The issue is not one of "formal logic" or of "formal validity," nor is it the presence or absence of all three parts of a dialectical syllogism. The issue is argumentation from "signs," which are considered to be "sure assumptions," or from "likelihoods," which are considered to be probable assumptions, rather than from decontextualized philosophical thinking. *Topoi* reside at the base of enthymemes, since *topoi* function persuasively in descriptive and explanatory discourse on the basis of pattern recognition.[16] The experience of "recognizing the pattern" gives credibility to the *topos,* evoking a conviction that the pattern is "sure" (based on a "sign") or "probable" (based on a "likelihood"). This credibility undergirds enthymematic argumentation, which moves in an inductive-deductive-abductive manner.[17] Thus, a *topos* is not simply a probable or sure "idea" or "theme"; it is "a nexus for enthymemes."[18] The inductive-deductive-abductive nature of enthymematic argumentation requires an interpreter to

---

[14] Carolyn R. Miller, "The Aristotelean *Topos:* Hunting for Novelty," in Gross and Walzer, *Rereading Aristotle's Rhetoric,* 141–42.

[15] Walter J. Ong, "Introduction" to "A Fuller Course in the Art of Logic (1672)," in *Complete Prose Works of John Milton,* vol. 8: *1666–1682* (ed. Maurice Kelley; New Haven: Yale University Press, 1982), 161; cf. David Hellholm, "Enthymemic Argumentation in Paul: The Case of Romans 6," in *Paul and His Hellenistic Context* (ed. Troels Engberg-Pedersen; Minneapolis: Fortress, 1995), 119–79.

[16] Warnick, "Two Systems of Invention," 110.

[17] Richard L. Lanigan, "From Enthymeme to Abduction: The Classical Law of Logic and the Postmodern Rule of Rhetoric," in *Recovering Pragmatism's Voice: The Classical Tradition, Rorty, and the Philosophy of Communication* (ed. Lenore Langsdorf and Andrew R. Smith; Albany, N.Y.: State University of New York Press, 1995), 49–70.

[18] I am grateful to L. Gregory Bloomquist for helping to nurture this insight; cf. Miller, "The Aristotelean *Topos,*" 136; Carey, "Introduction," 11, 13.

identify and display the constituents that function as Rule, Case, and Result, rather than Major Premise, Minor Premise, and Conclusion.[19] For example, the *topos* of "final catastrophe" functions as a resource for the invention of enthymematic argumentation in Rev 18:7–8:

> **Case:** (7b) Since in her heart she says, "I rule as a queen; I am no widow, and I will never see grief,"
> **Result:** (8) therefore her plagues will come in a single day—pestilence and mourning and famine—and she will be burned with fire;
> **Rule:** for mighty is the Lord God who judges her.

The *topos* of "final catastrophe" is stated in the Result. In this "enthymematic apocalyptic argumentation," the Result is a "logical" outcome of the nature of God's attributes and actions (the Rule, inferred from the story of God's actions and attributes in the past) and the nature of the attitudes and actions of Babylon (the Case). Whether or not it could be judged as "formally valid" by a logician, some early Christians considered this argumentation to be probable or sure on the basis of "likelihood" or "signs."[20]

A major challenge for enthymematic analysis and interpretation is to perceive the underlying Rule-Case-Result nature of different kinds of discourse.[21] This essay contains a description of the underlying enthymematic nature of different kinds of discourse as they become important for the analysis and interpretation.

1. Apocalyptic Topoi *and Argumentation in Mark 1:1–20*

From a sociorhetorical perspective, the Gospel of Mark is a biographical composition woven with prophetic, miracle, wisdom, apocalyptic, and

---

[19] Vernon K. Robbins, "Enthymemic Texture in the Gospel of Thomas," *SBL Seminar Papers, 1998* (SBLSP 37; Atlanta: Scholars Press, 1998), 343–66 (http://www.emory.edu/COLLEGE/RELIGION/faculty/robbins/enthymeme/enthymeme343.html); idem, "From Enthymeme to Theology in Luke 11:1–13," in *Literary Studies in Luke-Acts: A Collection of Essays in Honor of Joseph B. Tyson* (ed. R. P. Thompson and T. E. Phillips; Macon, Ga.: Mercer University Press, 1998), 191–214 (http://www.emory.edu/COLLEGE/RELIGION/faculty/robbins/Theology/theology191.html); idem, "Progymnastic Rhetorical Composition and Pre-Gospel Traditions: A New Approach," in *The Synoptic Gospels: Source Criticism and the New Literary Criticism* (ed. Camille Focant; BETL 110; Leuven: Leuven University Press, 1993), 111–47.

[20] See the discussion of "premonitory discourse" in Farrell, "Aristotle's Enthymeme As Tacit Reference," 104–5.

[21] Robbins, "Argumentative Textures in Socio-Rhetorical Interpretation."

suffering-death "rhetorolects" that were nurtured by early Christians in the rhetorical environment of Mediterranean discourse.[22] In the context of early Christian discourse, the obvious missing rhetorolect is precreation discourse, which functions dynamically in the Gospel of John, Ephesians, Colossians, 2 Timothy, Titus, and Hebrews.[23] The Gospel of Mark presents an account of the life of Jesus with the aid of all of the major modes of early Christian discourse except that which became its most distinctive mode: precreation discourse.

In contrast to the Gospel of John, which begins with a reconfiguration of Gen 1:1 that introduces precreation discourse,[24] the Gospel of Mark begins with a reconfiguration of prophetic discourse like that which appears in Hosea 1:2 LXX: "the beginning of the word of the Lord in Hosea."[25] Markan narration has reconfigured phrasing characteristic of prophetic discourse by replacing "the word of the Lord" with "the gospel of Jesus Christ [Son of God]" and attributing the beginning to "the prophet Isaiah" through the conventional oral-scribal formula "as it is written."[26] The result is an account of Jesus' adult life and death as the continuation of a redemptive story that began during the time of the prophets.[27] Immediately after these opening words, Markan narration presents an oral-scribal recitation of biblical discourse in a manner of prophetic fulfillment (1:2–3).[28]

---

[22] Vernon K. Robbins, *Jesus the Teacher: A Socio-Rhetorical Interpretation of Mark* (Minneapolis: Fortress, 1992); idem, "Argumentative Textures in Socio-Rhetorical Interpretation"; cf. idem, "Dialectical Nature of Early Christian Discourse."

[23] Precreation discourse focuses on the redemptive effect for humans and the cosmos of Christ's relation to God prior to creation. Cf. Robbins, "Argumentative Textures in Socio-Rhetorical Interpretation," 59–63.

[24] John 1:1–5 introduces precreation Rule-Case-Result argumentation as follows (cf. ibid.):
Rule: (1) In the beginning was the Word, and the Word was with God, and the Word was God.
(2) He was in the beginning with God;
(3) all things were made through him [by God], and without him was not anything made that was made [by God].
Case: (4) In him was life, and the life was the light of men.
Result: (5) The light shines in the darkness, and the darkness has not overcome it.

[25] Vincent Taylor, *The Gospel according to St. Mark* (London: Macmillan, 1952), 152.

[26] Cf. Robert A. Guelich, *Mark 1–8:26* (WBC 34A; Dallas: Word, 1989), 10.

[27] Norman R. Petersen, *Literary Criticism for New Testament Critics* (GBS; Philadelphia: Fortress, 1978), 50–53.

[28] For details concerning the content of the biblical discourse, see Guelich, *Mark*, 11

Rule: (2) "Behold, I send my messenger before thy face, who shall prepare thy way; (3) the voice of one crying in the wilderness: Prepare the way of the Lord, make his paths straight."
Case: (4–6) John the baptizer appeared in the wilderness....
Result: (7) And he preached saying, "After me comes he who is mightier than I.... (8) I have baptized you with water; but he will baptize you with the Holy Spirit.

In prophetic discourse, primary "Rules" regularly emerge from God's decisions to select certain people and groups to enact righteousness in the human realm.[29] Mark 1:2–3 present God's sending of a messenger to prepare the way of the Messiah. These oral-scribal verses function as the Rule in prophetic reasoning that governs the Case of John the Baptizer. The Result of John's appearance as God's messenger is his baptism of people with water as a preparation for the coming of another who will baptize with the Holy Spirit (cf. 13:11). In characteristic fashion, this prophetic narration is filled with vivid imagery about the present ("crying in the wilderness," "mak[ing] paths straight," "clothed with camel's hair," etc.) and tantalizing assertions about the future ("after me comes he who is mightier than I," etc.). Wolfgang Roth has accurately perceived that the kind of prophetic discourse conventionally associated with Elijah and Elisha in 1 Kgs 17–2 Kgs 13 is evoked by this opening recitation and continues throughout the Gospel.[30] The "messenger" to whom the recitation refers in Mark 1:2 has, through prophetic interpretation in Mal 3:1 and 4:5, become Elijah,[31] and *topoi* associated with Elijah continue in the account of John the Baptist (1:4–8), Jesus' temptation in the wilderness (1:12–13), and Jesus' calling of his first four disciples (1:16–20), which establishes the transition that sets the stage for Jesus' ministry.[32]

---

[29] Robbins, "Argumentative Textures in Socio-Rhetorical Interpretation," 44–50.

[30] Wolfgang Roth, *Hebrew Gospel: Cracking the Code of Mark* (Oak Park, Ill.: Meyer-Stone, 1988), 4.

[31] Guelich, *Mark,* 11.

[32] Vernon K. Robbins, "Mark 1.14–20: An Interpretation at the Intersection of Jewish and Graeco-Roman Traditions," *NTS* 28 (1982): 220–36; idem, *Jesus the Teacher,* 27–31. Topics associated with Elijah and Elisha continue in the account of the healing of the man with the unclean spirit in the synagogue in Capernaum (1:21–28; see Roth, *Hebrew Gospel,* 5, 30, 32, 46, 47, 72, 107). The middle of the Markan account explicitly evokes the name of Elijah seven times (Mark 6:15; 8:28; 9:4, 5, 11, 12, 13), and two of these occur in a context where Elijah appears as a personage in conversation with Jesus (9:4–5). The end of the Gospel evokes the name of Elijah twice (15:35, 36) when people refer to the possibility of Elijah's appearance during the crucifixion of Jesus (15:35–36). In other words, modes and

In the initial sequence of episodes in Mark 1:1–13, there are three potentially apocalyptic *topoi* that appear in descriptive discourse: (1) the splitting open of the heavens (1:10); (2) a voice coming out of the heavens (1:11); and (3) Jesus' being tested by Satan (1:13). While the opening of the heavens is a common *topos* in biblical discourse,[33] it acquired special meanings in biblical prophetic discourse. Isaiah 64:1 looks forward to the time when God will "split open" the heavens and come down on earth. In Ezek 1:1, the heavens are opened and the prophet sees "visions of God." Isaiah 24:18–23 moves this *topos* beyond prophetic reasoning into Case-Result-Rule protoapocalyptic reasoning when it presents a logical sequence in which the opening of the heavens calls forth an earthquake throughout the earth, punishment of powers on the earth and in the heavens, and shame on behalf of the moon and the sun:[34]

> **Case:** (17) Terror, and the pit, and the snare are upon you, O inhabitant of the earth!
> **Result:** (18a) Whoever flees at the sound of the terror shall fall into the pit; and whoever climbs out of the pit shall be caught in the snare.
> **Rule:** (18b) For the windows of heaven are opened, and the foundations of the earth tremble. (19) The earth is utterly broken, the earth is torn asunder, the earth is violently shaken.
> (20) The earth staggers like a drunkard, it sways like a hut; its transgression lies heavy upon it, and it falls, and will not rise again.
> **Case:** (21) On that day the Lord will punish the host of heaven in heaven, and on earth the kings of the earth.
> **Result:** (22) They will be gathered together like prisoners in a pit; they will be shut up in a prison, and after many days they will be punished. 23 Then the moon will be abashed, and the sun ashamed;
> **Rule:** (23) for the Lord of Hosts will reign on Mount Zion and in Jerusalem, and before his elders he will manifest his glory.

This reasoning moves beyond prophetic discourse in which the Rules enact the selection of specific individuals and groups with special responsibility to embody righteousness in the human realm. In this protoapocalyptic discourse, the Rules narrate God's attributes and actions that bring imminent judgment upon the earth and the heavens. The narration in Isa 24 focuses on the trembling of the earth, the response of the

---

topoi associated with prophetic discourse about Elijah and Elisha are present in the opening-middle-closing texture of the Gospel of Mark (see Robbins, *Tapestry of Early Christian Discourse*, 50–53; idem, *Exploring the Texture of Texts*, 19–21).

[33] E.g., Gen 7:11; Ps 78:23.

[34] Cf. Robbins, "Argumentative Textures in Socio-Rhetorical Interpretation," 54–59.

heavens, and the punishment of unrighteous people in the manner of proto-apocalyptic discourse. Unlike fully developed apocalyptic discourse, it does not detail the actions of angels or other representatives of God's authority, nor does it feature one or more voices speaking out of the heavens. The Apocalypse of John features the opening of the heavens accompanied by a voice out of the heavens in 4:1,[35] and the apocalyptic discourse in *2 Bar.* 22:1 and *T. Levi* 2:6 and 5:1 also feature such an occasion. As the voice comes forth in these passages, it engages its auditor in dialogue or invites the person to see things in the heavens that soon will take place. In addition, these passages feature a first-person singular account of the experience by the seer himself. While the splitting apart of the heavens and the coming forth of the voice in the Gospel of Mark has the potential for evoking apocalyptic reasoning, the amplificatory-descriptive narration of the *topos* is more characteristic of prophetic discourse than apocalyptic discourse.

Ernst Lohmeyer considered the opening of the heavens to establish definitively the apocalyptic texture of the Markan story.[36] The narration in the Gospel of Mark, however, exhibits a restraint of narration about heavenly things that is uncharacteristic of apocalyptic discourse. Jesus does not engage in dialogue with the voice. The voice does not invite Jesus to come up to heaven. Jesus does not see a throne or lightning, nor does he hear peals of thunder (cf. Rev 4:2–6). When Jesus sees the heavens split apart, he sees the spirit descend on him like a dove.[37] The descent of the spirit of the Lord is a special phenomenon in prophetic discourse (see Isa 11:2; 61:1), and Mark 1:11 features a recontextualization of Isa 42:1 interwoven with Ps 2:7. The Gospel of Mark, as most literature during the Hellenistic period, merges phenomena characteristic of multiple kinds of discourse. As Mark features God's selection of a personage on earth who will have a special role at the end of time, it merges prophetic and apocalyptic discourse in a manner similar to *T. Levi* 18:6, which presents the Case of a new priest who will function in a special way during the final days of time:

> (6) The heavens will be opened, and from the temple of glory sanctification will come upon him, with a fatherly voice, as from Abraham to Isaac. (7) And the glory of the Most High shall burst forth upon him. And the spirit of understanding and sanctification shall rest upon him.[38]

---

[35] Cf. Rev 11:19; 19:11.

[36] Ernst Lohmeyer, *Das Evangelium des Markus* (16th ed.; KEK 2; Göttingen: Vandenhoeck & Ruprecht, 1963), 22.

[37] Leander E. Keck, "The Spirit and the Dove," *NTS* 17 (1970–71): 41–67.

[38] See also *T. Jud.* 24:2.

When the narration continues with the spirit driving Jesus into the wilderness, it introduces another *topos* characteristic of Elijah-Elisha prophetic narration.[39] Apocalyptic discourse would feature Jesus being transported into another level of heaven[40] or engaging in dialogue with the voice to receive answers about things that appeared in heaven. However, when Jesus is in the wilderness, Satan tests him. The presence of Satan in the world is an apocalyptic *topos,* receiving the form it has in Mark from the influence of discourse like that in *1 Enoch, Jubilees,* and the writings at Qumran.[41] While Mark 1:13 takes the form of descriptive discourse, discussion of Satan becomes argumentative in Mark 3:23–30. There will be further discussion of *T. Levi* 18 in the section below on exorcisms in Mark.

After the appearance of potentially apocalyptic *topoi* in the descriptive discourse of Mark 1:9–13, two potentially apocalyptic *topoi* appear in argumentative discourse attributed to Jesus: (1) announcement that time is fulfilled (1:15); and (2) announcement that the kingdom of God is drawing near (or "has drawn" near) (1:15). The enthymematic nature of the discourse becomes evident in a Rule–Exhortative Result display:

> **Rule:** (15) The time is fulfilled, and the kingdom of God is at hand;
> **Exhortative Result:** repent, and believe in the gospel.

There are two *topoi* here that exhibit a close relation to biblical prophetic discourse: (1) fulfillment of time and (2) kingdom of God. When first approaching Mark 1:15, it would appear that the first two clauses present a Case rather than a Rule. But in apocalyptic discourse, assertions about time and the coming of a new age regularly are Rules emerging from the attributes and actions of God. This becomes evident when one sees the application of the Rule to a Case in Ezek 7:12–13:

> **Rule:** (12) The time has come, the day drawn near [when those who are righteous will be preserved by God, but those who are not righteous will have wrath upon them].
> **Case:** (13) For the vision concerns all their multitude; it shall not be revoked. Because of their iniquity,
> **Result:** they cannot maintain their lives.

In prophetic literature, the Rules are God's performative decisions and pronouncements in time. When God pronounces them, they occur. The

---

[39] See 1 Kgs 18:12; 2 Kgs 2:16; Acts 8:39.

[40] See *Apoc. Pet.* 9, 17; *Apoc. Paul* 3, 20, 21, 22, 23, 24, 25, 26, 27, 28, 29, 31, 41, 45.

[41] See Elaine Pagels, *The Origin of Satan* (New York: Random House, 1995), 3–62.

Cases are people whom God selects to perform specific tasks to enact righteousness and people whom God judges by the Rules to be performing righteousness or unrighteousness. The Results emerge from the application of the Rules to the Cases. In Ezekiel, as in portions of Isaiah, God's words are becoming apocalyptic Rules. The prophet presents God's Rule in Ezek 7:12. This leads to an exhortative Result as well as a deductive Result. Ezekiel 7:13 explains that the vision concerns the iniquitous multitude. Here one sees the Case over which the Rule governs. The Result of their inquiry is that "they cannot maintain their lives."

The second *topos* is the kingdom. This appears to be more specifically an apocalyptic topos, as is evident from Dan 7:21–22:

> **Case:** (21) As I looked, this horn made war with the holy ones and was prevailing over them,
> **Rule:** (22a) until the Ancient One came;
> **Case:** then judgment was given for the holy ones of the Most High,
> **Result:** (22b) and the time arrived when the holy ones gained possession of the kingdom.

In apocalyptic discourse, the attributes and actions of God and those whom God sends to perform his tasks during time function as the Rules. People on earth who are either righteous or unrighteous function as the Cases upon which the Rules produce the Results. The unrighteous actions of the horn against the holy ones in Dan 7:21 present the Case upon which God's actions of coming and judging in 7:22a function as the Rule that produces the unstated Result of ending the power of the horn and the stated Result of giving the kingdom to the holy ones in 7:22b. The result of the cultural intertexture of Mark 1:15 with prophetic texts such as Ezek 7:12–13 and Dan 7:21–22 suggests that Jesus' announcement of the fulfillment of time and the arrival of the kingdom functions as a prophetic-apocalyptic Rule. The Rule is at one and the same time a prophetic "word of God" (in Mark 1:14, called the "gospel" of God) that performs what it declares and an apocalyptic action of God that enacts the attributes and actions of God throughout all time in the past, present, and future.

Thus, Mark 1:1–20 has significant oral-scribal intertexture with prophetic biblical literature. Into this prophetic narration, the Gospel of Mark introduces apocalyptic *topoi* that evoke the recognition of a pattern of God's activity at the end of time. The narration does not fulfill the expectations of apocalyptic discourse, but it embeds potentially apocalyptic *topoi,* including an apocalyptic Rule in 1:15 that creates an enthymematic environment inviting apocalyptic patterns of expectation and fulfillment.

2. Apocalyptic Topoi and Argumentation in Miracle Discourse: Mark 1:21–8:26

In the context of the overall prophetic discourse of the Gospel of Mark, miracle discourse functions centripetally in 1:21–8:26.[42] Since miracle discourse is conventional in Elijah-Elisha prophetic discourse (1 Kgs 17–2 Kgs 5), Jesus' inauguration of his Galilean ministry in the Capernaum synagogue by healing a man (1:21–28) and his regular performance of miracles of various kinds throughout the first eight chapters of Mark would be considered highly acceptable, if not expected, by a first-century reader. The presence of unclean spirits or demons in the people to be healed, however, was not a conventional phenomenon in Elijah-Elisha discourse.[43] Mediterranean writers as early as Hesiod referred to good and evil δαίμονες,[44] and during the second century B.C.E. *1 En.* 15:6–12 presented an "apocalyptic" account of the origin of "evil spirits" through interpretation of Gen 6:1–4.[45] In both *1 Enoch* and *Jubilees*, these evil spirits "corrupt" the world, causing it to be "impure" and "unclean."[46] By the first century C.E. a writer like Josephus could use the term δαιμόνιον to refer either to a good or divine power (fate).[47] Out of fifteen occurrences of a singular or plural form of δαιμόνιον in the writings of Josephus, nine refer to evil demons.[48] In contrast to a phrase like "good δαίμων,"[49] Markan discourse uses the phrase "holy spirit," "spirit," or "angel."[50] In Mark, the term δαιμόνιον always refers to an evil spirit, which can be called an "unclean" spirit.[51]

---

[42] The language of "centripetal" function comes from the writings of M. M. Bakhtin. The most comprehensive guide to miracle discourse during the time of earliest Christianity, with its bibliographical references, currently is Wendy Cotter, *Miracles in Greco-Roman Antiquity: A Sourcebook for the Study of New Testament Miracle Stories* (London: Routledge, 1999).

[43] While Qumran's *Genesis Apocryphon* attributes Abram with an exorcism and Josephus attributes exorcistic powers to David and Solomon, the tradition did not associate Elijah and Elisha with exorcism; see ibid., 48–53, 96–105.

[44] Ibid., 75–89.

[45] Ibid., 106–12.

[46] *1 En.* 8:2; 15:11; *Jub.* 5:2–3, 10; 7:20–21; 10:5, 8; 11:4; 50:5.

[47] Everett Ferguson, *Demonology of the Early Christian World* (Symposium 12; Lewiston, N.Y.: Mellen, 1984), 84–86.

[48] Josephus, *War* 7.185; *Ant.* 6.166 (2), 168, 211; 8.45, 46, 47, 48. These may be equated to an evil spirit: πονηρὸν πνεῦμα (*Ant.* 6.211; cf. *War* 7.185) and are opposite of divine spirit (θεῖον πνεῦμα: *Ant.* 6.166).

[49] Josephus, *Ant.* 16.210; cf. *War* 6.47–48.

[50] See Ferguson, *Demonology of the Early Christian World*, 84.

[51] See Mark 7:25–26, 29–30. Mark 9:25 refers to a "dumb and deaf" spirit.

The Gospel of Mark contains only four exorcisms.[52] It is likely that, outside of their context in Mark, the exorcism of the legion of demons from the Gerasene man (5:1–20), the unclean spirit/demon from the Syrophoenician woman's daughter (7:24–30), and the dumb spirit from the boy with the believing father (9:14–29) evoked only general Mediterranean understanding of evil spirits, rather than anything specifically apocalyptic in nature. However, the placement and argumentative texture of the exorcism of the man with the unclean spirit in the Capernaum synagogue (1:21–28), which inaugurates Jesus' Galilean activity after he calls four disciples, moves what is otherwise an account of prophetic teaching toward apocalyptic discourse. The holy spirit that came down into Jesus after his baptism (1:10) and immediately drove him into the wilderness (1:12) is quite clearly the agent that equips Jesus to cast out "unclean spririts." This becomes evident when the unclean spirits fall down before Jesus and cry out to him that he is "the Son of God" (3:11), the natural designation to infer from the voice from heaven that called Jesus "my beloved Son" (1:11) in the context where the spirit came down into him. But all of this could be understood in the mode of prophetic discourse, since Elijah is a "man of God" (1 Kgs 17:18, 24) who heals by means of "the word of the Lord in [his] mouth" which "is truth" (1 Kgs 17:24; cf. Mark 1:24–27) and Elisha is a "holy man of God" (2 Kgs 4:9) upon whom the spirit of Elijah rested in double portion (2 Kgs 2:9–15). Mark 1:24 has the nature of oral-scribal recontextualization of 1 Kgs 17:18 and 2 Kgs 4:9, and Mark 1:27 may be oral-scribal reconfiguration of 1 Kgs 17:24.[53]

The narration, however, appears to call forth apocalyptic understanding when people refer to Jesus' action as "a new teaching" that "commands even the unclean spirits" and they obey him (Mark 1:27). If the new teaching includes 1:15 ("The time is fulfilled and the kingdom of God is drawing near") and if a result of the descent of the holy spirit is the empowerment of Jesus to encounter a large number of unclean spirits, then the discourse has moved beyond the reasoning of prophetic discourse, where evil in the world is a result of human disobedience, into a worldview where evil spirits have "corrupted" God's "good creation." In other words, here the narration appears to have apocalyptic "cultural

---

[52] The Gospel of Mark refers eleven times to unclean spirits (1:23, 26, 27; 3:11, 30; 5:2, 8, 13; 6:7; 7:25; 9:25), eleven times to demons (1:34 [2], 39; 3:15, 22 [2]; 6:13; 7:26, 29, 30; 9:38), and four times to people who are "demonized" (1:32; 5:15, 16, 18; cf. Josephus, *Ant.* 8.47). The longer ending in Mark contains two additional references to demons (16:9, 17).

[53] Robbins, *Tapestry of Early Christian Discourse,* 97–108, 129–42; idem, *Exploring the Texture of Texts,* 48–50.

intertexture." The invasion of the human realm of God's created world by unclean spirits and demons becomes clear in Markan summaries and other references (1:32–34, 39; 3:11–12, 15, 22; 6:7, 13) outside the four specific exorcisms. From all of these references, it seems obvious that the presence of unclean spirits and demons in people is the result of spirits "ris[ing] up against the children of the people and against the women" (*1 En.* 15:12). The general Markan discourse about unclean spirits and demons, then, appears to be apocalyptic in its worldview. There are no exorcisms in apocalyptic writings.[54] Part of the Markan achievement is to intertwine exorcisms with apocalyptic *topoi* in a manner that moves the casting out of unclean spirits/demons beyond the worldviews of basic Mediterranean miracle discourse or biblical prophetic discourse into apocalyptic discourse.

Markan discourse never explains how unclean spirits and demons came into being on earth or why they dwell in humans. The discourse takes on a decisive argumentative texture,[55] however, in Mark 3:19b–30, where scribes from Jerusalem accuse Jesus of casting out demons by the prince of demons (3:22). Into the topic of household (3:19, 21, 25, 27, 31–35), the argumentation embeds the topics of the public domain (3:20–21); scribes from Jerusalem (3:22); being "out of one's mind"/possessed by Beelzebul, Satan, a demon, or an unclean spirit (3:21–23, 26, 30); casting out demons (3:22–23); kingdom (3:24); sin (3:28–29); and holy spirit (3:29).[56] The opening of the account in 3:19b–22 introduces the concept of household and family, and it correlates being "out of one's mind" (3:21) with being possessed by Beelzebul[57] or casting out demons by the prince of demons (3:22). The scribes from Jerusalem function as those to whom God has given the responsibility for righteousness both in the public domain and in the private domain of the household. Jesus' response, therefore, functions in the mode of prophetic discourse that criticizes and corrects the reasoning of those who have been selected by

---

[54] Cotter, *Miracles in Greco-Roman Antiquity,* 119.

[55] Robbins, *Tapestry of Early Christian Discourse,* 58–64, 77–88; idem, *Exploring the Texture of Texts,* 21–29.

[56] Cf. Vernon K. Robbins, "Rhetorical Composition and the Beelzebul Controversy," in Burton L. Mack and Vernon K. Robbins, *Patterns of Persuasion in the Gospels* (Sonoma, Calif.: Polebridge, 1989), 171–77.

[57] For discussion of Beelzebul, see Edward Langton, *Essentials of Demonology* (London: Epworth, 1949), 165–67; Werner Foerster, "Βεεζεβούλ," *TDNT* 1:605–6; Ferguson, *Demonology of the Early Christian World,* 18–22; Ernest Best, *The Temptation and the Passion: The Markan Soteriology* (2d ed.; SNTSMS 2; Cambridge: Cambridge University Press, 1990), 11.

God to oversee righteousness but have not carried out their duties responsibly. As Jesus elaborates his response to the scribes, he uses the argumentative procedures of wisdom discourse that features parables, enthymemes, and contraries:

> **Proposition/Result:** (23) "How can Satan cast out Satan? [= Satan cannot cast out Satan.]
> **Rationale:**
>> **Case:** (24) If a kingdom is divided against itself,
>> **Result:** that kingdom cannot stand.
>> **Case:** (25) And if a house is divided against itself,
>> **Result:** that house will not be able to stand.
>> **Case:** (26) And if Satan has risen up against himself and is divided,
>> **Result:** he cannot stand, but is coming to an end."
>> [**Unstated Rule:** If a powerful domain rises up against itself, it will destroy itself.]
> **Argument from the Contrary:**
>> **Case:** (27) "But no one can enter a strong man's house and plunder his goods, unless he first binds the strong man;
>> **Result:** then indeed he may plunder his house."
>> [**Unstated Contrary Rule:** If one powerful domain overpowers another, it may plunder the domain it subdues.]
> **Conclusion As Authoritative Apocalyptic Judgment:**
>> **Rule:** (28) "Truly, I say to you, all sins will be forgiven the sons of men, and whatever blasphemies they utter; (29) but whoever blasphemes against the Holy Spirit never has forgiveness, but is guilty of an eternal sin"—
>> **Case:** (30) for they [the scribes] had said, "He has an unclean spirit."
>> [= they had said that he cast out unclean spirits by an unclean spirit (Beelzebul), thus blaspheming against the Holy Spirit.]
>> [**Unstated Result:** The scribes never have forgiveness for their assertion about Jesus.]

Markan narration asserts that Jesus responded to the scribes "in parables" (ἐν παραβολαῖς), which means in arguments from analogy characteristic of wisdom discourse.[58] The analogies come from the commonly understood social domains of kingdom and household, and the mode of elaboration is characteristic of wisdom discourse. The term "Satan," however, introduces an apocalyptic *topos*. Thus, the question that introduces the proposition that Satan cannot cast out Satan (an *interrogatio*) begins the

---

58 Ronald F. Hock and Edward N. O'Neil, *The Progymnasmata* (vol. 1 of *The Chreia in Ancient Rhetoric;* Atlanta: Scholars Press, 1986), 177; Mack and Robbins, *Patterns of Persuasion in the Gospels,* 54–57, 143–60, etc.

argumentation in a mode of apocalyptic reasoning. The argumentation presents three reasons for believing the apocalyptic assertion. The first two reasons, based on the nature of a kingdom and a house, argue in a mode characteristic of wisdom discourse. The third reason, standing in a natural position of "conclusion" in a series of three,[59] brings the "wisdom" reasoning to fruition in an "apocalyptic" conclusion about Satan "rising up" and "coming to an end."[60] The argument from the contrary, then, continues with a counterargument from analogy (παραβολή). By analogy, the strong man is Satan, and the one who enters the strong man's house is Jesus. Ernest Best has devoted two editions of a book to the issues embedded in this argumentation with special focus on 3:27. Following the interpretations of Roland Meynet and Jan Lambrecht, Best understands 3:27 to be "the rhetorical centre of iii.20–35."[61] For him, the key soteriological issue in Mark is Jesus' binding of Satan in the temptation account and Jesus' assertion about binding the strong man in Mark 3:27. Best asserts:

> The conception of the binding of evil spirits is common in the apocalyptic writings. It presumably takes its Jewish origin [the idea also existed in Persian circles] in Isa. xxiv.21 f. and becomes more explicit in Tob. viii.3; I Enoch x.4 f., 11 f.; xviii.12–xix.2; xxi.1–6; liv.4 f.; Test. Levi xviii.12; Jub. xlviii.15. It reappears in the New Testament in Rev. xx.2, where it is explicitly said that it is Satan who is bound.... Christ has already bound Satan according to Mark iii.27; δήσῃ, aorist subjunctive, would suggest one definite act, and this must be the trial of strength which he had with Satan in the desert—the Temptation.[62]

For Best, Jesus' confrontation of Satan in the temptation supplemented by the argument in Mark 3:27 establishes the environment for understanding the salvific effect of Jesus' activity in the entire Gospel of Mark. One of these effects is to empower his disciples to cast out demons. In the end, Best proposes that "The argument in Test. Levi xviii and in

---

[59] Vernon K. Robbins, "Summons and Outline in Mark: The Three-Step Progression," *NovT* 23 (1981): 97–114; repr. in *The Composition of Mark's Gospel: Selected Studies from Novum Testamentum* (ed. David E. Orton; Brill's Readers in Biblical Studies 3; Leiden: Brill, 1999), 103–20.

[60] *1 En.* 10:1–7; 15:6–12; 54:1–6; Cotter, *Miracles in Greco-Roman Antiquity,* 106–12.

[61] Best, *Temptation and the Passion,* xxii; Roland Meynet, "Qui donc est 'le plus fort'? Analyse rhétorique de Mc 3,22–30; Mt 12,22–37; Luc 11,14–26," *RB* 90 (1983): 334–50; cf. Jan Lambrecht, *Once More Astonished: The Parables of Jesus* (New York: Crossroad, 1981), 117.

[62] Best, *The Temptation and the Passion,* 12–13.

Mark is precisely the same."[63] In the terms of the present essay, Best has used the enthymematic "apocalyptic cultural reasoning" of *T. Levi* 18 as a guide for reading the amplificatory-descriptive narration of the Gospel of Mark:

> **Rule:** (6) The heavens will be opened [by God],
> **Case:** and from the temple of glory sanctification will come upon him, with a fatherly voice [from God], as from Abraham to Isaac.
> **Result:** (7) And the glory of the Most High shall burst forth upon him. And the spirit of understanding and sanctification shall rest upon him.…
> **Case:** (8) For he shall give the majesty of the Lord to those who are his sons in truth forever … (11) and he will grant to the saints to eat of the tree of life.
> **Result:** The spirit of holiness shall be upon them.
> **Case:** (12) And Beliar shall be bound by him. And he shall grant to his children the authority to trample on wicked spirits.
> **Result:** (14) … and all the saints shall be clothed in righteousness.

This is apocalyptic reasoning that moves enthymematically from the actions of God as Rule through a special envoy of God's attributes and actions as Case to the Result of special blessing on a group of righteous ones, which includes the ability to overpower demons.

The overall argumentative texture of the Markan account reveals vigorous claims by Christians over both the public domain and the domain of the household. After the argument in 3:23–27, the Markan Jesus presents an authoritative judgment in 3:28–29—a type of assertion that often supplements argument from analogy and example in Greco-Roman discourse.[64] The authoritative judgment interweaves the topic of forgiveness of sins with blasphemy against the holy spirit, explaining that the blasphemy occurred when people asserted in public that Jesus possessed an unclean spirit (rather than the holy spirit). This judgment uses apocalyptic reasoning that presupposes that primary attributes and actions of God are embodied in an agent of God's authority and judgment during the end time. From this reasoning, blasphemy in public against the holy spirit in Jesus has the effect of blaspheming against God, which has devastating results.

The closing of the Markan account (3:31–35) inverts the public and private domain in the opening (3:19b–22). At the end of the account, "a crowd" is sitting around Jesus in the house (3:32), and Jesus describes his "true kinfolk" as those who "do the will of God" (3:35). The insight by Robert G. Hall that "arguing like an apocalypse" includes "a call to join the

---

[63] Ibid., 13.

[64] Hock and O'Neil, *Progymnasmata,* 177, 181; Mack and Robbins, *Patterns of Persuasion in the Gospels,* 28–29, 54–57, passim.

righteous realm God rules and to repudiate the wicked realm ruled by other forces"[65] would appear to apply here. The "household of Jesus" contains "people who do the will of God" by gathering around Jesus, who possesses the holy spirit, versus those who "blaspheme against the holy spirit" by asserting that Jesus possesses an unclean spirit. The rhetorical effect of the unit is a call to repudiate the unrighteous public realm nurtured by the scribes and others (3:21–22) and to join the righteous household realm nurtured by Jesus, who teaches them how to "do the will of God."

For the present essay on the intertexture of apocalyptic discourse in Mark, it is important to notice that this unit uses "common social topics"[66] characteristic of wisdom discourse to present a public challenge characteristic of prophetic discourse that contains topics internal to apocalyptic discourse intertwined with miracle discourse. This merger of prophetic, wisdom, apocalyptic, and miracle discourse is highly characteristic of the manner in which early Christians participated in the creative intertwining of conventional discourses during the Hellenistic period. If one follows the lead of Best's analysis, Markan discourse in this account reveals "cultural intertexture" with contemporary apocalyptic discourse. There is no significant oral-scribal intertexture here with apocalyptic literature or with prophetic literature. Rather, the intertexture lies within enthymematic presentation of apocalyptic *topoi*.

3. *Apocalyptic* Topoi *in Wisdom Discourse and Seeking of Signs in Mark 1:21–8:26*

In the previous two sections we have seen apocalyptic *topoi* in descriptive prophetic narration (1:1–15, 21–28) and in argumentative discourse about exorcisms (3:20–35). Given the presence of apocalyptic *topoi* in the introduction and the dispute over exorcisms, it is surprising that no apocalyptic *topoi* appear in the healings and disputes in 1:29–3:6; the miracle stories and rejection of Jesus at Nazareth in 4:35–6:6; the death of John the Baptist, the feedings, the miracles, and the dispute with the Pharisees in 6:14–8:10; and Jesus' discussion with the disciples and the healing of a blind man in 8:14–26. *Topoi* that may be interpreted as apocalyptic in nature appear in the initial exorcism (1:21–28), Jesus' choosing of twelve disciples (3:7–19), the dispute over exorcisms (3:20–35), Jesus' teaching in parables (4:1–34), Jesus' sending out of the Twelve (6:7–13),

---

[65] Robert G. Hall, "Arguing Like an Apocalypse: Galatians and an Ancient *Topos* Outside the Greco-Roman Rhetorical Tradition," *NTS* 42 (1996): 436.

[66] Robbins, *Tapestry of Early Christian Discourse,* 159–66, 179–82; idem, *Exploring the Texture of Texts,* 75–86.

and the Pharisees' challenge to Jesus to give a sign (8:11–13). This means that all the potential apocalyptic *topoi* in 1:21–28 concern the casting out of demons, except for the parables of Jesus in 4:1–34 and the Pharisees' challenge of Jesus in 8:11–13.

Once an interpreter has read the five parables with well-developed apocalyptic features in Matthew (13:24–30, 35–43, 47–50; 25:1–13, 14–30), one might suppose that Mark 4:1–34 also contains well-developed apocalyptic parables. In fact, only explanatory discourse about the parable of the Sower (4:11–12), the reference to Satan in Jesus' retelling of the parable of the Sower (4:15), Jesus' saying about hidden things coming to light (4:22), and the parable of the Mustard Seed (4:30–32) contain potentially apocalyptic *topoi*. Mark 4:1–34 is not argumentative discourse, but a combination of descriptive and elaborative discourse. The overall elaboration introduces a cultural system of understanding that focuses on mystery rather than a well-articulated *paideia.*[67] The chapter begins with references to teaching in 4:1–2 that evoke a context of wisdom discourse, and parables are a natural part of this kind of discourse. After the initial parable (4:3–9), Jesus explains to the disciples that "the mystery of the kingdom of God" has been given to them, while everything is "in parables" to those outside (4:11). This statement introduces an apocalyptic *topos* into Jesus' wisdom discourse. Mystery had become a special *topos* in apocalyptic discourse by the first century. Daniel 2:28–30 exhibits primary enthymematic reasoning associated with this *topos:*

> **Rule:** (28) there is a God in heaven who reveals mysteries,
> **Case:** and he has disclosed to King Nebuchadnezzar what will happen at the end of days.
> **Result:** ... (29) ... the revealer of mysteries disclosed to you what is to be.
> **Contrary Case:** (30) But as for me, this mystery has not been revealed to me because of any wisdom that I have more than any other living being, but in order that the interpretation may be known to the king and that you may understand the thoughts of your mind.
> **Contrary Result:** ... (36) This was the dream; now we will tell the king its interpretation....

In Daniel 2, wisdom discourse is mysterious apocalyptic discourse. Mark 4:1–20 has cultural intertexture with this Rule-Case-Result reasoning in apocalyptic discourse. With Jesus' explanation in 4:11, the parable of the Sower in 4:3–9 receives the status of an "apocalyptic" message from God in heaven to the hearers. With this parable, Jesus has revealed to them

---

[67] Burton L. Mack, "Teaching in Parables: Elaboration in Mark 4:1–34," in Mack and Robbins, *Patterns of Persuasion in the Gospels,* 143–60.

some special insight into the end of days. Jesus has been given the wisdom to interpret the parable, which he does in 4:13–20. Thus, the sequence of the parable, the explanation, and the retelling of the parable has cultural intertexture with apocalyptic reasoning about God as a revealer of mysteries like that exhibited in Dan 2:28–45.

While Mark 4:11 has "cultural" intertexture with Dan 2:28–45, it does not have "oral-scribal" intertexture with it. Rather, in accordance with the underlying "prophetic" dynamic of Markan discourse, Jesus' explanation reconfigures the Rule/Case/Result reasoning of Isa 6:9–10 into apocalyptic reasoning. Isa 6:9–10 asserts:

> **Rule:** (9) [The voice of the Lord said:] "Go and say to this people: 'Keep listening, but do not comprehend; keep looking, but do not understand.'
> **Case:** (10a) Make the mind of this people dull, and stop their ears, and shut their eyes,
> **Result:** (10b) so that they may not look with their eyes, and listen with their ears, and comprehend with their minds, and turn and be healed."

Mark 4:11–12 has changed the Rule-Case-Result reasoning of Isa 6:9–10 into:

> **Case:** (11) To you has been given the mystery of the kingdom of God, but for those outside everything is in parables;
> **Result:** (12) so that they may indeed see but not perceive, and may indeed hear but not understand; lest they should turn again, and be forgiven.
> [**Unstated Rule:** God is a revealer of the mystery of the kingdom to special people.]

In other words, the unstated Rule for Mark 4:11–12 is well stated in Dan 2:28, and with this change Markan discourse reconfigures prophetic discourse into apocalyptic discourse.

According to *1 Enoch,* the earthly Watchers—the "evil spirits" on earth—know only the "rejected mysteries," not the true, deep mysteries of the entire cosmos. They, "out of the hardness of their hearts," have broadcast the "false mysteries" to women, and "by those mysteries the women and men multiply evil deeds upon the earth" (*1 En.* 16:3). In *1 Enoch,* to counter this false understanding—the rejected mysteries—various angels reveal "the hidden, secret things" either to Noah or Enoch (*1 En.* 60:10–13; 68:1; 71:3–4; 104:10–13; 107:3; 108:15). The Gospel of Mark presents a variant version of this apocalyptic view. To everyone outside the Twelve, everything is in parables (which means something like "stories that keep the 'hidden wisdom' secret"). Yet, Jesus says in Mark 4:22, "there is nothing hid, except to be made manifest; nor is anything secret, except to come to light." In an apocalyptic worldview, all secrets of the cosmos will become known when the end-time events play themselves out in full.

After these statements, Jesus says in Mark 4:24–25:

Case: (24) ... the measure you give
Result: will be the measure you get, and still more will be given you.
Rule: (25) For to him who has will more be given; and from him who has
not, even what he has will be taken away.

The saying about the measure appears in the context of wisdom argumentation in Matt 7:1–2:

Exhortative Result: (1) Judge not that you be not judged.
Rule: (2) For with the judgment you pronounce you will be judged, and
the measure you give will be the measure you get.

Hans Dieter Betz appropriately identifies this as a basic rule of
exchange within society: "it is a rule of business stipulating that the same
instruments for measuring (*to metron*) must be used for all business trans-
actions."[68] From the social arena of business, wisdom discourse applies
this by analogy to ethical standards and to God at the last judgment. Mark
4:24–25 moves beyond the analogical reasoning of wisdom discourse into
apocalyptic reasoning when "for to him who has will more be given; and
from him who has not, even what he has will be taken away" becomes the
Rule; "the measure you give" becomes the Case; and "will be the measure
you get, and still more will be given you" becomes the Result. Mark 4:25
expresses a Rule based on attributes and actions of God rather than basic
social rules of exchange. In turn, the Result contains a statement of "more
will be given" on the basis of God's attributes both of "blessing more" and
of "utterly destroying that which is unjust." Thus, the Markan discourse has
reconfigured the reasoning of a wisdom *topos* into apocalyptic reasoning
that evokes the *topos* of God's final judgment, which brings superabundant
blessings in the context of terrible destruction.

The elaboration in Mark 4 ends with the parable of the Mustard Seed.
The Markan version of the parable has dramatically reconfigured and
recontextualized language about "the birds of the air," conventionally associated with the great apocalyptic tree in Dan 4:12, 21, and "nesting in the
shade of its branches," conventionally associated with the great cedar of
Lebanon in Ezek 17:23.[69] In Mark, the kingdom of God is not like a tree
that will be destroyed (Daniel) or a cedar of Lebanon that will be plucked

---

[68] Hans Dieter Betz, *The Sermon on the Mount* (Hermeneia; Minneapolis:
Fortress, 1995), 491.

[69] Cf. John Dominic Crossan, *In Parables: The Challenge of the Historical Jesus*
(New York: Harper & Row, 1973), 45–48.

up and replanted (Ezekiel), but it is a mustard seed that "becomes the greatest of all shrubs." In contrast to other *topoi* that function apocalyptically in Mark, the *topoi* in Mark 4:30–32 present a critique of traditional Jewish imagery of Israel's destiny, which is being reconfigured by the Markan story.[70] When Markan wisdom discourse shows oral-scribal or cultural intertexture with apocalyptic discourse, therefore, it often reconfigures it toward prophetic discourse.

Just as Mark 4:30–32 refuses, rather than embellishes, the image of the great tree in Ezek 17 or the apocalyptic tree in Dan 4, so Jesus refuses to play the role of an apocalyptic seer in Mark 8:11–13. When Pharisees ask Jesus to show them a sign from heaven, he will not do it. Again, Markan discourse exhibits a restraint that is more characteristic of prophetic than apocalyptic discourse. When apocalyptic *topoi* appear, they regularly are redirected back to earth in a manner more characteristic of prophetic than apocalyptic discourse.

4. Apocalyptic Topoi *in Suffering-Death Discourse in Mark 8:27–12:44*

In the last half of the Gospel, 8:27–16:8, suffering-death discourse becomes the centripetal mode in the context of the overall prophetic discourse. Glimpses of suffering-death discourse appear in 1:14; 3:6, 19; 4:17; 6:4, 11, 14–29, but prophetic-miracle discourse, with apocalyptic and wisdom *topoi* embedded in it, dominates the first half of the Gospel. In Mark 8:34–9:1, Jesus introduces suffering-death discourse argumentatively in public—in other words, not only with his disciples, but also with the crowd (8:34). This sets the stage for narration that leads to Jesus' crucifixion, death, and resurrection from the tomb. The argumentative introduction of suffering-death discourse occurs in the following manner:

> (34) He called the crowd with his disciples, and said to them,
> **Proposition/Result:** "If anyone wishes to follow after me, let him deny himself and take up his cross and follow me.
> **Rationale Based on Opposite Consequences/Case:** (35) For whoever wishes to save his life will lose it, but whoever loses his life for my sake, and for the sake of the gospel, will save it.
> **Confirmation of Rationale Based on Wishing to Save Life/Rule:** (36) For what does it benefit a person to gain the whole world and forfeit his life? [= It does not benefit a person to gain the whole world and forfeit his life.]
> **Confirmation of Rationale Based on Losing Life/Rule:** (37) Indeed, what can a person give in exchange for his life? [= A person can give nothing in exchange for his life.]

---

[70] Cf. Mack, "Teaching in Parables," 158.

Enthymematic Argument by Contrary Example:
Case: (38) For whoever is ashamed of me and of my words in this adulterous and sinful generation,
Result: of him the Son of Man will also be ashamed when he comes in the glory of his Father with the holy angels."
[**Unstated Rule:** A person who honors the Son of Man will be honored and a person who is ashamed of the Son of Man will be shamed.]

Conclusion/Exhortation by Apocalyptic Rule: (9:1) And he said to them, "Truly I tell you, there are some standing here who will not taste death until they see that the kingdom of God has come with power."
[**Unstated Case:** Those who honor the Son of Man/
Result: will be saved by the power of the kingdom;
Case: those who are ashamed of the Son of Man/
Result: will experience negative consequences from the power of the kingdom.][71]

The primary challenge for rhetorical understanding of the sequence in Mark 8:34–9:1 is the shift from suffering-death argumentation in a mode of wisdom discourse to apocalyptic discourse when it moves from the opening enthymematic sequence to the argument and the conclusion. The sequence begins with an inductive-deductive syllogism characteristic of early Christian wisdom discourse. In enthymematic terms, the opening sequence consists of Result-Case-Rule-Rule. An unusual thing here is the presentation of two Rules: one that addresses the desire to save life (first part of the Case) and one that addresses the loss of life (second part of the Case). In other words, the Confirmation in Mark 8:36–37 proceeds according to an argument "from the parts."[72] Mark 8:36 presents a Rule that attempting to secure one's life by accumulating possessions results in throwing one's life away. Mark 8:37 presents a Rule that implies that a person has to give life over to a great cause, because it is impossible to buy it with anything. Luke 9:25 omits the second confirmation, evidently considering the Rule about attempting to secure one's life to be sufficient for the syllogistic reasoning.

After this syllogistic beginning, characteristic of an elaboration that begins with an enthymeme rather than a paradigm,[73] the elaboration presents an

---

[71] I am grateful for discussions over Rhetoric-L during January, 2001, with Fredrick J. Long and others, which helped to clarify a number of things about this and other sequences of argumentation in the Gospels.

[72] This appears to be what Theon means by "argument from the parts" (Hock and O'Neil, *Progymnasmata,* 72–73).

[73] The two ways an elaboration (or speech) can begin, as Aristotle observed in *Rhet.* 1.2.8 (1356b).

argument and a conclusion. In Mediterranean discourse outside of Jewish and Christian circles the content of the argument and conclusion is unusual, because at this point the elaboration shifts from argumentation characteristic of wisdom discourse to argumentation characteristic of apocalyptic discourse. It is characteristic of apocalyptic discourse for the Rules to articulate attributes and actions of God, his angels, and representatives (like the Son of Man).[74] One can see how a basic Rule about the Son of Man emerges from Dan 7:13–14:

> **Case:** (13) I saw one like a son of man coming with the clouds of heaven. And he came to the Ancient One and was presented before him.
> **Result:** (14a) To him was given dominion and glory and kingship, that all peoples, nations, and languages should serve him.
> **Rule:** (14b) His dominion is an everlasting dominion that shall not pass away, and his kingship is one that shall never be destroyed.

The descriptive discourse in Dan 7:13–14 introduces an apocalyptic *topos* about the power of the Son of Man in the form of an apocalyptic syllogism. All three parts of the syllogism function as resources for early Christian discourse. Mark 8:38 is a Case-Result enthymeme (see above) that presupposes a Rule about the consequences of being ashamed of the Son of Man. This enthymeme presupposes that the only hope for a person's not being destroyed is to honor the universal and everlasting power of the Son of Man. In other words, this argumentation presupposes dynamics of honor and shame that are central values in the Mediterranean world.[75] The shame concerns social identification with a person who has been publicly dishonored by Jerusalem temple authorities (Mark 8:31) and the "gospel" that recounts this humiliation (cf. Rom 1:16; Heb 2:11). It also evokes the dynamics of accepting alternative kinship relations (cf. 2 Tim 1:15–16) where people do the will of God rather than are ashamed of Jesus' words (cf. Mark 3:31–35). In Mark 8:34–9:1, then, apocalyptic *topoi* are present in suffering-death discourse that begins in a mode characteristic of wisdom discourse and progresses into an apocalyptic argument and conclusion.

Immediately after Jesus' elaborated argument with the crowd and his disciples about suffering and death (8:34–9:1), he takes three of his disciples to a high mountain, where he is transformed into a shining personage before them. When the writer of the *Apocalypse of Peter* wanted to compose an apocalypse out of episodes in the Synoptic Gospels, he started with Jesus' discourse on the Mount of Olives (Matt 24 par. Mark 13: *Apoc.*

---

[74] Robbins, "Argumentative Textures in Socio-Rhetorical Interpretation," 54–59.

[75] Malina, *New Testament World*, 26–62; Robbins, *Exploring the Texture of Texts,* 76–77.

Pet. 1–14 [Ethiopic]) and continued with the transfiguration of Jesus (Matt 17:1–8 par. Mark 9:2–8: *Apoc. Pet.* 15–17 [Ethiopic]).[76] To make the trans-figuration account function as fully apocalyptic discourse, the author describes with detailed imagery the shining faces and bodies of Jesus, Eli-jah, and Moses (*Apoc. Pet.* 15). In other words, in *Apocalypse of Peter* the disciples have followed Jesus into a region of heaven, where holy people "shine" with a brilliance that makes it impossible to "look upon their faces." When the disciples ask where Abraham, Isaac, Jacob, and the rest of the righteous fathers are, they are shown a great garden (*Apoc. Pet.* 16). Again, the presupposition is that Jesus has taken the disciples into a region beyond the earth, where places like Paradise exist. When Peter asks if he should make three tabernacles, Jesus says that his eyes must be opened and ears unstopped so that he may see a tabernacle not made with hands for Jesus and his elect (*Apoc. Pet.* 16). At this point, a voice comes from heaven, the heaven opens, and the disciples behold men traveling with Jesus, Moses, and Elijah "into another heaven" (*Apoc. Pet.* 17). After this, the heaven shuts, the disciples pray, and the disciples go down the moun-tain glorifying God.

In comparison with the apocalyptic version of the transfiguration in the *Apocalypse of Peter,* one can see that the Markan account has a restraint related to the Exodus account of Moses on Mount Sinai. In Mark, Jesus' body and garments, without description of his face, become glistening, intensely white, and the disciples hear a voice from a cloud that speaks about "my Son" (9:7). But the heavens do not open, the disciples do not see anything else in this "region of heaven," and the disciples do not see Jesus or any-one travel from one region of heaven to another. The Markan account proceeds in a manner much more characteristic of prophetic discourse than apocalyptic discourse. Yet, as one can see from the development of the transfiguration account both in Matthew and in the *Apocalypse of Peter,* the Markan account contains "potentially apocalyptic" *topoi.*

5 Apocalyptic Discourse in a Prophetic Context: Mark 13

After the transfiguration (Mark 9:2–8), the next major scene for apoca-lyptic *topoi* emerges in Mark 13. Things changed dramatically for the study of Mark 13 when the analysis of the SBL "Genre of Apocalypse" group brought forth the following definition of apocalypse in 1979:

---

[76] J. K. Elliott, ed., *The Apocryphal New Testament: A Collection of Apocryphal Christian Literature in an English Translation Based on M. R. James* (Oxford: Clarendon, 1993), 600–612; Edgar Hennecke, ed., *New Testament Apocrypha* (ed. Wilhelm Schneemelcher; trans. and ed. R. McL. Wilson; rev. ed.; 2 vols.; Louisville: Westminster John Knox, 1991–92), 2:620–38.

"apocalypse" is a genre of revelatory literature with a narrative framework in which a revelation is mediated by an otherworldly being to a human recipient, disclosing a transcendent reality which is both temporal, insofar as it envisages eschatological salvation, and spatial, insofar as it involves another, supernatural world.[77]

This description called into question the definition of Mark 13 and its parallels as an apocalypse, since "the revelation" is not "mediated by an otherworldly being to a human recipient."[78] Shortly after this, David E. Aune described Mark 13 as a Greco-Roman *"Tempeldialog,"*[79] and the author of the current essay combined Aune's insights with earlier work to describe the chapter as a temple dialogue "with features of the conventional farewell speech and the apocalypse."[80] Subsequently, Adela Yarbro Collins, a member of the SBL Genre of Apocalypse Group, criticized the "Little Apocalypse Theory" about Mark 13 and described the chapter as "a scholastic dialogue with prophetic or apocalyptic content."[81] These alternative points of view broaden the discussion of the cultural intertexture of Mark to include aspects of Greco-Roman culture as well as Jewish culture.

Brief comparison with *Apoc. Pet.* 1–14 can help the reader to see why the SBL Genre of Apocalypse Group decided that Mark 13 did not qualify as an apocalypse. First, *Apoc. Pet.* 1 declares the work to be a revelation from Christ "through Peter to those who died for their sins, because they did not keep the commandment of God, their creator."[82] The *Apocalypse of Peter* evokes the *topos* of "revelation" from Christ to a person who transmits the revelation to others. This is absent from Mark, where Jesus functions as an earthly teacher (13:1) of four of his disciples.

---

[77] John J. Collins, "Introduction: Towards the Morphology of a Genre," *Semeia* 14 (1979), 9; cf. Adela Yarbro Collins, "Early Christian Apocalyptic Literature," *ANRW* 25.6:4670.

[78] John J. Collins, "Introduction," 9; cf. Adela Yarbro Collins, "Early Christian Apocalyptic Literature," 25.6:4691; idem, *Cosmology and Eschatology in Jewish and Christian Apocalypticism* (JSJSup 50; Leiden: Brill, 1996), 7.

[79] David E. Aune, *Prophecy in Early Christianity and the Ancient Mediterranean World* (Grand Rapids: Eerdmans, 1983), 184–87.

[80] Robbins, *Jesus the Teacher,* 173–79, esp. 178; cf. Hans-Joachim Michel, *Die Abshiedsrede des Paulus an die Kirche Apg 20, 17–38* (SANT 35; Munich: Kösel, 1973).

[81] Adela Yarbro Collins, *The Beginnings of the Gospel: Probings of Mark in Context* (Minneapolis: Fortress, 1992), 77; cf. Egon Brandenburger, *Markus 13 und die Apokalyptik* (Göttingen: Vandenhoeck & Ruprecht, 1984), 15.

[82] All quotations of *Apocalypse of Peter* are from Elliott, *Apocryphal New Testament,* 600–609.

Second, in the *Apocalypse of Peter* Jesus speaks throughout in first-person singular about himself, the revealer, and Peter tells his experience in first-person singular to the reader in *Apoc. Pet.* 2–3, 15–17. This kind of first-person narration, which is a characteristic feature of apocalypses, also is absent from Mark 13.

Third, Jesus' revelation to Peter merges Mark 13:5–6 with 13:21 (*Apoc. Pet.* 1) to create an enthymeme at the beginning based on the Rule that "the coming of the Son of God will not be plain [unnoticeable]." This creates the context for an "amplified description" of the *topos* of Jesus' coming in great majesty. Jesus comes with his cross going before him as he shines seven times greater than the sun, with all his angels accompanying him in his majesty, and with the Father setting a crown on his head so he is empowered to judge the quick and the dead (*Apoc. Pet.* 1). Again, the restraint of Markan narration keeps the description and the argumentation closer to prophetic discourse, which describes the Day of the Lord without amplifying the details of the process in the manner of apocalyptic discourse. The narration in Mark 13:26–27 presents Case-Result argumentation that presupposes the results of God's transfer of power to one like a son of man in Dan 7:

> **Case:** (26) And then they will see the Son of man coming in clouds with great power and glory.[83]
> **Result:** (27) And then he will send out the angels, and gather his elect from the four winds, from the ends of the earth to the ends of heaven.[84]
> [**Unexpressed Rule:** The dominion of the one like a son of man is an everlasting dominion that shall not pass away, and his kingship is one that shall never be destroyed (Dan 7:14b).]

In contrast to the *Apocalypse of Peter* (and also Matt 24, which provided the base for the amplification in *Apoc. Pet.*), the Son of Man in Mark does not judge the quick and the dead. Rather, the Son of Man enacts only one role in Mark 13, the sending out of his angels to gather all of the elect together (13:27).[85]

---

[83] Cf. *4 Ezra* 13:30–32: "And bewilderment of mind shall come over those who dwell on the earth. And they shall plan to make war against one another, city against city, place against place, people against people, and kingdom against kingdom. And when these things come to pass and the signs occur which I showed you before, then my son will be revealed, whom you saw as a man coming up from the sea."

[84] Cf. Deut 30:4: "Even if you are exiled to the ends of the world, from there the Lord your God will gather you, and from there he will bring you back."

[85] Robbins, *Jesus the Teacher,* 173–79; idem, "Rhetorical Ritual: Apocalyptic Discourse in Mark 13," in Carey and Bloomquist, *Vision and Persuasion,* 114–16.

Fourth, Jesus moves directly from his description to Peter of his coming (*Apoc. Pet.* 1) to "learning" from "the parable of the fig tree" (*Apoc. Pet.*
2), which comes near the end of the Markan speech (13:28). This earlier
position in the discourse provides the setting for: (a) recitation of the parable; (b) first-person inquiry by Peter how "we" can understand it, because
"We do not know"; and (c) elaborated explanation of the meaning of the
parable. Jesus' explanation amplifies the nature of the fig tree as "the house
of Israel," leading to a concluding enthymeme that argues that whose who
die by the hand of the false Christs who come will be "reckoned among
the good and righteous martyrs who have pleased God in their life" (*Apoc.
Pet.* 2). In other words, *Apocalypse of Peter* omits the description of the
"tribulations" that are like "birth pangs" in Mark 13:7–20, which are conventional biblical and prophetic *topoi* about disturbances that will lead to
judgment by the Lord.[86] *Apocalypse of Peter* 2 builds the apocalyptic *topoi*
of "false Christs" and "dying as a martyr" into amplified descriptions and
enthymematic arguments about the end time.

Fifth, after these opening revelations, Jesus begins to show Peter things
in heaven. Jesus shows him "the souls of all men" in his right hand (*Apoc.
Pet.* 3), God commanding hell to open its bars when all people from the
east to the west gather together for the judgment of God (*Apoc. Pet.* 4), and
fire overtaking those "who have fallen away from faith in God and have
committed sin" (*Apoc. Pet.* 5). In other words, Jesus shows Peter what happens to "those who endure" (Mark 13:9–13) and those who are deceived
during the times of distress (Mark 13:14–23) rather than recounting, in conventional prophetic manner, the nature of the times of tribulation for them.

Sixth, when Jesus recounts his "coming upon an eternal cloud of
brightness" with the angels (cf. Mark 13:24–27), he amplifies the scene by
describing:

(1) the angel Uriel's burning of the souls of sinners (*Apoc. Pet.* 6),
(2) the pit of fire where sexually errant people are placed (*Apoc. Pet.* 7),
(3) another pit with excrement in addition to fire for parents who aborted
their unborn or delivered them to death after they were born (*Apoc. Pet.* 8),
(4) the angel Ezrael's leading of people to various places either to be tor-
mented or to see people in torment (*Apoc. Pet.* 9–12).

An overall enthymeme governs this activity, which is articulated by Jesus
in *Apoc. Pet.* 6:

Rule: Rewards shall be given to every man according to his deeds.
Case: As for the elect who have done good,

---

[86] E.g., 2 Chr 15:6; Isa 13:13; 14:30; 19:2; Jer 22:23.

Result: they shall come to me and not see death by the devouring fire.
Contrary Case: But the unrighteous, the sinners, and the hypocrites
Result: shall stand in the depths of darkness that shall not pass away, and
their chastisement is the fire, and angels bring forward their sins and prepare for them a place wherein they shall be punished for ever, every one
according to his transgression.

Mark 13:27 presents the conventional biblical and prophetic *topos* of gathering the elect as the one role enacted by the Son of Man. In contrast,
Apoc. Pet. 6–12 develops the role of the Son of Man as "judge" in a manner characteristic of "apocalyptic" discourse. *Apocalypse of Peter* 13 returns
to the *topos* of the elect (cf. Mark 13:27), amplifying it with a scene in
which the angels "clothe them with the raiment of life" in the sight of all
the unrighteous. Then the unrighteous develop the meaning of the action
with enthymematic argumentation (*Apoc. Pet.* 13). First they articulate an
enthymematic plea:

Petitionary Result: Have mercy upon us.
Case: We know the judgment of God, which he declared to us beforetime
and we did not believe.
[**Unexpressed Rule:** Coming to the knowledge of God's judgment
(repentance) brings mercy.]

When the angel Tatirokos tells them that the time for repentance has
passed, the unrighteous articulate an enthymeme that reflects the inner ideology of the narration:

Rule: Righteous is the judgment of God.
Case: We have heard and perceived that his judgment is good.
Result: We are recompensed according to our deeds.

This enthymeme shows the inner "apocalyptic" reasoning that guides the
amplification of the biblical and prophetic *topos* of gathering the elect into
"apocalyptic" discourse about the unrighteous versus the elect in the
Apocalypse of Peter. Matthew 24–25 also amplifies Mark 13 in an apocalyptic manner, but the *Apocalypse of Peter* shows even more clearly how
wisdom and prophetic *topoi* were nurtured into "apocalyptic" discourse
with amplificatory-descriptive and argumentative-enthymematic elaboration of certain *topoi*.

The conclusion to Jesus' revelation to Peter in *Apoc. Pet.* 14 contains
a charge to Peter to "Spread my gospel throughout all the world in peace"
(cf. Mark 13:10). In *Apocalypse of Peter* "the gospel" has attained a fully
apocalyptic form: "Jesus' words shall be the source of hope and of life,
and suddenly shall the world be ravished" (*Apoc. Pet.* 14). Mark, in contrast, ends with a parable about "living in a household" in a posture of

"watching," because only the Father knows the day or the hour. In a context of turmoil and anticipation of salvation when the Son of Man comes,
wisdom, miracle, suffering-death, and prophetic *topoi* deeply inform and
guide Markan discourse. Apocalyptic *topoi* appear in manifold places
throughout Mark. Nevertheless, the discourse exhibits a continual return
to wisdom, miracle, prophetic, and suffering-death *topoi* that is uncharacteristic of fully apocalyptic discourse.

6. Apocalyptic Topoi *in the Trial before the Sanhedrin: Mark 14–16*

In the context of the suffering-death discourse that dominates Mark
14–16, apocalyptic *topoi* appear in argumentative narration when Jesus
stands before the high priest and the Sanhedrin after he has been arrested.
In response to the high priest's question if he is "the Messiah, the Son of
the Blessed," Jesus answers:

> **Case:** (14:62) "I am [the Messiah, the Son of the Blessed];
> **Result:** and you will see the Son of Man
> seated at the right hand of the Power,
> and coming with the clouds of heaven.
> **[Unexpressed Rules:**
> (1) The Lord said to my Lord, "Sit at my right hand until I make your ene-
> mies your footstool" (Psalm 110:1);
> (2) The dominion of the one like a son of man is an everlasting domin-
> ion that shall not pass away, and his kingship is one that shall never be
> destroyed (Dan 7:14b).]

Daniel 7:14 first appears in Mark as a resource for a basic Rule in argumentative suffering-death discourse underlying Mark 8:38 (see above). Then
Dan 7:14 reappears as a basic Rule in argumentative prophetic discourse
about events when the end finally arrives (Mark 13:24–27). The appearance
of Dan 7:14 yet again in Jesus' trial before the high priest and the Sanhedrin
reveals its presence not only as cultural intertexture but also as oral-scribal
intertexture for Markan discourse. Thus, it is clear that Dan 7 is a substan-
tive oral-scribal resource for the Markan embedding of apocalyptic *topoi*
into prophetic, miracle, wisdom, and suffering-death discourse.

7. Conclusion

There are many *topoi* in Markan prophetic, miracle, wisdom, and
suffering-death discourse that can potentially evoke, but need not
definitively evoke, apocalyptic reasoning and argumentation. *Topoi*
such as the splitting open of the heavens (1:10), the descent of the spirit
(1:10), a voice coming out of heaven (1:11), and tribulations (4:17;
13:7–8, 19) are present in biblical and prophetic discourse in a manner

that does not call forth fully apocalyptic reasoning and argumentation. Also, unclean spirits and demons are present in Mediterranean miracle discourse with no apocalyptic overtones. In spite of this, the opening exorcism (1:21–28); the argumentation about exorcisms, Satan, and unclean spirits (3:20–30); and the repetitive reference to unclean spirits and demons in Markan miracle summaries naturally evoke the apocalyptic reasoning in *1 En.* 15:6–12. Much Markan wisdom discourse that features Jesus disputing with scribes, Pharisees, and Sadducees reveals little or no apocalyptic *topoi*. However, Jesus' presentation of parables in Mark 4 reveals an emphasis on "mystery" (4:11) characteristic of the book of Daniel, a view of everything hidden being revealed (4:22) that evokes apocalyptic revelation, and reasoning about receiving "more" than one's measure (4:24–25) that appears to be apocalyptic amplification of wisdom reasoning. In addition, the presence of Satan on earth (1:13; 4:15), the fulfillment of time (1:15), the drawing near of the kingdom of God (1:15), the binding of Satan (3:26–27), the beginning of "the end" (13:7–8), and the coming of the Son of Man (8:38; 13:26; 14:62) exhibit cultural and oral-scribal intertexture explicitly with apocalyptic discourse.

On the one hand, it could seem that there should be no debate that the Gospel of Mark is apocalyptic discourse. Our description throughout, however, has tried to indicate why interpreters have substantively different views of its function in Markan narration. Norman Perrin championed the view that the Gospel of Mark is apocalyptic discourse. Building on the work of interpreters such as Albert Schweitzer, Johannes Weiss, Ernst Lohmeyer, and Willi Marxsen, Perrin asserted in 1974:

> Fundamentally, Mark is an apocalypse in its purpose. For all that he writes realistic narrative, the intent of the evangelist is precisely that of the apocalyptic seers in the discourses in Mark 13 and its parallels or that of John of Patmos in the book of Revelation. . . . Like an apocalyptic seer, he views himself and his readers as caught up in a divine human drama.[87]

Viewing the Gospel of Mark as an apocalypse, Perrin understood the apocalyptic drama of its "realistic narrative" to unfold in three acts:

> (a) John the Baptist "preaches" and is "delivered up" [1:7, 14].
> (b) Jesus "preaches" and is "delivered up" [1:14; 9:31; 10:33].
> (c) The Christians "preach" and are to be "delivered up" [13:9–13].[88]

---

87 Norman Perrin, *The New Testament: An Introduction—Proclamation and Parenesis, Myth and History* (New York: Harcourt Brace Jovanovich, 1974), 162.
88 Ibid., 144.

"When the third act is complete," Perrin asserted, "the drama will reach its climax in the coming of Jesus as Son of man (13:26)."[89] In enthymematic terms, this is a Case-Result argument:

> **Case:** John the Baptist, Jesus, and the Christians preach and are delivered up.
> **Result:** Jesus will come as the Son of Man.

Like many enthymematic arguments, it is not entirely clear what Perrin presupposed to be the unstated Rule. If the argumentation is apocalyptic, the Rule would concern attributes and actions of God that are bringing imminent judgment upon both the earth and the heavens. Perhaps Perrin's proposal for the conceptual location of Mark presupposed a Rule something like: Within God's plan for the end of time, it will be necessary for God's righteous ones to preach God's good news and be delivered up before the Son of Man will come to gather the elect from the four corners of the earth. While few would argue, I think, that this enthymematic argumentation is not present in Mark, it is also clear that this emphasis can give us only a partial view of Markan discourse.

In contrast to Norman Perrin and others who follow his lead, Richard Horsley has argued that wisdom discourse in the Gospel of Mark guides "the author's main message," which is "to refuse to be distracted by ostensibly earth-shaking events from the concerns of the movement. But the concerns of the movement were renewal of Israel centered in Galilee, with a rejection of temple and high priests as exploitative and unfaithful stewards."[90] Horsley's assertion implies that the dominant enthymematic mode of Mark features *topoi* that present the attributes and actions of God as hidden in God's creation. In other words, implicit in Horsley's assertion is an argument that Markan discourse exhorts people to turn away from "apocalyptic signs" toward the establishment of justice on the basis of knowledge about walking the "path of life" and rejecting the lure of power and wealth. One could, perhaps, present an entire commentary on Mark in this mode by correlating Burton Mack's interpretation of Mark 4 as a "rhetorical elaboration"[91] with Mary Ann Tolbert's presentation of the "maps" for the Markan plot in Mark 4 and Mark 12:1–12[92] to argue for

---

[89] Ibid.

[90] Richard Horsley, "Wisdom and Apocalypticism in Mark," in *In Search of Wisdom: Essays in Memory of John G. Gammie* (ed. Leo G. Perdue et al.; Louisville: Westminster John Knox, 1993), 242.

[91] Mack and Robbins, *Patterns of Persuasion in the Gospels,* 143–60.

[92] Mary Ann Tolbert, *Sowing the Gospel: Mark's World in Literary-Historical Perspective* (Minneapolis: Fortress, 1989).

enthymematic wisdom at the center of the Gospel of Mark. But this also would give us a partial view of Markan discourse.

In contrast to these two interpretations, Robert H. Gundry has written a commentary based on the following presupposition: "Marks' meaning lies on the surface. He writes a straightforward apology of the Cross, for the shameful way in which the object of Christian faith and subject of Christian proclamation died, and hence for Jesus as the Crucified One."[93] From a sociorhetorical perspective, this is an assertion that suffering-death enthymematic argumentation dominates Markan narration. It is informative when Gundry writes twenty-one "No-sentences" introduced by "The Gospel of Mark contains no ciphers, no hidden meanings, no sleight of hand" to lead up to the statement quoted above. Following the lead sentence are sentences such as:

> No messianic secret designed to mask a theologically embarrassing absence of messianism from the ministry of the historical Jesus.... No covert attack on divine man Christology.... No discipular enlightenment in the miracles.... No apocalyptic code announcing the end. No de-apocalyptic code cooling down an expectation of the end. No open end celebrating faith over verifiability. No overarching concentric structure providing a key to meaning at midpoint. No riddle wrapped in a mystery inside an enigma.[94]

This sequence of assertions exhibits Gundry's attempt to reduce Markan narration to "one basic enthymeme" rather than to display the multiple kinds of enthymematic argumentation that interweave with one another in this early Christian discourse. When a sociorhetorical interpreter asks what mode of suffering-death discourse the Gospel of Mark presents, it becomes clear that Gundry is thinking beyond a wisdom or prophetic mode to an atonement mode like one finds in 1 Pet 2:22–24:

> **Case:** (22) He committed no sin; no guile was found on his lips.
> (23): When he was reviled, he did not revile in return; when he suffered, he did not threaten; but he trusted to him who judges justly.
> **Rule:** (24) He himself bore our sins in his body on the tree, that we might die to sin and live to righteousness.
> **Result:** By his wounds you have been healed.

This mode of reasoning would appear to be implied by the following interpretation by Gundry of Mark 10:41–45:

---

[93] Robert H. Gundry, *Mark: A Commentary on His Apology for the Cross* (Grand Rapids: Eerdmans, 1993), 1.

[94] Ibid.

In saying that his serving goes to the extent of giving his life as a ransom in substitution for many, Jesus interprets his approaching death as supremely self-sacrificial for the saving of many others' lives. Thus the Marcan apologetics of miraculous ability, of didactic authority, and of predictive power metamorphose into an apologetic of beneficial service. The Cross will not bring shame to its victim, but salvation to its followers.[95]

It is clear to most that suffering-death discourse is a very important feature in Markan discourse. But is it appropriate to argue for this discourse alone as dominant for understanding descriptive, explanatory, and argumentative discourse in the Gospel of Mark? The thesis of this essay is that the answer is not to be found in only one major kind of discourse in the Gospel of Mark. As an interpreter looks at the kinds of Christian discourse that had developed by the end of the first century c.e., it is obvious that both apocalyptic and precreation discourse had moved into a potentially "totalizing" position. On the one hand, the Revelation to John presented an overall view that could have absorbed all narratives and discourses into apocalyptic reasoning and argumentation. On the other hand, the Gospel of John presented a narrative about Jesus that could have absorbed all narratives and discourses into precreation reasoning and argumentation. By the fourth century, precreation discourse had won out over apocalyptic discourse in the centers of power in the Roman Empire. Nevertheless, apocalyptic discourse remained alive and well in many regions, and it has emerged in a vibrant fashion during virtually every century since.

The underlying thesis of this essay is that interpreters must not allow the dynamic interaction between apocalyptic and precreation discourse in early Christianity to obscure the manner in which most New Testament literature continually interweaves wisdom, miracle, prophetic, and suffering-death discourse into its narration. The Gospel of Mark is a foremost instance. Since precreation discourse is absent from it, one might imagine that apocalyptic discourse would totally dominate its presentation of Jesus. Prophetic discourse, however, lies at its base. Markan discourse interweaves apocalyptic, miracle, wisdom, and suffering-death discourse into prophetic discourse. Interpreters who focus on one of these discourses in a manner that excludes the others give a skewed view of the internal nature of Christian discourse during the first century, and after it to the present.

---

95 Ibid., 581.

The Intertexture of Lukan Apocalyptic Discourse

L. Gregory Bloomquist

1. Definitions

In analysis that is attentive to methodological accuracy, it is important to note that the definition of a subject will determine the eventual outcome of the results.[1] The situation is no different in the determination of "intertexture" or of "apocalyptic discourse." The definition of apocalyptic discourse that I will use for this study is the one assigned to us, namely, "Apocalyptic discourse reconfigures our perception of all regions of time and space, in the world and in the body, in light of the conviction that God will intervene to judge at some time in the future."[2] It should be clear from the above that a different definition will yield a different understanding of apocalyptic discourse and thus different results.

I understand "intertexture" as it has been used by Vernon Robbins in his sociorhetorical analysis of texts. By it, he means "the interaction of the language in the text with 'outside' material and physical 'objects,' historical events, texts, customs, values, roles, institutions, and systems."[3] Intertexture is, in other words, those points of intersection within our passages with other textual (oral or scribal), social, cultural, or historical worlds that are not the immediate, fictive world that is created by the text of Luke itself, a world that is discerned by what we might call "innertextural" analysis.[4] "Intertexture" is, then, as it were, the juncture of the inner world of the text, a world created by literary and narrative artifice, and the "outer world" within which the text arose and took its shape. Not everything

---

[1] L. Gregory Bloomquist, "Methodological Criteria for Apocalyptic Rhetoric: A Suggestion for the Expanded Use of Sociorhetorical Analysis," in *Vision and Persuasion: Rhetorical Dimensions of Apocalyptic Discourse* (ed. Gregory Carey and L. Gregory Bloomquist; St. Louis: Chalice, 1999), 181–203.

[2] The definition was determined by the editorial board of the Rhetoric of Religious Antiquity series (Deo Publishing).

[3] Vernon K. Robbins, *Exploring the Texture of Texts: A Guide to Socio-Rhetorical Interpretation* (Valley Forge, Pa.: Trinity Press International, 1996), 40.

[4] Ibid., 7–39.

in the latter world is found in our text; all that is and is not in the text is the subject of study of the outer world (social and cultural texture, sacred texture, etc.). So, we do not deal here with the larger social and cultural texture or sacred texture that does not "intersect" Lukan apocalyptic discourse, only with the intersection points themselves.

Furthermore, there are many "junctures" of worlds in Luke's two volumes that are not found in the specific apocalyptic discourse of Luke. There is miracle discourse, wisdom discourse, death-resurrection discourse, and the like. We omit the junctures within these discourses.

2. Identifications

Those verses in Luke-Acts that I have determined to contain apocalyptic discourse as defined above are given here. For Luke: 1:46–55, 68–79; 2:29–32, 34–38; 3:1–6, 16–17; 4:16–30; 6:21 and 25; 7:18–23; 9:23–27, 52–56; 10:8–24; 11:29–32; 12:2–12, 35–48, 49–53, 54–59; 13:1–9, 22–30, 34–35; 14:15–24; 16:19–31; 17:20–37; 19:11–27, 28–44; 20:9–19, 27–38; 21:5–36; 22:15–30, 67–70; 23:39–43; 24:19–27, 44–49. For Acts: 1:3–11; 2:14–36; 3:12–26 (specifically, vv. 18–26); 10:34–43; 13:26–47; 15:15–18; 17:30–31; 26:23; 28:25–28. I continue to have questions about certain of the above verses and their apocalyptic nature (specifically, Luke 24:44–49; Acts 13:26–41; 17:30–31). However, given their consistency with these other verses, and the fact that their exclusion does not change the overall picture, I have included even these verses in the discussion.

3. Intertexture in Apocalyptic Discourse Material in the Gospel according to Luke

Having identified those verses containing apocalyptic discourse, we can begin to discuss the intertexture made evident by them.

Luke 1:46–55. As has often been noted, a close Old Testament parallel appears to provide this hymn with its underlying structure. That parallel, the hymn of Hannah (1 Sam 2:1–11), or possibly (though less likely) the hymn of the prophet Habakkuk (Hab 3), is further supplemented with extensive reconfigurations of Old Testament texts: Ps 35:9 (1:47), Gen 29:32 (Leah), 30:13 (Leah), and *4 Ezra* 9:45 (barren Zion) (1:48); Deut 10:21 (Moses) and Zeph 3:17 LXX (1:49); Ps 103:17 and *Pss. Sol.* 13:11 (1:50); Ps 89:11 LXX, Sir 10.14, Job 12.19, Ezek 21:31, Ps 107:9, and 1QM XIV, 10–11 (1:51–53); and Isa 41:8–9, Ps 98:3 LXX, Mic 7:20, 2 Sam 22:51, and *Pss. Sol.* 10:4 (1:54–55). A clear cultural intertexture can also be found in the hymn's apparent focus on reversal, namely, that economic power and honor-shame roles are givens and that the deity alone can overturn them. Since there is no historical intertexture evident that ties the actions of God to any specific historical events, but only to the characteristic action of God, one is left with the impression that this action of the deity is characteristic of Israel's past experience.

Luke 1:68–79. There is no single Old Testament precedent for Zechariah's hymn as there is for the Magnificat. Nevertheless, the individual verses are equally definable in terms of intertexture: Pss 41:4, 72:18, 106:48 and 1 Kgs 1:48 (1:68a); Ps 111:9 (1:68b); Ps 18:3, 1 Sam 2:10 and 2 Sam 22:3 (1:69a); 2 Sam 7:12–13 (1:69b); Pss 18:18, 106:10 and 2 Sam 22:18 (1:71); Gen 24:12 (1:72a); Pss 105:8 and 106:45 (1:72b); Gen 26:3 (1:73); Josh 24:14 and Isa 38:20 (1:74b–75a); Mal 3:1 and Isa 40:3 (1:76b); Ps 107:10 (1:79a); and Isa 59:8 (1:79b). One is not left with the same sense of reversal here as is found in the previous verses. Rather, the notion of the faithfulness of the deity and prophetic fulfillment dominate. The former is clear in the abundant use of verses from the Psalms in Luke 1:68–75 and in the remaining verses of reconfigurations of texts from the prophets (e.g., Isa 40:3 in Luke 1:76).

Luke 2:29–35. The hymn of the aged Simeon is comprised, like the earlier two hymns noted, of text reconfigured from the Old Testament, and, in this case, primarily from Isaiah: Gen 15:15 LXX (2:29b); Isa 40:5 (2:30); Isa 52:10 (2:31); Isa 49:6 (2:32a); Isa 46:13 (2:32b); Ezek 14:17 (2:35). We are also introduced here to a theme that will accompany Lukan apocalyptic discourse, especially in its intertextural facet, until the very end of the corpus in Acts 28, namely, the notion of divine favor toward the Gentiles. The sense of fulfillment and a kind of realized apocalyptic is clear from the form that Simeon's enthymematic hymn takes: I should be able now to die in peace, since I have seen your salvation, since "one who has seen your salvation may die in peace." The salvation Simeon sees is, of course, not accomplished as such but it is in some way focused in the child Jesus.

Luke 3:1–6. Luke shares with the Synoptic and Johannine proclamation of John the Baptist in the wilderness the recitation of Isa 40:3 LXX (cf. 1QS VIII, 12–16). Unlike the Synoptic parallels, however, Luke also recites Isa 40:4–5b LXX. The fuller recitation builds on the enunciation by Simeon (from Isa 46 and 49) and continues to herald implicitly the apocalyptic notion of salvation for the whole earth (especially Luke 3:6, which directly parallels Simeon's prophetic utterance in Luke 2:30, echoing Luke 40:5).

Luke 3:16–17. The proclamation of John the Baptist echoes Old Testament passages such as Mal 3:1–2; 4:5–6; and Ps 118:26. It finds parallels in later Second Temple texts (*Mekilta* to Exod 21:2 and *b. Ketubbot* 96a in relation to 3:16b as well as in 1QS 4.20–21, though these may find their first echo in the Markan souce). The *Lives of the Prophets* 21:3 may be a parallel to or background for 3:17.

It is noteworthy that in two subsequent sections containing apocalyptic discourse, Luke will employ the proclamation of John found here. In Acts 1:3–11 the narrator will have the risen Jesus recall to his followers these words of John in 3:16, though now couched in Jesus' own proclamation. In Acts 13:24–25, Paul will use the fuller recitation Luke 3:16 to speak to the Jews in Pisidian Antioch of the fulfillment brought in Jesus. In neither case, however, is the apocalyptic preaching of John in 3:17 picked up, an absence reminiscent of the truncated recitation of Isaiah in the next section.

It is, perhaps, an indication that we will need to determine the *kind* of apocalyptic discourse in Luke-Acts, rather than just that it *is* present. For example, might John be evidencing one kind of apocalyptic expectation and Jesus another? If so, might it be that the content determines the kind of expectation? Might it be that John's expectation does not envision the same role for the Gentiles as that of Jesus?

Luke 4:16–30. Isaiah 61:1–2a LXX seems clearly to be the base-text from which Jesus' reading is drawn (cf. 4:18a, b, c and 19), though 4:18d appears to echo Isa 58:6 LXX. As is often noted, Isa 61:2b is not quoted. As in the previous section containing apocalyptic discourse (3:16–17), 4:18–19 is also echoed in the sermon of Paul in Pisidian Antioch (Acts 13:14–41). Echoes can also be found in Luke 7:18–23 (see below) and its use of Isaiah. The fuller story also incorporates Jesus' quote of an apparent maxim and allusions to the cultural *topoi* of Elijah and the Sidonian widow of Zarephath and of Elisha and Naaman the Syrian, two prophets who ministered to two Gentiles.

Luke 6:21 and 25. The social intertexture of these two verses is clear: both deal with common human realities. However, whether the two verses can be "localized" culturally or "referenced" in terms of oral-scribal texture is another matter. While the latter is unlikely, I have argued elsewhere for the extensive cultural location of both verses.[5]

Luke 7:18–23. Reminiscent of Luke 4:18–19, Jesus uses Isa 61:1 (7:22c), as he had done in the previous section, but also Isa 35:5 (7:22c and f) and Isa 26:19 (7:22g). These texts provide inductive examples that are the material for Jesus' suggestion to John's disciples that Jesus is indeed the one to be expected.

Luke 9:23–27. There is no clear oral-scribal material to be found here beyond, of course, Luke's apparent, extensive use of Mark (8:34–9:1). Nevertheless, extensive cultural intertexture is apparent and more than likely accounts for the echo of Plutarch's *Sera* 9.554a.[6]

Luke 9:52–56. Unique to Luke, the query of James and John— whether they should ask for fire from heaven to consume a Samaritan

---

[5] "The Rhetoric of the Historical Jesus," in *Whose Historical Jesus?* (ed. Michael Desjardins and William E. Arnal; Studies in Christianity and Judaism 7; Waterloo, Ont.: Wilfrid Laurier, 1997), 98–117.

[6] Joseph A. Fitzmyer, *The Gospel according to Luke* (2 vols.; AB 28–28A; Garden City, N.Y.: Doubleday, 1981), 1:785.

village that has not received Jesus—contains an echo of a similar story in 2 Kgs 1:10, 12 concerning Elijah and Ahaziah "the king of Samaria" (2 Kgs 1:3). It is unclear, though, whether this is oral-scribal reconfiguration or an echo of cultural intertexture. (See also, below, the comment on 12:49–53.)

Luke 10:8–24. In this extended mission exhortation, there are a limited number of Old Testament allusions. They are to stories or prophecies of cities characterized by wickedness. All of them are Gentile cities, namely, the destruction of Sodom and Gomorrah (Gen 19:24–28) and the prophesied destruction of Tyre and Sidon in Isa 14:13, 15 and Ezek 26–28.

Luke 11:29–32. The sign of Jonah that Jesus cites explicitly appears to be an allusion to the fate of Jonah in the belly of the whale (Jonah 1:17–2:10), a likely echo from cultural intertexture. So, too, would the reference to the Ninevites (11:30, 32) likely be a direct echo of those to whom Jonah preaches (Jonah 3:1–4:11) and the Queen of the South (Q 11:31) a reference to the Queen of Sheba and her visit to Solomon (cf. 1 Kgs 10:1–10 or 2 Chr 9:1–12). None of these three gives any indication of being oral-scribal intertexture. Nevertheless, it is significant that they incorporate three cultural images of Gentile acknowledgement of the divine in Jewish understanding. This is the only consistent element in these images, since only in the case of the Queen of the South is it clear that "acknowledgement" involves coming to Israel.

Luke 12:1–12. This section contains several elements of cultural intertexture. The reference to the Pharisees (12:1) does not appear to be so much historical as it is cultural, as is clear from the augmented reference to "leaven" (12:1). There appear to be two culturally relevant maxims (12:2 and 12:6; cf. 4:23–24) and a cultural intertexture echo of the "Son of Man" (12:8, 10), of the angels of God (12:8, 9), and of the Holy Spirit (12:10, 12).

Luke 12:35–48. The story that is told in 12:47–48 may have an Old Testament intertextural echo in Deut 25:2–3 and Num 15:29–30, but it necessitates clear cultural intertextural information about lamps and weddings and the normal activities of servants. In addition, it relies on information about the "Son of Man" to make the story applicable.

Luke 12:49–53. The connection of the positive desire of Jesus to "cast fire" on the earth expressed in the thesis of this elaboration, though in apparent tension with 9:52–56 above, does not have any clear oral-scribal connection. Nevertheless, the rationale of the contrary of the thesis (bringing division) finds an Old Testament echo in Mic 7:6, which is recited here with minor modification.

Luke 12:54–59. The elaboration found here begins with an allusion to cultural, meteorological knowledge (12:54–55). An analogy to the restatement of the thesis is drawn from cultural, socioeconomic knowledge (12:58), as is the conclusion (12:59).

Luke 13:1–9. The one element of historical intertexture in the apocalyptic discourse of Luke is found in this section. The events narrated are apparently actual cases of severe persecution (13:1–3) or tragic accidents (13:4–5). These severe cases form the paradigmatic theses for two elaborations, the latter of which leads to a paradigmatic story that is based on apparent cultural intertextural information.

Luke 13:22–30. This unusual elaboration, which Jesus offers in answer to an important query in the Lukan apocalyptic scheme, is hard to follow. The intertextural elements consist of the cultural information about policies of householders toward outsiders, as well as a reference to "Abraham and Isaac and Jacob and all the prophets in the kingdom of God," which is likely a cultural *topos* rather than an oral-scribal reference. The conclusion (which is that many will come from elsewhere into the kingdom) seems to overturn the initial thesis that *not* many will enter. However, as we shall see, this elaboration is consistent with a general theme in Lukan apocalyptic discourse—the overturning of the expectations of Israel that it will be treated in a preferential way by God over the Gentiles (cf. 13:29).

Luke 13:34–35. The reference to the execution of prophets and messengers by "Jerusalem" again appears to be more at the level of cultural *topos* than oral-scribal reference, thus suggesting the consistency of our understanding of the previous portion. An oral-scribal recitation can, though, be found in Jesus' recitation of what "Jerusalem" will say at the end (Jer 22:5 or Ps 118:26). In line with Lukan apocalyptic discourse, however, one wonders if the recitation is not here reconfigured from a positive acclamation in the original texts to a lament in Luke?

Luke 14:15–24. An oral-scribal reference may be found in this story, analogous to the "fables" in the *Progymnasmata*,[7] when reference is made to a man wedding a woman and being freed from obligatory responsibilities (cf. Deut 24:5 and Luke 14:20). More important appear to be the social and cultural violations of those who refuse to come to "a certain man's" banquet. Given the inadequate information about either the man or his relation to the invited guests, it is difficult to know.

Luke 16:19–31. The next element of apocalyptic discourse in Luke is also a fable. The figure of Abraham here is clearly not drawn from the Old Testament; likewise, the figure of Lazarus appears to be a cultural type. The rationale given by "Abraham" to the rich man is echoed in the apocalyptic discourse of James (Acts 15:21), when he provides a rationale for the apocalyptic, Gentile mission to proceed (see below).

---

[7] J. R. Butts, "The Progymnasmata of Theon: A New Text with Translation and Commentary" (Ph.D. diss., Claremont Graduate School, 1986), 256–89.

Luke 17:20–37. It appears that Luke does not confine the Markan-style passion-week apocalypse (Mark 13 and Matt 24) to one section of his Gospel but reconfigures that apocalypse by scattering elements of it throughout his Gospel and Acts. (Luke's treatment of the passion-week apocalyptic discourse in Mark and Q is thus similar to John's treatment of the passion trial: they can be found throughout the Gospel, rather than only at the end.[8]) The only clear intertextural elements are those that are related to cultural echoes associated with figures from the Old Testament and the actions of the people around them: Noah, Lot, and Lot's wife. The point of comparison appears to be that the Son of Man and those around him can be compared with these figures.

Luke 19:11–27. Unlike the man in the parable in Luke 14:15–24, the "certain man" here is described as "well-born," suggesting his wealth, a suspicion confirmed by his entrusting his servants with a considerable part of his wealth at his departure to receive a kingdom for himself. The well-known story contains no oral-scribal intertexture; it is based entirely on the cultural knowledge that alone makes this parable "work" rhetorically (see also the comment on Acts 1:3–11).

Luke 19:28–44. This passage is included in our overview because it seems to suggest the crowd's apocalyptic expectation. One notes that Luke does not have Matthew's apocalyptic fulfillment motif based on the oral-scribal reference found in Isa 62:11 LXX or Zech 9:9 (Matt 21:4), though Luke shares with Mark the reference to the colt on which Jesus will sit as a "tied-up colt, on which no person has yet sat." It is unclear whether this is an oral-scribal allusion, possibly pointing to the young cow that has not had a yoke (Num 19:2; Deut 21:3; 1 Sam 6:7) or to another cultural echo.

The echo in Luke 19:38 of Ps 118:26, however, appears clear. The origin of the welcome being extended to a king seems clearer in John 12:12–19 (namely, to Zeph 3:15) than it does in Luke, though the same reference is likely here, especially in light of the earlier use of Zeph 3:17 LXX (cf. Luke 1:49). Jesus' response to the Pharisees may be drawn from Hab 2:11, and Jesus' words concerning Jerusalem appear to be drawn from both the social and cultural *topoi* of sieges and oral-scribal rehearsals of sieges recorded in the Old Testament (e.g., Isa 29:3; Jer 6:6; Ezek 4:2).

Luke 20:9–19. The overall story here appears to draw on Isa 5:1–7. The conclusion is a recitation of Ps 118:22–23. Further allusions to the motif of the cornerstone can also be found in Isa 8:14 and 28:16.

---

[8] J. O. Tuñi Vancells, "El cuarto evangelio y el tiempo: Notas para un estudio de la concepción del tiempo en el cuarto Evangelio," *EstEcl* 57 (1982): 129–54.

Luke 20:27–38. In their questioning of Jesus, the Sadducees recite some words of *Moses* to the people (Deut 25:5). In his answer, Jesus recites the words of *God* to Moses (Exod 3:6), either as words of God or as a cultural *topos*. Jesus' contrasting action again appears to underscore an element of Lukan sacred intertexture, namely, the role of the divine in apocalyptic association with Jesus.

Luke 21:5–36. As I have noted elsewhere in detail,[9] the extensive Old Testament echoes found in this apocalyptic discourse suggest extensive interaction with Jewish oral-scribal material. It is an interaction that goes well beyond the recitation and reconfiguration found in Mark or his sources of the same traditions. While some of the abundant allusions are debatable (e.g., the added emphasis on nearness of the right time may be an echo of Dan 7:22, a reference that may also be behind mention of the "Son of Man" in other Lukan, apocalyptic discourse passages), most are clear. Luke 21:10–11 not only repeats the Old Testament echoes found in Mark 13:7 (e.g., Mic 4:3; Isa 2:4; 19:2), but also expands on them by adding, among others, a possible allusion to Ezek 3:12; Isa 19:17; and 29:6. The Lukan reference to the destruction of Jerusalem (21:20–24) echoes Deut 32:25, 35; Hos 9:7; 13:16; and especially Jer 46:10. Specifically, 21:23–24 echo Deut 28:64; Ezek 32:9; Esth 9:7; Zech 12:3; Sir 28:18; *Pss. Sol.* 17:25; Tob 14:5; and Dan 12:7. Luke 21:25–28 provides more Old Testament allusions in reference to the cosmic signs found in Mark 13:24–27: Joel 3:3–4 (see below Acts 2:14–21); Isa 24:19; Pss 65:8; 46:4; 89:10; Wis 5:22; Jonah 1:15. The final L warnings (21:34–36) also draw on Old Testament imagery: Isa 24:17 and Jer 25:29. Thus, in a passage that many would argue is drawn from unambiguously apocalyptic material, it is arguable that Luke heightens the apocalyptic discourse through intertextural elements.

Luke 22:15–30 (31–34?). Luke 22:21 echoes two texts from the Psalms: 41:9 and 55:12–13. The entire scene of 22:14–38 also appears to pick up the cultural echo of speeches of departing leaders, speeches common to us from Gen 48–49; Deut 31–34; Josh 23–24; 1 Kgs 2:1–10; and 1 Macc 2:49–70. The reference to the betrayer seems to be a reconfiguration of Ps 41:10, but it may also contain echoes of Isa 65:11–12 or Ezek 39:20–23. If it be the case that we should include 22:31–34 as an example of apocalyptic discourse, then we would find there an echo either of the

---

[9] L. Gregory Bloomquist, "Rhetorical Argumentation and the Culture of Apocalyptic: A Socio-Rhetorical Analysis of Luke 21," in *The Rhetorical Interpretation of Scripture: Essays from the 1996 Malibu Conference* (ed. Stanley E. Porter and Dennis L. Stamps; JSNTSup 180; Sheffield: Sheffield Academic Press, 1999), 173–209.

cultural *topos* of Satan testing the saints of God or an oral-scribal reference from Job 1:6–12.[10]

Luke 22:67–70. Again, reference is found on the lips of Jesus to the figure of the "Son of Man" (cf. Dan 7:13). (A clear Lukan parallel to this text is found in Acts 7:56, though that text does not appear to be apocalyptic discourse, as I shall note.) Here we find also "anointed one" and the phrase "Son of God," both of which are apparent cultural intertexture (since no oral-scribal reference is in view), though the latter is used only this once in the apocalyptic discourse of Luke (cf. Acts 13:33 below). There appears to be a kind of innertextural progression here from "anointed" to "Son of Man" to "Son of God."

Luke 23:39–43. The phrases "anointed one" and "the kingdom" suggest cultural intertexture, along with the element of challenge and riposte.

Luke 24:19–27. The intertextural references here are all cultural and, at this point in the story, could conceivably be drawn from material internal to the story told within Luke itself: prophet, relationship of God and the people, the particular religious leadership of Israel, the divine redemption of Israel, angels, resurrection, "anointed one," the sacred writings, and finally (perhaps) the breaking of bread. What is consistent, but perhaps also telling, is that the major intertextural references are picked up in large part in three other Lukan texts that can also be identified as apocalyptic discourse and that they are only picked up in these other three texts, namely, Luke 24:44–49; Acts 2:22–23; 10:37–39.

Luke 24:44–49. We again note how the elements of the cultural intertexture that is evidenced in 24:19–27 can be found here. We also note the progression created by the addition of other cultural intertextural elements: repentance, forgiveness of sins, preaching of both to all nations, power from heaven. Again, no oral-scribal intertexture is evident. We might also note the relation of this text to the first evidence of apocalyptic discourse in Acts, namely, 1:3–11.

4. Intertexture in Apocalyptic Discourse Material in the Acts of the Apostles

Acts 1:3–11. As noted above, this passage echoes Luke 24:44–49, as well as Luke 3:16–17 (see above) and Luke 19:11–27 (see above). Several elements of cultural intertexture reappear here, most prominently the notion of "kingdom," which becomes the *topos* (a social as well as cultural topic) for the discussion of the risen Jesus and his followers. The query from Jesus' followers (1:6) concerning the "kingdom" appears to echo Mal

---

[10] See further on this point the recent thesis of Ibitolu Oluseyi Jerome Megbelayin, "A Socio-rhetorical Analysis of the Lukan Narrative of the Last Supper" (Ph.D. diss., Saint Paul University, Ottowa).

3:23 LXX, while Jesus' response concerning not knowing the exact times appears to echo cultural intertexture notions common to other apocalyptic discourse. His statement about the empowerment of the spirit, while it may employ Isa 32:15, appears to echo a cultural intertexture *topos* of "power from heaven" (as in Luke 24:44–49). Jesus' consequent programmatic response may draw on verses such as Isa 49:6 (as in Luke 2:32) or *Pss. Sol.* 8:15, but it appears more clearly to echo the promise of witness to the Gentiles found throughout Luke (and explicitly in Luke 24:44–49). It appears also to be a further narrative (innertexture) progression from the initial words of the risen Jesus in Luke 24:19–27, to Luke 24:44–49, and now to here. The presence of two angel-interpreters can be found elsewhere in oral-scribal material (e.g., 2 Macc 3:26) but appears to be an element of cultural intertexture.

Acts 2:14–36. The speech by Peter begins with an extensive recitation of Joel 3:1–5 LXX (possibly alluded to in the apocalyptic discourse found in Luke 21:5–36), with echoes of Isa 2:2, 33; 10:45; and Num 11:29. This recitation occupies almost the entire first part of his speech.

A second major recitation, now of Ps 15:8–11 LXX, is found in the second part of the speech. Here it is introduced more extensively by Peter, who also incorporates in his own words cultural intertextural elements of apocalyptic signs and the *topos* of the just man who falls at the hands of the unjust leaders, as well as the cultural intertexture around the sufferings of death and the promise of resurrection (2:24: Pss 17:6; 114:3 LXX; and 2 Sam 22:6 LXX).

This last cultural theme introduces the third part of Peter's speech and touches not only on death and resurrection (2:29–30: 1 Kgs 2:10; Pss 89:4 and 132:11) but also incorporates a much shorter recitation, this time of Ps 109:1 LXX, as well as the cultural intertextural element of "anointed one" and David. Peter concludes the whole speech with an apparent allusion to Ps 20:7.

Acts 3:18–26. This section contains a reconfiguration of Deut 18:15–20, a passage used widely throughout the Gospel tradition, with elements of recitation. Only here, however, is the Deuteronomy passage conjoined with Lev 24:27 to denote the implications of not heeding the "coming" prophet like Moses. This, again, suggests a possible overturning of the Mosaic, apocalyptic expectation of Israel (and possibly of John the Baptist) in Lukan sacred intertexture. Confirmation of this view is the evidence of an echo of the opening hymns of Luke that is also found here in the recitation of Gen 22:18 or 26:4 in Acts 3:25 (which are echoes of Gen 12:3 and Gen 18:18).

Acts 10:34–43. Peter's speech to the Gentile Cornelius is replete with Old Testament allusions. They do not appear to be evidence of cultural intertexture as such but are brief oral-scribal echoes. Thus, Peter's initial

"perception" of God is an echo of Deut 10:17 and Sir 35:12–13; his awareness of those who do the law without the law (again to be underscored by
Paul in the next apocalyptic discourse, 13:26–43) may be an allusion to Ps
15:2; the "word" sent forth is referred to in Pss 107:20 and 147:18–19; the
good news of peace to Israel is likely drawn from Isa 52:7 or Nah 2:1 MT;
the anointing of Jesus in the power of the spirit may echo Isa 61:1 or
1 Sam 16:13; Peter may conclude his words by recalling Isa 33:24. There
are also echoes internal to Luke's body of material itself: the rehearsal of
the events of Jesus' life recites material from earlier in Luke (see above),
and the reference to the "third day" may be a part of the Christian tradition at this point (or an echo of Hos 6:2).

Acts 13:26–43. It is important to note the parallel between this text
and Jesus' speech in the synagogue (Luke 4:16–30), as well as between this
text and Peter's speech to Cornelius (10:34–43). In the section of Paul's
speech that employs apocalyptic discourse, there are four recitations of
Old Testament material: Ps 2:7 (13:33); Isa 55:3 LXX (13:34); Ps 16:10
(13:35); and Hab 1:5 (13:41). Reference to the healing word being sent
forth (Ps 107:20 and/or 147:18–19) is found here, as it was in the previous
section. In 13:46–47 we would note the presence again of Isa 49:6, already
employed twice in earlier apocalyptic discourse portions of Luke (above
Luke 2:29–32 and Acts 1:3–11).

Acts 15:15–18. James's concluding address to the Jerusalem assembly
employs apocalyptic discourse, in part through a recitation of Amos
9:11–12 LXX (with an introduction that may be drawn from Jer 12:15 and a
conclusion that may be drawn from Isa 45:21). In addition, James's speech
may open (15:14) with language drawn from Deut 14:2 LXX.

Acts 17:30–31. As in the case of Peter's speech to the Gentile Cornelius, the speech of Paul to the Athenian philosophers is replete with
Old Testament echoes, though there are no clear recitations, reconfigurations, or recontextualizations of any kind. (True, there are a couple of
recitations of Greco-Roman oral-scribal material. However, rhetorical
apocalyptic discourse is clear in this speech only in the concluding
verses and there is no Greco-Roman material there.) After introducing
elements from wisdom discourse, such as the denial of the reality of
idols in 17:29 (which is more than likely an echo of a cultural *topos,*
though oral-scribal echoes may be suggested: cf. Deut 4:28; Isa 40:18;
44:9–20; and Wis 13:10) and Paul's comments about the divine benevo-
lence toward those who behaved thus out of ignorance (cf. Sir 28:7),
Paul, as Peter had done in his speech to Cornelius, proclaims that the
divine has sent this holy person Jesus in preparation for the obligatory,
righteous judgment at the end of the age (Pss 9:9; 96:13; 98:9). It is at
the point of this abrupt shift from wisdom to apocalyptic discourse that
Paul's speech is halted by his audience.

Acts 26:23. At the end of Paul's extended biographical speech, he invokes an element of apocalyptic discourse that echoes earlier intertextural patterns used in Luke and Acts. The passage also reminds the reader of Isa 49:6 and 46:13 (see above on Luke 2:32).

Acts 28:25–28. Acts concludes with Paul's speech to the Jewish elders of Rome, a speech that includes a lengthy recitation of Isa 6:9–10 LXX, as well as concluding allusions to Pss 67:3; 98:3; and Isa 40:5 LXX.

5. Intertextural Map of the Apocalyptic Materials of Luke and Acts

I shall organize the intertextural resources noted above by the kind of intertexture in order to make some tentative conclusions regarding the map of intertexture in Lukan apocalyptic discourse.

5.1. Oral-Scribal

We note the presence in the Lukan apocalyptic texts of different kinds of oral-scribal intertexture. The first is the intertexture with other early Christian materials, primarily the Gospels. The second is the intertexture with Old Testament texts found in the Hebrew or Greek Old Testament. The third is the intertexture with Second Temple Jewish texts not found in the Old Testament. The fourth is the intertexture with Greco-Roman texts.

5.1.1. Early Christian Materials

According to the dominant scholarly consensus, Luke shows evidence of the use of three sets of early Christian materials: Mark, Q, and material known only to Luke (L). The bulk of early Christian material used by Luke in the sections identified as apocalyptic discourse appears to be from Q. Luke uses and modifies Q in the following apocalyptic discourse sections: 3:16–17; 6:21 and 25 (though see L); 7:18–23; 10:8–24; 11:29–32; 12:2–12 (though possibly Mark in 12:11–12), 35–48 (though 12:47–48 may not be from Q), 49–53, 54–59; 13:22–30, 34–35; 14:15–24; 17:20–37 (though possibly Mark in 17:31); 19:11–27; and 22:28–30. In the apocalyptic discourse of Luke, L material appears to be the next most common "source": 1:46–55, 68–79; 2:29–32, 34–38; 4:16–30; 6:21 and 25 (though see Q); 9:52–56; 13:1–9; 16:19–31; 23:39–43; 24:19–27, 44–49.

Surprisingly, perhaps, Luke uses and modifies Mark in only a few sections that employ apocalyptic discourse: 3:1–6; 9:23–27; 19:28–44 (though note the extensive redaction); 20:9–19 (or, less likely, Q), 27–40 (or, less likely, Q); 21:5–36 (though with extensive interaction with both Q and L material); 22:15–27 and possibly 67–70. As I noted above and have noted elsewhere,[11] Lukan apocalyptic discourse that does base itself on Markan

---

[11] Ibid.

apocalyptic discourse heightens the already-existing apocalyptic expectation we find in Mark by means of intertexture, specifically through the incorporation of Old Testament oral-scribal and cultural materials.

Luke's use of early Christian oral-scribal material almost assuredly continues in Acts, though opinions are much more divided about that material. The constancy, however, at the level of social and cultural *topoi* and of Old Testament references would suggest that in fact Luke is either incorporating fairly consistent sources without significant alteration or he is so much the master of whatever material he has incorporated that he has left his seal on it so prominently as to obliterate clear tracing of the source.

5.1.2. Old Testament Materials (Hebrew or Greek Bible)

I have chosen to group the assured and probable oral-scribal intertexture with Old Testament material found in Lukan apocalyptic discourse together in the three categories that Luke himself identifies. Luke, as is well known, echoes the Second Temple Jewish division of the Old Testament into Torah, Prophets, and Writings. I have, however, also included material found in the Greek Old Testament, though I have done so by classifying it in one of the three sections of the Hebrew Bible.

5.1.2.1. Torah. The assured and possible oral-scribal material from the Lukan apocalyptic discourse found in the Torah shows no clear pattern. However, in total, it is a relatively minor contribution, made even more minor by the probability that some of the following references are not actually oral-scribal but only cultural echoes. The material found in Lukan apocalyptic discourse comes from throughout the Torah, though with a preponderance of material deriving from Genesis and Deuteronomy: Gen 15:15 LXX; 19:24–28; 22:18; 24:12; 26:3, 4; 29:32; 30:13; Exod 3:6; Num 11:29; 15:29–30; Lev 24:27; Deut 10:17, 21; 14:2 LXX; 18:15–20; 25:2–3; 28:64; 32:35.

5.1.2.2. Prophets. The assured and possible oral-scribal material in Lukan apocalyptic discourse that is drawn from the division known as the Prophets is clearly dominant in Lukan apocalyptic discourse. Of course, the material in the Hebrew Bible and the LXX that is considered to be within the "canon" of the "prophets" is also the most extensive, so this "amount" of intertexture may not be significant. Lukan apocalyptic discourse material shows a clear predilection for Isaiah, followed most closely by Ezekiel (unless one assumes that the references to "Son of Man" in our texts are oral-scribal intertextural references to Dan 7; I believe that the references are cultural, not oral-scribal, intertexture): Josh 24:14; 1 Sam 2:1–11 (1 Sam 2:10); 16:13; 2 Sam 7:12–13; 22:6 LXX, 18, 32, 51; 1 Kgs 1:48; 2:10; 10:1–10 (cf. 2 Chr 9:1–12); 2 Kgs 1:10, 12; Esth 9:7; Ezek 3:12; 4:2;

14:17; 21:31; 26:1–28:26; 32:9; 39:20–23; Isa 2:2, 4, 33; 5:1–7; 6:9–10 LXX; 8:14 (?); 10:45; 14:13, 15; 19:2, 17; 24:17, 19; 26:19; 28:16 (?); 29:3, 6; 32:5; 33:24; 35:5; 38:20; 40:3 LXX (2x), 5 (2x); 41:8–9; 45:21 (?); 46:13 (2x); 49:6 (4x); 52:7, 10; 55:3 LXX; 58:6 LXX; 59:8; 61:1–2a LXX (3x); 65:11–12; Jer 6:6; 12:15 (?); 22:5; 25:29; 46:10; Dan 7:13 (several), 22; 12:7; Hos 6:2; 9:7; 13:16; Joel 3:1–5 LXX (2x); Amos 9:11–12; Jonah 1:15, 17ff.; 3:1ff..; Nah 2:1; Hab 1:5; 2:11; 3:1–11; Zeph 3:15, 17 LXX; Mic 4:3; 7:6, 20; Zech 12:3; Mal 3:1–2 (2x), 23 LXX; 4:5–6.[12]

5.1.2.3. Writings. The assured and possible oral-scribal intertextural materials from the Old Testament Writings in the Lukan apocalyptic discourse material is clearly weighted toward the use of materials from the Psalms. (Thus, while the risen Jesus' final words to his followers in Luke [24:44] are often understood to refer to the "Psalms" as the last section of the Hebrew canon [i.e., the Writings], it is clear at least from the apocalyptic discourse in Luke and Acts that it really is the book of Psalms that is of interest, and the other writings are so only very peripherally.) Other oral-scribal references are only possible, not probable. Material from the Psalms include: 2:7; 9:9; 15:2, 8 LXX; 16:10; 17:6; 18:3, 18; 20:7; 35:9; 41:4, 9, 10; 46:4; 55:2–13; 65:8; 67:3; 72:8; 89:4, 10, 11 LXX; 96:13; 98:3 LXX (2x?), 9; 103:17; 105:8; 106:5, 10, 48; 107:9, 10, 20 (2x); 109:1 LXX; 111:9; 114:3 LXX; 118:22–23, 26 (3x); 132:11; 147:18–19 (2x); material from other writings: Sir 10:14; 28:7, 18; 35:12–13; Job 1:6–12 (?); 12:19; Tob 14:5; Wis 5:22.

5.1.3. Second Temple Non-Old Testament Texts

There are only a few references that may possibly be identified as non-canonical Second Temple oral-scribal intertexture. Curiously, most of them stem from the *Psalms of Solomon:* 8:15; 10:4; 13:11; and 17:25. Nevertheless, the Lukan texts that may contain these references more than likely contain cultural echoes, not oral-scribal references. Other possible oral-scribal references within Lukan apocalyptic discourse (1QM XIV, 10–11; *Mekilta* to Exod 21:2; *b. Ketubbot* 96a, *Lives of the Prophets* 21:3; and *4 Ezra* 9:45) seem very unlikely and are also more likely to be cultural echoes.

5.1.4. Greco-Roman Texts

There is no likely evidence of oral-scribal intertexture from Greco-Roman texts in any of the Lukan apocalyptic discourse. The possibilities mentioned above are likely cultural intertexture, not oral-scribal.

---

[12] Though the books of Esther and Daniel are found among the Writings, rather than among the Prophets, in the canon of the Masoretic Text, the earlier canon of the Septuagint classifies them both as being among the Prophets (specifically, among the Former Prophets and the Prophets, respectively).

5.2. The Social, Cultural, and Historical Intertextural Map

Not all intertextural elements are oral-scribal, though as we have seen it is not always easy to know which ones are and which ones are not. First, there are a vast number of examples of cultural intertexture in terms of social and cultural practice. In apocalyptic discourse, these are significant. As Vernon Robbins has shown concerning the apocalyptic discourse found in Mark, even cultural practices such as sitting, standing, or moving around become highly charged. Attention to this broad cultural intertexture is often missed in less rhetorically sensitive forms of analysis.[13]

Second, this intertexture gives evidence of several significant elements of sacred texture, namely, particular ways of talking about divinity, spirit beings, holy persons, divine history, human redemption, and sacred communities and their practices.[14] This further localizes the apocalyptic discourse. The divine is, if not always an explicit player in the apocalyptic drama, certainly an implicit player. From the very first texts that employ apocalyptic discourse in Luke, it becomes clear that the divinity is the one who is bringing about the events that, as we shall see, overturn and reverse an existing order. In sociorhetorical terminology, it is deity, not humans, who overturns cultural assumptions and moves humans to new cultural settings. This has relevance not only for understanding the nature of apocalyptic in Luke but also for an eventual analysis of Lukan ideological texture. I believe that ideological texture charts "movements" of people, as opposed to their "static" placement, identified in social and cultural texture.[15]

Jesus, as a holy person, is clearly the central figure of Lukan apocalyptic discourse and is regularly identified as a holy person through, as we have seen above, a number of culturally sacred "titles": anointed one, Son of Man, and Son of God. The latter two titles may in fact also be means of associating Jesus with divinity or classing him as a divinized, spirit being. It is the preeminence of Jesus in Lukan apocalyptic discourse that probably accounts for the absence of (other) spirit beings. Confirmation of this is clear in the presence of "messengers" only when Jesus is absent. This appears to contrast very strongly with other Second Temple and even first-century Greco-Roman texts that employ apocalyptic discourse. In these

---

[13] "The Rhetorical Ritual: Apocalyptic Discourse in Mark 13," in Carey and Bloomquist, *Vision and Persuasion,* 95–121.

[14] Robbins, *Exploring the Texture of Texts,* 120–31.

[15] "Refining Ideological Texture" (paper presented at the Rhetoric and Early Christian Discourse Panel, Canadian Society of Biblical Studies and Canadian Society for the Study of Rhetoric, Edmonton, Alberta, 27 May 2000).

texts, spirit beings often become a defining feature and, thus, evidence of apocalyptic discourse.[16]

Divine history is also a prominent feature of Lukan apocalyptic discourse, though it is a selective history and not merely the recounting of God's action in the past. It is first of all a divine history that focuses on Israel and the divine promises to Israel. Second, it is a history that focuses on the scandalous nature of Israel's history in relation to surrounding peoples: for example, God exalted Israel in spite of Israel's weakness; God exalted the weak within Israel when the Israelite leadership became corrupt; and when all of Israel had appeared to become corrupt, God turned around and exalted those outside of Israel. All of this appears to be associated with a regular theme in Lukan apocalyptic discourse, namely, the kingdom. In a fuller analysis we would need to go on to show how Lukan apocalyptic discourse shows God's action in Jesus to be a kind of shaming of those who consider themselves honored as the kingdom is taken from ethnic Israel in its putative purity and given to all humanity in their alienation.[17]

Third and finally, the only historical intertexture is found in Luke 13:1–9, in which two tragic stories are told as the thesis of an elaboration about severity of suffering.

6. Tentative Results of the Study of the Selection of Intertextural Materials in the Invention of the Argument

It appears likely that Luke was not the first to tell or write a story of Jesus and that he has built his story of Jesus on earlier accounts. Thus, the argumentation that Jesus employs in Luke is not likely to have derived from argumentation exclusively in Luke's mind. Nevertheless, Luke does not accept without modification the argumentation to be found in those sources that we can more or less feel assured provided him with large parts of the story, namely, Mark, Q, and L. For example, as noted above, in Lukan apocalyptic discourse that bases itself on Markan apocalyptic discourse, Jesus' argumentation evidences a heightened apocalyptic expectation through the incorporation of Old Testament oral-scribal and cultural materials.

The assured or probable Old Testament oral-scribal intertexture of Lukan apocalyptic discourse may also derive in part from earlier Christian sources. Again, however, it is clear that Luke has used this and additional

---

[16] Greg Carey, "Introduction: Apocalyptic Discourse, Apocalyptic Rhetoric," in Carey and Bloomquist, *Vision and Persuasion*, 4.

[17] H. Moxnes, "Honor and Shame," in *The Social Sciences and New Testament Interpretation* (ed. Richard L. Rohrbaugh; Peabody, Mass.: Hendrickson, 1996), 19–40.

material to highlight or create the following three emphases: (1) the expectation of deliverance of the people of Israel in exilic bondage, (2) the praise of God, and (3) the promise of the extension of God's grace to those who have not always been perceived to experience it. Regarding the first emphasis, in Old Testament texts, the expectation of deliverance carries a prominent element of revenge on those who have mistreated Israel, an element that is almost entirely absent in Lukan reconfiguration. The second emphasis is generally recontextualized in that the material is recited in relation to a new context, namely, that of God's grace evidenced in Jesus. Finally, the most prominent characteristic of oral-scribal material in Lukan apocalyptic discourse is shared by the prominent cultural intertexture, namely, the element of grace to those not usually considered to be "worthy" recipients of grace.

In terms of cultural intertexture, Luke appears very selective in those intertextural materials that relate to the divine history and with a clear trajectory in mind. So, most prominently within the apocalyptic discourse of Luke-Acts we find not only Old Testament–based cultural *topoi* of both regular apocalyptic figures (e.g., the Son of Man) that we find in other New Testament texts, but also, and more strikingly, cultural *topoi* of other characters: Noah, Abraham, Lot and Lot's wife, Jonah, the Ninevites, David, the Queen of the South (and, through her, Solomon), Elijah, and Elisha. What is most noticeable about these unique figures in the intertexture of Lukan apocalyptic discourse is that they are all either Gentiles or are associated with Gentiles: Noah is a precursor of those saved from among the Gentiles, as is Abraham; Lot and Lot's wife live among the Gentiles; Jonah preaches to the Gentile Ninevites; the Queen of the South is a Gentile visiting the Hebrew king Solomon; Elijah and Elisha are invoked in Lukan apocalyptic discourse texts only because of miracles they perform for Gentiles. Even the Son of Man appears to the seer Daniel while the latter is in exile among the Gentiles.

The only figure who is not directly related to Gentiles happens to be David, the king of Israel's "golden age." He figures in the apocalyptic discourse of Luke-Acts, however, only because he is an example of one who prophesies the incorruption of the Jewish Messiah but who is himself corrupted in death! Contrasting with the positive light cast on the others—Gentiles or prophets to the Gentiles—David, as king, prophesies only how unlike his fate is to that of the one who is his Son!

7. *Argumentative Strategies Employed in Lukan Apocalyptic Discourse*

Luke and Acts contain argumentation that is characteristic of all Greco-Roman argumentation, namely, deductive enthymematic argumentation and inductive paradigmatic argumentation. Within these two broad categories, however, we find that Lukan apocalyptic discourse also evidences distinctive argumentative patterns. These patterns appear, in part at least, as a result of attention to intertextural material found in Lukan apocalyptic discourse.

7.1. The Influence of Prophetic Texts in Lukan Apocalyptic Argumentation
     Rhetorical argumentation from Aristotle to the modern period has been viewed as being built on the enthymeme for its structure. This debated but most fundamental building block of rhetorical argumentation is almost assuredly the form that rhetorical argumentation always takes, be it its most sophisticated form or its most simple.

     According to Stephen Toulmin, however, argumentation involves more than simply the form of argumentation employed, since the same logical form may be used by one speaker or writer, as well as another, to argue for opposite actions on the part of the audience. Toulmin has helped us to see that in order to get at the argumentation we need to do more than analyze the formal or enthymematic structure of a rhetorical argument for the criteria of *validity* for a particular argument. We need to get at that which allows the argument to have its *force* on a particular audience.[18]

     What provides the force of an argument on a particular audience is the background information that allows the warrants (or missing premises or conclusions in rhetorical arguments) to work. Toulmin does not disagree with Aristotle and the neo-Aristotelian tradition of analysis, according to whom the background information is the very stuff of the enthymeme, that is, what is to be supplied (at least in the rhetor's mind) by the audience both to engage the audience in the core of their convictions and to allow the rhetor not to have to say everything. What Toulmin is doing, however, is to ask what gives an argument not only its validity but its emotional force. Toulmin is, in fact, getting beyond the simple, analytical, or logical approach to the enthymeme and back to the Aristotelian rhetorical and psychological roots of the enthymeme.[19]

     Attention to this background information suggests that the arguments in Lukan apocalyptic discourse above have force with the writer's audience or implicit audience (that is, an audience that historically existed or only existed in Luke's mind) because they are drawn from commonly shared information and expectations. Given the prominent place of intertextural prophetic writings based on wisdom discourse in Lukan apocalyptic discourse, this seems to be an important feature that gives Lukan apocalyptic discourse its force, not its criteria. An early example is found in the Mag-

---

[18] *The Uses of Argument* (Cambridge: Cambridge University Press, 1964).

[19] A. B. Miller and J. D. Bee, "Enthymemes: Body and Soul," *Philosophy and Rhetoric* 5 (1972): 201–14.

nificat and Benedictus. In the latter we find Zechariah saying that the child will be called prophet of the Most High, since he will go before the Lord to prepare his way, suggesting in the mind of the audience that "one who goes before the Lord and prepares his way will be considered the prophet of the Most High." This is not an obvious conclusion in every culture, but it is one that certainly fits and has force in a culture conversant with these prophetic texts. Or again, only with the background knowledge that one who has experienced divine redemption may die in peace do Simeon's words "work" in 2:29–30: because my eyes have seen your salvation, you should let me go (i.e., die) in peace.

The blessings and woes containing apocalyptic discourse (Luke 6:21, 25) also use this simple enthymematic argumentation. For example, you who hunger are blessed since you shall be satisfied, suggesting that "those who shall be satisfied are the blessed." Here, too, the argumentation may not be evident in another cultural or ideological setting.

In Luke 7:18–23, at the request of John the Baptist, Jesus enunciates elements of Old Testament expectation so as to suggest that when the following things happen, the one who is to come has come, and since they are happening now, he must be the one who is to come! Here, the argumentation depends entirely on the intertextural (prophetic) recitations.

Having determined what gives the argumentation of Lukan apocalyptic discourse its force, we can discuss how it works and how that force is delivered to an audience.

7.2. The Prominence of Chreia-Elaboration As a Form of Argumentation in Lukan Apocalyptic Discourse

Chreia-elaboration is one of the main forms of rhetorical practice and argumentation in the first century. This is certainly the case in Lukan apocalyptic discourse. The dominant mode of Lukan apocalyptic discourse is chreia-elaboration by Jesus or by "apostles" in speeches about the holy events surrounding Jesus. In some cases intertextural material seems to provide the complete structure of the chreia-elaboration. One example is Luke 12:1–3, 4–7, and 8–12. Each of these elaborations, which form distinct units of apocalyptic discourse, underscore the theme of future reversal. First, we find a thesis (v. 1) that is dependent on the cultural intertexture of Pharisees and leaven (as well as the understanding of hypocrisy), a contrary (v. 2), and a rationale (v. 3). Second, we have a thesis (v. 4), a contrary and its immediate restatement (v. 5), a natural analogy drawn from a cultural maxim (v. 6a) with implicit rationale (v. 6b), a human analogy (v. 7a), followed by a restatement of the thesis (v. 7b), and an explicit rationale for the missing one in v. 6b (v. 7c). Third, we have a thesis built on necessary cultural intertextural information (v. 8) and a contrary (v. 9), followed by a restatement of the thesis (v. 10a) and a new contrary (v. 10b).

Furthermore, chreia-elaboration need not happen in the stark sayings-like texts such as Q and those portions of Q modified by Luke. Thus, even in the limited number of paradigmatic arguments found in Lukan apocalyptic discourse (specifically, those evidencing intertextural materials: Luke 14:15–24; 16:19–31; 19:11, 27; 20:9–19), a more important element of chreia-elaboration can be found. The story told in Luke 12:35–48 is an interesting example of chreia-elaboration in the telling of a tale. The cultural information is necessary to make the story work (vv. 36a–39, and retold in vv. 42a–48); the echo of "Son of Man" in the rationale of the conclusion to the elaboration (conclusion, v. 40a; rationale, v. 40b) is necessary for the story to reach its intended conclusion.

Finally, the rhetorical elaboration found in the speech materials in Acts is also chreia-elaboration. Acts 1:3–11 contains a simple enthymeme (vv. 4–5), and then a chreia-elaboration of minimal length: v. 6 (thesis by some of Jesus' followers), v. 7 (contrary by Jesus), v. 8 (conclusion). The remaining eight speeches have significant argumentative parallels. Of interest to us, however, are those parallels that relate specifically to the intertextural elements.

Within the chreia-elaboration, there are elements that make Lukan apocalyptic discourse unique.

7.2.1. No Oral Scribal Materials in Jesus' Thesis

Strikingly, there are no examples of Jesus' use of oral-scribal intertextural materials as the thesis or chreia of an elaboration (see Luke 20:28 and below). When oral-scribal intertextural materials are used in the apocalyptic discourse of Jesus in Luke-Acts or of others in Acts, it is always outside of the category of the thesis.

Apocalyptic discourse in Luke-Acts is intertexturally grounded but is not midrashic. The lack of oral-scribal intertextural elements in the thesis is a strong argument against seeing Lukan apocalyptic discourse as a midrash. The single exception to this rule confirms our observation: in Luke 20:27–40 it is the Sadducees who bring to Jesus a problem (in the form of a thesis) that arises in Deut 25:5. In this case, Jesus introduces his own thesis, which is not only not a contrary to theirs, but a different thesis with no oral-scribal intertexture. Jesus' authority to interpret Scripture, rather than the authority of Scripture itself, is one of the goals of apocalyptic discourse in Luke-Acts.[20]

7.2.2. A Contrary Following the Thesis

A distinctive pattern in the chreia-elaboration of Lukan apocalyptic discourse in the mouth of Jesus or in the mouth of those who appear to be

---

[20] Bloomquist, "Rhetorical Argumentation and the Culture of Apocalyptic," 190.

"at one" with Jesus reveals that the thesis or chreia is regularly followed not by a rationale for the thesis, but by a contrary which is then followed by a rationale. The example just cited in the previous section is followed characteristically by a contrary and rationale. (A difference in this specific case is that Jesus brings forward not just one but three rationales!)

7.3. Qualifiers to the Argumentative Logic of Others in Lukan Apocalyptic Discourse

A related phenomenon to contraries in chreia-elaboration is the regular presence of "qualifiers" in argumentation in Lukan apocalyptic discourse. Toulmin alerts us to the need to take into consideration argumentative "qualifiers," elements of an argument that nuance or make more complex a simple rhetorical syllogism. These qualifiers must usually be associated with a rebuttal.

Qualifiers are found among our material at a couple of points. Luke 17:25 is a good example of an apocalyptic qualification of Jesus' apocalyptic chreia concerning the coming of the kingdom. It suggests that, while there is no way to discern the impending end, there is nevertheless an ordered sequence of coming events, presumably within the control of God (note the use of δεῖ, which is often understood as an indication of divine will and is clearly used in the way I have understood it here in the final section of apocalyptic discourse in Luke, namely, 24:44). Another example is Luke 24:22. Here the disciples on the road to Emmaus do not finish with the conclusion (24:21b) to which 24:19–21a has led them (namely, that Jesus of Nazareth is not the hoped-for one), but rather are forced to advance subsequent theses (24:22b and 24:24a) and contraries for each (24:23 and 24:24b respectively), allowing Jesus to draw the "right" conclusion for them (24:25–27).

Jesus' rebuke of his followers' rhetorical argumentation may be compared here to Luke 9:52–56. In both Luke 24 and 9, apparent Old Testament textures or *topoi* might have led the followers to conclude something contrary to Jesus' own eventually explicit intention, thus necessitating Jesus' explicit rebuke of their rhetorical conclusions. This "qualifying" or contrasting aspect is, then, a distinctive of Lukan apocalyptic discourse, both in terms of correcting elaboration (e.g., 17:25) and in terms of outright rejection of an enthymeme (9:52–56).

7.4. Narrative Progression

Luke 24:44–53 picks up many of the same elements of cultural intertexture found in 24:19–43 but supplements them with further elements, particularly the notion of the preaching of repentance and forgiveness of sins to all nations and the notion of "power from heaven" being given to them in or for that process. This narrative progression is achieved through the supplemental use of cultural intertexture and becomes, therefore, a kind of argumentation: the risen Jesus tells them what had happened so that they might go and be the ones to tell others. This is not explicit at this point in Luke's narrative, but it is suggested, and it will be confirmed in the second volume of his work. In fact, Acts 1:3–11 continues the narrative progression and makes it more concrete by establishing a programmatic order for the extension of the preaching to all nations (Acts 1:8).

Another example, the narrative of Luke 9:52–56, is clear but has no clear conclusion: Jesus rebukes the argumentative logic of James and John (we should call down fire to consume them because the Samaritans have rejected you, and those who reject you should be consumed), but we are not told what Jesus would suggest. If, however, it is to be understood in light of the intertextural parallel in 2 Kgs 1, then, perhaps the conclusion of 9:52–56 is to be drawn from the earlier story, namely, that as the king of Samaria died, so, too, will these Samaritans who reject this newly revealed agent of the God of Israel, Jesus. Such a conclusion would depend on the argument being "fleshed out" through the progression that intertexture provides.

8. Summary Analysis

When we now consider the role that the intertexture plays in the argumentation present in the apocalyptic discourse in Luke and Acts, we find the following.

Using the intertextural map as guide through the apocalyptic discourse of Luke-Acts helps us to see that the focus of this apocalyptic discourse is found in the "third" section of Luke's Gospel, namely, 9:51–19:44, and in the "fourth" section of Luke's Gospel, namely, 19:45–21:38 (first, infancy narratives; second, mission in Galilee; third, mission on the road toward Jerusalem; fourth, mission in the temple in Jerusalem; fifth, passion and resurrection). This is not surprising: not only is this the longest section of the Gospel, but it is also the lead-up to the events that Luke sees as historically pivotal. So, while there is apocalyptic discourse, intertwined with intertextural, prophetic allusions in the events surrounding John the Baptist and Jesus, as well as during Jesus' Synoptic, Galilean ministry, Luke seems to regard Jesus' approach to Jerusalem and his time there as the rhetorical forum par excellence for apocalyptic discourse. One can see the extended apocalyptic discourse in chapter 21 as the core of that toward which previous apocalyptic discourse points and out of which subsequent apocalyptic discourse must be understood.

Apocalyptic discourse as found in Luke and in the first two chapters of Acts begins to wane in Acts as the speeches focus not on the coming judgment of God but on the past judgment of God evidenced in the death and resurrection of Jesus. Nevertheless, apocalyptic discourse is still interwoven into Acts 3–12, especially into the death-resurrection discourse that begins to appear more prominently. This is especially clear in the vision of Stephen (7:54–59), which picks up Jesus' earlier apocalyptic words from the context of his trial; Jesus' words may be identified as apocalyptic, but Stephen's words, though they come very close, do not fit our definition. Thus, the initial words of Jesus (Luke 22:67–70) may be considered an example of apocalyptic discourse in Luke; the restatement of these words by Stephen is already a recontextualization of apocalyptic discourse within the Lukan tradition.

The exceptions to this pattern of waning apocalyptic intertexture in Acts occur when (1) the gospel is introduced to the Gentiles in the person and authority of Cornelius (10:34–43) and is related to the community of Jerusalem as such (15:14–18), (2) when the gospel is introduced to Jewish and Gentile believers living in Pisidian Antioch, (3) James's "agreement" with the mission of Paul to the Gentiles, (4) Paul's speech in Athens, (5) Paul's defense before Agrippa, and (6) Paul's concluding speech before the Jewish elders in Rome. What characterizes each of these cases is that apocalyptic discourse is employed when mission to the Gentiles returns to the fore.

Using the intertextural map to navigate through Lukan apocalyptic discourse also helps us to see Luke's vision of how God is guiding the events of the Gentile mission as a part of God's divine redemption. It is for this reason, I suggest, that we find Paul employing the same text from Isaiah concerning salvation for the Gentiles when speaking to Agrippa as Simeon had when he sang the praise of God in the temple with the baby Jesus. The apocalyptic moment has not passed;[21] rather, it is taking place as a witness to Jesus and under his authority.

Finally, we can see Lukan apocalyptic not as the short-lived, revolutionist, and liminal cultural moment usually associated with a cataclysmic inbreaking, but as an enduring "revolutionist" and countercultural overthrow.[22] In the Lukan picture, Judaism is first presented with a challenge to believe in one who is believed to be the Messiah; failing to believe, however, Judaism is faced by the followers of Jesus with the unthinkable, namely, that the torch of God's election will pass from them to the rest of

---

[21] *Pace* H. Conzelmann, *The Theology of Luke* (trans. G. Buswell; New York: Harper & Row, 1961).

[22] Only a Leninist-Stalinist Marxist would argue that Trotsky's vision of a perpetual revolution was not a truly "revolutionary" or "socialist" position and that Lenin's hope of a "liminal" socialism leading to an enduring communist utopia was truly revolutionary. Just as revolution need not be understood as a liminal reality, so Lukan apocalyptic revolutionism need not be.

the peoples (the "Gentiles"). The final volume of Luke is played out on a stage in which the apocalyptic events happen in the context of (1) signs and wonders of apostolic teaching, (2) the mutual reciprocity of family life, (3) the meal-table of the family home, and finally (4) in the praise-filled prayer of the church in which there is neither Jew nor Greek (see Acts 2:42–47).

The Interaction of Social and Scribal Intertexture in Q's Apocalyptic Discourse

Russell B. Sisson

Over the past quarter century, scholars have debated how much discourse in Q can properly be called apocalyptic. Only a handful of Q sayings potentially evoke the dualistic configuration of space and time characteristic of apocalyptic discourse, but these sayings lack certain subjects and motifs commonly associated with apocalyptic discourse. For example, we find no tours of the heavenly realms with visions of impending cosmic upheavals and eschatological judgment. Neither is there a delineation of history into periods or ages, with a timetable of events leading up to a final showdown between cosmic forces of good and evil.

Perhaps most important, there is no explicit, unambiguous description of Christ's *parousia* similar to that found in Paul and Matthew. The closest Q comes to having a *parousia* is in the Son of Man sayings of Q 17:24–30, what some interpreters call the "Q apocalypse." Here we find allusions to future catastrophic events by way of analogy to catastrophic "days" of judgment in Israel's epic past. What the term "Son of Man" means here is not clear because there is little context from which to draw conclusions. Earlier in Q, Jesus speaks of a "Son of Man" who will stand as a judge of "this generation" (11:30) and who will acknowledge his disciples "before the angels of God" (12:8). Since Jesus does not explicitly identify himself as the coming Son of Man, it is not clear that he is referring to his own future return.[1] In Matthew's reworking of Q 17:24–30 (Matt 24:23–28, 37–42), there is a reference to the Son of Man's *parousia* (24:39), but this is generally regarded as a Matthean redaction.[2] There are no clear allusions to Dan 7:13–14 in any of Q's "Son of Man" sayings. It is thus not certain that this Jewish concept

---

[1] Heinz Tödt, *Der Menschensohn in der synoptischen Überlieferung* (Gütersloh: Mohn, 1959), 59–60, 206, 210. Tödt argues that Q 12:8–9 suggests a soteriological relationship between Jesus and the Son of Man.

[2] Richard Horsley, *Whoever Hears You Hears Me: Prophets, Performance, and Tradition in* Q (Harrisburg, Pa.: Trinity Press International, 1999), 74–75. Horsley argues that Q remains wholly within Israelite tradition with no distinctively "Christian" features.

of a heavenly redeemer lies behind the Q sayings.[3] Just as some interpreters
warn against reading into Q later "Christian" concepts of the Son of Man,
others warn against carrying over particular Jewish understandings of this
enigmatic figure. Nevertheless, Q's "Son of Man sayings" do seem to evoke
a temporal dualism, if not a spatial one, because following the sayings and
a parable about judgment, Jesus envisions his disciples, who have perse-
vered with him in his trials, sitting on thrones judging the twelve tribes of
Israel (22:28–30). Implicit in the allusion to sudden, unexpected destruction
preceding the restoration of Israel is the concept of a divinely initiated transition from an old age of disobedience to a new age of righteousness.[4]

The interpretation of Q's apocalyptic discourse is complicated by the
fact that, aside from the "Q apocalypse," Q contains only a small amount
of discourse that *potentially* evokes an apocalyptic configuration of space
and time. We find language of spatial orientation in references to heaven
(6:23; 12:33) and the underworld (10:5; 12:5) and to the inhabitants of
these transcendent realms and their agents on earth: Sophia (7:35; 11:49),
angels (12:8–9), the devil (4:1–13), and demons (11:14–26). On the temporal horizon looms a coming judgment (3:7–9; 10:13–15; 11:31–32; 22:28–
30) marked by the destruction of the impenitent (3:17; 17:26–30) and an
eschatological banquet (13:28–29). The presence of these few apocalyptic
motifs seems to justify the conclusion drawn by John Kloppenborg that the
Q community and its scribes "breathed the apocalyptic atmosphere" of
their time.[5] Assuming that apocalyptic thinking was ubiquitous in early
Christian communities, Kloppenborg seems to be saying that we should be
surprised if Q *lacked* apocalyptic motifs.[6]

---

[3] For a summary of the recent debate, see John Kloppenborg, "The Sayings
Gospel Q and the Quest of the Historical Jesus," *HTR* 89 (1996): 318. Kloppenborg
cites Q's lack of an explicit reference to Jesus' resurrection as evidence that Q's
"Son of Man" is not patterned after the same in Daniel.

[4] Horsley, *Whoever Hears You Hears Me*, 262–63. Noting that this closing saying
in Q is difficult to reconstruct because of how it is used in Matthew and Luke, Horsley proposes that 22:28–30 is about historical renewal of Israel that involves no
cosmological regeneration. He bases this on the possibility of reading κρίνειν in the
sense of "liberating, delivering, saving, effecting justice for." The paucity of cosmological imagery in the saying speaks for the plausibility of the reading, but
nothing more. The catastrophes alluded to in the "Son of Man" sayings, especially
the flood in the days of Noah, suggest that the restoration of Israel is based on
some renewal of the natural or cosmic order.

[5] John Kloppenborg, "Symbolic Eschatology and the Apocalypticism of Q," *HTR*
80 (1987): 291.

[6] Kloppenborg, "Symbolic Eschatology," 288–89. Kloppenborg challenges that
tradition of scholarship running from Johannes Weiss and Albert Schweitzer to

What is significant is that the apocalyptic topics are so few and scattered, making it difficult to discern a distinctive apocalyptic worldview underlying the Q discourses. Even more significant is the type of material surrounding these seemingly apocalyptic sayings—sayings that evoke a nonapocalyptic configuration of the world. Kloppenborg points out, for example, how discourse on confidence in prayer (Q 11:9–11) "directs attention not to apocalyptic liberation in the future, but instead towards God's sustaining help in the present."[7] In the discourse on earthly cares (Q 12:22–34), Jesus exhorts his hearers to seek the kingdom of God within the present world order. Of this discourse Kloppenborg writes: "An eschatological horizon is, in general terms, evident here but the metaphors of the Kingdom and incorruptible heavenly treasure serve primarily to undergird the appeal to utter dependence on God's providential care in the present."[8] Within this same discourse we find sayings about how God provides for the needs of birds and flowers (12:24–27), which Kloppenborg describes as affirming "God's intimate involvement in creation in quite positive terms."[9] He adds: "Instead of the spectre of a topsy-turvy cosmos, Q appeals to the normalcy of biological and social processes."[10] Where Q does have warnings about the imminent judgment and destruction of the impenitent, there are no suggestions that the present age is not in divine control. Where Jesus speaks of divisions within families (12:51–53), Kloppenborg says: "The focus is not upon the decay of society in general, but upon the divisive effects of the responding to the call of the Kingdom."[11] If the overall tenor of Q is nonapocalyptic, as Kloppenborg concludes, then what is the function of the apocalyptic discourse we find there? If it does not evoke a configuration of space and time that is truly apocalyptic, what is its rhetorical function?

1. The Function of Apocalyptic Discourse in the Redaction of Q

Recently, the function of the apocalyptic sayings has been discussed in the context of speculation about Q's composition history. In his groundbreaking work on the redaction of Q, Dieter Lührmann assigns the sections of Q attacking "this generation" to a later redaction of the original collection

---

Ernst Käsemann that affirms the thoroughly apocalyptic character of the earliest Jesus traditions.

[7] Ibid., 293.

[8] Ibid., 293–94.

[9] Ibid., 297.

[10] Ibid.

[11] Ibid., 299.

of Q sayings.[12] Lührmann proposes that this redaction occurred when the Q community lost hope that Israel would respond positively to its preaching.[13] He does not, however, assign the "Son of Man" sayings to the later redaction, claiming that the Q community had already identified Jesus with the Son of Man. Siegfried Schulz also assigns apocalyptic material to the earliest stratum of Q, arguing that the earliest Q community understood itself as the community of the end time.[14] For Schulz, the apocalyptic sayings in Q informed the prophetic self-understanding of a community that proclaimed a radicalized Torah in an apocalyptic framework.[15] A variation of this view holds that apocalyptic material is found both in the earliest form of Q as well as later redactions. Eugene Boring, for example, argues that the presence of the Son of Man sayings in the earliest version of Q explains the persecution that the community addresses in later versions. He writes: "'Son of Man' is the only christological title found in Q and was both fundamental to the community's confession of Jesus and the cause of its persecution."[16]

Arland Jacobson also proposes that apocalyptic materials function at different stages in the development of Q. Like Schulz, Jacobson believes that the earliest Q community had a prophetic self-understanding. It viewed Jesus and John as rejected messengers of Wisdom in line with earlier prophets rejected by Israel. He proposes that the Q community met rejection in its mission to reform Israel until it eventually abandoned that mission.[17] He assigns the sayings in 17:23—a warning against false signs of the end time—to the earlier stratum of Q. Together with 17:37b, the saying functions as a warning against apocalyptic watching and waiting. As he explains, "The group was apparently vulnerable to any eschatological excitement in the Jewish community at large."[18] The "Son of Man" sayings, Jacobson argues, were added later to denounce and threaten unreformed Israel.[19] Yet even in the later redaction, the warning against watching and waiting still holds. The Q scribes, Jacobson says, paradoxically "use

---

[12] Dieter Lührmann, *Die Redaktion der Logienquelle* (WMANT 33; Neukirchen-Vluyn: Neukirchener Verlag, 1969), 93.

[13] Ibid., 40–41.

[14] Siegfried Schulz, *Q: Die Spruchquelle der Evangelisten* (Zürich: Theologischer Verlag, 1972), 68.

[15] Ibid., 82.

[16] Eugene Boring, *Sayings of the Risen Jesus* (SNTSMS 46; Cambridge: Cambridge University Press, 1982), 141.

[17] Arland Jacobson, *The First Gospel: An Introduction to Q* (Sonoma, Calif.: Polebridge, 1992), 255–56.

[18] Ibid., 236.

[19] Ibid., 236–37.

apocalyptic language against apocalypticism."[20] What emerges in these constructions of Q's redactional history is the view that apocalyptic discourse functions primarily to motivate the Q community in its prophetic mission and, when facing rejection, to denounce its persecutors.

Other reconstructions of Q's compositional history assign all the apocalyptic material to later stages of redaction. The basis of these reconstructions has been James Robinson's proposal that the literary genre, or *Gattung,* of the earliest stratum of Q is an ancient genre that he identifies as "the sayings of the wise."[21] Helmut Koester, following Robinson and using the *Gospel of Thomas* as a model for the genre, proposes that Q was originally a wisdom book to which apocalyptic sayings were later added.

> If the genre of the wisdom book was the catalyst for composition of the sayings of Jesus into a "gospel," and if the christological concept of Jesus as the teacher of wisdom and as the presence of heavenly Wisdom dominated its creation, the apocalyptic orientation of the *Synoptic Sayings Source* with its christology of the coming Son of Man is due to the secondary redaction of an older wisdom book.[22]

Building on the theories of Robinson and Koester, Kloppenborg regards the "wisdom book" genre as formative for the development of Q. Genre, he asserts, is the key to function. To explain, he quotes Paul Riceour: "The function of genre is 'to mediate between the speaker and hearer by establishing a common dynamics capable of ruling both the production of the discourse as work of a certain kind and its interpretation according to the rules of that genre.'"[23] Anything that does not fit the formative genre, Kloppenborg concludes, must be the result of later redaction. He thus assigns to a later redactional stratum five clusters of sayings that function as pronouncements of judgment—3:7–9, 16–17; 7:1–10, 18–35; 11:14–26, 29–32, 39–53; 12:39–57; 17:23–35—the last of these being the "Q apocalypse." Opponents of the community's preaching are the projected audience of these discourses.[24] Although he argues

---

[20] Ibid., 236.

[21] James Robinson, "LOGOI SOPHON: On the Gattung of Q," in idem and Helmut Koester, *Trajectories through Early Christianity* (Philadelphia: Fortress, 1971), 71–113.

[22] Helmut Koester, "Apocryphal and Canonical Gospels," *HTR* 73 (1980): 112–13.

[23] John Kloppenborg, *The Formation of Q* (Philadelphia: Fortress, 1987), 3; Paul Ricoeur, "The Hermeneutic Function of Distanciation," *Philosophy Today* 17 (1973): 136.

[24] Kloppenborg, *Formation of Q,* 166–70.

that the "wisdom" sayings of the earliest stratum reflect the earliest preaching, Kloppenborg is hesitant to characterize this preaching as nonapocalyptic, for he believes the apocalyptic sayings added in later redaction may have functioned in the earliest missionary preaching. In their redactional form, these sayings with their apocalyptic motifs function "to define more clearly group boundaries, to enhance internal cohesion and to reinforce group identity."[25] However, if Q's apocalyptic discourse could function this way in a later redaction, why could it not function that way in the earliest stratum? Kloppenborg himself suggests as much when he says that the redactional changes in Q are not due to the introduction of previously unknown material, nor do they represent a shift from a "noneschatological" to an "apocalyptic" document.[26] Kloppenborg's reconstruction does not presume that the Q community's rejection and possible persecution caused it to become apocalyptic in its outlook; rather, it suggests that situations that developed later may have caused the community to modify the "wisdom" eschatology reflected in the original formative stratum. That is to say, Kloppenborg understands the rhetorical function of the apocalyptic discourse in relation to a particular underlying problem.

Kloppenborg's reconstruction of Q's composition history presumes a basic continuity in eschatology throughout the earliest stratum. However, as Richard Horsley asks, what if the clusters of wisdom sayings functioned originally as separate discourses and not as part of a "formative document?"[27] Should we not ask how the apocalyptic discourse in Q potentially transforms the wisdom discourse within individual discourse, putting on hold judgments about basic continuity in eschatology throughout Q? Also at issue here is the historical meaningfulness of the concepts "sapiential" and "apocalyptic," especially in theories about formative genres. As Horsley points out, the concept of "apocalyptic," as it is used to describe a textual genre or a type of discourse, is a synthetic concept of modern interpreters.[28] He explains: "It has often been assumed in scholarly discourse that if a particular symbol, motif, or form, often understood in a somewhat literalistic way, has been identified as typical of apocalyptic, it carries with it and indicates an apocalyptic theology wherever it

---

[25] Ibid., 167–68.

[26] Kloppenborg, "Sayings Gospel Q," 336.

[27] Horsley, *Whoever Hears You Hears Me,* 67. A similar point is made by Christopher Tuckett (*Q and the History of Early Christianity* [Edinburgh: T&T Clark, 1996], 72–73), who argues that it is clear that the allegedly "prophetic" material in Kloppenborg's later stratum may just as well be addressed to "insiders"—the audience of the alleged "sapiential" material—as to "outsiders."

[28] Horsley, *Whoever Hears You Hears Me,* 69–75.

occurs."[29] However, even if particular symbols and motifs point to an underlying theology, which is not always the case, there is no "typical" apocalyptic theology. As Frederick Murphy observes, "There is tremendous variation in apocalypses with respect to form and content, beliefs, expectations, historical circumstances, political positions, and so on."[30] There existed no standard apocalyptic text and no single apocalyptic movement; instead, there were undoubtedly a variety of sources and settings for the rise of apocalyptic in early Christianity.[31] Similarly, there is no single standard for judging what constitutes sapiential discourse. Kloppenborg, in his most recent work on Q, notes a trajectory in the Jewish wisdom tradition in which "the reign of God" is offered as an alternative to the current political and social order.[32] This trajectory represents a shift from an earlier Jewish wisdom tradition that envisions "a divine order that permeates and sustains the current order of things, from king down to individual clans and families."[33] Noting several Q sayings that speak against the permanence of the current order (e.g., 11:49–51; 13:34–35), Kloppenborg asserts that Q, while lacking typical apocalyptic elements, "clearly undergirds its ethical appeals by involving the impermanence of the present and the hope of a divinely established future."[34]

If there are these problems with the use of the term *apocalyptic,* then there are problems in defining "sapiential" discourse as essentially "non-apocalyptic." We should be cautious about attempting to reconstruct the theology of a scribe or a community from any text, especially from a text that is essentially a collection of discourses on various topics, as is Q. There may be thematic connections between these discourses that allow interpreters to speculate about the underlying theology or eschatology, but as long as the theology or eschatology is implicit, we must respect the vagueness of the text on these matters. Instead of separating the "apocalyptic" and "sapiential" material in order to recover a consistent eschatology, coherent by modern standards, perhaps we should examine how these

---

[29] Ibid., 69–71,

[30] Frederick J. Murphy, "Introduction to Apocalyptic Literature," *NIB* 7:1.

[31] Ibid., 7:4–7.

[32] John S. Kloppenborg Verbin, *Excavating Q: The History and Setting of the Sayings Gospel* (Minneapolis: Fortress, 2000), 386–87.

[33] Ibid., 386. The trajectories of the Jewish wisdom tradition noted by Kloppenborg Verbin are those identified by John Gammie in "From Prudentialism to Apocalypticism: The House of the Sages amid the Varying Forms of Wisdom," in *The Sage in Israel and the Ancient Near East* (ed. John Gammie and Leo Perdue; Winona Lake, Ind.: Eisenbrauns, 1990), 479–97.

[34] Kloppenborg Verbin, *Excavating Q,* 387.

supposedly distinct types of discourse might interact, each potentially modifying the other.

2. Apocalyptic Discourse and the Social Intertexture of Q

Hans D. Betz has proposed that apocalyptic discourse be defined not on the basis of literary elements or theological motifs but on the basis of an "underlying problem"—namely, the pollution of the cosmos by oppressive forces that leave humanity helpless and lost.[35] Apocalyptic discourse creates a transcendent perspective from which this underlying problem and its solution are viewed. Betz explains, "Redemption can only come from the deity, who rules over the elementary and celestial spirits. God's saving acts result in the 'purification' of the earth, the restitution of righteousness and worship of the deity among men, and announcement of an era of paradise."[36] Accepting Betz's definition, Kloppenborg questions whether the "problem" underlying the eschatological warnings in Q can properly be called apocalyptic. He writes: "It is precisely this sense of anomie, of devastating and inescapable pollution, of demonic domination which is not evidenced in Q."[37] For example, Q envisions a cosmos that is still in divine control (Q 11:3–4, 9–13; 12:4–7, 22–31), not one under the control of demonic forces.[38]

The understanding of the "underlying problem" that Betz proposes and Kloppenborg follows is based on the type of problems addressed in *1 Enoch* and Revelation, texts that describe cosmic disorder in terms of "pollution" and "purification." In defining "apocalyptic" discourse, we must also avoid presuming that such discourse addresses a standard type of underlying problem. For instance, it is not clear that all first-century Jews would have viewed the anomic phenomena around them through cultic lenses. That is to say, the particular way the "underlying problem" and its resolution are described in any text reflects a particular sociocultural perspective. What is absent from Q is not an underlying problem like that Betz defines, but the particular sociocultural understanding of the problem that Betz's definition

---

[35] Hans Dieter Betz, "On the Problem of the Religio-Historical Understanding of Apocalypticism," *JTC* 6 (1969): 148.

[36] Ibid.

[37] Kloppenborg, "Symbolic Eschatology," 298.

[38] Ibid., 298–99. Kloppenborg acknowledges that in the Q temptation story the devil claims to be able to deliver "all the kingdoms of earth and their glory" (4:5–7). But, he argues, "It is unjustified to interpret the story of Q on the analogy of the function of Mark 1:12–13—as the inauguration of the eschatological struggle in which Satan and his minions are bound and the Kingdom manifest—because Q elsewhere show such little interest in exorcisms, demons, and Satan."

presumes. Q may envision a corruption of the present order so devastating that only divine intervention can rectify the problem, even though the problem or its solution is not described in terms of pollution and purification.

Failing to identify a typically apocalyptic problem, Kloppenborg explains how apocalyptic motifs are transformed to describe a nonapocalyptic problem, namely, the rejection of the Q community's message and messengers. There is nothing fundamentally apocalyptic in warnings about impending judgment and destruction, if, as Kloppenborg proposes, these warnings function "to rationalize failure and to strengthen the boundaries between insiders and outsiders."[39] Like Jacobson, who argues that Q "uses apocalyptic language against apocalypticism," Kloppenborg describes an interpretative "problem" that results when apocalyptic language is used in nonapocalyptic ways:

> The framers of Q no doubt apprehended the transformative powers resident in traditional apocalyptic motifs. Their innovation was to deploy these motifs in non-traditional, non-apocalyptic ways. In Q apocalyptic language becomes the servant of an ethic of antistructure and a tool for boundary definition.[40]

The rejection of the Q prophets might count as an apocalyptic problem if the Q community viewed the rejection as a case of national apostasy. Horsley rejects this view of the underlying problem, arguing that Q's polemic against "this generation" is not a polemic against "all Israel." To get at the real problem, Horsley challenges the stratification theories that assign the apocalyptic discourse to a secondary "judgmental" stratum. He notes how Helmut Koester uses parallels in the *Gospel of Thomas* to argue that the original stratum of Q contained sayings that point to the fulfillment of prophetic longings in Jesus' inauguration of the kingdom of God.[41] Horsley, however, calls attention to an important difference between the *Gospel of Thomas* and Q on the basis of different "implicit hermeneutics."[42] With the *Gospel of Thomas,* "the sayings require studying or pondering by an *individual* in order to penetrate their meaning." If Q had the same implicit hermeneutic as Thomas, then Q's pronouncements of judgment and condemnation would be out of place, and assigning them to a later stratum

---

[39] Ibid., 306.

[40] Ibid.

[41] Horsley, *Whoever Hears You Hears Me,* 81; Helmut Koester, *Ancient Christian Gospels: Their History and Development* (London: SCM; Philadelphia: Trinity Press International, 1990), 137–38.

[42] Horsley, *Whoever Hears You Hears Me,* 85–86, emphasis added.

would be in order. Horsley instead identifies a different implicit hermeneutic based on the inclusion of the judgment and condemnation sayings alongside the "sapiential" material. He explains, "The hermeneutics implicit in Q is straightforward exhortation of a community of people regarding socio-economic-political interaction sanctioned by prophetic threats of reward and punishment."[43] He cites as examples Jesus' inaugural sermon (6:20– 49), which includes instructions on socioeconomic relations, and the instructions dealing with fear and anxiety (12:2–12, 22–31). This hermeneutic is also implicit in discourses that condemn the opponents of the Q community. In 11:39–52, the opponents are Pharisees who receive seats of honor in synagogues and salutations in the marketplaces and who tithe but neglect the justice and love of God by neglecting others. In 13:28–30, 34–35 and 14:16–24, the opponents are rulers of the temple-state in Jerusalem.[44] Instead of supposing that Q's polemic is directed at all Israel, Horsley proposes that the polemic aimed at Pharisees and rulers in Jerusalem come from within Judaism. The polemic against "this generation," then, does not begin with the rejection of the Q messengers, but the polemic is central to the messengers' original preaching.

Horsley explains how a community situated in Galilee—the commonly accepted location of the Q community—would have regarded these groups as opponents. After Galilee came under Hasmonean control in 104 B.C.E., when Galileans were forced to live under the "laws of the Judeans,"[45] scribes and Pharisees began to operate as agents of the temple-state in Jerusalem within Gaililee. Horsley proposes that scribes and Pharisees, in their role as interpreters of the law, represented the political-economic-religious interests of the temple-state.[46] The resentment Galileans felt toward the temple-state's exploitative taxation would also have been directed toward the scribes and Pharisees they encountered. The villagers who experienced such economic exploitation thus became increasingly alienated from Galilean cities that housed garrisons and served as base for the agents of the temple-state. This explains the "village versus city" character of the social conflict reflected in several Q sayings.

As Jonathan Reed shows, the village versus city mentality is evident in the ways agricultural and urban images are used.[47] For example, in the

---

[43] Ibid., 86.

[44] Ibid.

[45] Josephus, *Ant.* 13.257–258.

[46] Horsley, *Whoever Hears You Hears Me*, 56.

[47] Jonathan Reed, "The Social Map of Q," in *Conflict and Invention: Literary, Rhetorical, and Social Studies on the Sayings Gospel Q* (ed. John Kloppenborg; Valley Forge, Pa.: Trinity Press International, 1995), 24–29.

mission discourse Jesus tells his followers that they can expect opposition in cities (10:8–11). The agora, an urban institution, is the locale of the Pharisees criticized in 11:43. It is also the locale of children playing the flute and singing, to whose music Jesus and John are seen being out of step (7:32). Cities would also be the location of the rulers and magistrates before whom the members of the Q community might be brought (12:4–12, 59). In the parable of the banquet (14:16–24), a servant goes *outside* the city to invite people to the banquet after members of the wealthy urbanites turn down their invitations. Divine judgment is described with agricultural images. In John's warnings about judgment, there are references to the ax being laid to the root (3:8–9) and to clearing the thrashing floor and burning the chaff (3:17). Q on the whole, Reed concludes, uses such images to express anxiety and apprehension about urban, civilized life.[48] Such attitudes toward urban society are quite common in traditional agricultural societies, but as Horsley notes, Roman political administration of Palestine likely exacerbated the resentment and cynicism of the village people in first-century Galilee.[49]

3. Social and Scribal Intertexture in Q 17:23–27

If a "political-economic-religious rift" between Galilean villages and cities is the "underlying problem" addressed by the apocalyptic discourse in Q, then how does it address it? Is the eschatological judgment to occur in the "days of the Son of Man" a condemnation of an urban culture from which the Q community is alienated? The way Reed and Horsley describe the sociopolitical context of the Q discourses suggests the need to examine two dimensions of the rhetorical intertexture—the social and scribal-oral. Social intertexture is reflected in the way a text evokes knowledge of social phenomena "readily accessible to all people through general interaction."[50] The scribal-oral intertexture is reflected in the way "a text uses any other text outside of itself"[51]—either written or orally transmitted tradition. No canonical texts are recited in any of the apocalyptic discourse in Q. In 17:26–29, we find references to Noah and Lot, heroes in the Hebrew epic tradition. How the Q sayings describe the "days" of Noah and the "days" of Lot are at some variance from the canonical accounts. This

---

[48] Ibid., 29.

[49] Richard Horsley, "Social Conflict in the Synoptic Sayings Source Q," in Kloppenborg, *Conflict and Invention,* 45.

[50] Vernon Robbins, *Exploring the Texture of Texts: A Guide to Socio-Rhetorical Interpretation* (Valley Forge, Pa.: Trinity Press International, 1996), 62.

[51] Ibid., 40.

difference reflects a *reconfiguration* of the two traditions. That is to say, the old traditions are recounted in a manner that creates a "new" event, one that "replaces" or "outshines" the previous event.[52] The social intertexture and scribal-oral intertexture become intertwined at this point, for the social intertexture evokes the consciousness of social context in which the epic traditions are engendered with meaning.

At first glance, the references to "the days of Noah" and "the days of Lot" appear to serve as examples of sudden, unexpected expressions of divine wrath. The warnings about destruction "in the days of the Son of Man" are preceded by warnings about the suddenness of the judgment: "For as lightning flashes and lights up the sky from one side to the other, so will the Son of Man be in his day" (17:24). Matthew describes how judgment and destruction came upon people unexpectedly in the days of Noah: "And they knew nothing until the flood came and swept them all away" (24:38). The words "they did not know until" (οὐκ ἔγνωσαν ἕως) do not appear in Luke. The words are probably a Matthean redaction, since Matthew also interprets the coming days of the Son of Man as a παρουσία.[53] Since Q lacks the explicit reference to the *parousia* and the description of people "not knowing" until it is too late, the sayings in 17:26–30 probably function as more than warnings about the need for preparedness in the last days. References to "the days of Noah" and "the days of Lot" evoke images of God destroying entire populations by means of cataclysmic events—flood and fire. The theme of total devastation is explicit: καὶ ἦλθεν ὁ κατακλυσμὸς καὶ ἀπώλεσεν πάντας (17:27).[54]

Q's descriptions of what people are doing when the cataclysmic events come do not correspond with epic traditions as known through the canonical texts. The Q scribes may have known oral versions of the traditions that differed from the canonical versions, but to assert this would be pure speculation. In Q's description of "the days of Noah" we are told that people were "eating, drinking, marrying, and being married" (17:27). There are no references to humans engaging in these activities at the moment of the flood in the Genesis account. The birth of the Nephilim (Gen 6:1–5), the offspring of the sons of God and human daughters, is presented as the

---

[52] Ibid., 50.

[53] Matthew's use of the Q sayings in what amounts to a discourse on the *parousia* may explain why the analogy to "the days of Lot" is absent in Matthew. Noah is given time to prepare for the coming catastrophe. Lot has only enough time to flee from the moment the impending destruction of Sodom is revealed to him. Matthew envisions people having time to prepare for the impending *parousia* (see 25:1–13).

[54] Matthew reads ἦρεν instead of ἀπώλεσεν.

cause of the spread of unrighteous upon the earth, prompting God to destroy the earth with a flood. The language of marriage, however, is not used in Genesis to describe this illicit union. "The days of Lot" are described here as times when people were "eating, drinking, buying, selling, planting, building." However, in the biblical account of the destruction of Sodom and the circumstances leading up to it (Gen 18:16–19:26), these human activities are not mentioned.

The Q sayings are clearly a reconfiguration of the epic tradition, but for what purpose have they been reconfigured? It is possible that the human activities mentioned in these two sayings represent the type of everyday activities people will be engaged in when the day of divine judgment comes. If so, it reinforces the idea set forth in the opening of the discourse that this day will come so unexpectedly that it is futile for people to try to predict it (17:21–23). In this case, the human activities described are not the cause of the imminent judgment. However, when interpreted this way, the discourse provides no indications of how people might be prepared for that day, other than not to believe those people who do in fact predict when it will be. The canonical versions of the Noah and Lot traditions say nothing about people being led astray by false prophets.

The meaning of Q's reconfigurations of Noah and Lot traditions may be discerned by examining reconfigurations of the two traditions side by side in other texts. In 3 Maccabees, for example, when Simon the high priest entreats God to thwart Ptolemy IV's attempt to enter the temple, he recalls past instances when God, "the creator of all things," destroyed the insolent and arrogant (2:3). First, he recalls how the "strong and bold" giants were washed away in a flood (2:4). Next, he recalls how the "arrogant" people of Sodom were destroyed with fire and sulfur to be "an example to those who should come afterward" (2:5). Another example of parallel reconfigurations is found in the Wisdom of Solomon. Here allusions to both the Noah and Lot traditions are found in a list of Wisdom's great acts in history, where the emphasis is on the saving role of Wisdom. Wisdom is credited with saving "the righteous man" during the flood (10:4) and another "righteous man" when "fire ... descended on the Five Cities" (10:6). The writer of the Wisdom of Solomon understands the flood as the consequence not of the Nephilim (Gen 6:1–5), but of Cain's murder of Abel (Gen 4:1–6). Cain is described as "an unrighteous man [who] departed from [wisdom] in his anger" (Wis 10:3). Similarly, we are told that the five cities were destroyed "because they passed wisdom by" (10:8). In these examples, the saving power of Wisdom is manifested in acts of divine judgment and destruction brought on by the rejection of Wisdom. In both 3 Maccabees and Wisdom of Solomon, these catastrophic events from the epic past represent the predisposition of the Creator to intervene in history to rectify some disruption of the order of creation—disregard and contempt either for the Creator or for God's agent in creation, Wisdom.

Examination of the social intertexture of the discourse in 17:26–30 suggests that the Q scribes reconfigure the Noah and Lot traditions to function in a way similar to what we find in 3 Maccabees and Wisdom of Solomon. The social intertexture here is represented by references to such common human activities as eating and drinking (mentioned twice), marrying and being given in marriage, buying and selling, planting, and building. At first we might consider these activities to be the type of activities all people engage in at some point in time. However, from the standpoint of politically and economically oppressed people, which the Q community appears to be, some of these activities might be associated with wealth and power. Not everyone, for example, would have been a builder. When Jewish elders approach Jesus about healing the sick slave of a centurion, they commend the centurion for having "built" a synagogue for them (Luke 7:4–5, possibly in Q).[55] If the centurion did not pay for the building of the synagogue, he could have at least supplied the forced labor. Q 11:46–47 pronounces "woes" on lawyers who overburden people—presumably the poor—and who "build" tombs for prophets, even though their fathers killed prophets. Implicit in these charges is that the lawyers have the financial resources to build tombs and perhaps acquire these resources from those with the least to contribute. Having the resources to build resulted from power and quite possibly was a sign of social status.

A similar point can be made about planting. If the exploitative taxation of the Romans resulted in a large landless underclass in Galilee, as Horsley's analysis suggests, then planting and harvesting would have been under the control of a powerful few, probably the type of absentee landlords described in Jesus' parables (Q 19:11–27). The image of the agora, where "buying and selling" would have occurred, no doubt carried connotations of wealth and power concentrated in cities. Village peasants would not have been among those making a livelihood buying and selling in the agora of the city. The "marrying" need not evoke images of social power and privilege, but "being given in marriage" (ἐγαμίζοντο) could refer to arranged marriages by which political alliances were created and the inheritance of wealth was controlled. As for "eating and drinking," at first glance there is no reason to associate these actions with power or privilege,

---

[55] The Jewish elders with their words praising the centurion are absent in Matthew, so this part of the tradition may not have been in the Q account. Even if the reference to the centurion "building" a synagogue is Lukan, there is still no reason to doubt that the Q community would have associated the deed with wealth or social power.

since all people eat and drink to survive. However, when mentioned alongside these other activities that carry connotations of wealth and power, Q's audience may have readily associated "eating and drinking" with lavish banquets for the wealthy and their friends, such as the one described in Jesus' parable about a great banquet (14:16–24).

Using the social intertexture as a guide to interpreting the scribal intertexture of 17:26–30, the catastrophic events that will mark the "day of the Son of Man," like those in the days of Noah and Lot, represent God's judgment against people responsible for some type of corruption of the created order. The destruction alluded to in the Q saying is divine retribution against those who procure wealth and power at the expense of the poor. As an eschatological vision, it sanctions exhortations and warnings in preceding discourses of Q. For example, it supports the beatitudes beginning the opening sermon: "Blessed are you poor, for yours is the kingdom of God. Blessed are you who hunger now, for you shall be filled" (6:20–21). It supports also the warning at the end of the opening sermon that houses not built on a solid foundations will be washed away (6:49), the pronouncement of judgment on "cities" that reject the community's prophets (10:12), and the parable of the Talents that follow (19:12–13, 15b–26). Alongside this eschatological vision of judgment and condemnation, there is a place for a vision of Wisdom and her children vindicated, similar to what we find in Wisdom of Solomon 10. So we find in Q 11:29–32 Jesus foretelling how the children of wisdom will stand in condemnation of "this" evil, sign-seeking "generation."

4. Conclusion

Can the sayings in Q 17:26–30 and the discourse of Q 17:20–37 properly be described as apocalyptic discourse within sapential discourse? The sayings seem to evoke a dualistic configuration of space and time within which the Q community envisions God's imminent redemption of the social order. How Q views the redemption of the social order is how the Q community views the renewal of Israel. But the renewal depends on divine judgment and destruction of those responsible for the disruption of the present social order. Q does not envision the whole of the created order out of control, only part of it, namely, the urban societies controlled by an aristocratic elite. Those alienated from this sector of Galilean society no doubt felt powerless to deliver themselves from its oppression. So convinced were they that God did not tolerate this disruption of the social order that they expected God to intervene and rectify the situation. Such a belief would not represent a total rejection of the tradition sapiential view of the present world order, but it does entail a modification of that outlook.

As Leo Perdue notes, wisdom sages in the Hebrew tradition occasionally draw on images of the city in their representations of Wisdom. He cites

Prov 1, 8, and 9, where Wisdom is described entering the city and seeking students to learn from her. "She walks along its walls, teaches in its gates, stands on its street corners, and takes up residence on its acropolis, exhorting the simple to learn from her."[56] Perdue notes also how Wisdom in Ben Sira dwells in the holy city and its temple (Sir 24). Such descriptions, he argues, "not only suggest the social location of wisdom teaching, but also construes reality."[57]

Q seems intent on locating wisdom outside cities—it is there and only there that wisdom can be sought and found. Such a countercultural view of wisdom needs sanction to stand over and against a tradition that locates wisdom in cities. The "Son of Man" sayings in 17:26–30, read as apocalyptic sayings, provide such a sanction. Given the type of pervasive, systemic corruption of urban society in Galilee that Horsley believes is the social context of Q, it is difficult to believe that the Q community developed this countercultural view of wisdom only after some attempt to reform urban society failed. That is to say, in order to explain the presence of "apocalyptic" saying alongside "sapiential" material, one need not posit a scenario in which a reform-minded religious community became disillusioned as the result of rejection and thus decided Wisdom no longer dwelt in the city. For there is no evidence in Q that the community ever sought wisdom there. The exhortation to seek the kingdom of God here and now is general, with no specification about where wisdom can be found. This is perhaps because the community already knew where it could be found and where it could not.

Apocalyptic sayings modifying sapiential material can be found elsewhere in Q. In 10:21–22, for example, which Horsley says contains the most explicitly apocalyptic language in Q, Jesus thanks God for having revealed to children things "hidden" from the wise and learned.[58] Because Jesus proceeds to note the special relation with God that allows him to know and impart these revelations, it can be argued that he is implicitly identifying himself with Wisdom. Horsley cites this along with other examples from canonical and noncanonical Jewish writings as evidence that a sharp dichotomy between "sapiential" and "apocalyptic" discourse is unwarranted. The "Son of Man" sayings in 17:26–30, coming as they do at the end of Q, sanction the saying in 10:21–22 as well as the preaching

---

[56] *Wisdom and Creation: The Theology of Wisdom Literature* (Nashville: Abingdon, 1994), 338.

[57] Ibid.

[58] Richard Horsley, "Wisdom Justified by Her Children: Examining Allegedly Disparate Traditions in Q," *SBL Seminar Papers, 1994* (SBLSP 31; Atlanta: Scholars Press, 1994), 735.

of John—a warning of imminent judgment and destruction that is ripe with agrarian imagery (3:7–9, 16–17). It also sanctions the pronouncement of eschatological condemnation against those who reject the community's itinerant prophets (10:12), rejection that occurs in cities. Horsley points out that agrarian societies often produce their own "wisdom" tradition, sometimes counter to other wisdom traditions around them.[59] It is plausible that the Q community did this in its conflict with the Judean temple-state and its agents in Galilee. It is also plausible that the community created its own apocalyptic discourse in the process. Instead of "apocalyptic" discourse being foreign to the "sapiential," the two are so tightly interwoven in Q that the association of each discourse with a different redactional stratum is unwarranted. Also, if one holds to a theory of Q's compositional history such as that proposed by Kloppenborg, the theory needs to account for this basic continuity in eschatological outlook throughout the different redactional strata. As Kloppenborg says, "The polemical and defensive cast of the main redaction inevitably extended what was already in play in Q1."[60]

There is no reason to posit a typical "apocalyptic situation" as the background for Q's apocalyptic discourse. Similarly, Q does not represent a type of sapiential eschatology within which the few apocalyptic sayings and motifs seem out of place. Q's worldview defies characterization as either typically "apocalyptic" or typically "sapiential," thus illustrating how these categories for describing discourse need to be fluid in order to be useful to modern interpreters. The worldview projected by Q integrates elements from both genres of discourse. For the Q scribes and audience, the prospect that the urban-based agents of socioreligious corruption will be judged and destroyed is affirmed, but not in a manner that engenders a passive, "let's wait it out" attitude. The development of such an attitude is effectively checked by the sayings that precede the "Son of Man" sayings (17:20–21, 23–25). There is nothing the community can do to hasten the "day of the Son of Man," so it should not allow itself to be distracted by apocalyptic expectations. Nevertheless, the belief that divine intervention is imminent is important to the Q community because it warrants a continued polemic against the current social and political order and the ongoing search for Wisdom outside that order.

---

[59] Ibid., 749–50.
[60] *Excavating Q,* 394.

Echoes of Isaiah in the Rhetoric of Paul: New Exodus, Wisdom, and the Humility of the Cross in Utopian-Apocalyptic Expectations

B. J. Oropeza

Within the last decade a growing number of rhetorical studies have focused of 1 Corinthians.[1] Perhaps the most influential of these works has been Margaret Mitchell's *Paul and the Rhetoric of Reconciliation* (1991).[2] Mitchell argues that the primary problem in the Corinthian congregation involves factions. Through the use of deliberative rhetoric Paul attempts to persuade the congregation to accept unity and concord rather than division. The structure of the letter points to 1:10 as the *prothesis*. In this passage Paul exhorts the members to be unified. After a brief statement of facts (1 Cor 1:11–17), he presents four major supporting proofs, which are topically/logically arranged and related to the error of factionalism: (1) the censure of factionalism and need for the apostle's advice (1:18–4:21); (2) the integrity of the community against outside defilement (5:1–11:1); (3) the manifestations of the factionalism when "coming together" (11:2–14:40);

---

[1] See, for example, Anders Eriksson, *Traditions As Rhetorical Proof: Pauline Argumentation in 1 Corinthians* (ConBNT 29; Stockholm: Almqvist & Wiksell, 1998); Laurence L. Welborn, *Politics and Rhetoric in the Corinthian Epistles* (Macon, Ga.: Mercer University Press, 1997); Rollin A. Ramsaran, *Liberating Words: Paul's Use of Rhetorical Maxims in 1 Corinthians 1–10* (Valley Forge, Pa.: Trinity Press International, 1996); Khiok-khng Yeo, *Rhetorical Interaction in 1 Corinthians 8 and 10: A Formal Analysis with Preliminary Suggestions for a Chinese, Cross-Cultural Hermeneutic* (BibInt 9; Leiden: Brill, 1995); Ben Witherington, *Conflict and Community in Corinth: A Socio-Rhetorical Commentary on 1 and 2 Corinthians* (Grand Rapids: Eerdmans, 1995); Stephen M. Pogoloff, *Logos and Sophia: The Rhetorical Situation of 1 Corinthians* (Atlanta: Scholars Press, 1992); Hermann Probst, *Paulus und der Brief: Die Rhetorik des antiken Briefes als Form der paulinischen Korintherkorrespondenz (1 Kor 8–10)* (WUNT 2/45; Tübingen: Mohr Siebeck, 1991). For an overview of some major rhetorical works on 1 Corinthians before 1991, consult Duane F. Watson, "Rhetorical Criticism of the Pauline Epistles since 1975," *CurBS* 3 (1995): 228–30.

[2] Louisville: Westminster John Knox, 1991.

and (4) the resurrection and final community goal (15:1–58). Mitchell concludes that Paul is attempting to dissuade the Corinthians from factionalism
and appeals to what is most advantageous for the body of Christ. The
importance of this theme in 1 Corinthians is rightly identified by Mitchell,
and I do not wish to contend with her thesis. My intention is to posit a reason why factionalism was an issue for the Corinthian congregation in the
first place and to suggest some strategies Paul uses to combat the situation.

A number of scholars have maintained that the discord in Corinth was
instigated either primarily or partially by the congregation's misunder-
standing of issues related to the in-breaking of the new era as understood
by the early Christians.[3] This particular problem is best argued by Anthony
Thiselton, who posits that the Corinthians' view of the culmination of the
eschaton was overrealized. They were convinced by the practice of their
spiritual activities that God's kingdom had become fully realized. The completion of the eschaton seemed evident in their ability to operate through
God's Spirit in areas related to speech, wisdom, knowledge, tongues, and
prophecy.[4] The congregation, along with many of the early Christians,
believed the manifestation of God's Spirit was a defining mark that the
kingdom had arrived (Luke 3:16–17; Acts 2:17–21; Matt 12:28–29; cf. Heb
6:4–5). Since the spiritual manifestations were excessive in the Corinthian
congregation (e.g., 1 Cor 12–14), the members likely assumed this as an
indication that God's reign was fully realized in them. It also appears that
a wedge had developed between those who claimed to possess a special
kind of knowledge/gnosis into spiritual matters and those who did not.
Knowing that there was no other God but one, the "strong" congregation
members approved of eating meat sacrificed to idols in various social settings; the "weak" members found this to be offensive (contrast 1 Cor 8:1
with 8:7–13).[5] Hence, in the Corinthian situation, we find an interaction
between congregational discord and an overconfident sense of spirituality

---

[3] E.g., Gordon D. Fee, *The First Epistle to the Corinthians* (NICNT; Grand Rapids:
Eerdmans, 1987), 12–13; Richard A. Horsley, "'How Can Some of You Say There Is
No Resurrection?' Spiritual Eliticism in Corinth," *NovT* 20 (1978): 203–31; Wayne A.
Meeks, "Social Functions of Apocalyptic Language in Pauline Christianity," in *Apocalypticism in the Mediterranean World and the Near East* (ed. David Hellholm; SHR
14; Tübingen: Mohr Siebeck, 1983), 687–705; Witherington, *Conflict and Community in Corinth,* 139–40.

[4] Anthony C. Thiselton, "Realized Eschatology at Corinth," *NTS* 24 (1977–78):
510–26.

[5] If the members claimed to follow different leaders in 1:12 (those who claimed
to belong to Paul, Apollos, Cephas, or Christ), it is not entirely clear how the strong
and weak fit into this categorization. The evidence seems too tentative to affirm that
all the strong cleaved to one certain leader while all the weak followed another.

involving leadership disputes, pride and boasting, insistence on liberty, and indifference toward the human body (1:12–19; 2:15–3:4; 5:2; 6:13–20; 10:23; 15:12–19).

Although his view is more reserved than that of the Corinthians, Paul himself thinks in terms of apocalyptic time frames.[6] His scheme begins with Christ's resurrection, but the culmination of the kingdom does not take place until all of God's enemies, including death, are defeated (1 Cor 15:20–28, 51–55). The return of Christ remains future (1 Cor 1:4–9; 15:23; 16:22).[7] Paul uses irony as he addresses the Corinthians who think themselves to be already perfected and reigning as kings (4:7–8, 20; cf. 3:1–4; 15:34). Yet Paul's contention with the Corinthians is not simply over a

---

[6] See J. Christiaan Beker, *Paul the Apostle: The Triumph of God in Life and Thought* (Philadelphia: Fortress, 1980); Martinus C. De Boer, "Paul and Apocalyptic Eschatology," in *The Origins of Apocalypticism in Judaism and Christianity* (vol. 1 of *The Encyclopedia of Apocalypticism;* ed. J. J. Collins; New York: Continuum, 1998), 345–47; John M. Court, "Paul and the Apocalyptic Pattern," in *In Paul and Paulinism: Essays in Honour of C. K. Barrett* (ed. Morna D. Hooker and Stephen G. Wilson; London: SPCK, 1982), 57–66; Richard B. Hays, *Echoes of Scripture in the Letters of Paul* (New Haven: Yale University Press, 1989), 191–215; Ernst Käsemann, "Zum Thema der urchristlichen Apokalyptic," *ZTK* 59 (1962): 257–84; ET in *New Testament Questions of Today* (trans. W. J. Montague; Philadelphia: Fortress, 1969), 108–38; B. J. Oropeza, *Paul and Apostasy: Eschatology, Perseverance and Falling Away in the Corinthian Congregation* (WUNT 2/115; Tübingen: Mohr Siebeck, 2000); Albert Schweitzer, *The Mysticism of Saint Paul* (trans. William Montgomery; New York: Henry Holt, 1931); Marion L. Soards, "Paul: Apostle and Apocalyptic Visionary," *BTB* 16 (1986): 148–50. R. Barry Matlock (*Unveiling the Apocalyptic Paul: Paul's Interpreters and the Rhetoric of Criticism* [JSNTSup 127; Sheffield: Sheffield Academic Press, 1996]) surveys some of the most prominent interpreters of Paul and apocalyptic in the twentieth century. Seldom is there any uniformity regarding apocalyptic motifs in New Testament studies. Perhaps the phrase "mere apocalyptic motifs" would help to identify some shared characteristics rather than all the differences. I agree with three of Meeks's motifs: (1) in such literature, there are revelations/visions given to a person/mediator; (2) there is a cosmic transformation involving a contrast between two (or more) ages; (3) there is a divine overthrow of the current order in which the wicked are punished and the righteous are rewarded ("Social Functions of Apocalyptic Language," 689).

[7] Paul affirmed that the *parousia* was unpredictable (1 Thess 5:1–3; cf. Matt 24:32–25:14). Passages related to an imminent return (e.g., 1 Cor 7:26–31; Rom 13:11–12; 1 Thess 4:16–18) must be tempered with other texts that anticipate Paul's death before the end (Phil 1:20–23; cf. 2 Cor 1:9; 5:1–11; 2 Tim 4:6–7). The Pauline anticipation of "nearness" in relation to the eschaton reflects Jewish apocalyptic/eschatological language (e.g., Joel 2:1, 15; Obad 15; Ezek 12:23–25; *4 Ezra* 11:44; cf. Rev 1:1–3). It is not a consistent indication that Paul believed he would live to see the *parousia* in his own lifetime.

disagreement about the timing of the eschaton. He seems primarily concerned that the congregations' viewpoint was leading them to moral misbehavior and divisive conduct. An example of how Paul addresses the problem in Corinth is found in his agape discourse. He calls on the congregation to operate in love, which is a sign of perfection. By way of contrast, spiritual gifts do not indicate ethical maturity. Paul intimates some of the Corinthians' own imperfections in relation to their overconfidence in wisdom, spirituality, and perspective on the new era (13:1–3, 8–9). If some of the members prided themselves in speaking in heavenly languages as a sign of a perfected status, Paul bursts their bubble by claiming that in the future age all such tongues will cease (13:8–9).[8] The vices he mentions in this pericope have a peculiar resemblance to the factional behavior he describes in the earlier chapters; they include jealousy, boasting, rejoicing in wrongdoing, rudeness, and insisting on one's own way (3:3, 21; 5:2; 6:7; 8:5–13; 11:21–22). Moreover, Paul points out the current state of incompletion in terms of "now" (ἄρτι) and sets this in contrast to the perfect "then" (τότε) in 13:8–12. Although Paul believes that the Spirit is significant for the new age (e.g., Gal 6:8; Rom 8:11; 14:17; 2 Cor 5:5), the completion of that age had not been fulfilled. In this regard Paul's own view is that the followers of Christ experience spiritual blessings related to God's kingdom in the "now," but the future culmination is "not yet."

If the tension underlying the Corinthian discord has something to do with such time frames, Paul's intention would seem to be directed to persuading the Corinthians not only to be united in mind and thought but also to reevaluate their presuppositions about themselves in relation to the age in which they lived. Paul's task was to answer the Corinthians' misperceptions. What might Paul's strategy be in attempting to persuade them to accept a more sober alternative? We will unpack two: (1) Paul appeals and alludes to the Isaianic tradition as an authoritative source to buttress his claims; (2) Paul's argumentation involves turning the congregation's thoughts from utopia to humility.

1. Strategy One: Appeal to Isaiah As the Primary Focus of Israel's Traditions

Paul frequently cites from or alludes to the early traditions of Israel. Hans Hübner has listed hundreds of citations or possible allusions that

---

[8] Some of the Corinthians, it seems, believed that they were speaking with "tongues of angels" (13:1b; cf. 14:2; *T. Job* 48; *Apoc. Ab.* 17). In this letter angels are associated with the end of the age (1 Cor 6:2) and worship (11:10). The Corinthians' low view of marriage and sexuality may be associated with their desire to mimic the angels. According to early Christian belief, angels do not marry or die (see Luke 20:35–36).

Paul makes to earlier Jewish/Hebrew traditions in his letters. The Isaianic and Psalm traditions head the list of writings that Paul seems to echo the most.[9] The reason why he refers to Israel's traditions so often seems rooted in the fact that he mentions some of these sources as "scripture." They were sacred writings that he considered to be "the oracles of God" (τὰ λόγια τοῦ θεοῦ—Rom 3:1–2; cf. 1:2). As such the ancient writings provided him with an authoritative resource applicable to both himself and his churches.[10]

The hermeneutical pattern for Paul's interpretation of the Hebrew/Jewish scriptures seems to center on a comparative dimension that relates Israel's redemptive history to those who confess Jesus as the Christ. Paul readily actualized these traditions because he believed that the Christ event had altered history as he understood it. What was originally written to Israel now pointed to the Christ followers, and fresh meaning could be given to the old texts in light of the new era (Rom 4:23–24; 15:4; 1 Cor 9:14). In 1 Cor 10:6 and 11 Paul leaves no doubt that his churches are to be a people who have inherited the writings of the Israelites. The things that happened to Israel in ancient times are set forth as hypothetical types for the Pauline community, which stands at a transitional point in time ("the end[s] of the ages") as it distinguishes itself from the earlier epoch(s) of God's elect people.[11]

1.1. Prominence of the Isaianic Tradition

The Hebrew/Jewish tradition most frequently referred to by Paul in 1 Corinthians is Isaiah. F. Malan lists seven of the clearest references to the Isaianic tradition in the letter (1 Cor 1:19/Isa 29:14; 1 Cor 2:9/Isa 64:4; 52:15; 65:16; 1 Cor 2:16/Isa 40:13; 1 Cor 14:21/Isa 28:11–12; 1 Cor 14:25/Isa 45:14; 1 Cor 15:32/Isa 22:13; 1 Cor 15:54–55/Isa 25:8).[12] Paul's apparent fondness

---

[9] Hans Hübner, *Corpus Paulinum* (vol. 2 of *Vetus Testamentum in Novo;* Göttingen: Vanderhoeck & Ruprecht, 1997). See also E. Earle Ellis, *Paul's Use of the Old Testament* (Edinburgh and London: Oliver & Boyd, 1957); Hays, *Echoes of Scripture;* Dietrich-Alex Koch, *Die Schrift als Zeuge des Evangeliums: Untersuchungen zur Verwendung und zum Verständnis der Schrift bei Paulus* (Tübingen: Mohr Siebeck, 1986); and Moisés Silva, "Old Testament in Paul," in *Dictionary of Paul and His Letters* (ed. Gerald F. Hawthrorne et al.; Downers Grove, Ill.: InterVarsity, 1993), 630–42.

[10] On Paul's attitude toward these writings, see Ellis, *Paul's Use of the Old Testament,* 20–37.

[11] For elaboration on this point, see Oropeza, *Paul and Apostasy,* 128–32, 167–70.

[12] F. S. Malan, "The Use of the Old Testament in 1 Corinthians," *Neot* 14 (1981): 134–70. See Hübner (*Corpus Paulinum,* 221–305) for a number of other possible allusions to Isaiah in 1 Corinthians. Florian Wilk (*Die Bedeutung des Jesajabuch*

for the tradition likely stems from his belief that its message had special significance for his churches (see below). Consequently, even non-Pauline writings such as Acts present discourse material attributed to Paul in which the apostle alludes to the Isaianic tradition when proclaiming the gospel (e.g., Acts 13:34/Isa 55:3; Acts 13:47/Isa 49:6). Paul considered the tradition to be sacred and authoritative, identifying it as scripture (cf. 1 Cor 15:3 with Isa 53:5).

Paul reconfigures at least three major motifs in the Isaiah texts in an effort to address the Corinthian situation. First, he considered the Corinthian congregation to be participating in a new exodus-wilderness journey. This perspective provided him with a framework for defining the new era and for adjusting Corinthian misperceptions about it. Second, the Corinthians not only practiced spiritual extremism related to faulty views about the eschaton (seen primarily in 1 Cor 4, 7, 10, 15), but they also had a problem understanding the true nature of wisdom (chs. 1–4). Third, they were in danger of committing idolatry and justifying their consumption of idol meats in non-Christian precincts (chs. 8, 10). It does not seem to be coincidental that the opponents in Isaianic literature happen to be the "wise" and "strong" princes in the community and that the tradition provides a polemic against dumb idols. Such discourses would be highly relevant for Paul's response to the problems in the Corinthian church.

1.2. The New Exodus Motif

What is often neglected by scholars in studies on 1 Corinthians is the ramification of space/time parameters in which the original events in Israel's past pointed to the Corinthians (1 Cor 10:1–11). These events happened while Israel made its journey "in the desert" (10:5) during the forty-year-period in which God tested the hearts of God's people. Paul elaborates on how the majority of Israelites were destroyed in the wilderness after they were delivered from Egypt by Moses at the Red Sea. They never made it to the promised land because they committed acts of apostasy in the wilderness. Hence, the rebellions and subsequent punishments arising from the episode become the thrust of the comparison. This is what was "written" for the Corinthians' admonition and set forth as "types" for the Corinthians. They are warned *not* to follow the behavior of their predecessors or else they too would suffer a similar fate before they ever get to the "promised land" of eternal rest. By comparing the Israelites with the

---

für Paulus [FRLANT; Göttingen: Vanderhoeck & Ruprecht, 1998]) recognizes the prominence of this tradition in the writings of Paul. His study primarily examines Isaianic references in Romans.

Corinthians, it seems quite clear that Paul considers the followers of Christ to have embarked on a new exodus-wilderness journey.

There are certainly a number of exodus patterns that were transformed by the early Christians (e.g., Matt 1–5; Mark 1; John 6; Heb 3–4; 1 Pet 1; Jude 5; Rev 15).[13] It is always possible that Paul's ideas about the people of God experiencing a new exodus were derived from the non-Isaianic traditions of his ancestors (e.g., Amos 2; Jer 31:31–34; Ezek 20; Hab 3; Zech 10:8–12) or from the earliest Christian proclamations that seemed to regard Jesus as a type of Moses (e.g., Matt 1–5; Acts 7:20–44). Both trajectories probably influenced him, but this explanation alone does not properly explain his use of the motif in 1 Corinthians. The Isaianic language that we find Paul using has a special affinity with the exodus tradition. Several references/allusions from Isaiah in 1 Corinthians are originally located in the context of (or are in proximity to) new exodus discourses (e.g., 1 Cor 2:9–16/Isa 40; 1 Cor 12:7–8/Isa 11; 1 Cor 15:3/Isa 52–53).

Some scholars identify the new exodus theme in Isa 40–55 as the main subject of Deutero-Isaiah and recognize its presence in an *inclusio* that spans the entire text (40:1–11; 55:12–13).[14] The motif portrays images of

---

[13] See Dale C. Allison, *The New Moses: A Matthean Typology* (Edinburgh: T&T Clark, 1993); David Daube, *The Exodus Pattern in the Bible* (All Souls Studies 2; London: Faber & Faber, 1963); Fred L. Fisher, "The New and Greater Exodus: The Exodus Pattern in the New Testament," *SWJT* 20 (1977): 69–79; Ulrich Mauser, *Christ in the Wilderness: The Wilderness Theme in the Second Gospel and Its Basis in the Biblical Tradition* (London: SCM, 1963); R. E. Nixon, *The Exodus in the New Testament* (London: Tyndale, 1963); Otto A. Piper, "Unchanging Promises: Exodus in the New Testament," *Int* 11 (1957): 3–22; Rikki E. Watts, *Isaiah's New Exodus and Mark* (WUNT 2/88; Tübingen: Mohr Siebeck, 1997).

[14] Cf. Gordon P. Hunsberger, "The Servant of the Lord in the 'Servant Songs' of Isaiah: A Second Moses Figure," in *The Lord's Anointed: Interpretation of Old Testament Messianic Texts* (ed. Philip E. Satterthwaite et al.; Grand Rapids: Baker, 1995), 122; Anthony R. Ceresko, "The Rhetorical Strategy of the Fourth Servant Song (Isaiah 52:13–53:12): Poetry and the Exodus-New Exodus," *CBQ* 56 (1994): 47; Carroll Stuhlmueller, *Creative Redemption in Deutero-Isaiah* (AnBib 43; Rome: Biblical Institute Press, 1970), 59; Shemaryahu Talmon, "The 'Desert Motif' in the Bible and in Qumran Literature," in *Biblical Motifs: Origins and Transformations* (ed. Alexander Altmann and Philip W. Lown; Institute of Advanced Judaic Studies—Studies and Texts 3; Cambridge, Mass.: Harvard University Press, 1966), 54; Walther Zimmerli, "Le nouvel 'exode' dans le message des deux grandes prophètes de l'exil," in *Maqqél Shâqédh: La Branche D'Amandier: Hommage á Wilhelm Vischer* (Montpellier, Vt.: Causse, Graille & Castelnau, 1960), 221. See Rikki E. Watts ("Consolation or Confrontation? Isaiah 40–55 and the Delay of the New Exodus," *TynB* 41 [1990]: 33 n. 8) for a brief list of those who mitigate the motif's importance.

the people of God experiencing a new deliverance and destination similar to the Hebrews' departure from Egypt under Moses. It reflects concerns about the Israelite community during its Babylonian captivity and also depicts a homecoming for all of Israel's exilic people among the nations.[15] The wilderness is associated with a new creation and becomes transformed into a place of abundant water and fruitfulness. The final place of rest becomes Zion. Bernhard Anderson lists a total of ten passages that describe the theme (Isa 40:3–5; 41:17–20; 42:14–17; 43:1–7, 14–21; 48:20–21; 49:8–12; 51:9–10; 52:11–12; 55:12–13), while Carroll Stuhlmueller adds three more (44:1–5; 44:27; 50:2).[16] Discourses related to the exodus

---

Bernhard W. Anderson ("Exodus Typology in Second Isaiah," in *Israel's Prophetic Heritage: Essays in Honor of James Muilenburg* [ed. Bernhard W. Anderson and Walter Harrelson; London: SCM, 1962], 182–84) recognizes nine major similarities between the original exodus tradition and Isa 40–55: (1) the glory of YHWH is revealed by delivering Israel; (2) YHWH protects his people via his presence; (3) YHWH is a warrior who fights on behalf of Israel; (4) a victory song accompanies the deliverance; (5) YHWH prepares a way in the wilderness; (6) Israel is sustained by food and drink; (7) a covenant is established between YHWH and his people; (8) Zion/Canaan is the land apportioned to Israel; and (9) Israel consists of a tribal confederation.

[15] Hans M. Barstad (*A Way in the Wilderness: The Second Exodus in the Message of Second Isaiah* [Journal of Semitic Studies Monograph 12; Manchester: University of Manchester Press, 1989], 6, 26, 37, 107–12) contends against the idea that Israel's return from the Babylonian exile is the concern of the text; it concerns those who stayed behind in Judah and Jerusalem. Much of what is considered new-exodus imagery functions in a strongly metaphorical way that comforts God's people about their restoration and prosperous future with YHWH. My own view is that references to Cyrus as a deliverer implicitly associate him with Moses (e.g., Isa 44:28; 45:1, 13–14; 48:14–16; cf. 2 Chr 36:15–23; Ezra 1; see also Graham S. Ogden, "Moses and Cyrus: Literary Affinities between the Priestly Presentation of Moses in Exodus vi–vii and the Cyrus Song in Isaiah xliv 24–xlv 13," *VT* 28 [1978]: 195–203). This makes it probable that Deutero-Isaiah is more concerned about the Babylonian exiles than Barstad affirms. On possible reconstruction of tradition-historical events as they relate to the Isaianic texts, see Jörg Barthel, *Prophetenwort und Geschichte: Die Jesajaüberlieferung in Jes 6–8 und 28–31* (FAT 19; Tübingen: Mohr Siebeck, 1997); David G. Meade, *Pseudonymity and Canon: An Investigation into the Relationship of Authorship and Authority in Jewish and Earliest Christian Tradition* (Grand Rapids: Eerdmans, 1987), 26–42; Paul D. Hanson, *The Dawn of Apocalyptic: The Historical and Sociological Roots of Jewish Apocalyptic Eschatology* (rev. ed.; Philadelphia: Fortress, 1979), 32–208.

[16] Anderson, "Exodus Typology in Second Isaiah," 181–82; Stuhlmueller, *Creative Redemption in Deutero-Isaiah,* 66. For other possible references, see Hunsberger, "Servant of the Lord," 122–23. For a compilation of various scholars on the issue, see Stuhlmueller, *Creative Redemption in Deutero-Isaiah,* 272.

motif, however, are not limited to Second Isaiah; they also appear in First and Third Isaiah (Isa 4:2–6; 10:20–27; 11:10–16; 14:1–6; 26:20; 27:12–13; 31:5; 32:14–20; 34:16–17; 58:8; 60:2; 61:4–7; 63:8–14). This observation suggests that the authors and redactors of the three major Isaianic sections (chs. 1–39; 40–55; 56–66) were well aware of the motif. It is possible to consider the entire book as a complex unity with the redactors of Third Isaiah editing through the two previous Isaiah texts.[17] The upshot of this perspective for our study is that if some of Paul's arguments in 1 Corinthians resonate from Isaianic motifs, those motifs would not necessarily be limited to one particular Isaianic section. It is not wrong to assume that Paul considered the work we know today as "Isaiah" in a unified manner.

Important topics within the Isaiah-exodus rubric include re-creation/restoration in the desert by water/Spirit, monotheism/theodicy, the appearance of God's servant/deliverer, and language related to the "new" and "former" things. The "new" and "former" dialectic may be understood in terms of God's knowledge and control of past and future events. This view is set in contrast to all other deities, which are created by human hands and lack any power or knowledge of their own (Isa 41:21–29; 42:8–9; 43:9–13; 44:6–8; 45:11–13, 20–21; 46:9–11; 48:3–16). It is recorded that God's control of former events ensures that the new ones will also be fulfilled, yet the Israelites are told to forget about the past greatness of their exodus out of Egypt. God will do a new thing, raising up a servant like Moses, making a way for Israel in the wilderness, and creating streams in the desert. This imagery of "new" and "old" suggests a second release of Israel from the oppression of a foreign power into a new and greater exodus experience (see Isa 43:16–21).[18] Anderson connects the "former things" to the events of Israel's *Heilsgeschichte* (salvation history). He understands these former

---

[17] On the complex unity view, see Rolf Rendtorff, "The Book of Isaiah: A Complex Unity Synchronic and Diachronic Reading," in *New Visions of Isaiah* (ed. Roy F. Melgin and Marvin A. Sweeney; JSOTSup 214; Sheffield: Sheffield Academic Press, 1996), 32–49; idem, "Zur Komposition des Buches Jesaja," *VT* 34 (1984): 295–320. For other scholars in the unified camp, see Barstad, *Way in the Wilderness,* notes on pp. 1–2, 45–46.

[18] See C. R. North, "The 'Former Things' and the 'New Things' in Deutero-Isaiah," in *Studies in Old Testament Prophecy: Presented to Theodore H. Robinson* (ed. H. H. Rowley; Edinburgh: T&T Clark, 1957), 116. Although God's servant-deliverer appears in these texts, it is not so clear or consistent that the term always has the same referent. Sometimes it appears to be Cyrus, other times Jacob-Israel, and other times a futuristic messiah. One thing seems clear: if we are dealing with resonances from the exodus tradition, then at least some of the servant imagery points back to Moses. For the various alternatives and criticisms, see Hunsberger, "Servant of the Lord," 105–40.

events in terms of *Urzeit*. The new exodus would be considered the "new things" or *Endzeit*.[19] Rikki Watts nevertheless argues that the Isaianic tradition replaces the old exodus with the new exodus as the saving event. Cyrus is the agent whom God chooses to bring about deliverance. YHWH appeals to Jacob-Israel to trust in his wisdom and choice, but the people remain blind, deaf, idolatrous, and rebellious. Thus, the new exodus failed to be completely fulfilled, and so the tradition looks to a future deliverance with a future servant.[20] If this is the case, the new exodus is not really *the end* but the beginning of the end. Zion may be the place of rest in Second Isaiah, but Third Isaiah transforms this notion by embracing an even greater fulfillment in terms of a period of judgment and then the appearance of a new heaven and new earth (Isa 65:17–25).[21] Here we find the dawning of the apocalyptic perspective of two ages with the new exodus as its prototype. The Isaianic perspective, then, directs us to a new age.

Another aspect about this motif is that the wilderness marks a location/ space in between the two polarities of deliverance and rest. In both the Isaianic and earlier exodus-wilderness traditions, God's people are sustained by water in the desert. Yet Isaiah begins to disassociate the concept of "water in the desert" from the earlier records of Israel's murmuring and Moses' unfaithfulness (Exod 15:22–27; 17:1–7; Num 20:1–13). "Streams in the desert" are now linked with the Spirit of God as the source of life for God's people during their long journey (Isa 32:15–19; 34:16–35:10; 44:3–4).

When writing to the Corinthians, Paul (like the Isaianic writings) transforms earlier exodus traditions. His thoughts probably gravitated toward the Isaianic new exodus when he began to address the Corinthians' perspective about the end times. The new age had arrived for them, and they believed themselves to be already at the end of time. If Paul's own perspective was present realization/future anticipation (see above) he most likely considered the new exodus as a workable model for depicting his own era. And since Paul identifies Jesus as the Isaianic servant of God and the royal messianic

---

[19] Anderson, "Exodus Typology in Second Isaiah," 188–89.

[20] R. E. Watts, "Consolation or Confrontation?" 31–59. On the Isaianic actualization of earlier traditions, Michael Fishbane ("The 'Exodus' Motif/The Paradigm of Historical Renewal," in *Text and Texture: Close Readings of Selected Biblical Texts* [ed. Michael Fishbane; New York: Schocken, 1979], 129) notes how Isaiah transforms the original exodus conception of Egypt as the oppressor to Egypt as the oppressed, which is sent a deliverer and is called "my people" (Isa 19:19–25). Similarly, Meade (*Pseudonymity and Canon*, 29–31, 41) suggests several transformations of the term "remnant" within the Isaianic tradition depending on which historical situation is being addressed.

[21] See Hanson, *Dawn of Apocalyptic*, 185–86; Meade, *Pseudonymity and Canon*, 41; cf. 35–40; Fishbane, "'Exodus' Motif," 133.

figure (e.g., 1 Cor 15:3/Isa 53:5; Rom 4:25/Isa 53:12; Rom 15:8–12/Isa 11:1–2; Rom 15:20–21/Isa 52:15), the new deliverance would seem to have occurred because of Jesus. For Paul, then, the followers of Christ were presently making their way through the wilderness of the present age with the Spirit of God sustaining them and the final rest ahead of them.

1.3. Polemic against the Wise and Proud

Isaianic literature presents a polemic against those who relied on human wisdom to make political choices.[22] In the original situation it seems that Isaiah confronted the "wise" counselors of King Hezekiah and Ahaz during the threat of foreign oppression. The counselors apparently adopted human wisdom, such as that of counselors from Egypt, rather than consulting the mind of YHWH. This resulted in their giving misguided advice (see Isa 19:11–12).[23] The leaders of the people who desire the influence of Egypt are rebuked (Isa 29:14; 30:1–7; 31:1), and God is said to overthrow the wisdom of the world by God's sovereignty over history (Isa 44:24–28). Yet it seems that Isaiah is not opposed to all forms of wisdom. Isaianic messages are highly poetic and embedded with the wisdom genre. In essence, Isaiah utilizes wisdom against the wise to persuade his listeners against misguided direction. James Whedbee astutely writes: "Isaiah had borrowed the vocabulary and traditions of wisdom in order to combat the apostasy engendered in part by the royal wise men.... by using wisdom traditions—both to condemn the ostensibly wise and to defend the true Yahwistic wisdom—Isaiah was able to speak a pertinent message to the particular problems of his own situation."[24]

In Isa 28–33 we find perhaps the strongest polemic against the wise (Isa 28:7–13, 23–29; 29:13–16; 32:1–8; 33:6). The message presents the wise

---

[22] See Johannes Fichtner, "Isaiah among the Wise," in *Studies in Ancient Israelite Wisdom* (ed. James L. Crenshaw; New York: Ktav, 1976), 429–38; Joseph Jensen, *The Use of tôrâ by Isaiah: His Debate with the Wisdom Tradition* (CBQMS 3; Washington, D.C.: Catholic Biblical Association of America, 1973); Robert Martin-Achard, "Sagesse de Dieu et sagesse humaine chez Ésaie," in *Maqqél Shâqédh*, 137–44; James Whedbee, *Isaiah and Wisdom* (Nashville: Abingdon, 1971).

[23] See Gary Stansell, "Isaiah 28–33: Blest Be the Tie That Binds (Isaiah Together)," in Melugin and Sweeney, *New Visions of Isaiah*, 78, 87, 89, 94.

[24] Whedbee, *Isaiah and Wisdom*, 147. The illustration of the farmer in Isa 28:23–28, for instance, is universally recognized as wisdom genre (cf. Jensen, *Use of tôrâ by Isaiah*, 50). For examples of parables, proverbs, woe oracles, and other teaching devises in Isaiah, see Whedbee, *Isaiah and Wisdom*, chs. 2–3. On the Isaianic use of rhetoric as persuasion, see Yehoshua Gitay, *Prophecy and Persuasion: A Study of Isaiah 40–48* (Forum Theologiae Linguisticae 14; Bonn: Linguistica Biblica, 1981); Ceresko, "Rhetorical Strategy," 42–43, 54.

advisers of Jerusalem as bumbling drunkards who can only teach children extremely elementary points (28:5–11). They make a covenant with "death" by consulting Egypt (28:18–19).[25] But the wise leaders of Israel will be confounded and their eloquence of words will be brought to naught. They are portrayed as murmurers, and this conception alludes to the rebels who grumbled in the wilderness after the exodus event (Isa 29:24; 30:12 LXX).[26] Gary Stansell demonstrates the connection of themes in Isa 28–33—YHWH's exaltation, the place of Zion/Jerusalem, Israel's "seeing" and "hearing," and Israel's alliances in relation to the Assyrian threat—with every major section of the book. He argues that this section should be considered not merely as supplementary but complementary to Isa 1–12: chapters 28–33 operate as a "functional doublette" to 1–12.[27]

A central motif in this section that permeates the entire Isaianic tradition is the paradoxical manner in which Israel and its guides are blind and deaf, lacking special insight (Isa 28:7, 12; 29:9–14; 30:9–11; 33:18; cf. 6:9–10; 19:11; 43:8; 44:24–25; 48:8, 18–20). The Isaianic writer encourages the listeners to hear and gain wisdom (28:23–29).[28] In the time of the new exodus, a reversal of blindness and deafness takes place in passages directed toward Israel's restoration and righteous king. At that time the blind and deaf will see and hear again (29:18; 30:20–22; 32:1–5; 33:17–22; cf. 35:1–10; 42:16–19; 43:8; 61:1–11).

Another important aspect of wisdom involves its association with God's Spirit. The "spirit of wisdom" heads the list of virtues coming from YHWH's Spirit and resting on the royal figure known as the "root of Jesse" and wonderful "counselor" (Isa 11:1–2; cf. 9:5–7).[29] The Spirit of YHWH is set against the foolish conduct and overconfidence of the wise. The counselors and rich women exploit the poor and will suffer divine judgment; afterward, a restoration takes place in which the Spirit of God will be poured out upon the desert so as to make a fertile region where the righteous will be at peace (32:6–20; cf. 58:4–7; 59:4, 15). Whereas the people are blind to true wisdom, the Spirit of God anoints the servant to give sight to the blind (61:1 LXX; cf. 42:1). God's Spirit is therefore combined with

[25] See Hans Wildberger, *Jesaja* (3 vols.; BKAT; Neukirchen-Vluyn: Neukirchener Verlag, 1974–82), 3:1078.

[26] See Georg Fohrer, *Das Buch Jesaja* (2 vols.; ZBK; Zürich and Stuttgart: Zwingli, 1962, 1966) 2:85; Wildberger, *Jesaja,* 3:1145.

[27] Stansell, "Isaiah 28–33," 99–101.

[28] See ibid., 75–77, 85–86, 97–98.

[29] For background information on the motif of royalty/leadership in this verse, see P. Robert Koch, "Der Gottesgeist und der Messias," *Bib* 27 (1946): 250–55; Fichtner, "Isaiah among the Wise," 437.

the theme of restoration, and this connection is often situated in the matrix of the new exodus (11:1–16; 32:15–19; 34:16–35:2; 44:3–4; 59:21; 63:7–14). Water and Spirit provide life and a new creation in the wilderness.[30] In addition, the Spirit seems to be analogous with God's glorious presence that guided and protected Israel in the wilderness (4:4–6; 40:5; 63:7–14; cf. 19:1).[31]

The Isaianic discourses also come against the proud, wealthy, and rebellious people in Israel as well as the nations. The princes of the community are considered the "strong ones" of Israel who commit idolatry and are identified as apostates (Isa 1:24–31; 2:20).[32] The arrogant are depicted as being wise in their own eyes, drunkards, eating, banqueting, exploiting, and depriving the rights of weaker people (5:8–25). Despite their wealth and arrogance, they are taken captive because they have "no knowledge" (5:13). Their punishment involves destruction in which the great men of the world (and women—3:1, 16–17; 32:9–20) hide among rocks and in caves trying to escape divine wrath. Captivity and humility will replace their haughtiness (1:24–31; 2:10–3:3; 5:1–30; 11:33–34). Afterward a remnant will arise and trust the mighty God (2:2–4; 4:2–6; 6:13; 10:20–3; 11:10–11). Rebellion and consequent judgment thus play a major role in the Isaianic tradition. Although Isa 13–27 focus essentially on God's judgment against other nations, the theme of pride and haughtiness remains. The nations are brought down to humility by the power of God.[33]

The Isaianic polemic against the wise would have appealed to Paul in dealing with the misguided Corinthian members who boasted about themselves and their leaders as wise and spiritual. Wisdom and eloquence of speech seemed to play a factor in determining for the Corinthians who was a spiritual leader and who was not (1 Cor 1–4, 12–14). Paul likewise confronts a faction in the church caused by a group identified as the "strong"

---

[30] Such language reflects the creation tradition of the work of the Spirit in Gen 1:2.

[31] The missing premise that connects the Spirit with both the cloud-presence and water might be stated as follows. Clouds produce rain that becomes streams of living water. The first exodus associated a rainstorm with the pillar cloud (Exod 13:17–14:31; Ps 77:16–20). Other traditions developed the idea of the outpouring/rainstorm of the Spirit in a new era (see Ezek 47:1–12; Zech 14:8; *1 En.* 48:1; cf. Ps 68:7–18; Eph 4:8–12; Acts 1:5; 2:3–4).

[32] The LXX seems to equate the "strong" of Isa 1:24 with those who are denounced in 1:31. In the Hebrew text, Wildberger (*Jesaja,* 1:59) identifies the term in 1:24 with YHWH. The "strong one" of Israel (1:24) denounces the strong rebels and will make them weak (1:31). For Hebrew terms related to the concept of "rebellion" in Isa 1, consult John D. W. Watts, *Isaiah* (2 vols.; WBC 24, 25; Waco, Tex.: Word, 1985, 1987), 1:18–19.

[33] See Christopher R. Seitz, *Isaiah 1–39* (IBC; Louisville: Knox, 1993), 122.

or those "having knowledge" (chs. 8–11). In an effort to combat these problems at Corinth, Paul, like Isaiah, seems to use his own set of rhetorical wisdom structures to refute the words of the wise and proud. It is not that Paul considers wisdom or rhetoric a bad thing; for him the issue is whether such forms of communicating are genuinely guided by the Spirit of God (1 Cor 2). Here Paul resonates the Isaianic idea that the Spirit of God is the true giver of wisdom. The "root of Jesse," whom Paul identifies as Jesus, was the possessor of the spirit of wisdom (Isa 11:1–2/Rom 15:12). No doubt Paul recognized that the passage (Isa 11) associated a messianic figure with the spirit of wisdom in the context of a new exodus-wilderness journey. In fact, as the spirit of wisdom, understanding, and knowledge head the list of virtues in Isa 11:2, so the spirit of wisdom and knowledge head Paul's list of spiritual gifts (1 Cor 12:8–9). Most likely, then, Paul considers God's Spirit to be an insignia for a new age that was initiated by Jesus. Both he and the Isaianic tradition testified that true wisdom comes from the divine Spirit.

1.4. Monotheism and Idolatry

In the face of oppression from foreign powers and temptation to seek after other gods, a prominent theme in Deutero-Isaiah centers on the monotheistic and sovereign nature of Yhwh. The text emphasizes that Yhwh is one God who is not comparable to other gods or idols of the nations (Isa 40:18–19; 42:8; 43:10–11; 44:6–7; 45:19–25). The motif appears in other Isaianic units as well (e.g., 2:20; 16:12; 21:9; 27:9; 31:7; 37:18–20). Against false sages and gods, the writer affirms that God alone declares things from the beginning to the end (41:28–29). Idols will only bring shame to those who trust in them. In humorous fashion the Isaianic tradition maintains that those who trust in idols are like them: they become deaf and blind (42:17–20; 44:9–20; 46:5–7; 48:1–8). The polemical language in Deutero-Isaiah gravitates towards a confrontation with Yhwh against both Jacob-Israel and the gods of the nations. Israel lacks knowledge and complains that God has rejected the nation, but Yhwh affirms his sovereignty and how he renews those who wait on him (40:12–31). It appears that anti-wisdom and anti-idolatrous categories interact in Deutero-Isaiah. The problem, as Watts suggests, may be that "Jacob-Israel is still bound by the idolatrous categories of wisdom which led to the exile in the first place."[34] The punishment for Israel's errors resonates the language of blessing and curses from the Deuteronomic covenant, which condemns idolatry and apostasy (Deut 28–32). Yhwh calls heaven and earth to witness his proclamation that his people have become rebellious (Isa 1:2–4; cf. Deut 30:19; 32:1). When Israel turns against God, he reverses his blessings and applies

---

[34] R. E. Watts, "Consolation or Confrontation?" 44; cf. 37–38.

the covenant curses to them (e.g., Isa 1:19–20; 7:23–25; 30:15–26; cf. Deut 30:15–20; 32:30).[35]

It is noteworthy to observe the dialectical manner in which divine judgment and salvific language are played off against one another in the Isaianic tapestry. In the same pericope in which God punishes the proud, the wise, and the idolaters, the offer of restoration is given by God's Spirit, God's servant, and the new-exodus imagery (e.g., Isa 1:24–2:5; chs. 40–55). In the very context of YHWH's "woes" against Israel, the offer of salvation is extended (e.g., Isa 28:1–6; 29:5–8; 30:1–26).[36] Paul repeats a similar pattern in the Corinthian correspondence. He begins his letter with a word of encouragement (1 Cor 1:4–9) before delivering severe warnings (1 Cor 5–6). When he warns the Corinthians that they are in danger of committing idolatry "in the wilderness," he turns right around and comforts them with a word about perseverance (1 Cor 10:5, 12–13).

Both Isaiah and Deuteronomic traditions emphasize monotheism and covenant curses, and both are echoed frequently in 1 Corinthians. Paul, for example, alludes to the Shema (1 Cor 8:4–6/Deut 6:4), which establishes his entire discussion on meat sacrificed to idols (1 Cor 8–10). The Deuteronomic tradition surfaces most clearly in this section,[37] but the idea of the new exodus comes primarily from Isaiah. Idolatry, as it relates to these traditions, turns the blessing of God into a curse. The Corinthians are warned to flee idolatry, to avoid fellowship with demons, and to be considerate to weaker congregation members who may not be able to accept their eating of idol meats.

2. Strategy Two: Argumentation from Utopia to Humility

Thomas Boomershine suggests that in 2 Cor 5:16–17 Paul may be working with dialectic structures in relation to the Corinthians' assumptions about the eschaton. His opponents in Corinth claimed to know things according to the new age of the Spirit (*kata pneuma*) rather than the old age of the flesh (*kata sarka*). In response to this, "Paul relates to the traditions of apocalyptic and particularly the possibility of a new age

---

[35] Similarly, Sungsoo Kim ("A Study of the Exodus Motif in Isaiah" [thesis, Calvin Theological Seminary, 1983]) argues that in Isaiah divine judgment is the reversal of *Heilsgeschichte*.

[36] See Stansell ("Isaiah 28–33," 71) for a fuller list of passages in Isa 28–33.

[37] It is more than coincidental that Paul resonates the Song of Moses (Deut 32), which warns against apostasy and idolatry as it uplifts the monotheistic nature of God. For further treatment on Deuteronomic echoes in Paul's letter, see B. J. Oropeza, "Laying to Rest the Midrash: Paul's Message on Meat Sacrificed to Idols in Light of the Deuteronomic Tradition," *Bib* 79 (1998): 57–68.

epistemology in what can be called a dialectical manner. 'Yes,' in the resurrection we know Christ and, therefore, ourselves *kata pneuma;* 'no,' until the *parousia* we do not know either Christ or ourselves *kata pneuma* but only *kata stauron.*"[38] Paul's answer may have not been what the Corinthian readers expected. He does affirm a new age of the Spirit, but not their overconfidence about that age; he speaks of the age in terms of the cross (*kata stauron*). In this manner, he intended to compel his readers to reevaluate their assumptions in an effort to get them to embrace humility. The readers were expected to arrive at a conclusion that is different from what they previously embraced—a type of enlightenment by a breaking or undoing. In discussing literary presentations, Stanley E. Fish describes this type of process as "an uncomfortable and unsettling experience [that] is offered as the way to self-knowledge, in the hope that self-knowledge will be preliminary to the emergence of a better self, with a better (or at least more self-aware) mind."[39]

In 1 Corinthians, Paul resists the Corinthians' premature state of utopia without denying utopianism altogether. In early Jewish traditions the opposite end of utopia was despair. This involved the idea that God's people were oppressed under foreign rule in the present age. The Gentiles are often regarded as the "wicked" while Israel is considered the "righteous."[40] The attitude of apocalyptic writers maintained that the godly await the destruction of God's enemies (e.g., *2 Bar.* 13:4–12; *Jub.* 23:13–15; *Sib. Or.* 3:542, 690–691; *As. Mos.* 10:7–10; Rev 6; 12–13). The problems arising in the Corinthian congregation make it evident that the church consisted mostly of Gentiles rather than Jews.[41] As the earliest Christians adjusted

---

[38] "Epistemology at the Turn of the Ages in Paul, Jesus, and Mark: Rhetoric and Dialectic in Apocalyptic and the New Testament," in *Apocalyptic and the New Testament: Essays in Honor of J. Louis Martyn* (ed. Joel Marcus and Marion L. Soards; JSNTSup 24; Sheffield: Sheffield Academic Press, 1989), 148. Boomershine's work also covers some of the parables of Jesus and the Markan tradition. It does not address 1 Corinthians.

[39] Stanley E. Fish, *Self-Consuming Artifacts: The Experience of Seventeenth-Century Literature* (Berkeley and Los Angeles: University of California Press, 1972), 371; cf. 1–2. Fish identifies two types of literary presentation: a presentation that flatters the readers by affirming their worldview ("rhetoric") and one that disturbs the readers by causing them to scrutinize their worldview ("dialectic").

[40] See D. S. Russell, *The Method and Message of Apocalyptic: 200 BC–AD 100* (OTL; London: SCM, 1964), 297.

[41] In 1 Cor 8–10, for example, the "weak" who opposed idol meats were not Jews (see 1 Cor 9:20, 22) but Christian Gentiles who were once involved in idolatry (1 Cor 8:7–13; cf. 12:2). In Acts and Galatians, idol meat is an issue of dispute among Jews and Gentiles.

earlier Jewish thought, the positive influence of Jesus' resurrection as the hallmark of the new age may have overshadowed previous Jewish conceptions related to foreign domination. Hence, Gentile believers in Corinth probably did not empathize well with Jewish despair. Rather than embrace the concept of despair and humility, the Corinthians leaned in the opposite direction toward the notion of utopianism in the new era. Perfection had arrived for them, and the powers of the old epoch would not be able to dominate the new community. The manifestation of God's Spirit became tangible evidence of this (e.g., Mark 3:28; Acts 2; cf. Joel 2:28–32; *1 En.* 49:1–4; 62:1–3; *T. Jud.* 24:2–3; *T. Levi* 18:3–11). Christians lived in the age of *pneuma,* and since the Corinthians operated in the abundance of spiritual manifestations (1 Cor 1:4–9; 12–14), they would have assumed that the new era was already in some significant sense fully realized. Paul's strategy was to make humility rather than utopia their present concern.

3. Strategy Three: The Humility of the Cross

Paul challenges the Corinthian assumptions by using the language of temporal dualism against the congregation. He affirms that the new age has arrived but denies that the old age has been rendered powerless. On close examination, Paul is echoing new-exodus and polemic motifs that for him provide an adequate description of the tension between the two ages. The way Paul uses the imagery of a second exodus involves polarity: it is first intended to be a positive example for the Corinthians' own perspective. They are called to be sojourners who have been freed from a slavemaster and are now on their way to the promised place of rest. It also is intended to be a negative example. The exodus involves a second wilderness journey in which the place of rest is "not yet," and this awareness involves humility rather than elation. The Corinthians expected Paul, a new-epoch thinker himself, to flatter their worldview—Paul gives them an unsettling dose of humility instead. In this sense he appears to be using the Isaianic tradition in a way that stresses a reversal of expectation. The age of *pneuma* is to be reconsidered as the age of *stauros,* and utopianism must be turned in the direction of humility. Paul combines authoritative statements from the scriptures with argumentation that aims to undermine the Corinthians' high-minded thoughts. His aim is to redirect their utopian assumptions to more sobering conclusions related to the cross of Christ, true wisdom, the resurrection of the body, and divine judgment.

3.1. The Message of the Cross: Humility Rather Than Boasting in the Present Age

In the first supporting proof of Paul's argument beginning in 1 Cor 1:18, the apostle seeks to encourage concord by affirming that true wisdom and power come from the cross of Christ and through God's Spirit

(1 Cor 1:18–4:21). Paul, as an imitator of Christ, refers to himself as the paradigm for the Corinthians to follow (2:1–6; 4:1; cf. 4:9–17; 11:1). He is not trying to compete with other spiritual leaders in relation to baptism or wisdom of speech (1:13–17; 3:4–15; 4:1–5). Instead, he exemplifies a model of humility, coming to the Corinthians with "fear and trembling" and with God's Spirit rather than with great eloquence or human wisdom (2:1–5). It is possible that Paul adopts the phrase "fear and trembling" from the context of an Isaianic oracle against Egypt and its wise counselors (Isa 19:16). In the original context, the wise and proud Egyptians will be humbled, trembling with fear at God's visitation. Paul may have reconfigured the phrase and applied it to himself. He intends to persuade the congregation to accept humility rather than human wisdom. It is not that Paul is against all wisdom; rather, he appears to be arguing against a certain type of wisdom—a wisdom in which the oratory aspect is an end in itself divorced from an attitude of humility exemplified by the message of the cross. The preaching of the cross represents lowliness and is set in contrast to a boasting attitude (1 Cor 1:29–30). More than this, the cross is a unifying rather than dividing force (1:24; cf. Eph 2).

All too often the intertextual backdrop to Paul's message of the cross is not properly appreciated. In 1 Cor 1:18, Paul associates those who think the message of the cross is foolishness and are "perishing" with the "wise" of the Isaianic tradition: "I will destroy the wisdom of the wise and the understanding of the clever I will make invalid" (1 Cor 1:19/Isa 29:14). Paul chooses to land in an Isaianic context rich with polemical denunciations against the wise (Isa 28–33). The gist of this section is that the counsel of the wise advisers of Judah, who relied on Egypt's wisdom, will prove to be foolish. They have replaced authentic Yhwh worship with human instruction and fail to seek his guidance properly. This section of the Isaianic tradition rests on a reverse ordering of society. In the future days linked with the new exodus, it is said that the humble, the needy, and the blind will be filled with joy and exalted (Isa 29:18–19), while the proud leaders and ungodly are humbled and "cut down" (see Isa 27:1; 29:1–8, 19–20; 31).[42] Through Paul's reading of Isaiah, we can surmise that the wisdom the Corinthians were adopting did not embrace humility. Their "spiritual" status did not prevent them from holding on to a human philosophy headed for destruction.

---

[42] There also might exist some faint vestiges in Paul about the proud men and wealthy women of the Isaianic tradition. Ideas and phrases appear to be borrowed in terms of the "wise architect" (Isa 3:3 lxx/1 Cor 3:10), denunciation against shaming the poor (Isa 3:15; 32:9/1 Cor 11:22), and apparel related to wealthy women (Isa 3:16–26; 32:9–20/1 Cor 11:2–6).

Paul alludes to this section of Isaiah in 1 Cor 1:20 when he asks, "Where is the one who is wise? Where is the scribe? Where is the debater of this age? Has not God made foolish the wisdom of the world?" In the Isaianic context, the ethically righteous of the new era will no longer see the wise counselors and people of obscure speech (1 Cor 1:20/Isa 33:18–19; cf. 19:11–12; 44:25). It is not by coincidence that Paul faces factions in Corinth in which spiritual wisdom and the obscure language of speaking in tongues got out of hand. In fact, Paul echoes this pericope in Isaiah again when correcting the misuse of speaking in tongues (1 Cor 14:21/Isa 28:11–12; cf. 32:4; 33:6 lxx). Paul, like his Isaianic predecessor, believes that the future era will do away with worldly wisdom and unknown "tongues" altogether (1 Cor 13:7–13). The irony here is that the clever wisdom and speaking in tongues of the Corinthians, believed by the congregation to be signs of realized perfection, were in fact demonstrations that their utopia had not arrived!

Moreover, the Isaianic tradition mentions that the Israelites who were obstinate and rebellious rely on Egyptian wisdom, and this coincides with the older wilderness traditions in which the rebels murmur and say that they want to go back to Egypt (Isa 29:24; 30:1–12 lxx; 31:1–3; cf. 19:11–12; Num 13–14). They refuse to find "rest" and peace through repentance (Isa 30:15; 32:18). God, who appears in a "cloud of smoke" and a "consuming fire," will afflict Egypt and shield Jerusalem (31:1–5; cf. 30:27–29; 33:14). The Deuteronomic blessings are realized in the people of Zion who will experience prosperity in their land (30:23–26; cf. Deut 27–30), and similar to the Deuteronomic curses, the rebellious will be put to flight by the least of their enemies (Isa 30:16–18). Paul thus transforms the Isaianic "wisdom of Egypt" into the "wisdom of the present world/*cosmos*" (1 Cor 1:20, 26; 2:4–8). For Paul the present *cosmos* is fallen, temporal, run by Satan, and slated to be destroyed (e.g., 1 Cor 5). To go back to the *cosmos* would be akin to the wilderness murmurers desiring to go back to Egypt and to lose the covenantal blessings of God.

It does not appear to be the case that Paul is citing random passages from Isaiah. He echoes the Isaianic polemic against the wise that is associated with the new exodus in order to buttress his argument against the misguided Corinthian notions of wisdom, the eschaton, and spiritual realities. Paul actualizes the Isaianic version of the new exodus to address his own situation. He likewise uses his own form of wisdom against the wise.[43] Paul encourages the imitation of Christ on the cross in relation to unity and humility. The reversal of expectation here is that the Corinthians

---

[43] A noteworthy example of Paul's ability to resonate the wisdom genre of Isa 28:24 appears in 1 Cor 9:10.

thought their wisdom to be spiritual. Paul says it is worldly, divisive, foolish, and totally misses the true meaning of the cross (1 Cor 1:18–26; 2:1–16; 3:18–23).

3.2. Wisdom of the Spirit Rather Than Wisdom of This Age

Paul also differentiates the Spirit of God from the spirit of the present age. The former, not the latter, is the teacher of true wisdom (1 Cor 1:20–21; 2:6–8, 12), and Christ is the source of that wisdom (1:30–31). In 1 Cor 1:31 Paul seems to be citing 1 Kgdms [1 Sam] 2:8–10 (LXX)/Jer 9:22–23: "the one who boasts, let him boast in the Lord."[44] Still, the Isaianic tradition does not appear to have left Paul's thoughts when he contrasts human wisdom with wisdom that comes from the Spirit (1 Cor 2:6–16). In 1 Cor 2:16 Paul refers to Second Isaiah when he argues that the Spirit of God interprets the thoughts of God (1 Cor 2:11–16/Isa 40:13). The concept he alludes to in 1 Cor 2:9 originates from Third Isaiah, which mentions God's ability to act on behalf of his people and points to the blessings of the future age (Isa 64:34; 65:16–17).[45] These passages stand at the end of another exodus account in which God's presence in the wilderness is associated with the Holy Spirit (Isa 63:7–14; cf. 19:1; Ps 106:32–33). The text relates how YHWH placed his Spirit among the Israelites and led them through the Red Sea (Isa 63:11–14; cf. 52:12), but they rebelled and grieved God's Spirit in the wilderness (Isa 63:9–10). Jesús Luzarraga argues that the Isaianic "Spirit of glory" mimics the cloud of glory and that the language of birds hovering over their nests is to be associated with the cloud of the presence in Exodus (Isa 4:5; 31:5).[46] Paul seems to acknowledge this tradition when he compares the Corinthians' baptism in the Spirit with the Israelites' baptism "in the cloud" (1 Cor 10:2, 6; cf. 12:13). This sets him up to warn the Corinthians about their own potential rebellion related to idols and idol meats.

Paul claims that Jesus is the "Lord of glory" (1 Cor 2:8). This term comes close to Third Isaiah 61:3–4 LXX (a passage that is remotely heard again in 1 Cor 3:8–9 when Paul discusses building and planting in terms of the work of Apollos and himself). The "Spirit of glory" and the "planting of the Lord for glory" may be closely related. Perhaps the correlational aspect between the Spirit and Christ has as its backdrop the Isaianic idea that the messianic "root of Jesse" is the possessor of God's Spirit (Isa

---

[44] Malan ("Use of the Old Testament in 1 Corinthians," 141) suggests that both traditions may be utilized here.

[45] This Pauline text is later mentioned by Clement in his own letter to the Corinthians (1 Clem. 34), and he connects 1 Cor 2:9 with Isa 64:3–4.

[46] Las tradiciones de la nube en la biblia y en judaismo primitivo (AnBib 54; Rome: Biblical Institute Press, 1973), 234–35; cf. 114, 131, 236–45.

11:1–2). As we noted earlier, the "spirit of wisdom" and subsequent virtues in Isa 11:2 are mimicked by Paul when he discusses the "spirit of wisdom" and subsequent spiritual gifts (1 Cor 12:8–14:40).[47] Paul stresses that true wisdom comes from the Spirit and argues that the kingdom of God rests not in wisdom of words but in the power of God (1 Cor 2:4–5; 4:20). The unsettling twist of all this is that the Corinthians considered themselves to be spiritual *because* they operated in the gifts of the Spirit. Opposite of what they might have expected to hear, Paul tells them that he could not speak to them as "spiritual," but only as "worldly." They were not mature at all; they were spiritual babies exemplifying their worldliness through factions and boasting (3:1–4). Beyond this their worship in the Spirit was tainted with elitism, chaos, and disorder (chs. 12, 14). The very hallmark by which they deemed themselves to be perfected proved them to be too immature to have arrived at the culmination of God's kingdom.

Moreover, although the Corinthians possessed the Spirit, they were in danger of defiling their bodies and the church (both of which are called the "temple of the Holy Spirit") due to their divisions and sexual misconduct (1 Cor 3:16–17; 6:19–20). Paul describes a scenario in which each person's work would be tried by fire on the "day" of the Lord. Some would receive rewards while the works of others would be burned up. Still others who defiled the temple would be destroyed (3:10–17). Judgment by fire appears to be a common theme in early Jewish apocalyptic literature (*Pss. Sol.* 15:6–8; *2 Bar.* 48:39; Mal 4:1; *T. Ab.* 13), but Paul's source need not go much further than the Isaianic tradition. It is plausible that 1 Cor 3:13 resonates Isa 66:15–24: the same Isaianic macro-text that Paul echoed in 1 Cor 2:8–9. Here the author laments that the temple in Zion has been burned with fire (Isa 64:10–11). The object of "fire" changes, however, when the coming of Yʜᴡʜ is anticipated. To be sure, a fiery judgment awaits the nations who oppressed Israel (64:1–2; see also 13:13; 29:6–7; 30:27–28; 34:8–17), but a similar fate is pronounced against the Israelites who rebelled against Yʜᴡʜ. They will be burned with unquenchable flame (66:24; cf. 33:14; 1:2).[48] Judgment by fire also depicts the Spirit's activity in relation to the divine presence (4:4–6; cf. 43:2). In 1 Cor 3:10–17, then, Paul may have adopted a connection between judgment and fire from the Isaianic tradition. If so, Paul seems to follow Isa 66:24 by anticipating a fiery judgment against God's own people. The ones who are going to be judged in 1 Cor 3, however, are not apostate Israelites but the Corinthian Christians.

---

[47] Here Wildberger (*Jesaja*, 1:484) recognizes a relationship between Isa 11:2 and New Testament spiritual gifts, but he does not mention 1 Cor 12.

[48] See John L. McKenzie, *Second Isaiah* (AB 20; Garden City, N.Y.: Doubleday, 1968), 208.

The way to avoid negative consequences on that "day" is to lay aside their worldly wisdom and divisions as they embrace the humility of the cross (1 Cor 3:11, 18–20; cf. 1:18; 2:2; 4:16).

3.3. Future Resurrection of the Body Rather Than Present Realization

Another way the Corinthians needed to be redirected involves their misperceptions about the resurrection of the body (1 Cor 15:12, 35–58). For the Corinthians the body was not considered important, and perhaps some members thought the body would not participate in a future resurrection (e.g., the Corinthian slogan in 6:13–14). Christopher Mearns suggests that the Corinthians may have asserted that if "Christ is risen, we are risen too."[49] Paul begins his argument against such members by affirming the past resurrection of Jesus who died for the sins of the believers. (The atoning aspect of Jesus' death seems to come from the suffering servant message in Deutero-Isaiah: 1 Cor 15:3/Isa 53:5, 12.) Paul argues that Jesus' resurrection affirms the future resurrection of his followers at the close of the kingdom age (1 Cor 15:12–28, 51–58). Contrary to what some of the Corinthians might have believed, Paul posits different time frames in 15:20–28: the resurrection of Christ has already taken place, but the resurrection of those who belong to Christ at the time of the *parousia* has not.[50] After this event comes the "end" in which everything, including death, will be placed in submission to Christ (cf. Ps 110:1; 8:6–7), and Christ will then subject himself under his Father. Submission language here implies humility.[51] Paul continues his argument by describing the nature of bodily resurrection (1 Cor 15:29–49).

Although 1 Cor 15 carries ideas in common with Jewish apocalyptic sources such as a royal/conquering messiah figure, the kingdom of God, multiple epochs, and the resurrection from the dead (Dan 2:44; 12:2–3; *Pss. Sol.* 17; 2 Macc 12:43; *Sib. Or.* 4:181–187; *1 En.* 91; *4 Ezra* 7; *2 Bar.* 21:13), the Isaianic tradition probably did not entirely escape the apostle's thoughts. It too affirms a bodily resurrection in terms of a futuristic epoch (Isa 26:19; cf. 1 Cor 15:12).[52] Reminiscent of the first passover/exodus, the

---

[49] "Early Eschatological Development in Paul: The Evidence of 1 Corinthians," *JSNT* 22 (1984): 26.

[50] De Boer ("Paul and Apocalyptic Eschatology," 346–47; cf. 357) rightly affirms that "Paul's understanding of Christ and his saving work is permeated from beginning to end (from Christ's resurrection to his *parousia*) by the categories and the perspectives of apocalyptic eschatology."

[51] Similarly, Mitchell, *Paul and the Rhetoric of Reconciliation*, 289.

[52] Isaiah 24–27 has often been considered a section in which various apocalyptic concepts are portrayed (see Wildberger, *Jesaja*, 2:439–67; Watts, *Isaiah*, 1:309–12;

day of the Lord's visitation involves God's vengeance upon God's enemies, but the people of God will hide safely in their chambers (Isa 26:20–21). Another visitation or "day of YHWH" does not result in Jerusalem's lamentation but its celebration, drinking, and revelry (22:5–14; cf. 5:11–13; 28:1–4). Paul transforms this passage to make a hypothetical point about the resurrection. If the dead are not raised, then moral restraints could be cast aside to live for the moment: "let us eat and drink for tomorrow we die" (1 Cor 15:32–33/Isa 22:13). Apparently some of the Corinthians actually embraced an amoral attitude about the present time in relation to their bodies. Paul warns them to "stop sinning" (1 Cor 15:33–34).

In 1 Cor 15:54–55 Paul returns to his earlier discussion about the defeat of death (15:26). This concept echoes Isa 25:6–8, which is set in the context of a messianic banquet that is provided for all peoples (see also 1 Cor 15:52/Isa 27:13–14). It is important to note that Paul does not argue for the resurrection of Christ's followers during the age of "now" and "not yet"— this event still remains in the Corinthians' future. Paul's final echo from Isaiah in this pericope confirms this (1 Cor 15:58/Isa 65:23; cf. 49:4). The Isaianic tradition here implies that the new-exodus and wilderness journey is replaced by a new heaven and new earth (Isa. 65:17–25). This final place of rest will be the culmination, the ultimate promised land, the utopia, and the age of resurrection/*anastasis* where the Corinthians' efforts will be rewarded. Until then they are called to continue working and persevering in the age of *stauros*. All these innuendoes function together to provide Paul with a perspective that is intended to act as a wake-up call for the Corinthians. He teaches them that a future resurrection awaits them.

3.4. Divine Judgment Rather Than Present Blessing

Both of Paul's recollections about the exodus event in 1 Corinthians arise in the context of judgment. In 1 Cor 5:7–8, Paul confronts a situation in which a man in the congregation was living immorally his stepmother. Instead of being ashamed, the congregation was boasting about this man's actions. Paul reproves them, claiming that a little leaven has a way of permeating an entire loaf. He charges them to get rid of the old leaven (i.e., the incestuous man, and by extension, the vices of wickedness and malice) so that their congregation may become "unleavened" and a "new loaf" (cf. 1 Cor 10:16–17). Christ, the Passover lamb, has been sacrificed for them. Paul adapts the language of the original Feast of Unleavened Bread

---

Jean Steinmann, *Le Prophète Isaïe: Sa Vie, Son Oeuvre et Son Temps* [2d ed.; Paris: Cerf, 1955], 348–65). But this Isaianic section does not appear to be the only one related to resurrection ideas. Hezekiah's recovery from near death, for instance, may be seen as a type of raising from the dead (Isa 38).

associated with the Passover meal and the departure from Egypt. The death of the lamb now points to the sacrificial death of Christ, the one who purifies the community. As a result, God's people become a new people of God embarking on a new journey that is perpetrated by the celebration of the Lord's death (the Eucharist) "until he comes" (1 Cor 11:26).[53] The sexually immoral man, however, is cast out of the congregation into the *cosmos* where Satan is said to await him for the "destruction" of his "flesh." This is done with the hope that the man might be saved "on the day of the Lord" (5:5, 13). Paul's new-exodus imagery is thus connected with present judgment (expulsion from the community) and a futuristic divine judgment in which the final fate of the fornicator will be determined.

Paul elaborates on the motif of judgment in relation to the exodus in 1 Cor 10:1–11. The analogy between the baptism in Moses and in Christ is evident in 10:1–2 (see also 12:13; cf. 1:13; Gal 3:27–28). Paul's decision to mention Moses fits well with the Jewish idea that the new messianic redeemer would be like Moses, the first redeemer of Israel (Deut 18:18–19; 34:10–12; cf. Isa 63:11–19). Dale Allison maintains that first-century messiah/Moses correlations probably arose from the idea that the Jews' eschatological redemption would involve a new exodus, and this notion was linked with a Moses figure.[54] For Paul the second redeemer (Jesus) would lead his people through a new wilderness experience, even as the first redeemer (Moses) led Israel.

Paul then takes his imagery a step further to ensure humility among the Corinthians. When he compares them with the Israelites, he stresses Israel's deliverance at the Red Sea and how the people were sustained on their journey by "spiritual" water and food (1 Cor 10:3–4). Paul seems to use the word *pneumatikon* here to set up the Corinthians for a humbling word of warning. As the Corinthians thought themselves to be "spiritual" in terms of operating in God's Spirit, Paul argues that the Israelites of old were also "spiritual." They were miraculously delivered, blessed, and sustained in the desert. A shocking turn of events occurs in 10:5. *Despite* Israel's spiritual privileges, many of them were rejected by God and punished in the wilderness. Many Israelites committed vices in the wilderness and were destroyed by various plagues (10:5–10). This took place *after* they experienced deliverance in the Red Sea through Moses. After they experienced the spiritual blessings and God provided for them in the wilderness, many were destroyed in the wilderness and never made it to the promised land.

---

[53] See J. K. Howard, "'Christ Our Passover': A Study of the Passover-Exodus Theme in 1 Corinthians," *EvQ* 41 (1969): 97–108.

[54] Allison, *The New Moses,* 88–90, see also 165–72, 194–207, 267–68, 307–11.

Because the Isaianic new exodus stresses a restoration/renewal motif, plagues against Israel in the wilderness are rare in the tradition.[55] Paul reworks his version of the new exodus to include the category of hypothetical "new plagues" (1 Cor 10:5–11). This appears to be one reason why he resonates the older Exodus and Numbers traditions more than Isaiah in the latter portion of the pericope. They complement the intention he wishes to convey: what was intended as a positive restoration turns out to be a negative rebellion with dire consequences.

The Israelites of old committed acts of covetousness, idolatry, *porneia,* tempting the Lord, and murmuring in the wilderness (1 Cor 10:6–10). The Corinthians faced similar temptations in terms of factions and questioning leadership authority (chs. 1–4, 9, 11), sexual misconduct (chs. 5–7), and meat sacrificed to idols (chs. 8, 10). Paul's metaphor of a footrace in 1 Cor 9:24–27 sets the stage for the wilderness journey in 10:1–11. Both images are concerned about enduring and finishing a course. The "wilderness" functions as the present era of "now" and "not yet." The prize for completion of the course involves a reward at the culmination of the rest (9:25); incompletion is associated with a punishment that excludes the participant from the final rest (9:27; 10:5–12). Paul is thus warning the Corinthians that if they persist in vices related to their past behavior when they belonged to the fallen *cosmos,* they might find themselves excluded from the final rest at the end of the eschaton. His arguments would have come as a shock to the Corinthian readers. In essence Paul was saying to them that the blessings the Corinthians were experiencing through the Spirit did not bring about a genuine state of utopianism. More intense, however, would be the insinuation that Paul makes regarding their sense of overconfidence and security. Possession of the Spirit does not automatically guarantee a place in the final eschaton because the Corinthians, like their Israelite predecessors, could be destroyed in their present age of *pneuma* before they ever make it to the age of *anastasis!* The warning again involves humility: those who think they stand need to take heed lest they fall away (1 Cor 10:12). The new

---

[55] Isaiah 66:24 and passages with parallel ideas about fire by judgment might point to the wilderness plagues against Israel. Ceresko ("Rhetorical Strategy," 49–50) notices that the suffering servant in Isa 52:13–53:12 takes upon himself the covenant curses of Deuteronomy and suffering associated with the Egyptian bondage and plagues. On allusions to the exodus plagues in other Jewish traditions, see Samuel E. Loewenstamm, *The Evolution of the Exodus Tradition* (trans. Baruch J. Schwartz; Jerusalem: Magnes, 1992), 69–188. Anderson ("Exodus Typology in Second Isaiah," 183) claims that there is no specific allusion to the Egyptian plagues in Deutero-Isaiah.

exodus-wilderness conception provides the necessary framework so that Paul could make this impact on his readers.

4. Conclusion

Paul's echoes from the Isaianic tradition and his appeal to the message of the cross for humility are not his only strategies in 1 Corinthians. But these two approaches do involve intertextual discourse and apocalyptic relevance. The regions of the spatial and temporal intersect with his resonances from the Isaianic new exodus. God's people are on a metaphorical journey, and this involves the overlap of eras. Paul affirms that the present era is the age of the new exodus experience. For "those who are perishing" with the old age of the flesh, the preaching of the cross of Christ is foolishness, but for "those who are being saved" unto the age of resurrection, it involves true spiritual wisdom and power (1 Cor 1:18–31). The Corinthians are to pattern their lives after the humility exemplified by the message of the cross. For Paul salvation through the preaching of the cross involves a process, a journey from one's former disposition to a place of rest and complete utopia. Paul affirms that the Corinthians have entered into the spiritual blessings of that journey. They belong to the new people of God, and the "Spirit" provides them with life and sustenance on their new journey through the "wilderness." Yet the Corinthians' factional behavior and other vices confirmed that they were not perfected; they were in fact spiritually immature (1:10–17; 3:1–4). Despite their leanings toward a present utopia, the culmination of the eschaton remained in their future. Every member of the congregation needed to make sure that he or she continued on the spiritual journey in humility. The Corinthians' view of the present age of the spirit needed to be reexamined as the age of the cross. Paul's approach was to unsettle the Corinthians' self-confidence so that they might reevaluate their patterns and assumptions. Overall, this approach encouraged the Corinthians to stand away from factional behavior, arrogant wisdom, idolatry, and other vices that might cause them to be judged by God.

Ambivalent Apocalypse: Apocalyptic Rhetoric and Intertextuality in 2 Corinthians

Edith M. Humphrey

It is perhaps a misconceived task to examine texts in Paul's letters in order to find rhetorical argument that is typically apocalyptic. Paul himself would be the first to admit that he is not typical in any way, and he would have insisted that he was a custodian of a wisdom that breaks molds. The text that we call 2 Corinthians is a case in point. Whatever our definition of the weasel word "apocalyptic," this letter is replete with it, engaging in language, imagery, and ideas that are normally associated with both apocalyptic thought and form. "Revelation" and "veiling," "transformation," "light and darkness," and "death and resurrection" run throughout as constant themes, counterpointed by specific references to "mystery," "the Day of the Lord", "the [satanic] god of this world," and "the judgment of God." This perspective, that cosmic and future realities impinge upon our present world, informs the whole letter and affords it a certain unity, despite the near consensus that this text is a composite. An investigation of Paul's peculiar use of apocalyptic language provides an intriguing starting point in the analysis of 2 Corinthians and is bound to disclose both his rhetorical acumen and the multivalent potential of "open" symbolic discourse in argument.

Already the wise will perceive that our working definition of "apocalyptic" has been reshaped, so as to take the weight slightly off the eschatological. Eschatology is, after all, only one of the mysterious aspects disclosed by apocalypses. A concrete understanding of apocalyptic discourse begins by observing actual specimens of the genre apocalypse. Such observation confirms that this discourse "reconfigures time and space both in the realm of the world and the body in the light of God's future intervening judgment"[1]—but also *in the light of past, present, and future salvation and in view of the impinging reality of other mysterious worlds, both heavenly and infernal.*[2]

---

[1] This is the working definition of apocalyptic discourse adopted for this volume.

[2] The elasticity of the word *apocalyptic,* especially as applied to Pauline thought (and his so-called "apocalyptic eschatology"), is well documented. Following on the

Paul himself writes no full-blown apocalypse. Yet 2 Corinthians, along with his other letters, displays a complete familiarity with the apocalyptic tradition, while using its themes, forms, and ideas in ways that surprise the reader. Paul in fact reconfigured apocalyptic discourse itself, in the light of his own conviction that the "future intervening judgment and salvation" and the "impinging reality of another world" had in a definitive sense *already occurred* in the person of Jesus the Christ and continued to be disclosed in the body of Christ through the Spirit. The future dimension, of course, is not wholly subsumed, as Paul anticipates the fulfilment of what has begun, in the life of the church and in the world as a whole. Paul's rhetoric is of necessity subtle, since it is governed as much by his reserve toward things normally construed as apocalyptic as it is by his acceptance and experience of them. His complete repository of resources, pulled from various sources—Hebrew Bible, Second Temple, Greco-Roman, and varied cultures—is directed toward a careful and enticing presentation of how the body of Christ should live together in the light of the apocalypse par excellence that he declared had already been revealed, but has yet to be grasped fully.

A complete reckoning of apocalyptic discourse in 2 Corinthians would embrace every chapter, including the unlikely topics of Paul's collection for God's people, exhortation to ethical living, and apostolic ministry. A quick flight over the letter shows every part (despite all its textual complications) informed by apocalyptic perspective, themes, or even form.[3] Paul begins

---

generic studies of the SBL group, published first in *Semeia* 14 (1979), then refined in *Semeia* 36 (1986), I have myself understood "apocalyptic" as an adjective related (in the first instance) to examples of apocalypses, in which a certain configuration of content, form, and function can be observed. Thus, "apocalyptic discourse" would be discourse that employs a cluster of motifs normally associated with the content of an apocalypse (mysteries to do with space and time) and/or a combination of formal elements such as a mediating angel, visions, and the like. In my own work, *The Ladies and the Cities: Transformation and Apocalyptic Identity in Joseph and Aseneth, 4 Ezra, the Apocalypse and the Shepherd of Hermas* (JSPSup 18; Sheffield: JSOT Press, 1995), I argued that apocalypses answer not only to questions of "what" and "when" but also to "who," so that an axis of identity is seen as crossing the temporal and spatial axes. It is thus pleasing to note that the definition employed for this volume also includes identity, in its individual and corporate aspect.

[3] "Apocalypse is a genre of revelatory literature *with a narrative framework*, in which a revelation is *mediated by an otherworldly being* to a human recipient, disclosing a transcendent reality" (John J. Collins, "Introduction: Towards the Morphology of a Genre," *Semeia* 14 [1979]: 9). My added italics indicate attention to formal features.

by treating affliction and consolation (1:3–11) in terms of the consoling God "who raises the dead" (1:9) and in terms of a future hope (1:13–14). He goes on to tackle problems in Corinth by providing for them a dual stance: actions done "before the face of Christ" and in full knowledge of Satan's "machinations" (2:10–11). Similarly, the apostolic ministry is depicted in dualistic terms (2:14–17), from the perspective of life and death (and perhaps with an echo of *merkabah* mysticism,[4] a practice not unrelated to that of the apocalyptic visionary). Chapters 3 and 4, drawing as they do on key revelatory moments in Israel's history, are fully framed in apocalyptic terms (but see especially 3:7–18, 4:3–14), as will soon become apparent. In chapter 5 the future hope typically is disclosed in terms of both positive hope and judgment (5:1–10), and then the apostolic ministry is viewed from the perspective of Paul's reformulated apocalyptic worldview (5:14–17). The thematically connected sections of 6:1–13 and 7:2–5 deal with the "Day" (now present) and the open heart and are punctuated by the textually controversial and decidedly apocalyptic discourse of 6:14–7:1. Paul's subsequent discourse on repentance (7:5–16) is perhaps atypical for him, but its contrast of "godly" and "worldly" grief, and their diverse fruits of "salvation" and "death" (7:10–11), is clearly informed by an apocalyptic perspective. Chapters 8 and 9 discuss the collection, apostolic ministry ("the glory of Christ!" 8:23) and human giving in the light of the revealed gift of Jesus Christ (8:9), which is at the same time God's "indescribable" gift (9:14). Chapter 10 describes Paul's own apostolic rhetoric in terms of cosmic battle (10:3–6), and 11:2–3 employs the protological and eschatological imagery of virginity and the serpent (cf. Rev 12). In contrast, Paul's opponents are described as using an inverse apocalyptic discourse that obscures rather than reveals (11:13–14) and as having undergone a twisted transfiguration (μετασχηματιζόμενοι, 11:14) that corresponds diabolically to the transformation of the saints. While the "chaste virgin" has her high calling, these pseudo-ministers will reap their own end (τέλος, 11:15). As a climax to Paul's argument, 12:1–10 employs the form of apocalypse with rhetorical flair and to surprising effect. Finally, the letter closes by relativizing notions of power and weakness through Paul's underlying revelatory story of Christ (13:4).

Even contingent matters are thus framed in terms of typical apocalyptic topics, while the deeper issues of the letter verify Ernst Käsemann's dictum that "apocalyptic" (especially as construed beyond eschatological concerns) is indeed the matrix of Christianity. Throughout the letter, the contingent and the theological in fact merge, with Paul laboring as mid-

---

[4] Such allusions, as echoes, are notoriously difficult to nail down. See below, note 10, for a discussion of a possible allusion to *merkabah* mysticism in 2 Cor 2:14.

wife to "present the church as a chaste virgin" to the one to whom she is already betrothed (2 Cor 11:2), or as an inverse Jeremian prophet to "build up and not tear down" (Jer 10:17). Always his rhetoric is given a particular Pauline twist, in line with his view that the most important apocalypse (the revealing of the Son) had already occurred. For example, in the appeal of 1 Cor 9 for support, harvest imagery is used, along with a quotation from Ps 112:9 that implies a future dualism between the generous righteous and the envious wicked. Yet this future-oriented ethic is mitigated by Paul's conclusion to the discussion at 9:15, where God's present and ineffable gift overshadows all human giving: "Thanks be to God for his indescribable gift."

For the purposes of this paper, I will more closely consider the "intertexture"[5] of three passages, thus representing Paul's varied use of apocalyptic discourse in 2 Corinthians: the midrashic 2:14–4:18, the exhortative 6:1–7:4, and the highly polemical 12:1–12. These three passages provide a natural entrée into the discussion of Paul's apocalyptic discourse, since the first and last have already been identified as tied to revelatory themes or forms by virtue of their relation to the paradigmatic biblical (e.g., Exodus, Ezekiel, and Daniel), apocalyptic (*1 Enoch, Apocalypse of Abraham, Ascension of Isaiah*), and mystical material.[6] As for the second passage, embedded within it is that dualistic ethical "interruption" (6:14–7:1), which has been dubbed "an Essene fragment" because of its apocalyptic flavor. However, I will see that the entire sequence of 6:1–7:4 is couched in apocalyptic terms, as set out in the working definition. A detailed analysis of these text-complexes, in terms of resources (oral-scribal, social, cultural, and historical) and regions (Hebrew Bible, Second Temple, Greco-Roman) will give a good idea both of Paul's modus operandi in the invention of verses and of the distinctive ways that Paul uses apocalyptic discourse to conceptually and/or practically further his gospel. As a bonus to the analysis, some of the aspects of argumentation observed here will emerge as probably distinctive to apocalyptic discourse.

---

[5] Terms used to describe intertextuality are borrowed from the work of Vernon K. Robbins, *Exploring the Texture of Texts: A Guide to Socio-Rhetorical Interpretation* (Valley Forge, Pa: Trinity Press International, 1996); and idem, *The Tapestry of Early Christian Discourse: Rhetoric, Society and Ideology* (New York: Routledge, 1996).

[6] Alan Segal treats these passages in relation to esoteric experience, establishing Paul as a first-century mystic, an early instance of a developing tradition with "a special Christian cast." See *Paul the Convert: The Apostolate and Apostasy of Saul the Pharisee* (New Haven: Yale University Press, 1990).

1. *Midrash and Re-velation: 2 Corinthians 2:14–4:18*

1.1. Oral-Scribal Intertextuality

Within the longer passage of 2:14–4:18, 3:1–18 has undergone much debate due to the subtlety of Paul's argumentation and the allusiveness of his imagery. Those analyzing the chapter have also differed with regards to the delimitation of the section, many suggesting a slightly shorter unified argument, that is, 2:14–4:6. However, 4:7–18 is rightly included as part of this discourse, since it recapitulates the themes of thanksgiving (2:14; cf. 4:15) and life and death (2:15–16; 4:8–11) with which the section began. Moreover, the final verses (4:7–18) also sum up Paul's discussion of δόξα (4:17), a term that pervades chapters 3 and 4, occurring fifteen times, eight of which are emphatically placed as the conclusion of a clause.[7] The flow of Paul's argument, beginning at 2:14, indeed continues unabated until 4:18, while the final verses (4:7–18) also anticipate the eschatological concerns of chapter 5, providing a bridge into this next discussion (5:1–10).

Since this section has been labelled "midrashic," I am not be surprised to observe an oral-scribal component and, more particularly, the use of creative recitation. Especially noteworthy, Paul retells the story of Moses before the Lord and the people in Exod 32–34 and Deut 9–10 with a double effect. That is, the proto-seer Moses becomes for Paul and for the Corinthians a model and also an *inverse* model of perception and of ministry. (Paul also follows this procedure with reference to that other noteworthy visionary, Ezekiel, although the references here remain more allusive and thus may be more properly considered as "cultural" rather than "oral-scribal" intertexture.) Throughout the section, Paul displays his characteristic ambivalence toward all things visionary.

I begin with the retelling itself, which is substantively in Paul's own words, but which also uses key terms or phrases from Exodus and Deuteronomy. The Mosaic theme is first introduced unannounced as Paul slides from the historical/cultural texture (his own ministry [2:14–17] and letters of recommendation [3:1]) into a personal appeal. This appeal combines various phrases from the Hebrew Bible in a sophisticated rhetoric. In 3:2–5 the phrase "written ... on tablets of stone" (3:3, 7; cf. Exod 24:12; 31:18; Deut 9:10) sits alongside other poignant phrases and contrasting key words

---

[7] The term hardly recurs after 4:17 in the rest of the letter. Two exceptions are 6:8, where it has quite patently has the alternate sense of "honor," and 8:19, 23, where it arguably also carries the meaning of "honor" rather than of "splendor." As a point of comparison, it is interesting to note that δόξα is found scattered throughout the chapters of the letter to the Romans, from beginning to end, rather than clustered in two chapters, as is virtually the case in the letter to the Corinthians (1:20; 6:8; 8:19, 23 being the only exceptions).

drawn from Jer 31:33 ("the law" written "on their hearts") and Ezek 11:19 and 36:26–27 ("hearts of stone ... of flesh"). The Moses narrative, though not specifically named at this initial point, is here used both directly and inversely as a model. Paul has recalled the divine writing on the tablets by a negative reference to it ("*not* written on tablets"). At the same time he also verges on retelling the Sinai story, or at least the central part of it, while recontextualizing: he speaks of the Corinthians themselves as a letter "written not with ink but *with the Spirit of the living* God." The phrase is a well-known substitute for the more anthropomorphic "finger of God" used in both Exodus and Deuteronomy (Exod 31:18; Deut 9:10; cf. Luke 11:10 par. Matt 12:28). The "letter" that is the Corinthian church is thus deftly related both directly to the Moses narrative (like the commandments, the church has been "written" by the living God) and inversely (the writing is not on *stone* tablets)—all this before Paul actually names the story. Likewise, Paul relates himself (or perhaps the apostles in general) both positively to the narrative (he, too, is the "minister of a ... covenant," 3:6) and inversely (here he characterizes himself as "bold" rather than "humble"; cf. Moses, Num 12:3; Sir 45:4). It is not until 3:7, however, that these allusive phrases are enriched by further elements from the Sinai story; now we are tantalized by reference to divine chiselling, the people of Israel, the ministerial Moses with shining face, and the outcome of the ministry—lost glory and condemnation. Paul is not content simply to draw upon the imagery of Exodus/Deuteronomy but goes on to recall with increasing intensity the drama of that high event. Verses 12–14 allude further to its glory, its shame (cf. "stiff-necked people" who need "circumcised hearts," Exod 32–34 passim; Deut 10:16), and its raised or lowered veil of intimacy or mystery.

    Much ink has been spilled concerning the veil on Moses' face. (Present-day scribes, lured by the scribal ambience of Paul's argument, have not heeded the apostle's warning regarding the transience of ink and the killing power of the letter!) Indeed, the veil is a versatile image, operating on the oral-scribal level to recall the Moses story, but also directed toward the more general cultural phenomenon of *re-velatio* desired by the pious (see Ps 119:18) and experienced by the visionary. Later commentators, drawn by Paul's talk of covenant, connected the veil with the curtain blocking the holy of holies and its tearing in the Gospel narratives.[8] Such connections are not clearly supportable from the perspective of authorial intent, although they could be defended in terms of openings in the text itself. What can be demonstrated more easily is that Paul selectively retells the Exodus story for

---

[8] The words used for Moses' veil (τὸ κάλυμμα) and for the temple veil (τὸ καταπέτασμα) are almost consistently different in the Hebrew and Greek texts; it is not at all clear that Paul was aware of the torn-curtain tradition.

his own purposes, offering a new story about the veil. I am not referring here to the supposed novelty of fading glory on Moses' face. Despite the scholarly wrangling on the point, it is not clear that Paul forwarded this non-pentateuchal detail, either in echo of a lost midrash or by route of his own creativity. The repetition of καταργέω (vv. 7, 11, 13, 14 and elsewhere in Paul) suggests strongly that it is not Moses' face that fades in the Pauline retelling, but the Torah that was to be set aside. It is at another point that we see Paul's creative selection for the purposes of argument. Exodus 34:29–35 describes the Israelites' fear of Moses' shining face and his putting on the veil, which Paul recounts. However, the full story in Exodus is as follows: Moses descends from Sinai with shining face, terrifies the people by his reflective epiphany, calls them back to him, and reveals to them God's word *with face uncovered*. Only after Moses finishes the revelation does he cover his face, presumably to resume normal life. From this point on, the veil is off during his intimacy with God, and *also* during times of revelation, but put on after-wards (Exod 34:34–35). Paul does not recount this intermediate stage, that is, the continued baring of the face during Moses' mediated revelation to the Israelites—presumably because for his purposes, the veil was still substan-tially there, on "hardened hearts" (2 Cor 3:14). Blinded as they were by the glory, they did not understand that the covenant was to be set aside.

Paul's silence about the face-to-face contact of the Israelites with Moses is eloquent. Moreover, in his retelling of the story, Paul places the veil not only on Moses' face, but collectively "over the heart" (ἐπὶ τὴν καρδίαν, despite the NRSV translation "minds") of Paul's own contemporary Jewish listeners. Just as the contemporaries with Moses had hardened hearts (3:14), a detail picked up legitimately from the traditional stories by Paul, so his own contemporaries have a *veiled* heart. Thus, Paul argues, they cannot receive the revelation when it is read any more than the orig-inal audience understood the full import of Moses' words. Paul is briefer here than in Rom 9–11 about what is being missed by these hearts, since his point is to instruct the Corinthians rather than to rehearse the entire his-tory of his own people. We can surely glean what has been missed by Paul's *un*ideal readership, those who do not have open faces. Those for whom the veil has not been lifted miss, says Paul, the divine "setting aside" of the first glory, Torah. This is a detail belabored in these verses (3:7–10) and often missed again as analysts gaze, uninvited by Paul, upon Moses' face. Paul will go on to exploit Moses' "normal" wearing of the veil, and the metaphorical multiplication of Israelite veils, by contrasting these bar-riers to "open hearts" and "open faces" (2:17; 3:2; 4:2 in our section, but also 5:16; 6:11–13; 7:2). It is the open heart and face that he sets forward as the customary attitude of the new people of God.

It may be, too, that Paul's silence regarding the intermediate step—the shining and mediating Moses—is occasioned by his understanding of the new covenant. Could Paul, in his own thinking during the composition of these verses, have progressed from the talk of "hearts" in Jer 31:33 to the next verse, which describes a time when "they shall all know me, from the least of them to the greatest"? Although it is exigent here for Paul to defend his ministry, he is also reserved in casting himself as a new Moses—this role has already been taken, in his view, by the Christ. Moreover, his new story about God's people reaches its very climax in the ongoing trans-figuration of "all of us" (3:18), rather than an exceptional and veiled metamorphosis, such as that experienced by Moses. Again, as he moves fur-ther in the argument, Paul suggests the unity of the apostolic "we" and the community: first, he speaks of the apostles as "slaves" to the church for Jesus' sake (4:5); next, he recomposes a divine oracle ("Let light shine out of darkness," 4:6) by conflating Genesis with the Isaianic prophecy about the Gentiles (Gen 1:3; Isa 9:2; 49:6). Thus, Paul both establishes his author-ity and argues for the equal illumination of the entire faithful people. This equalizing strain may be illuminated by comparing closure in the two covenant stories (that of Exodus and the new story intimated here by Paul). The Exodus account closed by highlighting the dramatic glory of the taber-nacle, so heavy with God's presence that even Moses had difficulty entering (Exod 40:34–38). This sign, before the eyes of all the house of Israel, con-trasts starkly with Paul's vision of the "weight of glory beyond all measure" (4:17)—a glory prepared for the entire new household, as even affliction is transformed into life for the sake of the other (4:12), and as they gaze together not on what can be seen but on what is eternal. Paul's clinching and self-conscious citation (4:13; cf. Ps 115:10 LXX) commends to the Corinthians an ideal of mutuality. Bold belief and open speech is the stance of or perhaps the gift of both apostle and community—"Having the same s/Spirit of faith(fullness?)" (Ἔχοντες δὲ τὸ αὐτὸ πνεῦμα τῆς πίστεως, 4:13).

Attention to these strands of the oral-scribal texture discloses several strategies at play. Paul retells the story (with a few brush strokes, using tra-ditional and original phrases). He also recontextualizes it so that it applies to his ministry and to the Corinthian church (a recontextualization fully played out in 4:1–18). Finally, he engages in a clear reconfiguration of the textual traditions, in which the new event subsumes the first one, quite lit-erally, to use the words of Vernon Robbins, "outshining" it.[9] "Much more has the permanent come in glory!" (3:11). Many have pointed to the typical rabbinic rhetoric of *qal wahomer* (from lesser to greater) employed here by Paul. However, such is the power of Paul's rhetoric that the argument from lesser to greater does not entirely obscure the "glory" of the original story. By using both direct and inverse connections, Paul establishes the unfading

---

[9] Robbins, *Exploring the Texture of Texts,* 50.

glory of the new covenant without disparaging the old. Paul's method of having his cake and eating it too may be maddening to analysts who prefer a neater picture, but it is not unique to this letter and is found, for example, also in the letter to the Romans (note especially Rom 7:13).

These chapters are also intriguing because in them Paul combines the elements of retelling, recontextualization, and reconfiguration toward two ends. First, he mounts an explicit argument, using thematic elaboration, for the purpose of healing his relationship with the Corinthians. At the same time he implicitly offers, using the technique of narrative amplification, a new story about God's people. These two layers, discursive and narratival, interconnect at various points. In suggesting an outline for the thematic elaboration, it is easy to observe how it is nourished by the narratival elements:

Introduction (2:14–16): Thanksgiving and setting forth of Paul's ministry in context

Proposition (2:17–3:1): "We speak as persons of sincerity, sent from God … in his presence … nor do we need recommendation"

Rationale (3:2–3a): For you are our letter, written on our hearts, read by all

Opposite (3:3b): not like at Sinai, temporary and leading to death

Analogy (3:4–15): Like Moses' glory, only permanent and vital

Example (3:16–18): community all unveiled and the mirror/reflection/reflecting

Amplification (4:1–5): honest and cunning ministry, sight and blindness

Citation (4:6): "Let light shine out of darkness"

Example (4:7–12): treasure in jars; things are not as they seem.

Citation (4:13): "I believed and so I spoke"

Conclusion (4:16–18): We do not lose heart; what is unseen is eternal.

The explicit argument has to do with Paul's role as apostle of the Corinthian church and his desire that they recognize this amidst times of difficulty and stress. While Paul pleads for their ear, he also recounts a narrative of hope, a narrative that plays itself off against the tragic drama of the Exodus account. Moreover, Paul's narrative about the faithful community spins off from his underlying metanarrative, the story of the ministry, suffering, death, resurrection, and continued presence, through the Spirit, of the Christ. By invoking the Exodus story, Paul can set off unspoken contrasts and warnings for the Corinthians. May their community not be as in the Exodus story, where leaders were disappointed and disparaged, where people alternately stood in awe of revelation and ignored it, where the laws remained on tablets and were not assumed inwardly. By reference to being "in Christ" and to the light "shining in the hearts" so that God's glory is seen "in the face of Jesus," Paul also sets up an alternate story where each believer and all together are pictured as embraced by glory, a growing glory that is furthered and not diluted by affliction. The lines of argument are complex, since Paul is not simply advancing an apology for his ministry but setting forth a new perspective into which he is inviting his readers to place themselves. While he seems at first to be establishing his own *ethos* ("sent from God ... standing in his presence"), he ends by picturing the community *together* engaged in the same ministry of reflection (3:18), "extended ... more and more" (4:15) and brought "into God's presence" (4:14). The "we" is supple, as is the kaleidoscope of intertextual resources.

1.2. Cultural (and Historical) Intertextuality

Alongside the oral-scribal layer of Paul's argument appears to be a cultural layer of Jewish mystical tradition that peeks out at the reader from time to time throughout this section. It is indeed possible that the Moses citations are not wholly circumscribed by the biblical text but have been mediated through later cultural or textual traditions in which Moses is cast as one who of ancient times "descended" to the chariot and so was transformed.[10] This second overtone is rendered more likely by veiled references to the book and person of the mystical prophet Ezekiel throughout chapters 3 and 4. Allusions to "heart," "flesh," and "stone" recall Ezek 11:19 and 36:26, while the "Spirit [that] gives life" recalls Ezekiel's great vision of chapter 37—that is, the vivification of the house of Israel.[11] It is indeed a variation of this story that we have heard Paul telling in his recontextualization and alternate underlying narrative about the community of Christ.

The reference to "metamorphosis" is, it would seem, culturally ambiguous. The Hellenistic world knew various stories about transformation

---

[10] See *Midr. Pss.* 68:19, where Moses receives Torah as a gift for Israel in a *merkabah*-like ascent to Sinai, and the treatment of this midrash in relation to the introductory verses of our passage by James M. Scott in "The Triumph of God in 2 Cor 2:14," *NTS* 42 (1996): 270. If Scott's hypothesis is entertained, then the subsequent references to Moses in chapter 3 already may have been set in the context of the visionary and transformative at 2:14, even before Paul begins his own midrash and alternate narrative for the benefit of the Corinthians.

[11] See especially the treatment of Paul in relation to Ezekiel and subsequent mystics by Segal (*Paul the Convert*, 323 n. 94), who points out the importance of "glory" for Paul's expression of Christian community and transformation. He would consider even the "mirror" in 2 Cor 3:18 as a reference to mystical technique, hearkening back to Ezekiel 1 (*'eyyin* as a "magicomystical theme" with origins in Ezekiel, but later in the magical papyri).

through various texts, including those of Ovid and Apuleius. However, the notion of transformation through contact with the divine was expressed in particular ways in the Jewish context. The apocalypses and rabbinical mystical texts picturing transformation that we possess postdate the letter to the Corinthians, but it is not impossible that such ideas were already well known. Qumran texts, especially 1QS VI, 28–29; 1QS II, 2–4; 1QH IV, 5–6; and 1QH IV, 27–29, provide some parallels.[12] The Gospel accounts of Jesus' transfiguration provide relatively close temporal parallels, if not an indication of precedent (oral?) traditions. That there is some relationship between Paul's vision of the community's transformation and the lore of visionaries is supported by his own references to personal mystical experience (2 Cor 12) and by the intertextual allusions to Ezekiel throughout 2 Cor 3 and 4, since Ezekiel was the source par excellence of later mystic and apocalyptic experiences/writings.[13]

Particularly intriguing as an example of Paul's use of Ezekiel is the allusion to Ezekiel's vision of the chariot and God's *kābôd*, which occurs at 4:6, toward the conclusion of Paul's discourse in this section. The reader here encounters a phrase that borders on oral-scribal textuality, except that it has been so thoroughly reconfigured so as to be an echo rather than an outright citation. For ears attuned to mystical language, and well versed in the major source of these (Ezekiel's vision of the *merkabah*), the allusion is irresistible. Paul performs for such readers a kind of inverse recital that is then both recontextualized and reconfigured within the context of Paul and the Corinthian community. Ezekiel, in his epiphany, beheld an exceptional vision of "the appearance of the likeness of the glory of God" (1:28). His language carefully distances the seer from the God whom no one can see and live. Paul reconfigures this language, also using a string of linked terms, so as to evoke the unhindered and common sight of believers: "God … give[s] us the light of the knowledge of the glory of God" (4:6). In the invention of the echoed verse, Paul also

---

[12] See the treatment of Joseph A. Fitzmyer, "Glory Reflected on the Face of Christ (2 Cor 3:7–4:6) and a Palestinian Jewish Motif," *TS* 42 (1981): 630–44.

[13] It is difficult to trace the complex relationship between mystical practice and the experience implied by the Jewish apocalypses. Hints in a Jewish text written not much later than Paul's time suggest both a strong reserve toward esoteric journeys (*4 Ezra* 4:7–8) and an implied visit of the seer to the celestial Jerusalem (10:55). *Fourth Ezra* also cites preparatory techniques for such experiences, showing that these were not the preserve of mystics alone but found their way into written apocalypses (3:1–2; 5:21; 6:35; 9:26–28). Segal suggests that both types of literature (mystical texts and apocalypses) reflect "not unrelated experiences" (*Paul the Convert,* 38). Certainly, there are Jewish mystical texts that conform to the apocalypse genre in substance and form (e.g., *Sefer Hekhaloth* = *3 Enoch*).

reverses the direction or the impact of Ezekiel's mystical sequence. That is, the light of the knowledge of the glory of God are not distancing, but approaching terms. Paul clinches his anti-esoteric stance by insisting that the epiphany is commonly seen "in the face of Christ" and understood in "our hearts" (ἐν ταῖς καρδίαις ἡμῶν, 2 Cor 4:6.).[14] This common intimacy is further explained by the context that Paul has already provided through his discussion of glory at 3:18 and through reference to the protological purposes of God. Light is to come out of darkness, and the called community is, along with Christ, to bear the divine image: "For God, who said, 'Let light shine out of darkness,' made his light shine in our hearts, to give us the light of the knowledge of the glory of God in the face of Christ."[15] Here is a reconfiguration of the body, specifically the body of Christ, understood "dyadically"[16] and in the light of Paul's conviction about apocalypse.

By oblique reference to Ezekiel (along with the clear reference to Moses) Paul evokes the awesome presence of the Lord. Probably Paul is also drawing on a specific "historical" resource, his own visionary experiences, to which he will later testify (reluctantly) in the letter; yet, the thrust of Paul's polemic is to emphasize neither the ineffability of revelation nor his special apostolic privilege. Of course, there is an inherent risk in this method, as there remains the potential for actual collision between the directed discourse and the evocative visionary imagery. Paul is playing a dangerous game in co-opting apocalyptic discourse, not wholly taming it to the purposes of his argument, but continuing to allow it its own vitality. The danger remains that readers may pick up only on one side of the allusions. For example, some many simply note Paul's association with Ezekiel and mysticism without also commenting on his reserve. Paul's purpose goes beyond an appeal to such esotericism. Rather, he aims to highlight the glory (now identified with Jesus and the Spirit) that now dwells intimately with all of God's people. Something has happened so that the light of the knowledge of the glory of God has been brought near in the face of Christ; that same glory, says Paul, is still vibrantly present to the whole community through the Holy Spirit (2 Cor 3:17). Segal recognizes this

---

[14] That this is not a royal or apostolic "we" is clear from Paul's argument, which extends the transformation attendant upon this vision to "us all" (2 Cor 3:18) and which distinguishes between those whose eyes are veiled and those for whom the veil has been removed.

[15] Interestingly, Paul includes not only the typical *merkabah* themes of mysticism, but also the *bereshit* themes, implying a new creation.

[16] For this term, see Bruce J. Malina, *The New Testament World: Insights from Cultural Anthropology* (rev. ed.; Atlanta: Knox, 1993), 63–89; as used by Robbins, *Exploring the Texture of Texts,* 77–78.

dynamic without emphasizing the reluctance of Paul, who refuses to cite his own ecstatic visions as authoritative proof for this new state of affairs: "[Paul's] point is that some Christian believers also make such an ascent and that its effects are more permanent than the vision that Moses received. The church has witnessed a theophany as important as the one vouchsafed to Moses, but the Christian theophany is greater still, as Paul himself has experienced."[17]

In light of Paul's reticence, we should, perhaps, modify Segal's statement: Paul's point is that the church has witnessed a theophany greater (and more intimate) than that of Moses, and that some, like Paul, have done so through ecstasy, but all are *together* promised the resultant transformation.[18]

1.3. Social Intertextuality

This ancient dyadic (polyadic?) perspective, framed in particular Christian terms, leads us naturally into a discussion of the social resources drawn upon in these chapters. Paul appeals to many facets of life: public smells (2:14–16), processions of victor and slaves (2:14; 4:5), directed and open letters (3:1–3), veils and unveiled faces (3:12–18), selling and giving (2:27; 4:1–2), treasures in clay jars (4:7), and health and disease (4:15). Such images and activities are used by Paul to further his own defense before the Corinthians, as well as to conjure the alternative apocalyptic narrative about God's people and their life in Christ. Paul encloses this extended section of 2:14–4:17 with references to the heavenly world—God who "in Christ always leads us in triumphal procession" (2:14) and "that which is eternal" (4:17). Likewise, toward his conclusion, he refers to the great creative and recreative activity of God (4:6, 11, 14). Thus, he seeks to move his hearers so that they consider themselves, as he does, as those who dwell in the presence of God (2:17; God who is greater than the "god of this world," 4:4). Further, they are to see themselves as those who are beneficiaries of God's creative activity (4:6), including Jesus' recreating death and resurrection (to be recapitulated in their own experience, 4:11–14). In this way he provides for them a carefully shaped apocalyptic perspective, which includes both a vertical axis (the divine world and its

---

[17] Segal, *Paul the Convert*, 60.

[18] Note also the emphasis upon suspect transformation in 2 Cor 11:13–15 as Paul moves into the polemical conclusion of his "boasting" section. The super-apostles claim to be transformed, μετασχηματιζόμενοι (2 Cor 11:13)—just as Satan "transforms himself into an angel of light." Their transformation is thus into seeming to be "ministers of righteousness." They will, ironically, be judged on the basis of their works (works that include apocalyptic exploits?; cf. 12:11–12)—presumably because this is the apt fulfilment (τέλος, 11:15) of what they have emphasized in their pursuit of righteousness.

shadow) and a horizontal axis (primordial and significant past events pointing forward to the eschaton). Images painted and arguments construed in
terms of these two axes join to construct a third axis, by which they may
understand their own identity. Mundane symbols such as clay jars and mir-
rors, as well as potentially sacred images such as fragrance and veils, are all
taken up into a dramatic vision of the life of the people of God.

In the case of some of the cultural images, the line between "ordinary"
and "sacred" is blurred—a softness of barriers that we should expect, given
the polyvalence of language and also the ancient refusal to make an
absolute distinction between sacred and "secular." Is the "aroma" of 2 Cor
2:14–15 evocative of sacred incense and the altar, or more earthy smells,
such as blossoms from a fruit tree and erotic perfume (in reference to Wisdom as pictured in Sir 24:14–17) over against the stench of death? Is the
procession of 2:14 a reference to Roman parades, or to the *merkabah?* Is
the "veil" imagery polyvalent enough to go beyond its scribal Mosaic reference so as to evoke also the marriage ceremony and the intimate open
face between husband and wife?[19] As for vessels, we know from another
context (Rom 9:19–21) that Paul can use this image to evoke sacred and
everyday use. The effect of this unfolding repertoire of images and the cru-
ciform background story is that the "everyday" is itself assumed into a
cosmic drama, without losing significance.[20] Paul's own struggles with his
Corinthian "children" are also taken up into a bigger narrative, as apocalyptic story and discourse pull up the veil. The effect of this unveiling is
that much is tinged with glory but that darker contours or shadows are also
seen in some of the corners.

2. Holy Ministry and Revelation: 2 Corinthians 6:1–7:4

Our second selection actually continues the themes that Paul has
sounded in chapters 3 and 4—that of ministry and his desired intimate relationship to the Corinthian church—so that some have considered 2:14–7:4
to be a larger unified section. Thus, we might see ourselves as moving from

---

[19] Cf. the ancient custom of veiling, probably suggested by Gen 24:65, and Paul's
own symbolism at 2 Cor 11:2.

[20] An earlier generation of scholars (unsympathetic to "apocalyptic") saw it as
decadent prophecy, as losing touch with the world because of the larger picture
that it offered. It is more accurate to say that the apocalyptic perspective both
"pans out," adding a cosmic perspective, but also "pans in" to historical and cultural details, showing the lights and shadows that are cast upon the earthly realm
by the actors and events of the larger drama. Certainly Paul does not dismiss the
everyday but sees it as connected with and contributing toward the "eternal
weight of glory."

the initial part of Paul's argument (2:14–4:18), in which Paul has established *ethos*, to consider his conclusion (chs. 6 and 7), where *pathos* is the dominant tone. This second section, 6:1–7:4, focuses specifically upon the theme of "working together" and so has a more practical character than the midrashic passage. Also included is that problematic section 6:14–7:1, which has received various "solutions" because of a perceived mismatch between it and the surrounding verses. Attention to the various currents of apocalyptic discourse in the letter as a whole mitigates the problem. Some (though certainly not all)[21] of the language found here may be unusual for Paul, but so is his extensive midrashic argument at 3:1–18. Certainly, the use of rhetorical interrogation (6:14–16) or stringed citations (6:16–18) is characteristically Pauline, particularly at passionate points of argument. The major question, then, is whether this shorter section is an absolute digression or whether it is related to the plea that frames it—that the Corinthians open their hearts to him. It may be that too narrow a focus upon Paul's personal dilemma, and not enough attention to Paul's implied metanarrative, disclosed through apocalyptic discourse, has prevented analysts from seeing how this section fits into the whole. My purpose here is, at any rate, not to argue for the integrity of the passage but to see the various intertexts that are conjured.

2.1. Oral-Scribal Intertextuality

This passage is particularly strong in the first layer of intertextuality, since it is dependent upon actual citations. Paul begins his exhortation to live the separate or "holy" life, characterized as "working together," with the declaration that salvation is "now" (6:2, cf. Isa 49:8). He then goes on in 6:14–7:1 to reconfigure the present body, or "temple" of believers, in dualistic language and through a string of scriptural recitations (the composition of which has been suspected to have Essene roots). *If* this exhortative passage is foreign in origin, it is thoroughly recontextualized by Paul through its placement here. Moreover, the passage itself is consonant with Paul's gospel of righteousness and his message of incorporation into the family of God—which themes both have present and future aspects, in Paul's thought.

The string of citations (6:16–18) dealing with God's dwelling place includes two prominent references to Second Isaiah (6:17 = Isa 52:11; 6:18 = Isa 43:6), thus sustaining Paul's use of this material, which began at 6:2. Sources used besides Deutero-Isaiah are Ezek 37:27 (a closer match to 6:16 than Lev 26:12) and Ezek 20:34 LXX (also corresponding to v. 18). Verses of

---

21 Found elsewhere in Paul, for example, are the terms δικαιοσύνη, ἀνομία (cf. 2 Thess 2:3 7, also in an apocalyptic context), ναός, πιστός, θεοῦ, ζῶντος, ἀγαπητοί.

"promise" (2 Cor 7:1) from the Hebrew Bible are thus commingled and reformulated to give a dramatic and urgent backdrop to Paul's ethical injunctions. For Paul and his hearers, the accomplishment of the resurrection of Jesus means that, in one sense, there is already the new exodus, the new creation, and the new temple promised by the prophets. From this new perspective, holy living is the appropriate mode, not simply of the apostles, but of all the faithful. They become, in their turn after Jesus, the δικαιοσύνη of God (5:21).

2.2. Cultural and Social Intertextuality

Few commentators have missed (nor would Paul's informed readers have ignored) the similarities between Paul's rhetoric in 6:4–7 and Greco-Roman methods of self-commendation,[22] commendations that would frequently include paradox. However, also striking is the contrast between such virtuous models and the paradoxes here set up by Paul.[23] It has been suggested that Paul is relying on the death/resurrection imagery of Ps 118:17–18 in the invention of these verses, particularly in 2 Cor 6:8–10.[24] Such a scribal layer of texture is not readily apparent here, however, since only thematic echoes are to be heard, and no clear repetition of phrases. Instead, given the ubiquitousness of Deutero-Isaiah throughout this entire passage and the manner in which Paul has here established his apostolic identity as "servant of God" (2 Cor 6:3), it seems probable that Paul is modifying the Hellenistic notion of wisdom by reference to a figure well used in early Christian discourse— ʿebed YHWH, the servant of God who suffers.

Early Christian culture seems to have been thoroughly familiar with this figure because of its frequent association in early proclamation with Jesus himself. Here it is seemingly applied not to Jesus but to the apostolic ministry of reconciliation. It is not as though Paul expects the Corinthians to go rifling through Isa 42–53 in order to trace the images associated with this figure, for they are already part of the culture, part of their understanding of the "perfect" one of faithful speech and justice. Through reference to the servant, honored by God but dishonored in the human realm, Paul situates his ministry in a world of contrasts. As a servant, he is

---

[22] See, for example, the treatment of the second letter of Demosthenes in George Kennedy, *The Art of Rhetoric in the Graeco-Roman World* (Princeton, N.J.: Princeton University Press, 1972), 553–54.

[23] On the differences between Paul's rhetoric and both the *res gestae* and sophistic literature, see Linda L. Belleville, "A Letter of Apologetic Self-Commendation" *NovT* 31 (1989): 142–63, esp. 158–60.

[24] See the comments in the *HarperCollins Study Bible, NRSV with the Deuterocanonical Books* (New York: HarperCollins, 1993), 2173, note on 6:8–10.

unknown—yet well known, dying—yet alive, poor—yet making many rich. Paul thus sees himself as reflecting the ministry of Jesus, which he makes explicit in 8:9. As his own role is colored by the Isaianic figure, Paul casts himself as the voice calling "the peoples far away," bringing back God's people and gathering others to God as well. The Corinthians are invited to see themselves as a part of this drama, either in solidarity with Paul as the "we" (cf. 5:15) or (more likely at this point in his argument) as those being recalled from darkness to light.[25]

Thus, the "today" of salvation and the already visible (yet unseen) "new creation" gives shape to the drama of Paul's ministry among the Corinthians. In this new world, shame and honor are not only reversed, but also (in an eerie way) exchanged.[26] Things are not as they seem, once it is acknowledged that the greatest apocalypse has already been revealed. What appears to be apostolic shame actually partakes in the highest honor, and so the two meanings of δόξα merge. Moreover, his shame and the glory of the Corinthians live in a kind of symbiosis. Yet in reversing shame and honor, it is not Paul's motive to attribute shame to the Corinthians. Rather, he calls them to imitate him ("Open wide your hearts also. . . . Make room for us," 6:13; 7:2) and sees their life as intimately tied to his ("you are in our hearts, to die together and to live together," 7:3).

2.3. Historical Intertextuality

The pattern of death then life, of shame then glory, is actually laid down for the Corinthians in the sequence of Paul's argument, and they must tread it. Paul takes on the role of compassionate parent (6:13), perhaps even echoing the divine parent of Isa 49, who will never forget. He then moves on, predictably, to discipline the family. There may be a paradox regarding shame and honor, but there is still a stark and unbridgeable contrast between light and dark that the Corinthians are called to acknowledge. Paul's apocalyptic discourse carries with it a subversion of values, without negating the traditional prophetic call to purity. What may have been in another context a general exhortation to holiness (6:14–7:1) approaches historical specificity in the letter, though the details of the historical are not named. Paul does, however, move from a colorful description of his own situation (6:3–10), to an appeal in which he directly

---

[25] See the well-argued monograph of W. J. Webb, *Returning Home: New Covenant and Second Exodus As the Context for 2 Corinthians 6:14–7:1* (JSNTSup 85; Sheffield: JSOT Press, 1993). Webb places the Corinthians in the role of those being called out of exile by the "servant" Paul.

[26] For an interesting study of the "economics of exchange," see Frances Young and David F. Ford, *Meaning and Truth in 2 Corinthians* (Cambridge: SPCK, 1987), 166–85.

names the church ("We have spoken frankly to you Corinthians," 6:11), and finally to this dramatic exhortation to holiness. Such a progression implies a particular historical context for the cultural discourse to which they are attending. Specifically, if the Corinthians are to return Paul's affections, they must break with the faithless.[27] The placement of the dualisms of 6:14–7:1 between Paul's double call for reconciliation (6:13; 7:2) is a masterful stroke. In this so-called foreign passage he now places his opponents within the grand drama, alongside himself and the Corinthians—they are the lawless, the dark, the followers of Beliar, the devotees of idols, the unclean. Apocalyptic space is evoked as the enemies of the church are connected with the unseen (and here) insubstantial world. The promises of God, the apocalyptic perspective that declares that God does and will live with his people, demands a "priestly" cleansing of God's church. To work alongside Paul (6:1) means separation from these false workers.

Nor is this the only place where Paul will pull out such weapons from the cultural arsenal. Those who have commented upon the *hapax legomena* in this passage must also deal with Paul's extravagance of language later in this letter (or in a separate Corinthian correspondence, depending on one's view), where the enemies of Paul (and, in his view, of the church) are described as satanically "changing their appearance [to look like] apostles of Christ" (11:13). As Paul brings his exhortation home, he issues at 7:1 a priestly injunction to "cleanse oneself" so that all comes to fulfilment. Ethical conduct and community ties are given apocalyptic dimensions. Paul's perspective means that he regards no one "according to the flesh." He sees both the glory of God's people but also the darkness of those who are not legitimately part of God's temple. What he does throughout this section is to call upon the Corinthians to see the same picture, light and darkness included. Revelation sheds its light, and reconciliation casts its shadow. Here, as elsewhere, Paul's apocalyptic discourse provides for his readers a dramatic shared identity, a ministry and a world in which they are to die and live together, through an appeal to mysterious time and cosmic space.

3. Mystery and Revelation: 2 Corinthians 12:1–12

3.1. Oral-Scribal Intertextuality

Our first two examples presented themselves as apocalyptic discourse because of their connection with imagery and ideas normally associated

---

[27] If Paul's opponents are in view here, the translation "faithless" for ἄπιστοι is more appropriate than "unbelievers" [so NRSV] since the latter term suggests to the English-speaking reader those actually outside the institutional church household. Paul is throughout his argument distancing his opponents from the church, but it is undeniable that they are presently part of the social group.

with the visionary, the protological, and the eschatological. Rather more unusual is 2 Cor 12. Here Paul again touches upon what we could label as apocalyptic "content." More strikingly, however, he plays with, as well as against, the apocalyptic *form*. The oral-scribal intertext here seems to be the whole body of apocalyptic literature with which Paul and his readers would have been familiar. The contours of the *genre* provide the link, rather than specific verses from this apocalypse or that. We might be tempted, because of the abstraction, the implicit appeal to overall genre, to consider this as a cultural intertext. However, that would be a peculiar move, since one of the characteristics of the apocalypse genre is its inscribed nature—scrolls are ingested, writing is commanded, the vision-ary is pictured as scribe and not simply as prophet. Certainly, Paul's discourse here may be appropriately considered on the cultural level (informed not only by Jewish but also Hellenistic culture). Oral-scribal intertextuality, however (alongside the historical context of Paul's own life) dominates chapter 12.

Several of the apocalypses (e.g., various passages in *1 Enoch,* some of which were extant in Paul's day, plus later works such as the *Ascension of Isaiah*)[28] include the rapture of the visionary into the heavenlies. Such writings stress the spatial axis, over against historical apocalypses, which are more oriented to the temporal. Frequently Paul's apocalypticism has been understood only in terms of features that are to be plotted along the temporal axis. This is not entirely misguided, since Paul's greatest *apoka-lypsis* is of course the historical revealing of the Son of God in a surprising resurrection. However, as we have seen in this letter, Paul also has a sense of standing "in the presence of God" and sees an ongoing connection between the unseen world and the life of the church. This final section of the letter, though it is framed ironically, demonstrates that Paul was per-sonally knowledgeable about those visionary experiences that informed the "apocalypses with otherworldly journey." Moreover, his uses (and play-ful "abuse") of various formal features of these writings indicate that he was aware not only of the experience, but also of the writings.

Paul's method here is not citation, nor simple recontextualization, but a total reconfiguration of the genre, so that it becomes at the same time a supreme apocalypse and an anti-apocalypse. The mold is broken. After all, scribes recorded their visions in order to give their readers a proxy experi-ence of their exploits and, through the visions, to lend them a knowledge of the supreme drama, a reason for patience, and a desire for holy living. The

---

28 These apocalypses were called type II, "Apocalypses with Otherworldly Jour-ney," by the SBL group and subdivided into three categories. See the chart in Collins, "Introduction," 14–15.

apocalypticist typically offered his visions pseudonymously; Paul declines to name a notable namesake, but simply speaks anonymously of "a person [ἄνθρωπος] in Christ" whom he "knows" (12:2). The name by which he wants to be known, the only boast he can make (12:5), is that this person is "in Christ." Further, unlike the visionary, Paul never actually passes on to his hearers a single detail of the vision(s) or audition. They are, in any case, not to be told (the "sealing" of visions is also an apocalyptic feature) but to relate them would also do Paul and his hearers no good. Besides presenting to his reader a narrative framework, a third person account, and an (undisclosed) audition and vision, Paul also refers to an *angelus interpres,* or interpreting angel (12:7)—of the satanic variety. Paul sets up the expectations of the reader in order to frustrate: we receive little more than an "apparatus" of a revelation and are given, instead, an "un-vision," an "un-audition," and an "un-interpretation." Those conversant with the formal features of the apocalypse expect an interpretation. The surprising interpretation given through Paul's inverse angel is that these mysteries are not meant to elate but that rather weakness means strength. Whatever the identity of the "thorn," it serves as a memorial to the visions, a kind of inverse stigmata, over against the resultant "glory" of seers like Moses. It is permanent rather than fading, a seeming shame, but a sign that points to true glory.

It has been assumed by many that Paul's reserve and irony are directed in this section against the importance of visions and ecstatic experiences per se. Such assumptions have been less frequent since James Tabor launched his persuasive argument that Paul's reticence is due to a sense of the sacredness of the vision, rather than its unimportance. He concludes that Paul is reporting "a privilege of the highest order" and that "nothing in the context of 2 Cor 12 should lead one to conclude that Paul disparaged such experiences"[29]—or apocalyptic literature informed by the visionary, we might add.

3.2. Cultural Intertextuality

If, then, Paul is not implying that visions or apocalypses are irrelevant, why the irony? It seems that the answer lies in the use to which he puts the report. Whatever one's view of the letter's integrity, chapter 12 comes at a high point in the longer section 2 Cor 10:1–13:10. In this section, well marked because of the closure at 9:15 and the new invocation at 10:1, Paul is engaged in a subtle argument, both judicial (apologetic)[30] and

---

[29] James D. Tabor, *Things Unutterable: Paul's Ascent to Paradise in Its Greco-Roman, Judaic, and Early Christian Contexts* (Lanham, Md.: University Press of America, 1986), 21.

[30] See Hans D. Betz, who compares this to the "socratic apology" in *Der Apostel Paulus und die sokratische Tradition: Eine exegetische Untersuchung zu seiner*

deliberative, that plays with Hellenistic rhetorical conventions. While the tone is apologetic, the form is that of the "foolish speech"; the apology can therefore not be taken at face value. The proliferation of irony and sarcasm throughout the section means that the apology is not made for its own sake but is subordinated to a greater cause (as Paul himself declares at the conclusion, 12:19). The apology, then, is placed within a larger context of edification, as Paul's major concern is to direct his hearer toward attitudes and actions for the future—clearly a deliberative stance.[31] Readers aware of the various cultural regions from which Paul draws had (and still have) a complex and engaging task. It is as though, through the completion of difficult homework, Paul leads his hearers to make his worldview their own.

In considering 2 Cor 10:1–13:10 as a unit, Paul's vision-report and its sequelae (12:1–10) may be seen as coming at the high point of the *argumentatio* section, after the *exordium* of 10:1–6 and the statement of the case in 10:7–18. What is being put before the Corinthians is this: self-evaluation and self-commendation are not seemly; rather, the Lord's commendation is valuable, and boasting in the Lord is fruitful. The proofs begin at 11:1, where Paul introduces his own self-evaluation and commendation as "foolishness," going on to his past experience with the Corinthians, his pedigree, his experiences of humility, and a parody of the *corona muralis*. Paul, the first down the wall of the earthly city, then goes on in 12:1–10 to describe one who surpassed others in ascending to the heavenly realm—only to learn that there is no human glory in such experiences! So then, the impassioned arguments for his human pedigree and exploits are capped by reference to his otherworldly experiences and ensuing identity as one who is "weak, and therefore strong." The final clinching argument is followed by the conclusion at 12:11–13:10, in which Paul comments on the methods that he has used during his "apology" and goes on directly to address his audience, letting them in on his motives and encouraging them to act accordingly.

3.3. Social and Historical

While appealing to his own exploits, he has refused to give content to the vision, although it is just possible that the "content" of the vision is "the Lord" himself (reading ἀποκαλύψεις κυρίου in 12:1 as a subjective genitive).

"Apologie" 2 Korinther 10–13 (Tübingen: Mohr Siebeck, 1972); and Jerry W. McCant, who prefers the "philosopher's apology" as a model, in "Paul's Thorn of Rejected Apostleship," *NTS* 34 (1988): 555.

[31] In support of the pastoral function of 2 Cor 10–13, see the compositional analysis of Max-Alain Chevallier, in "L'argumentation de Paul dans II Corinthiens 10 à 13," *RHPR* 70 (1990): 3–15.

More than this, however, we do not hear. Nor do we get a description of the "paradise," or an explanation of the numbered heavens, or a description of the visionary conquest of each gate at each heaven, such as we might have expected in reference to Paul's excellence as a seer. In fact, he makes much of spurning the fine distinctions of the mode of ascent ("whether in or out of the body, I don't know, God knows"), perhaps himself acknowledging that this is in fact a matter of much speculation among some (the pseudo-apostles?). But mirror-reading, always a risky enterprise, is frequently frustrated in this letter. The reader is hampered by Paul's seemingly deliberate lack of disclosure at this point—a reticence that he does not follow in dealing with more practical matters, such as his support by the churches in Macedonia.

Paul's vision, then, functions as a proof, establishing the apostle's authority in an ironic manner. His very reticence to boast of his supernatural exploits is an indication of his apostleship. His obedience in the matter of not divulging that which is not to be uttered and his turning back to the theme of weakness for the sake of glorifying the Lord serve as an example to his listeners of what they should value. The argument works on several levels: if the listeners require this kind of proof, he could give it, but he won't. Paul's reserve itself should be an indication to them of his real motives and trustworthiness. Paul claims the fact of the heavenly journey without inviting his listeners to enter into its intricacies, all the while insisting that such talk is futile. Indeed, his accusers' accusation of weakness is turned around to have a positive value: the only enduring lesson to be learned is that of human weakness and divine grace. In handling this contest of spirituality, silence becomes a preferred weapon in Paul's hands, as he directs his hearers away from ordinary means of judging shame and glory, and away even from the debate in which he is embroiled, toward a larger canvas, a larger drama, within which he urges them to see his, and their, place. "Have you been thinking all along that we have been defending ourselves before you? We are speaking in Christ before God ... for the sake of building you up" (13:19).

4. Conclusion: The Dangers of Apocalyptic Discourse

Intriguingly, the double-edged sword of irony and the speculative atmosphere of the vision account may assume their own unruly life. Contrary to Paul's stated intent, the hearer may be tantalized by the brevity of his vision account. (And we know that later some devotees to Paul did precisely what he directed them against, speculating about his vision in the *Apocalypse of Paul*.) The hearer is led to muse about the contents of the vision. Has Paul given us a hint in his phrase "visions *of the Lord*"? Is there a two-stage journey from third heaven to paradise? What did Paul hear? What exactly is the difference between an in-the-body and an out-of-the-body rapture? Within the context of Paul's argument, such speculative details are quickly abandoned, but they are nonetheless raised in the encounter of this report that refuses to report. The same risk is met, though with perhaps less force, in our first two examples, as the reader may be tempted to think more about fading glory on faces than about Paul's argument for the reflected glory of God's people (2:14–4:18), or to spin off in the direction of dramatic, dualistic thinking that focuses upon the identity of Beliar and his cohorts (6:1–7:4). Paul is obviously prepared for such risks, for he does his readers the courtesy of inviting them to think, see, and enter the story with him. "Spaces" for readerly action are amply provided in the argument and in the narrative. The liminality and vitality of apocalyptic discourse is a mixed blessing, enlivening Paul's argument but also threatening to break its moorings. As Karl A. Plank points out, "Writing and reading are fraught with risk. . . . The risk: both writers and readers may be surprised by what occurs through the collaboration of the other."[32]

Indeed, we have seen that intertextual links occur not only at the level of writing and reading but also at the cultural, social, and historical levels. Paul's readers are at liberty to pause at the forbidden points in the discourse and interact with the various textures we have noted, thus entering a provisional or marginal part of the evoked world. The danger is that the reader may stop at her or his preferred (or most detested) point, rather than going on to see the entire horizon. The reader may well be unwilling to entertain a rhetoric that "reconfigures time and space both in the realm of the world and the body in the light of God's future intervening judgement"[33]—let alone in the light of past, present, and future salvation and in view of the impinging reality of other mysterious worlds, both heavenly and infernal. Dualisms, appeals to unseen worlds with "soft" barriers interconnected with ours, and deferred hope may be to some perspectives that are unpalatable or "polyanna-ish." Indeed, the resistant reader of the twenty-first century may refuse to place Paul's rhetoric, apocalyptic or otherwise, within Paul's proffered metanarrative. Without the central lifted veil, Paul's talk of weakness and strength becomes a mere powerplay, and his reserve toward personal visionary experience is rendered insincere. The complexity of his rhetoric is flattened, and Paul's "authority to build up," as well as his motivation, is subjected to cynical questioning. The only answer to such questioning is to change vantage points, as Paul himself pleads, so that the reader herself adopts a new identity within a larger readership, an identity disclosed through a new vantage point, discerned from a new "where" and "when."

---

[32] Karl Plank, *Paul and the Irony of Affliction* (Atlanta: Scholars Press, 1987), 91.

[33] The working definition of apocalyptic discourse adopted for this volume.

Apocalyptic Discourse in 1 Thessalonians

James D. Hester

Assuming for the moment that 1 Thessalonians is among the earliest writ-ten evidence we have of discussions of primitive Christian theology,[1] it seems clear that issues of eschatology and apocalypticism[2] were a part of the dia-logue being carried on among some of the first generation of Christian believers. It is also clear that Paul did not write apocalypses in response to this dialogue, if one limits the understanding of apocalypse to issues of genre. Having recognized that, however, leaves us with the task of identifying apoc-alyptic elements in his argumentation. Robert Hall, Louis Martyn, and Duane Watson have argued that Paul is capable of formulating an apocalyptic rhet-oric that makes use of, or focuses, the topics typically found in apocalypses and in the process of doing so changes the function of apocalypticism to fit the needs of his audiences.[3] Apocalyptic discourse can occur in genres other than an apocalypse and can be analyzed without appeal to that genre.

---

[1] Thomas Söding ("Der Erste Thessalonicherbrief und die frühepaulinische Evan-geliumsverkündigung: Zur Frage einer Entwicklung der paulinischen Theologie," *BZ* 35 [1991]: 180–203) reviews the major arguments and evidence for dating the letter around 50 C.E. He concludes that it does in fact contain the earliest example we have of Pauline theology and that its basic theological teaching anticipates con-cepts found in the later major letters. He does not address the issue of Paul's apocalyptic teaching in the letter.

[2] Calvin Roetzel ("Paul As Organic Intellectual: The Shaper of Apocalyptic Myths," in *Common Life in the Early Church* [ed. Julian Hills; Harrisburg, Pa.: Trinity Press International, 1998], 222 n. 3) makes the point that Käsemann's German word, "Apokalyptik," is typically translated erroneously as "apocalyptic," an adjective in English, rather than as the noun "apocalypticism." Greg Carey ("Introduction: Apoc-alyptic Discourse, Apocalyptic Rhetoric," in *Vision and Persuasion: Rhetorical Dimensions of Apocalyptic Discourse* [ed. Greg Carey and L. Gregory Bloomquist; St. Louis: Chalice, 1999], 3, 10) also makes it clear that "apocalyptic" is an adjective.

[3] Robert Hall, "Arguing Like an Apocalypse: Galatians As an Ancient Topos out-side the Greco-Roman Rhetorical Tradition," *NTS* 42 (1996): 434–53; J. L. Martyn, *Galatians* (AB 33A; New York: Doubleday, 1997); Duane F. Watson, "Paul's Appro-priation of Apocalyptic Discourse: The Rhetorical Strategy of 1 Thessalonians," in Carey and Bloomquist, *Vision and Persuasion*, 61–80.

I am indebted to Greg Carey for the definition of "apocalyptic discourse" I adopt in this paper.[4] After describing various modern attempts to understand the dimensions of the concepts of apocalypse, apocalyptic eschatology, and apocalypticism, Carey defines apocalyptic discourse in this manner: "Apocalyptic discourse refers to the constellation of apocalyptic topics as they function in larger early Jewish and Christian literary and social contexts. Thus apocalyptic discourse should be treated as a flexible set of resources that early Jews and Christians could employ for a variety of persuasive tasks."[5]

The importance of this definition for me lies in the insight that apocalyptic topics can function persuasively outside the context of an apocalypse. Said differently, and now being increasingly widely acknowledged, apocalyptic discourse exists in early Christian literature outside of the context of an apocalyptic literature and without necessary recourse to the full conceptual matrix of an apocalypse!

The concept I want to elaborate in the definition is "discourse." Carey highlights the concept of the rhetorical function of discourse, but he tends to focus on the social dimensions of functionality.[6] I want to expand the notion a bit. In the context of modern literary criticism and rhetorical theory, it seems as though it is better to talk about what discourse "does" rather than what discourse "is."[7] It is possible to think of discourse as the communication of ideas concerning things that are of interest to all members of a community.[8] Discourses arise in a variety of social settings, institutions, and disciplines, each of which have coding systems understood by members of those entities, and for which the use of a coding system can both generate and elaborate knowledge. New sets of knowledge are created through communicative exchange. The truths of these discourses are relative to their disciplinary and institutional contexts. That in turn means that those truths can have some claim to authority only within those contexts.[9]

Discourses not only sustain the knowledge created by institutions and disciplines but also make it possible for them to distribute knowledge by

---

[4] Carey, "Introduction," 2–10.

[5] Ibid., 10.

[6] Ibid., 12–14.

[7] I will use the word *discourse* in the singular, but I do not mean to imply by that use that I think there is a single, foundational discourse. It would be more accurate to speak of multiple "discourses" that arise contextually from various historical and cultural contexts.

[8] Renato Barilli, *Rhetoric* (Minneapolis: University of Minnesota Press, 1989), vii.

[9] Paul A. Bové, "Discourse," in *Critical Terms for Literary Study* (ed. F. Lentricchia and T. McLaughlin; Chicago: University of Chicago Press, 1990), 54–56.

entering into discourse about that knowledge. In doing so such discourses become authoritative for the group and exercise some power over the members of the group and those who choose to join in the discursive exchanges.[10]

The analytical method I want to use to analyze apocalyptic discourse is Fantasy Theme Analysis (FTA), the major topics of which are described in the glossary at the end of this essay. The argument I want to make is that in 1 Thessalonians apocalyptic discourse encompasses Paul's dramatizing messages *and* apocalyptic argumentation, thus functioning without recourse to the typical markers of the apocalyptic genre. It is placed within the framework of epistolary discourse and functions to give a specific content to the fantasy type, eschatological hope. It also functions to sustain the rhetorical vision of eschatological hope that Paul had preached among them and the group consciousness of the Thessalonians based on that hope. The expression of that vision through apocalyptic discourse sustains their identity as "insiders," the righteous of God who, through their holiness and purity, will escape the wrath to come and will be caught up into heaven at the *parousia*. It also provides a moral imperative that grows out of the shared values that had developed as the vision was chained out while Paul was in Thessalonica. FTA allows us to analyze how Paul's rhetoric functions to sustain group consciousness and set the stage for further consciousness raising.

1. Symbolic Convergence Theory (SCT)

In an earlier essay I have described in fuller detail the concept and claims of SCT and FTA.[11] In what follows I will, therefore, give only a basic overview of the theory. SCT is a general theory of communication[12] that

---

[10] The reader might recognize my loose dependence on the theories of Michael Foucault concerning the functionality of discourse. However, I am also indebted to Chaim Perelman and Lucie Olbrechts-Tyteca and their neo-Aristotelian construction of the Universal Audience (*The New Rhetoric: A Treatise on Argumentation* [trans. John Wilkinson and Purcell Weaver; Notre Dame, Ind.: University of Notre Dame Press, 1969], 30–35).

[11] "A Fantasy Theme Analysis of 1 Thessalonians," in *Rhetorical Criticism and the Bible* (ed. Stanley Porter and Dennis Stamps; JSNTSup 195; Sheffield: Sheffield Academic Press, 2002), 504–25.

[12] Ernest G. Bormann (*Small Group Communication: Theory and Practice* [3d ed.; New York: Harper & Row, 1990] 3–5) is careful to distinguish between "special theory," which he understands as useful in explaining how to conduct communication within the constraints of a certain time and place, and "general theory." "General theory" he defines as being able to account for "broad classes of

provides an account of the formation of group consciousness through the use by the group of imaginative language that creates for it a shared sense of reality. It assumes that the rhetoric of an individual, a "dramatic message," can be shared and "chained out" in a process of communication within a group that produces a "convergence" or overlapping of private symbolic worlds so that a common consciousness or "rhetorical vision" emerges. A group of individuals finds ways of talking about attitudes or emotions they have shared in response to some person or event in a world that they may find chaotic, threatening, or hostile. They produce "fantasies" that are imaginative interpretations of events that have occurred in a particular time and place. These fantasies use metaphorical or other forms of "insider" language that "interprets events in the past, envisions events in the future, or depicts current events that are removed in time and/or space from the actual activities of the group."[13] Thus a rhetorical community, made up of those who share a common rhetorical vision, is formed. SCT posits that the social reality constructed by the group allows for discursive argument within the group and is a source of motivation for action.[14]

The "dramatizing message" is the rhetorical foundation of fantasy sharing. It is set somewhere other than the here and now and makes use of metaphors, analogies, puns, allegories, anecdotes, narratives, and other imaginative language to talk about some past conflict or envision some future conflict and interpret them so that they make sense to the group.[15] It is the dramatizing message that is incorporated into the members' fantasies. It causes the group to share individual fantasies and to internalize the style, tone, and implications of the original message. This results in the expansion of the content of the original message to include shared group fantasies. An illustration of this process can be seen in the road to Emmaus story (Luke 24:13–35). This story not only chains out the dramatizing message of the resurrection but also incorporates the group sharing of postresurrection appearances. These are then further chained out by Jesus' appearance to the disciples in Luke 24:36–43.

---

events" and "tendencies in human communications events that cannot be ignored or rescinded by the participants" (Ernest G. Bormann, John F. Cragan, and Donald C. Shields, "In Defense of Symbolic Convergence Theory: A Look at the Theory and Its Criticisms After Two Decades," *Communications Theory* 4 [1994]: 266).

[13] Sonja K. Foss, compiler, *Rhetorical Criticism: Exploration and Practice* (Prospect Heights, Ill.: Waveland, 1989), 290.

[14] Ernest G. Bormann, "Colloquy: I. Fantasy and Rhetorical Vision Ten Years Later," *Quarterly Journal of Speech* 68 (1982): 289, 304.

[15] Bormann, Cragan, and Shields, "In Defense of Symbolic Convergence Theory," 280.

Dramatizing messages can make use of fantasy themes. These themes are orderly, shared interpretations of an experience that allow members to talk with one another about a shared experience. They use insider references, or "symbolic cues," that can cause emotional response to that experience. These cues help hearers understand what the theme means and to feel again the response they had when they first heard the dramatizing message. The language of fantasy themes characterizes the event or experience, giving it a "spin" that allows members of the group to account for differing perceptions of what happened.[16] The important distinction to be made here is that dramatizing messages trigger shared fantasies, which are a result of such sharing on the group consciousness. Chaining of fantasies can then occur as a result of a group member taking a fantasy theme and making use of it in a "new" dramatic message, which can then trigger further fantasy sharing that can impact group consciousness.

Fantasy themes can be organized under fantasy types, which are general scenarios, reference to which can help explain or interpret new experiences. Stock scenarios and generalized persona are synthesized from various themes shared by the group. Types undergird the group culture. In conventional terms, it is within fantasy types that commonplaces are found.

Finally, fantasy themes and types can be organized into a larger rhetorical vision, a coherent vision of social reality that can be conjured by the use of key words or slogans.[17] A group's rhetorical vision provides a "common set of assumptions about the nature and reality of proof" that is necessary for discursive argument. Evidence need not be tied to empirical experience, or even dialectic, but can be based on such things as "revelation."[18]

FTA of the rhetoric, or public discourse, of a group may allow a critic to anticipate the behavior of a group.[19] For example, an analysis of a group's rhetorical vision could suggest at what stage the social reality of a group finds itself—consciousness creating, consciousness raising, or consciousness sustaining—and therefore predict the viability of the vision for maintaining the group's definition of reality and anticipate actions by the

---

[16] Bormann, *Small Group Communication,* 107.

[17] Bormann, Cragan, and Shields, "In Defense of Symbolic Convergence Theory," 281.

[18] Ernest G. Bormann, *The Force of Fantasy: Restoring the American Dream* (Carbondale: Southern Illinois University Press, 1985).

[19] Bormann, "Colloquy," 304; Ernest G. Bormann, John F. Cragan, and Donald C. Shields, "An Expansion of the Rhetorical Vision Component of the Symbolic Convergence Theory: The Cold War Paradigm Case," *Communication Monographs* 63 (1996): 10.

group to make changes in the vision in order to cope with new experiences or events.

Consciousness creating occurs when fantasy sharing generates "new symbolic ground" for people, which in turns creates a group consciousness. New rhetorical visions that explain new experiences help the group to cope with and even re-create social realities.[20] Consciousness raising communication is predominantly fantasy sharing that is aimed at newcomers. It is "proselytizing" communication that seeks to enlarge the world of social reality created by the new rhetorical vision of the group.[21] To some degree both consciousness-creating and consciousness-sustaining communication occur throughout the life cycle of a given rhetorical vision.

The final stage of the life cycle, consciousness sustaining, deals with keeping those who have been converted to a rhetorical vision committed to that vision. The communications challenge is to keep converts from falling away from the rhetorical vision that has sustained the group. If the rhetorical vision is flexible enough, symbolic fantasies can be reconstructed using new characters, plot lines, and scenes.[22] If not, little or no accommodation is made to change features of the rhetorical vision in order to deal with changes in the world around a group, and the predominant rhetorical strategy is preservation. However, preservation may not work as a strategy, and failure to adapt the vision may lead to its inability to maintain group consciousness.

2. An FTA of Apocalyptic Discourse in 1 Thessalonians

It seems to me that discourse in 1 Thessalonians is designed to interact with a stage in community consciousness somewhere between consciousness raising and consciousness sustaining.[23] While Paul's appeal to what the Thessalonians already know suggests that he was concerned with sustaining the apocalyptic vision he helped create for and with the group, there is also evidence to suggest that the process of fantasy chaining in his absence had created problems, or at least raised questions (e.g.,

---

[20] Bormann, Cragan, and Shields, "Expansion of the Rhetorical Vision Component," 2–3.

[21] Ibid., 10–12.

[22] Ibid., 13.

[23] Bormann, Cragan, and Shields (ibid., 25) claim to have identified "12 operative rhetorical principles. Three—novelty, explanatory power and imitation—operate primarily in the consciousness creating stage. Two—critical mass and dedication—during the conscious raising stage. Three—shielding, rededication and reiteration—during consciousness sustaining. Others operate during the decline and terminus state of a vision." "Conservation" is my term.

4:2–8, 13–17). In other words, the Thessalonians may have chained out the original vision in ways that threatened to distort its central features or incorporate fantasies that were not derived from Paul's original description of the paideia.[24]

To offset those problems, Paul has to elaborate certain fantasy themes in order that the group will raise its consciousness beyond the here and now and see the full power of his vision. In effect, he has to remind his audience of earlier dramatizing messages and build new ones that will help them chain out new fantasies concerning their ultimate fate and what is expected of them in the meantime. By doing so he would expect to extend the power of his rhetorical vision by making it theirs.

There appear to be four major fantasy themes[25] in the letter: imitation of persons crucial to the life of the community (1:5–6; 2:4, 14); persecution that resulted from that behavior (1:6; 2:2, 14–16, 18; 3:3, 7); vindication of the faithful in the form of resurrection/glorification (1:10; 3:13; 4:6, 13; 5:1–9); and escape from the "coming wrath" for those who persist in righteous behavior (1:10; 5:23).[26] These themes share aspects of the elements of apocalyptic argumentation outlined by Robert Hall: a claim to inspiration; revelation of divine judgement against unrighteousness; exhortation to join the realm of the righteous and reject unrighteousness; and expectation of righteous activity.[27]

---

[24] I use the term "paideia" here to mean more than "instruction." For me it is the matrix of elements in Paul's gospel that convey not only the basic components of the gospel he preached but also the pragmatic outcomes he expected from those who believed the gospel. In other words, both theology and ethics make up "paideia."

[25] In an earlier paper ("A Fantasy Theme Analysis of 1 Thessalonians") I identified three major themes, but in order to highlight the apocalyptic tenor of Paul's paideia in this letter, I decided to separate the theme of escape from wrath from its allied theme of vindication. Both share, however, the notion of righteous behavior as a precondition.

[26] Vernon Robbins ("Socio-Rhetorical Hemeneutics and Commentary," in *EPI TO AUTO* [ed. J. Mrazek et al.; Praha-Trebenice: Mlyn, 1998], 284–97) has pointed out that in 1 Thess 1–3, Paul seems to be using a story line that has three elements to it: rejection, imitation, and glory. Compare David deSilva's sociorhetorical study of honor discourse in 1 Thessalonians, in which he refers to "the group's counter-definitions of reality (including its evaluation of outsiders)" ("'Worthy of His Honor': Honor Discourse and Social Engineering in 1 Thessalonians," *JSNT* 64 [1996]: 57). Throughout the study deSilva refers to Paul's concern for group maintenance, using honor/shame discourse, by defining group boundaries, one of the points FTA also identifies.

[27] "Arguing Like an Apocalypse," 436.

It is important to distinguish between the two levels of dramatizing messages in this letter: earlier messages that have been accepted by the group and incorporated into their consciousness; and new messages intended to trigger new chaining important to sustaining the rhetorical vision of the group free of novel distortions. There are at least two major insider cues pointing to earlier messages: the repeated reference to things the Thessalonians "know" and the reference to some form of "persecution."

The topic or insider cue of "knowing" is scattered throughout the letter. It functions as a reminder of a dramatizing message in 3:3–4; 4:2; and 5:2.[28] Each of those messages apparently had apocalyptic themes in them: persecution of the faithful; description of righteous behavior necessary to avoid wrath; and eschatological expectation. Furthermore, the knowledge they have had is an "insiders" knowledge; this is made clear by reference to various "outsiders" who have rejected it, oppose it, or act unrighteously (2:14, 18; 4:5, 12, 13; 5:6, 15).

The new dramatizing message includes the assurance that Paul had been deeply concerned for them during his enforced separation from them because he recognized that there was more they needed to know in order to be ready for the return of the Lord Jesus (2:18–3:10). This new knowledge includes apocalyptic teaching, based on divine inspiration—"a word of the Lord"—concerning the *parousia* and the resurrection of the believers who have died (4:13–18). The reference to grief over the implied death of at least one member of the congregation suggests that the original message and its underlying rhetorical vision had failed to sustain them in the face of death. An insider cue to the old message of resurrection is used in 4:14, but the larger drama of the resurrection is elaborated by the apocalyptic images described in 4:16–17. Those who have died in Christ will be resurrected at the same time as the *parousia* and accompany the remaining members of the group to meet the Lord in the air. That Paul expects this message to be chained out into the group consciousness is indicated by his exhortation to them to "encourage one another" (παρακαλεῖτε ἀλλήλους, 4:18) with this new knowledge and to share the letter with others in the Christian community (5:27). Furthermore, the pragmatic result of this new knowledge is a state of readiness for the return of the Lord, an old message that is chained out in 5:2–10.

The narrative of Paul's work among them, which was carried out in the midst of persecution (1:6), presumably of Paul, and the reference to persecution of the Thessalonians themselves (2:14), is meant to remind the Thessalonians of the fantasy theme of imitation of the faithful, both Paul

---

[28] In every instance where it refers to the Thessalonians and knowledge they have, οἴδατε is an "aorist perfect."

and believers in Judea. The fact that an earlier message had produced this theme can be found in Paul's report that the Thessalonians turned from idols and became a model for believers in Macedonia and Achaia. John Barclay has reviewed the role that persecution played in creating what he calls "apocalyptic excitement" in Thessalonica and points out that the symbolic world created by this excitement is "markedly dualistic," including the "social dualism of 'insiders' and 'outsiders.'"[29] Barclay goes on to argue that this excitement enhanced a sense of social alienation from the larger community and thus reinforced an "us versus them" view of their social world. This social dislocation contributed to a dualistic, apocalyptic worldview in which "insiders" stood against "outsiders" waiting for future vindication and destruction of the unrighteous.

The new dramatizing message elaborates Paul's insider persona. There is an implied reference to his apostolic persona, his more public persona (2:4, 7), but he is careful to remind the Thessalonians that his "public" face, which could invite comparison with others (2:5–6), is different from their experience of his work while he was with them. It is the private, insider Paul, the loving father (2:11), they should remember and imitate. The nature of that imitation is elaborated in 4:9–12. Although he does not say so explicitly in this letter, it is clear from other letters that Paul thought of himself as God-taught (e.g., Gal 1:1–2, 11–12; Rom 1:1–6). He now identifies them as taught by God to love one another (4:9). They have done so (4:10) and can continue to do so by imitating the insider persona of Paul. But he also implies that they have to modify, or at least be more attentive to, their public persona. They need to live quietly, minding their own business and avoiding confrontation with outsiders (4:11–12). Again, the pragmatic result of this new message is sanctification, a state of purity that will make them able to participate in the resurrection (5:23). Thus imitation of the faithful is portrayed as eschatological behavior.

Now to look more directly at the apocalyptic discourse in the letter, for it is by the use of that type of argumentation that Paul seeks to sustain the consciousness of the group, I see the following as the major sections of apocalyptic discourse: 1:4–10; 2:17–20; 3:12–13; 4:13–17; 5:1–10, 23.[30] Although claims of inspiration are not as explicit here as they are, for example, in the Galatian letter, references to the gospel coming to the Thessalonians "in power and in the Holy Spirit" (1:5) and to the fact that the Thessalonians have been "taught by God " (4:9) imply some form of inspiration having been experienced by members of the community. Paul

---

[29] "Conflict in Thessalonica," *CBQ* 55 (1993): 517.

[30] Translations of the Old Testament, Old Testament Apocrypha, and the New Testament are taken from the NRSV.

himself claims inspiration indirectly by his reminding the Thessalonians that he seeks to please God, not people, and that he speaks the word of the Lord (4:15). He also claims warrant for his authority from God (4:8).

Whether or not one could argue that there is evidence of a "divine revelation" against unrighteousness manifest in the argument in the letter, clearly such teaching occurs. Reference to "the coming wrath" (1:10) and the function of the Lord as an "avenger" (4:6) imply an earlier dramatizing message against unrighteousness. These references are complemented by the message to reject unrighteous behavior, including the need for "holiness" and to remain "blameless" before God at the coming of the Lord (3:13; 5:23), the need to be protected in the struggle against "darkness" (5:8), and the need to abstain from evil (5:22).

Pragmatic discourse (4:3–6a, 9–12; 5:11–22) is interwoven with apocalyptic discourse in those sections outlining an expectation of righteous activity. The whole argumentative unit, 4:2–5:23, has been called the *probatio* by some rhetorical critics.[31] It is typical to identify it as the paranetic section of the letter.[32] However one identifies the unit as a whole, discursively it functions in part to detail the content of righteous behavior and point toward the consequences of failure to behave righteously.[33] It is within this unit that Paul seems to make his most direct argument for the consequences of ignoring his rhetorical vision: rejection of God (4:8); exposure to the wrath of God (4:6; 5:9); and the collapse of insider ethics (4:10b–12; 5:12–22).

Now let us look at some of the important details of the argumentation. The argument beginning in 1:4 is the second element in "case-result" form of argumentation. It is the case that Paul gives thanks for Thessalonians, with the result that he (1) remembers them (μνημονεύοντες ὑμῶν) before God and (2) knows (εἰδότες) that they are the elect of God. This knowledge is confirmed by their behavior in receiving the Spirit and becoming imitators of Paul, with the result that their faith is known throughout Macedonia and Achaia. Among the things reported about them is their hospitality,

---

[31] Charles Wanamaker, *The Epistles to the Thessalonians* (NIGTC; Grand Rapids: Eerdmans, 1990), 146–204; Watson, "Paul's Appropriation of Apocalyptic Discourse," 72–78.

[32] F. F. Bruce, *1 and 2 Thessalonians* (WBC 45; Waco, Tex.: Word, 1982), 770.

[33] I have identified the epistolary framework of the letter in an earlier essay ("The Invention of 1 Thessalonians: A Proposal," in *Rhetoric, Theology and Scripture* [ed. Stanley Porter and Tom Olbricht; JSNTSup 131; Sheffield: Sheffield Academic Press, 1996], 275–76]. I have defined the argumentative units as 1:2–10; 2:1–3:13; 4:1–5:10; and 5:11–25 ("Speaker, Audience and Situations: A Modified Interactional Model," *Neot* 32 [1998]: 260–67).

their conversion from paganism, and their expectation of the *parousia*. These three things are cited as expressions of their faith, and all three will be the topic of elaboration in chapters 4 and 5. The presence of these topics in 1:2–10, as has been pointed out frequently before, is characteristic of the function of the thanksgiving period of the letter, and the whole section is epistolary discourse.

However, 1:9–10 introduces topics associated with apocalyptic discourse and is part of the topography of the argument laid out first in 1:3. Karl Donfried has argued that the reference in 1:9 to "turning from idols" may refer to abandoning such cults as those of Dionysius and Cabrius, as well as the imperial cult of Caesar.[34] A direct reference to idol worship is part of the cultural intertexture of the argument, but it also has elements of a historical intertexture and might have reminded some hearers of the Maccabean period. In any case, as Barclay makes clear, such action would have caused considerable problems for believers, including the possible charge of treason and antisocial behavior.[35] Such a radical turning away from the world and its political and religious institutions would be characteristic of a group who thought themselves to be already living in the end time. That perspective is enforced by the reference to the expectation of the *parousia* and attendant events in 1:10.

There are two apocalyptic insider cues in this verse: the Son from heaven (τὸν υἱὸν αὐτοῦ ἐκ τῶν οὐρανῶν) and the coming wrath (ὀργῆς τῆς ἐρχομένης). Although Paul uses the phrase "his son" eight other times (Rom 1:3, 9; 5:10; 8:29; 1 Cor 1:9; Gal 1:16; 4:4, 6), this is the only occurrence in an eschatological context. Charles Wanamaker suggests that the phrase "from heaven" is added both to indicate the place of the Lord's present rule and to remind the Thessalonians of Paul's earlier mission proclamation that promised "the return of Jesus from heaven to complete the eschatological beliefs begun with the resurrection."[36] From my point of view the insider cue of "his Son" is recontextualized with the addition of "from heaven" to elaborate an earlier dramatizing message of the resurrection—thus the reason for the insertion of the stylistically clumsy "whom he raised from the dead" (1:10b)—and adds to the texture of Paul's rhetorical vision.

The noun ὀργή is used in the undisputed Pauline literature only in 1 Thessalonians and Romans. From the point of view of SCT, it is possible to argue that 1:10 is chained out by Paul in Rom 2 and 3. There we find a

---

[34] "The Cults of Thessalonica and the Thessalonian Correspondence," *NTS* 31 (1985): 338–47.

[35] "Conflict in Thessalonica," 514–18.

[36] *Epistles to the Thessalonians,* 87.

much more elaborate description of the same kind of teaching found in 1 Thess 1 and 5. Therefore, we might be able to reason that Paul had, from a very early time in his preaching, been consistent in teaching that unrighteous behavior led to exposure to the wrath of God, while righteousness, both as a product of belief and a way of life, protected the believer from that wrath of God. However, the addition of the qualifying phrase τῆς ἐρχομένης distinguishes between "wrath" as the operation of God's judgment against the unrighteous within history and makes it clear that Paul is referring to the final judgment that will occur at the time of the *parousia*. The distinction can be seen by Paul's reference to "wrath" in 2:16.

The discourses in 2:17–20; 3:12–13; and 5:23 refer to the status of believers at the coming of the Lord Jesus (Christ). In 2:19–20, the "believer" is Paul who seems to see the righteous behavior of the Thessalonians as evidence for the success of his mission and, therefore, as eschatologically significant for him. This view of converts functioning as *apologia pro vita sua* can be seen in other places in his letters (Rom 1:13; 1 Cor 9:2; Phil 4:1). Here, as in Galatians 2:2, he expresses concern that something or someone, in the case of the Thessalonians, the Tempter (ὁ πειράζων), had caused his work to be "in vain" (εἰς κένον) (3:5).[37] However, the apocalyptic nature of the argument suggests that Paul reconfigured the figure of Satan or the Tempter, whose typical work of hindering the operation of the will of God in the course of history now has cosmic consequences. The implication for cooperating with the work of Satan is that believers who do so will not be holy and blameless at the time of the *parousia* (3:12–13; 5:23).

The teaching in 4:13–17 is the only new information conveyed in the entire letter.[38] Old dramatizing messages have been elaborated or reconfigured, but this material is not only identified as new (4:13) but seems to fit the category of teaching mentioned in 3:10, providing something they were lacking in their faith. Alan Segal makes the claim that in this passage Paul "forever alters" the quality of apocalyptic prophecies of the resurrection.[39] Resurrection is the fate not only of Jesus but also of those who have died in Christ. Their resurrection will occur shortly after the *parousia* (4:16), which is described here as an "explicit second coming bodily to earth from heaven on clouds of glory."[40]

---

37 Bruce, *1 and 2 Thessalonians*, 56.

38 Contra Longenecker, who characterizes 4:13–5:11 as "almost tacked on as afterthoughts, written in view of further concerns for those at Thessalonica" ("The Nature of Paul's Early Eschatology," *NTS* 31 [1985]: 88).

39 "Paul's Thinking about Resurrection in Its Jewish Context," *NTS* 44 (1998): 401.

40 C. L. Mearns, "Early Eschatological Development in Paul: The Evidence of I and II Thessalonians," *NTS* 27 (1981): 144.

The analogies for basic elements of the passage can be found in older apocalyptic texts such as Dan 12:1–3.[41] There the "wise" who are "asleep" shall "awake" and receive "everlasting life." But the teaching about resurrection is reconfigured here by the word of the Lord (ἐν λόγῳ κυρίου, 4:15). The fantasy theme of resurrection, which Paul undoubtedly preached while he was in Thessalonica,[42] is chained out by a new dramatizing message that describes the fate of all believers at the time of the *parousia*.[43] Paul moves beyond Old Testament and Jewish apocalyptic teaching about the living being assumed into heaven and consoles the Thessalonians with a new message that those who have died in Christ will also be part of the assumption that occurs at the *parousia*.[44] Paul needs to extend the trajectory of resurrection from Jesus, to those who have died in Christ, to those who are alive at his coming. In light of this new understanding of the function of resurrection—not judgment but vindication and transition into glory—it is possible to argue that Paul's resurrection theology is grounded in apocalypticism[45]

Although the assertion in 5:1–2 makes it appear that the Thessalonians knew about the Day of the Lord, an insider cue that must have been part of an earlier dramatizing message, it also appears that the Thessalonians had not understood Paul's earlier teaching and may have chained out the fantasy to teach that that Day had already come. Perhaps the Thessalonians had understood Paul to say that Jesus' appearance as Lord to him and the other apostles constituted the substance of the Day of the Lord and that the *parousia* would be the time of vindication of the righteous. Paul has to reconstruct the temporal relations between these two events while maintaining their distinctiveness and to argue for balance and perspective in interpreting experiences influencing the Thessalonians' social and political world. It may well be that at the time Paul wrote this letter, he expected

---

[41] William Baird ("Pauline Eschatology in Hermeneutical Perspective," *NTS* 7 [1971]: 324) points out that images in 1 Thess 4:16–17 find parallels in Mic 1:3; *4 Ezra* 4:36; 6:23; and *2 En.* 3:1.

[42] John Gillman, "Signals of Transformation in 1 Thessalonians 4:13–18," *CBQ* 47 (1985): 270–71.

[43] Wolfgang Weifel ("Die Hauptrichtung des Wandels im eschatalogischen Denken des Paulus," *TZ* 30 [1974]: 69–70) notes that in this passage Paul does not address the fate of all the dead, unrighteous as well as righteous, as in the case, for example, in Dan 12, but answers only the question of the fate of those who have died in Christ.

[44] Wanamaker, *Epistles to the Thessalonians,* 165–66.

[45] Segal, "Paul's Thinking about Resurrection," 402–5; cf. Longenecker, "The Nature of Paul's Eschatology," 89.

that the *parousia* would occur in his lifetime (4:17),[46] but he had also to make clear that the Day of the Lord had not occurred and in fact may be imminent (5:6). Again, this apocalyptic teaching gives imperative to morality. The future defines the pragmatic present.

Argumentatively 5:1–10 serves to dramatize the responsibility of those who are "awake" and waiting for the return of the Lord. The metaphors Paul uses to do so shift during the course of the argument. The initial metaphor is one containing the elements of surprise or even stealth, the activity of a "thief in the night." That image is elaborated to include loss of peace and security. At 5:4 the metaphor has to do with the location or condition of believers. They are not in darkness but are children of the light. This state of being is characterized as one of sobriety, wakefulness, and preparedness.

The use of the hortatory subjunctive in 5:6 and 8 follows on the declaration in 5:5b that the righteous are "not of the night or of darkness." The switch in the pronominal in 5:5b is significant. Paul's use of the insider cue of "children of light"[47] in 5:5a is elaborated by inclusion of himself with the Thessalonians, "*we* are not. . . . " This reinforces the theme of imitation and implies that the Thessalonians somehow share Paul's insider persona. It reinforces the idea that Paul is in solidarity with them despite his absence from them. He is part of their social world, sharing their dislocation and the consequent persecution and sharing their need to be vigilant!

The use of the insider cue word "wrath" in 5:9 recontextualizes the metaphors of "light," "night," "day," and "darkness." The original context was righteous behavior in daily life. That seems clear from the paranetic instruction in 4:3–12. The new context is the Day of the Lord. Children of the light are ready for the Day. Righteousness is an eschatological condition. As such it is now possible to understand that death does not affect the status of being children of light. Even when believers are "asleep," they live with the Lord (5:10).

The recontextualization of the metaphors in 5:4–10 also serves to chain out paranetic aspects of the fantasy theme of escape from the coming wrath. John Collins has noted that apocalypses do have analogies to wisdom

---

[46] Wanamaker, *Epistles to the Thessalonians,* 172–73.

[47] The metaphor of "light" as the estate of the believer is part of Pauline theology (2 Cor 6:14). Compare Rom 13:12: "Let us then lay aside the works of darkness and put on the armor of light." This condition is directly related to the revelation of Christ in the present (2 Cor 4:4–6), who will bring further illumination at his *parousia* (1 Cor 4:5). Compare 1QM, *The War of the Sons of Light against the Sons of Darkness,* where the battle is conducted by the righteous, whereas in Paul the armor of the righteous protects them against the coming wrath!

literature in that both can treat the subject of divine justice and that a writing such as *2 Enoch* can contain "apocalyptic wisdom" because it "shares with the Jewish wisdom tradition the conviction that right conduct depends on right understanding," while teaching that the source of understanding transcends human understanding and proverbial wisdom and comes from revelation.[48] In the body of the letter (2:1–3:13) Paul had made it clear that the Thessalonians knew that the source of his teaching was from God (1:4–5; 2:4, 13) and that God was also the source of support for living a blameless life (3:13). In his paranetic teaching in chapters 4 and 5, Paul goes on to make it clear that right conduct is a precondition to escape and vindication (e.g., 4:6–7; 5:23). His teaching in these chapters can be summarized by a phrase found in the opening greeting of Romans, "obedience of faith" (Rom 1:5), which in this context must be understood as "apocalyptic wisdom."

3. Examples of Apocalyptic Intertexture in 1 Thessalonians in Relation to SCT and FTA

In his description of the components of sociorhetorical criticism, Vernon Robbins defines intertexture as "the relation of data in the text to various kinds of phenomena outside the text."[49] He identifies four types of intertexture: oral-scribal, historical, social, and cultural. For the purposes of this essay, I want to focus on just one of these: oral-scribal. I recognize that at least one other category of intertexture could be discussed, that of "cultural intertexture." However, that would lead me into a much larger project than I want to undertake here.

Robbins subdivides oral-scribal texture into three kinds: recitation, recontextualization, and reconfiguration. Recitation is the "presentation of speech or narrative or both, either from oral or written tradition, in words identical to or different from those the person has received."[50] Recontextualization uses wording from texts without citing their use elsewhere.[51] Reconfiguration restructures an earlier tradition; it depicts an earlier situation in such a way as to make that situation seem new.[52]

---

[48] *The Apocalyptic Imagination: An Introduction to the Jewish Matrix of Christianity* (New York: Crossroad, 1987), 17, 197.

[49] *The Tapestry of Early Christian Discourse: Rhetoric, Society and Ideology* (New York: Routledge, 1996), 96.

[50] Ibid., 103.

[51] Ibid., 107.

[52] Vernon Robbins, *Exploring the Texture of Texts: A Guide to Socio-Rhetorical Criticism* (Valley Forge, Pa.: Trinity Press International, 1996), 50.

Each of these terms could be used to describe communication processes identified in SCT. All three can occur in fantasy sharing as the community refers to earlier expressions of fantasy themes and types that have been central to their self-understanding. Recontextualization of themes and types could occur when the community is going through consciousness raising, and reconfiguration when the community is engaged in consciousness sustaining while adapting a master analog or rhetorical vision to changed circumstances.

The implication of my argument above is that the intertextural features of apocalyptic discourse in the Thessalonian correspondence are due to fantasy sharing and fantasy chaining done by Paul within the argumentative situation shared by Paul and the Thessalonians. Obviously apocalyptic *topoi* had been generated within Palestinian and Hellenistic Jewish communities and had been influenced by religious and historical developments in the centuries before the emergence of Christianity. However, these *topoi* are given new meaning in the letter from the dynamic of the view of social reality that was shaped by the rhetorical vision of Paul and the Thessalonians.

In the sections that follow, I have selected pieces of apocalyptic discourse found in 1 Thessalonians and representative texts from prophetic and intertestamental literature typically cited by commentators and interpreters as possible sources for the concepts and/or language used by Paul in the letter. I comment on each section, pointing out fantasy themes and types that might have been used by Paul in chaining out his paideia for the Thessalonians.

3.1. 1 Thessalonians 1:8–10; 2:13–16; *Testament of Levi* 6:5–11; and 2 Maccabees 6:1–17

(8) For the word of the Lord has sounded forth from you not only in Macedonia and Achaia, but in every place your faith in God has become known, so that we have no need to speak about it. (9) For the people of those regions report about us what kind of welcome we had among you, and how you turned to God from idols, to serve a living and true God, (10) and to wait for his Son from heaven, whom he raised from the dead— Jesus, who rescues us from the wrath that is coming. (1 Thess 1:8–10)

(13) We also constantly give thanks to God for this, that when you received the word of God that you heard from us, you accepted it not as a human word but as what it really is, God's word, which is also at work in you believers. (14) For you, brothers and sisters, became imitators of the churches of God in Christ Jesus that are in Judea, for you suffered the same things from your own compatriots as they did from the Jews, (15) who killed both the Lord Jesus and the prophets, and drove us out; they displease God and oppose everyone (16) by hindering us from speaking to the Gentiles so that they may be saved. Thus

they have constantly been filling up the measure of their sins; but God's wrath has overtaken them at last. (1 Thess 2:13–16)

(6) When my father heard of this he was angry and sorrowful, because they had received circumcision and died, and so he passed us by in his blessings. (7) Thus we sinned in doing this contrary to his opinion, and he became sick that very day. (8) But I saw that God's sentence was "Guilty," because they had wanted to do the same thing to Sarah and Rebecca that they did to Dinah, our sister. But the Lord prevented them. (9) They persecuted Abraham when he was a nomad, and they harassed his flocks when they were pregnant, and they grossly mistreated Eblaen, who had been born in this house. (10) This is how they treated the nomadic people, seizing their wives and murdering them. (11) But the wrath of God ultimately came upon them. (*T. Levi* 6:5–11)[53]

First Thessalonians 1:8–10 is part of the thanksgiving of the letter. As such, it contains one of the topics of the letter: hope. Hope is also a fantasy type within the rhetorical vision of the letter. The language in 1:10 anticipates the apocalyptic discourse found in 4:13–18 and 5:1–10.

The fantasy theme, the "wrath that is coming" (1:10), is a theme that has been recontextualized from examples found in the prophetic and intertestamental literature. In Paul's rhetorical vision God's wrath is reserved for the unrighteous and will be experienced by them at the *parousia*. It is not that which can enter the experience of the faithful in the course of history; they may experience persecution in everyday circumstances but not God's wrath. Thus 1:10 is clearly apocalyptic in concept.

First Thessalonians 2:16 seems to be a recitation of *T. Levi* 6:11. It is also recontextualized to refer to the unrighteous persecutors of the Thessalonians. The theme is an expression of God's attitude toward unrighteousness and unbelief. "God's wrath" here, as can be seen in analyzing *T. Levi* 6:11, does not lie in the future but is an expression of God's nature and a response to unrighteousness expressed in everyday life.

The distinction between the "wrath that is coming" (1:10) and "God's wrath" (2:16) is important because God's wrath as part of God's nature would seem to be beyond considerations of time, while the expression of the "coming" wrath is very much an issue of time. Thus 1:10 is apocalyptic teaching, but 2:16 is not, if εἰς τέλος in 2:16 has no eschatological significance. That it does not seems to be born out by the intertexturality of 2:16. *Testament of Levi* 6:11 follows on a story of the destruction of the unrighteous, a sign that God's wrath had been manifest in that destruction, which had been carried out by Levi and others. Thus "God's wrath," in the

---

[53] Quotation is from the *OTP* 1:790.

form of action taken by Levi and his brothers as the self-appointed agents of God, had indeed come upon Shechem "completely," "utterly," or "in full" rather than "at the end."

Another point: some interpreters have argued that the reference to the wrath of God having overtaken the Jews "completely" in 2:16 must refer to the destruction of Jerusalem in 70 c.e. and conclude, therefore, that 2:13–16 is an interpolation. However, given that the fantasy theme of God's wrath as a form of punishment for the sins of the unrighteous is found so widely in Hebrew scripture and Jewish writings of the intertestamental period, it is not necessary to seek a historical reference for the phrase. It is simply a topic in the argumentation of the letter.

Another passage bearing on our discussion is 2 Macc 6:1–17. This passage narrates the attempt by Jason to hellenize temple practices in Jerusalem during the reign of Antiochus IV Epiphanes (175–164 b.c.e.). It is part of the larger dramatizing message of 2 Maccabees, which tries to interpret the crises produced in Palestine by the actions of the Seleucid Empire as foundation for the work of Judas Maccabeus and the Jewish Festival of Hanukkah, thus making sense of the period of persecution as preparation for the defeat of the enemies of God's people.

(1) Not long after this, the king sent an Athenian senator to compel the Jews to forsake the laws of their ancestors and no longer to live by the laws of God; (2) also to pollute the temple in Jerusalem and to call it the temple of Olympian Zeus, and to call the one in Gerizim the temple of Zeus-the-friend-of-strangers, as did the people who lived in that place.

(3) Harsh and utterly grievous was the onslaught of evil. (4) For the temple was filled with debauchery and reveling by the Gentiles, who dallied with prostitutes and had intercourse with women within the sacred precincts, and besides brought in things for sacrifice that were unfit. (5) The altar was covered with abominable offerings that were forbidden by the laws. (6) People could neither keep the sabbath, nor observe the festivals of their ancestors, nor so much as confess themselves to be Jews.

(7) On the monthly celebration of the king's birthday, the Jews were taken, under bitter constraint, to partake of the sacrifices; and when a festival of Dionysus was celebrated, they were compelled to wear wreathes of ivy and to walk in the procession in honor of Dionysus.

(8) At the suggestion of the people of Ptolemais a decree was issued to the neighboring Greek cities that they should adopt the same policy toward the Jews and make them partake of the sacrifices, (9) and should kill those who did not choose to change over to Greek customs. One could see, therefore, the misery that had come upon them. (10) For example, two women were brought in for having circumcised their children. They publicly paraded them around the city, with their babies hanging at their breasts, and then hurled them down headlong from the wall. (11) Others who had assembled in the caves nearby, in order to observe the

seventh day secretly, were betrayed to Philip and were all burned together, because their piety kept them from defending themselves, in view of their regard for that most holy day.

(12) Now I urge those who read this book not to be depressed by such calamities, but to recognize that these punishments were designed not to destroy but to discipline our people. (13) In fact, it is a sign of great kindness not to let the impious alone for long, but to punish them immediately. (14) For in the case of the other nations the Lord waits patiently to punish them until they have reached the full measure of their sins; but he does not deal in this way with us, (15) in order that he may not take vengeance on us afterward when our sins have reached their height. (16) Therefore he never withdraws his mercy from us. Although he disciplines us with calamities, he does not forsake his own people. (17) Let what we have said serve as a reminder; we must go on briefly with the story. (2 Macc 6:1–17)

The narrative discourse of 6:1–11 reflects a time when "Jews" were persecuting their countrymen; thus it is referred to by commentators as providing background for 1 Thess 2:13–16. Where there are no distinctly apocalyptic themes in 2 Macc 6:1–17, in sociorhetorical terms it is possible to understand this narrative as having been reconfigured and recontextualized for the purpose of the argument in 2:13–16. The exhortatory discourse of 2 Macc 6:12–17 contains moral instruction and elaborates the fantasy theme of God's vengeance on the unrighteous (6:14–15), which will be visited upon unrighteous Jews and Greeks alike. The difference here is that God punishes the sins of God's people during the course of experience (6:14b–15), while those of the "other nations" God punishes when their sins have reached their extreme. The passages illustrate the different concepts of God's wrath found in 1 Thess 1:10 and 2:16.

3.2. 1 Thessalonians 4:16–17; Micah 1:3–4; and *4 Ezra* 6:23

(16) For the Lord himself, with a cry of command, with the archangel's call and with the sound of God's trumpet, will descend from heaven, and the dead in Christ will rise first. (17) Then we who are alive, who are left, will be caught up in the clouds together with them to meet the Lord in the air; and so we will be with the Lord forever. (1 Thess 4:16–17)

(3) For lo, the LORD is coming out of his place, and will come down and tread upon the high places of the earth. (4) Then the mountains will melt under him and the valleys will burst open, like wax near the fire, like waters poured down a steep place. (Mic 1:3–4)

And the trumpet shall sound aloud, at which all men, when they hear it, shall be struck with sudden fear. (*4 Ezra* 6:23)

Throughout the Old Testament the trumpet is referred to as an instrument of warning and in particular as a signal of the coming of an enemy or a call to battle. In at least two places in the prophetic literature, Isa 27:13 and Joel 2:1, the trumpet is associated with the presence of the Day of the Lord. In Zech 9:14, God uses the trumpet to signal God's arrival as divine warrior.

In 1 Thess 4:16–17 Paul recontextualizes the image of God as divine warrior, both as to character and context. The reference to the Lord in 4:16 presupposes 1:10 and its reference to the Son from heaven. It is he, not God, who issues the command to protect the righteous; he is the divine warrior. The context is now the *parousia* of the Son from heaven, which will result in the resurrection and glorification of the righteous. That is the new significance of the Day of the Lord. It is interesting to note that, unlike most apocalyptists, nowhere in the letter does Paul engage in a description of the fate of the unrighteous. They are subject to the wrath of God and faithful believers are not. That is his apocalyptic message to the Thessalonians.

3.3. 1 Thessalonians 5:1–10; Joel 2:30–32; Amos 5:18–20; Zephaniah 1:14–18; Malachi 4:1–5; Daniel 12:1–4; Isaiah 59:15b–20; and Wisdom of Solomon 5:15–23

(1) Now concerning the times and the seasons, brothers and sisters, you do not need to have anything written to you. (2) For you yourselves know very well that the day of the Lord will come like a thief in the night. (3) When they say, "There is peace and security,"[54] then sudden destruction will come upon them, as labor pains come upon a pregnant woman, and there will be no escape! (4) But you, beloved, are not in darkness, for that day to surprise you like a thief; (5) for you are all children of light and children of the day; we are not of the night or of darkness. (6) So then let us not fall asleep as others do, but let us keep awake and be sober; (7) for those who sleep sleep at night, and those who are drunk get drunk at night. (8) But since we belong to the day, let us be sober, and put on the breastplate of faith and love, and for a helmet the hope of salvation. (9) For God has destined us not for wrath but for obtaining salvation through our Lord Jesus Christ, (10) who died for us, so that whether we are awake or asleep we may live with him. (1 Thess 5:1–10)

(30) I will show portents in the heavens and on the earth, blood and fire and columns of smoke. (31) The sun shall be turned to darkness, and the

---

[54] Commentators also point out that the statement "There is peace and security" may refer to Roman propaganda claims to social stability under Roman rule. The claim is ironic given the Thessalonians' experience of persecution.

moon to blood, before the great and terrible day of the LORD comes. (32) Then everyone who calls on the name of the LORD shall be saved; for in Mount Zion and in Jerusalem there shall be those who escape, as the LORD has said, and among the survivors shall be those whom the LORD calls. (Joel 2:30–32)

(18) Alas for you who desire the day of the LORD! Why do you want the day of the LORD? It is darkness, not light; (19) as if someone fled from a lion, and was met by a bear; or went into the house and rested a hand against the wall, and was bitten by a snake. (20) Is not the day of the LORD darkness, not light, and gloom with no brightness in it? (Amos 5:18–20)

(14) The great day of the LORD is near, near and hastening fast; the sound of the day of the LORD is bitter, the warrior cries aloud there. (15) That day will be a day of wrath, a day of distress and anguish, a day of ruin and devastation, a day of darkness and gloom, a day of clouds and thick darkness, (16) a day of trumpet blast and battle cry against the fortified cities and against the lofty battlements.

(17) I will bring such distress upon people that they shall walk like the blind; because they have sinned against the LORD, their blood shall be poured out like dust, and their flesh like dung. (18) Neither their silver nor their gold will be able to save them on the day of the LORD's wrath; in the fire of his passion the whole earth shall be consumed; for a full, a terrible end he will make of all the inhabitants of the earth. (Zeph 1:14–18)

(1) See, the day is coming, burning like an oven, when all the arrogant and all evildoers will be stubble; the day that comes shall burn them up, says the LORD of hosts, so that it will leave them neither root nor branch. (2) But for you who revere my name the sun of righteousness shall rise, with healing in its wings. You shall go out leaping like calves from the stall. (3) And you shall tread down the wicked, for they will be ashes under the soles of your feet, on the day when I act, says the LORD of hosts. (4) Remember the teaching of my servant Moses, the statutes and ordinances that I commanded him at Horeb for all Israel. (5) Lo, I will send you the prophet Elijah before the great and terrible day of the LORD comes. (Mal 4:1–5)

(1) At that time Michael, the great prince, the protector of your people, shall arise. There shall be a time of anguish, such as has never occurred since nations first came into existence. But at that time your people shall be delivered, everyone who is found written in the book. (2) Many of those who sleep in the dust of the earth shall awake, some to everlasting life, and some to shame and everlasting contempt. (3) Those who are wise shall shine like the brightness of the sky, and those who lead many to righteousness, like the stars forever and ever. (4) But you, Daniel, keep the words secret and the book sealed until the time of the end. Many shall be running back and forth, and evil shall increase. (Dan 12:1–4)

(15b) The LORD saw it, and it displeased him that there was no justice. (16) He saw that there was no one, and was appalled that there was no one to intervene; so his own arm brought him victory, and his righteousness upheld him. (17) He put on righteousness like a breastplate, and a helmet of salvation on his head; he put on garments of vengeance for clothing, and wrapped himself in fury as in a mantle. (18) According to their deeds, so will he repay; wrath to his adversaries, requital to his enemies; to the coastlands he will render requital. (19) So those in the west shall fear the name of the LORD, and those in the east, his glory; for he will come like a pent-up stream that the wind of the LORD drives on. (20) And he will come to Zion as Redeemer, to those in Jacob who turn from transgression, says the LORD. (Isa 59:15b–20)

(15) But the righteous live forever, and their reward is with the Lord; the Most High takes care of them. (16) Therefore they will receive a glorious crown and a beautiful diadem from the hand of the Lord, because with his right hand he will cover them, and with his arm he will shield them. (17) The Lord will take his zeal as his whole armor, and will arm all creation to repel his enemies; (18) he will put on righteousness as a breastplate, and wear impartial justice as a helmet; (19) he will take holiness as an invincible shield, (20) and sharpen stern wrath for a sword, and creation will join with him to fight against his frenzied foes. (21) Shafts of lightning will fly with true aim, and will leap from the clouds to the target, as from a well-drawn bow, (22) and hailstones full of wrath will be hurled as from a catapult; the water of the sea will rage against them, and rivers will relentlessly overwhelm them; (23) a mighty wind will rise against them, and like a tempest it will winnow them away. Lawlessness will lay waste the whole earth, and evildoing will overturn the thrones of rulers. (Wis 5:15–23)

In these passages there are two fantasy types: the Day of the Lord and the divine warrior. It would appear that the chaining out of these two types by Paul is meant to suggest that the persecution the Thessalonians were experiencing is a precursor to that which will be encountered at the end of time. The future is met in the experience of the faithful.

As noted above, Paul recontextualizes the Day of the Lord teachings in that he sets it within the larger event of the *parousia* and relates it to the end of history. He recites and recontextualizes elements of Dan 12 so that those who "sleep" are nonetheless alive in the Lord and participate in the resurrection at the *parousia*. The apocalyptic force of the image is maintained.

He also reconfigures the concept of the divine warrior. In prophetic and intertestamental literature, God is the divine warrior who dons armor and goes to battle to destroy the unrighteous (e.g., Isa 59 or Wis 5). For Paul spiritual armor is available to the believer and is defensive. In making this change he reflects one of the generic features of an apocalypse: nonviolent resistance in the face of persecution, and consolation and exhortation to remain faithful to the tradition he taught them.[55] He does not tell the Thessalonians to prepare for battle but to protect themselves against the consequences of the Day of the Lord. The imagery is fully apocalyptic.

4. Conclusion

An empirical analysis of the narrative discourse in the letter has led some commentators to portray the situation in Thessalonica as deeply troubled. They had experienced some form of persecution; their founder was unable to visit them and was worried about their response to persecution; one or more of their members had died before the return of the Lord Jesus; their community was having trouble fully enacting moral principles they had been taught. A Fantasy Theme Analysis of the apocalyptic discourse of the letter has shown that the Thessalonians had shared in a rhetorical vision that promised them a glorious future and helped them participate in the larger people of God by giving a value system to share and models to imitate. The drama of the resurrection and the *parousia* changed their understanding of their destiny and provided motivation for holy and blameless living. It also created a new social reality and with it a new understanding of how they were to live in a chosen community and to interact with the nonelect outsider. Paul redefines the preferred location of believers and the believing community in the prevailing social order. He affirms their social reality as that of "insiders" but argues that that does not relieve them of responsible behavior when dealing with the outside world as well. Insider persona entails maintenance of group boundary conditions, observance of group value systems, and a discrete behavior in the outside community. God is the judge of the outsiders, whose wrath is manifest temporally and eschatologically. The morality and destiny of the insider is defined by the future and enacted in the present as they wait for the Day of the Lord. Eschatology becomes the hermeneutic that allows believers to understand history and be confident of their destiny.

Apocalyptic discourse is also used to sustain Paul's rhetorical vision and provide enhanced fantasy themes to help the Thessalonians share in it. His original vision included instruction on the consequences of becoming part of the eschatological people of God. However, the exigence of the death of one or more church members required him to elaborate that vision so that the future could empower morality and not undermine it. That this was important to Paul personally can be seen in 2:18–3:13. James

---

[55] Louis F. Hartmann and Alexander A. Di Lella, *The Book of Daniel* (AB 23; New York: Doubleday, 1978), 71.

Dunn says that 4:13–18 is "the single clearest statement of [Paul's] parousia belief."[56] To that observation it should be added that this passage and his teaching on the Day of the Lord (5:1–10) are bracketed by paranetic material. Apocalyptic teaching is at the heart of ethics; righteousness is the pragmatic expression of apocalypticism. This is the substance of eschatological hope!

Thus despite the troubling aspects of their situation, the Thessalonians had reason for hope and could be motivated to engage in further discourse among themselves about the implications of their shared rhetorical vision. Furthermore, as 5:10–22 demonstrates, hope was the foundation for sustaining not only the inner symbolic of members of the community but also the pragmatic operations of daily communal life.

It is important to note that within the apocalyptic discourse of 1 Thessalonians, fantasy sharing and fantasy chaining recites, recontextualizes, and reconfigures themes and types from texts that might not have been part of earlier apocalyptic discourse. Thus, as has been argued above and has been demonstrated by this very general description of oral-scribal textures in the apocalyptic discourse of 1 Thessalonians, rhetorical criticism of apocalyptic discourse has no inherent need to limit its search for sources used by such discourse to the genre of apocalypse. A rhetorical community, seeking to interpret and communicate the meaning of exigences in its social world, can fashion apocalyptic discourse from a variety of texts and cultural phenomena.

A GLOSSARY FOR SYMBOLIC CONVERGENCE THEORY (SCT) AND
FANTASY THEME ANALYSIS (FTA)

Symbolic Convergence Theory: a general theory of communication that attempts to offer an explanation of the presence of a common consciousness on the part of members of a group. It posits that the sharing of group fantasies and the chaining out of those fantasies are responsible for that consciousness and group cohesiveness. As fantasies are "dramatized," a convergence of symbols on which participants agree occurs, and fantasy themes and fantasy types help the group understand unexpected, confusing, or even chaotic events or experiences. The process of convergence creates social reality for the group until new exigences cause new fantasies and moments of sharing, which in turn produce new group realities. These realities provide the underlying assumptions used by the group in discursive argumentation.

Fantasy Theme Analysis: a method of rhetorical criticism designed to analyze and describe the rhetorical artifacts produced by symbolic

---

[56] *The Theology of Paul the Apostle* (Grand Rapids: Eerdmans, 1998), 299.

convergence, not just in small-group communication but also in social movements, political campaigns, and the like. Analysis focuses on the content of the message and the relationship among message elements.

Dramatizing message (DM): a story that contains a pun, double entendre, personification, figure of speech, analogy, anecdote, allegory, fable, or narrative. The story often deals with past conflict or the potential of future conflict and is thus set in time references of somewhere/sometime rather than the here and now. It is based on some original facts. A DM is the basis for group fantasy sharing. If it is accepted by the group and is chained out in a process of elaboration and other responses, then it becomes a group fantasy. Acceptance may be due to the rhetorical skill of the one conveying the message.

Fantasy: "The creative and imaginative shared interpretation of events that fulfills a group's psychological and rhetorical need to make sense out of its experience and anticipate its future."[57] Fantasies are dramatic reconstructions of past events and experiences that create a social reality for a group and its participants. Fantasy "chains" are created when a group member tells about an experience or event and others who shared in that experience add their view of it until it becomes the experience of the group. Fantasy sharing is a means whereby groups establish identity and set boundary conditions for identifying insiders from outsiders. It is also a way in which group history and traditions are developed, thus enabling the group to think of itself as unique.[58]

Fantasy theme: Themes become part of the group consciousness; are artistic and organized; and are slanted, ordered, and interpretive. As a result, they provide a way for two or more groups of people to explain an event in different ways. An illustration of a FT is, "Illegal immigrants consume more in social services than they contribute in taxes."

Fantasy type: a general scenario that covers several concrete fantasy themes. This scenario may be repeated with similar characters and may take the same form. It can be generalized so that characters become persona who act in predictable fashion. Rhetors simply make use of a familiar type and the audience fills in the particulars. "Fantasy types allow a group to fit new events or experiences into familiar patterns."[59] An example of a fantasy type is "the American dream" or "family values."

Rhetorical vision: a unified construction of themes and types that gives those sharing fantasy types and themes a broader view of things. A rhetorical vision may be indexed by a symbolic cue or key word. A number

---

[57] Bormann, *Small Group Communication,* 104.

[58] Ibid., 115.

[59] Foss, *Rhetorical Criticism,* 292.

of rhetorical visions can be integrated by means of a master analogy.[60] Seven principles apply to all rhetorical visions: novelty, explanatory power, imitation, critical mass, dedication, rededication, and reiteration.[61] It is a rhetorical vision that can attract and help integrate larger groups of people into a common symbolic reality.[62]

Sanctioning agent: "The source which justifies the acceptance and promulgation of a rhetorical drama."[63] Agent can refer to an external source of authority such as God or to a dominant feature of a culture or a moment in history, such as a war or the crucifixion.

FTA ELEMENTS IN 1 THESSALONIANS: A PRELIMINARY TAXONOMY

Overall fantasy type: Eschatological Hope

Fantasy themes:
1. Imitation of faithful and reliable persons or groups: 1:5–6; 2:3–13
2. Persecution experienced by heroes of the faith and by believers who imitate those heroes: 2:1–2, 14–16; 3:1–7
3. Vindication of the pure and holy, which takes place in the form of resurrection of the dead and ascension of all believers to "heaven": 4:2–5:10
4. Escape from coming wrath: 1:10; 5:9, 23

Fantasy types used in apocalyptic teaching: Hope, Divine Warrior, Savior

Rhetorical vision
Present persecution: both Paul and church have suffered it to some degree, and Paul's message is and has been that persecution is the lot of the believer.

Praxis: fantasy has a practical side that has to be expressed if vindication is to be experienced and God's wrath avoided. ("You know what has to be done.")

Future glory: it is the past that guarantees future outcomes; present events and experiences do not. (All you need is more description of the future so that you can make sense of the present.)

---

[60] Ibid., 293.

[61] Bormann, Cragan, and Shields, "Expansion of the Rhetorical Vision Component," 25.

[62] John F. Cragan and Donald C. Shields, *Applied Communication Research: A Dramatistic Approach* (Prospect Heights, Ill.: Waveland, 1981), 6.

[63] Ibid., 7.

Master analog for rhetorical vision: resurrection of the dead/ascension of believers

Goal of rhetorical vision: maintenance of fantasy chain, thereby sustaining group consciousness: 5:11–22

Major insider cue words: holiness, affliction, Lord/Son from heaven, Satan/the Tempter, wrath

The Apocalyptic Intertexture of the Epistle of James

Wesley Hiram Wachob

Our concern in this essay is the apocalyptic intertexture of the Epistle of James.[1] Approaching the letter of James as an instance of written rhetorical discourse, our objective is to discover and scrutinize the ways in which the language in James interacts with apocalyptic phenomena in the world outside James.[2] In no sense is our exploration meant to be exhaustive; it is more of a brief excursion. Thus we shall touch briefly James's use of several topics that are frequently found in apocalyptic literature. Our discussion will be limited to the following items: the trials of faith, justice, judgment, the kingdom of God, the rich and the poor, and the *parousia* of the Lord. The configuration and function of these topics and other related motifs within the thoroughly deliberative discourse of the Epistle of James are what we hope to ascertain and elucidate.

1. Topics: The Parousia *and the Judgment of the Lord*

The *exordium* (1:2–12) and *peroratio* (5:7–20) of the letter feature several apocalyptic topics. Of these, perhaps the most obviously apocalyptic are the *parousia* of the Lord and the judgment of the Lord. The *parousia* is mentioned twice, in successive verses: "the *parousia* of the Lord" (5:7) and "the *parousia* of the Lord is at hand" (5:8). The reference to the judgment immediately follows: "the judge is standing at the doors" (5:9). That these

---

[1] On the intertexture of texts, see Vernon K. Robbins, *Exploring the Texture of Texts: A Guide to Socio-Rhetorical Interpretation* (Valley Forge, Pa.: Trinity Press International, 1996), 40–70. The various other textures of the Epistle of James, its inner texture, social and cultural texture, sacred texture, and ideological texture, are beyond the scope of this inquiry.

[2] My tentative outline of James as a rhetorical discourse is as follows: *inscriptio* (1:1); *exordium* (1:2–12); *narratio* (1:13–27); *argumentatio* (2:1–5:6); and *peroratio* (5:7–20). The letter-*propositio* is 1:12. See W. H. Wachob, "'The Rich in Faith' and 'The Poor in Spirit': The Socio-Rhetorical Function of a Saying of Jesus in the Epistle of James" (Ph.D. diss., Emory University, 1993); and idem, *The Voice of Jesus in the Social Rhetoric of James* (SNTSMS 106; Cambridge: Cambridge University Press, 2000), 1–24, 52–58.

topics occur together in the concluding section of James, which is marked by exhortations to communal solidarity and the patient endurance of suffering in the world, is an important rhetorical and theological fact, to which we shall return.

The Greek noun παρουσία means "presence" (2 Macc 15:21; 3 Macc 3:17; 1 Cor 16:17; Phil 2:12; Josephus, *Ant.* 3.80) or "arrival" (2 Macc 8:12; Jdt 10:18) and was regularly used of the coming of a royal figure (Polybius 18.48.4), a person of rank (1 Cor 16:17; 2 Cor 7:6, 7; 10:10; Phil 1:26), or a deity (Diodorus Siculus 3.65.1). In the New Testament it occurs twenty-five times, and in eleven instances it clearly refers to the eschatological coming of the Lord Jesus Christ (Matt 24:3, 27, 37, 39; 1 Cor 15:23; 1 Thess 2:19; 3:13; 4:15; 5:23; 2 Thess 2:1, 8, 9 ["the *parousia* of the lawless one"]; 2 Pet 1:16; 3:4; and 1 John 2:28). Moreover, the coming of the Lord Jesus is frequently associated with eschatological judgment (e.g., 1 Thess 2:19; 3:13; 5:2, 23; 1 John 2:28; 2 Pet 3:4, 12 ["the *parousia*" of "the Day of God"]; cf. Acts 10:42; Heb 10:25). These facts warrant the conclusion that in the New Testament the term *parousia* is practically a technical reference to the messianic coming of Jesus Christ, and this seems to be way it is used in James.[3]

In the Septuagint the term *parousia* is never associated with the coming of the Lord or with the eschatological judgment (Jdt 10:18; 2 Macc 8:12; 15:21; 3 Macc 3:17). On the other hand, the future judgment is associated with the coming of God (Isa 66:15–16; Zech 14:5; Mal 3:1–2; Pss 50:3; 96:13; 98:9).[4] This association is a well-established tradition in the prophets and is expressed in their proclamation of the "Day of Yнwн" (see Amos 5:18–20; Isa 2:12; 13:6, 9; 22:5; 34:8; Jer 46:10; Ezek 7:19; 13:5; 30:3; Joel 1:15; 2:1, 11, 31; 3:14; Obad 15; Zeph 1:7, 14–18; Zech 14:1; Mal 4:5; Lam 2:22).

"That Day" sometimes appears imminent; at other times it seems more or less remote. But for the prophets, "the Day of the Lord" means "the end of days."[5] This end, however, is not the end of the world; it marks a radi-

---

[3] Martin Dibelius, *James: A Commentary on the Epistle of James* (rev. H. Greeven; trans. M. A. Williams; Hermeneia; Philadelphia: Fortress, 1975), 242; Sophie Laws, *The Epistle of James* (HNTC; San Francisco: Harper & Row, 1980), 208; Luke Timothy Johnson, "Friendship with the World/Friendship with God: A Study of Discipleship in James," in *Discipleship in the New Testament* (ed. Fernando Segovia; Philadelphia: Fortress), 314.

[4] Marius Reiser, *Jesus and Judgment: The Eschatological Proclamation in Its Jewish Context* (Minneapolis: Fortress, 1997), 144–63.

[5] Isa 2:2; Jer 23:20; 30:24; 48:47; 49:39; Ezek 38:16; Hos 3:5; Mic 4:1; Dan 10:14; see Gerhard von Rad, "ἡμέρα," *TDNT* 2:946.

cally new beginning in time.[6] Thus there is nothing "eschatological per se" in "the concepts connected with the Day of Jahweh."[7]

Prior to the exile, the prophets proclaim God's future judgment as one of doom, though there are glimpses of hope and restoration (Amos 5:18–20; 5:4, 6, 14, 15).[8] Toward the end of the exile and in the postexilic period, while "the Day of the Lord" is associated with destruction and salvation, prophetic conceptions of judgment and restoration begin to be marked by an eschatologizing tendency and intensification (Ezek 38–39). Similarly, reflections on the promises of God and conceptions of God's kingship (especially in the Psalms) are colored with notions of a new, radical, decisive turn in history (Isa 40–55; 56–66). In the late postexilic period this eschatologizing tendency leads to conceptions of a future judgment of cosmic and universal dimensions in the proto-apocalyptic traditions (Isa 24–27; Zech 1–8; 9–14; Joel 3). Finally, with the book of Daniel and full-blown apocalyptic conceptions of the world and God, the coming of God for judgment is indeed an eschatological event, the fixed, final, cosmic consummation: history ends and the kingdom of God begins.

In apocalyptic literature there are numerous references to the coming of God for judgment (*1 En.* 1:4, 9; 25:3–4; 37:1; 90:26; 92–105; *Pss. Sol.* 9:9–10; 15:12; *T. Mos.* 10:1–7; *2 En.* 32:1; 42:5; Wis 5:17–22; *Sib. Or.* 5:344–360), and some of them employ the Greek term παρουσία (*T. Jud.* 22:2; *T. Levi* 8:11; in 8:15 παρουσία means "presence").[9] In the *Testament of Abraham* (ca. 100 C.E.), "the judgment and recompense of the world is made through three tribunals" (13:8). Abel, the twelve tribes of Israel, and God are the three judges (13:2–3, 6, 7). The term παρουσία occurs with reference to the judgment by the twelve tribes (13:6) and by God (12:4). Though the judgment scene is "unmistakably Jewish," it is possible that the use of the term παρουσία is the result of Christian revision.[10]

---

[6] J. Lindblom, *Prophecy in Ancient Israel* (Philadelphia: Fortress, 1962), 360–75.

[7] Gerhard von Rad, *Old Testament Theology* (2 vols.; New York: Harper & Row, 1965), 2:124.

[8] See also Hos 4:1; 5:12, 14 (3:1; 11:8–9); Isa 2:12–22 (1:8–9; 2:2–4, 7:3, 10–23; 9:2–7; 10:12; 31:4–5); Mic 3:12 (5:2–6); Zeph 1:2–2:3 (2:9; 3:11–13); Jer 24:15–38 (3:12–13; 24:4–7; 31:31–34).

[9] Moreover, if *T. Levi* 8:15 and *T. Jud.* 22:2 are of Christian origin, this usage may have been created by the Christian community. On the uncertainty of these texts, see Dibelius, *James,* 242–43.

[10] E. P. Sanders, "The Testament of Abraham," *OTP* 1:872–73. On the other hand, Sanders believes that "the term was probably more common in Jewish literature than can now be directly demonstrated" (1:890 n. 13a). See also Albrecht Oepke, "παρουσία, πάρειμι," *TDNT* 5:864.

At this point in our discussion, the conception of the *parousia* of Jesus Christ for the final judgment appears to have its basis in the prophetic conceptions of the Day of the Lord. Moreover, expressions such as "the day of the Lord Jesus Christ" (1 Cor 1:8; 5:5; Phil 1:6, 10; 2:16; 2 Cor 1:14; cf. 1 Thess 5:2; Rom 2:16), "the judgment seat of God" (Rom 14:10) and "the judgment seat of Christ" (1 Cor 5:10), as well as "the *parousia* of the Day of God" (2 Pet 3:12; "the day of the Lord," 3:10) and its intimate connection with the *parousia* of the Lord Jesus Christ for judgment (2 Pet 1:16; 3:4), suggest the idea of the transference of the final judgment by God to Jesus Christ at his *parousia*.[11]

Let us take a closer look at James's use of παρουσία. In Jas 5:7a we have an imperatival sentence: "Be patient, therefore, brothers [and sisters], until the coming of the Lord." Then in 5:8 the phrase "the coming of the Lord" and the exhortation "be patient" are repeated, but now in a statement made more emphatic by the additions of (1) a personal pronoun (ὑμεῖς), (2) an adverb (καί), and (3) an additional exhortation to firm resolve, "establish [στηρίξατε] your hearts," with (4) a motive clause that is marked temporally by a concluding and emphatic adverb (ὅτι ... ἤγγικεν). While there are various texts that exhibit meanings associated with James's statements, comparisons show that his particular employment of these terms is not replicated exactly in any known text.[12] Therefore, in referring to the *parousia* and judgment of the Lord, James does not appear to recite another text; he alludes to well-known cultural topics in early Christianity.

Numerous scholars have raised the question of the identity of "the judge" in verse 9: Is this a reference to God or to Jesus Christ?[13] First of all, James's use of the term κύριος is ambiguous: it occurs fourteen times and is used to identify both God and Jesus Christ.[14] Apart from these ambiguous references to "the Lord" and the two explicit mentions of his name (1:1; 2:1), it is only in possible allusions to some of his sayings that we hear of Jesus (e.g., in 2:5; 5:12).[15] Over against this is the fact that

---

[11] David E. Aune, "Early Christian Eschatology," *ABD* 2:602.

[12] Dibelius, *James,* 242–43.

[13] Ibid., 242; Laws, *James,* 208–9.

[14] James uses κύριος 14x: κύριον—3:9 (of God, the Father); κύριος—4:15 (of God or Jesus Messiah?); 5:11 (of God); 5:15 (of God or Jesus Messiah?); κυρίου 10x—1:7 (of God); 2:1 (of Jesus Messiah); 5:4 (of God); 5:7, 8 (of the *parousia* of the Lord: God or Jesus Messiah?); 5:14 ("in the name of the Lord": God or Jesus Messiah?); without the article: 1:1 (of Jesus Messiah); 4:10 (of God or Jesus Messiah?); 5:10, 11 (of God). See Wachob, *Voice of Jesus,* 68.

[15] See most recently, Wesley H. Wachob and Luke T. Johnson, "The Sayings of Jesus in the Letter of James," in *Authenticating the Words of Jesus* (ed. Bruce Chilton

James's discourse is undeniably theocentric (e.g., θεός ["God"] occurs 16x: Jas 1:1, 5, 13 [2x], 20, 27; 2:5, 19, 23 [2x]; 3:9; 4:4 [2x], 6, 7, 8). Further, in Jas 5:10 and 11 "the Lord" occurs in close association with both "the prophets" and "Job," and in both cases "the Lord" appears to be a reference to God. In close proximity, also, is "the one lawgiver and judge who is able to save and to destroy" (4:12); this, too, is a reference to God. Accordingly, some hold that "the judge standing at the doors" (5:9) is a reference to God,[16] and, based on this conclusion they suggest that "the *parousia* of the Lord" in verses 7 and 8 should be understood as referring to the coming of God for judgment.[17]

However, we have seen that in the New Testament "the *parousia* of the Lord" predominantly refers to the messianic coming of Jesus Christ. Further, the letter-prescript presumes a unity of will and purpose for God and Jesus Christ (1:1), and this unity is subsumed under a reference to "the faith of our Lord Jesus Christ" (2:1), which is then elaborated in terms of Jesus' interpretation of the Torah (= "the royal law") and summarized in the love-command (Lev 19:18).[18] Most scholars have argued, therefore, that "the *parousia* of the Lord" (5:7, 8) is probably a reference to the coming of Jesus Christ, and, given the association of the latter with eschatological judgment, they have concluded that the judge is Jesus Christ. Additional support for this view may be found in noting the terminological agreements between "the judge is standing at the doors" (πρὸ τῶν θυρῶν ἕστηκεν, Jas 5:9) and "Behold, I stand at the door [ἕστηκα ἐπὶ τὴν θύραν] and knock" (Rev 3:20).

In the various strands of apocalyptic literature references to the eschatological judgment by God are juxtaposed to references to judgment by God's agents.[19] For example, we have the archangel Michael (*T. Mos.* 10; cf. 1QM); the Messiah (*Pss. Sol.* 17); the Son of Man (*1 En.* 27–71); Melchizedek (11QMelch); Abel and the twelve tribes of Israel (*T. Ab.* 13). The authors of these texts apparently saw nothing contradictory in this, for

---

and Craig A. Evans; Leiden: Brill, 1999), 430–50. On the possibility of "the righteous one" in Jas 5:6 being an allusion to Jesus, see Richard B. Hays, "'The Righteous One' As Eschatological Deliverer: A Case Study in Paul's Apocalyptic Hermeneutics," in *Apocalyptic and the New Testament: Essays in Honor of J. Louis Martyn* (ed. Joel Marcus and Marion L. Soards; JSNTSup 24; Sheffield: JSOT Press, 1989), 191–215.

[16] Jean C. Cantinat, *Les Épitres de Saint Jacques et de Saint Jude* (SB; Paris: Gabalda, 1973), 232.

[17] Wilhelm Bousset, *Kyrios Christos* (trans. John E. Steely; Nashville: Abingdon, 1970), 291.

[18] See Wachob, *Voice of Jesus*, 117–22.

[19] Reiser, *Jesus and Judgment*, 86.

no effort is made to reconcile these ideas. It seems that in the New Testament we have a similar phenomenon (Acts 17:31). As already noted, Paul speaks of both God and Christ as judge of the world (1 Thess 2:19; 1 Cor 4:5; Rom 14:10; 2 Cor 5:10). Then there are references to Christ's reign rather than God's reign (Col 1:13; 2 Tim 4:1, 18; 2 Pet 1:11; cf. 1 Cor 15:24); in Eph 5:5 they are simply combined: "in the kingdom of Christ and of God."[20]

In summary, it is probable that Jas 5:7 and 8 refer to the *parousia* of the Lord Jesus Christ. It is also likely that the judge in Jas 5:9 is Jesus, but of this I am not certain. From the context, I am inclined to think this a reference to God. This coheres with the use of the terms in James, as well as with the practice of juxtaposing God and God's representatives in references to eschatological judgment. Sophie Laws, in my opinion, is correct in saying that, "the phrase *the judge at the doors* would not seem to have the established christological connection that *parousia* has," and in view of Jas 4:12, "it is probable that his [James's] reminder here [5:9] is of the coming judgment of God. (There is, of course, no scope for a definition of the relation between the coming of Christ and the judgment of God; all that can be said is that both are elements in James' eschatological expectation)." In any case, James's use of the topics of the *parousia* of the Lord and the judgment of the Lord are readily understood within an oral-scribal culture as allusions to well-known cultural topics among early Christians.[21]

There are numerous other references to the topic of judgment in James, and we shall have opportunity to touch several of them as we look at other apocalyptic topics in the text. At this point, however, we need to remember that, from a rhetorical perspective, the topic of "judgment" is but one aspect of the much larger topic of "justice" (*Rhet. Her.* 2.3.4). And both of the latter are typically regarded as subtopics of "honor" (Cicero, *Inv.* 2.53.160). This is fundamentally important in James's reference to Jesus as "our *glorious* Lord Jesus Christ" (2:1).

2. Topic: Justice

In the New Testament the term δόξα ("glory") is always related to the basic idea of "honor," "value," and "reputation"; thus it refers to the splendor of kings and kingdoms (Luke 4:6 par. Matt 4:8; Luke 12:27 par. Matt 6:29; Rev 21:24, 26), throne motifs (Matt 19:28; 25:31, 34), and is appropriate to the heavenly-divine sphere (Acts 7:55).[22] Sometimes it is simply

---

[20] Rudolf Bultmann, *Theology of the New Testament* (trans. K. Grobel; 2 vols. New York: Scribner's, 1951–55), 1:63–92.

[21] Laws, *James*, 213.

[22] Von Rad, "ἡμέρα," 2:232–55; Harald Heggermann, "δόξα, ης, ἡ," *EDNT* 1:344–49.

synonymous with "honor" (τιμή, Luke 14:10; 1 Cor 11:15; opp. ἀτιμία, 11:14; 2 Cor 6:8; 1 Thess 2:6, 20; Eph 3:13; Phil 3:19). It occurs but once in James, as an honorific designation of Jesus Christ (2:1). I think that this designation presupposes the resurrection, though James never mentions the passion and resurrection of Jesus.

In passing we may note that some scholars, observing that δόξα is used in the Septuagint to translate the Hebrew term *kābôd* ("honor," "nobility," "glory"; Gen 31:1; 45:13; Exod 24:16; Pss 8:5 [MT 6]; 49:16 [MT 17]; Isa 5:13; 16:14; 17:4; 1 Kgs 3:13),[23] some scholars want to read in Jas 2:1 a reference to Jesus as the visible manifestation of God's person and power.[24] Such a reading is possible, but the lack of any further textual specificity for the decisive meaning of the term warrants caution. I do not doubt that James has christological conceptions; the text simply does not provide much explicit information about them.[25] Nonetheless, there are other elements of James that fit rather nicely with the honorific designation of Jesus in 2:1 to suggest the presence of a messianic sensibility. The imagery of "the twelve tribes" in the letter prescript (1:1), for example, is an important intertextual feature in some early formulations of the Messiah and his role in the restoration of Israel (*Sib. Or.* 2:171; 3:249; Sir 44:23; *T. Mos.* 2:4–5; *2 Bar.* 1:2; 62:5; 63:3; 64:5; 77:2; 78:1, 4; 84:3; *T. Benj.* 9:2; Acts 26:7; Exod 24:4; 28:21; 39:14; Josh 4:5).[26] Furthermore, in those formulations the topics of

---

[23] G. Warmuth, "הָדָר," *TDOT* 3:335–41; Johannes Schneider, "τιμή, τιμάω," *TDNT* 8:169–80.

[24] Peter H. Davids, *The Epistle of James: A Commentary on the Greek Text* (NIGTC; Grand Rapids: Eerdmans, 1982), 107.

[25] Observing that James "relies heavily on the Jewish wisdom tradition in its understanding of man and the world," Roy Ward ("James, Letter of," *IDBSup*, 470) suggests that the author's "Christology may be a wisdom Christology." Rudolf Hoppe, *Der theologische Hintergrund des Jakobusbriefes* (FB 28; Würzburg: Echter Verlag, 1977); and Patrick J. Hartin, *James and the Q Sayings of Jesus* (JSNTSup 47; Sheffield: JSOT Press, 1991). Richard Bauckham (*James: Wisdom of James, Disciple of Jesus the Sage* [New York: Routledge, 1999], 31) correctly, in my view, disagrees with the notion that James identifies Jesus with personified wisdom; thus also John S. Kloppenborg, review of P. J. Hartin, *James and the Q Sayings of Jesus, CBQ* 54 (1992): 567–68; and Todd C. Penner, *The Epistle of James and Eschatology: Re-reading an Ancient Christian Letter* (JSNTSup 121; Sheffield: JSOT Press, 1996).

[26] E. Schürer, *The History of the Jewish People in the Age of Jesus Christ (175 B.C.–A.D. 135)* (rev. and ed. G. Vermes et al.; vols. 1–3.2; Edinburgh: T&T Clark, 1973-87), 2:530–31; James H. Ropes, *A Critical and Exegetical Commentary on the Epistle of St. James* (ICC 40; Edinburgh: T&T Clark, 1916), 120–25; Karl H. Rengstorf, "δώδεκα ... δωδέκατος, δωδεκάφυλον," *TDNT* 2:321–28; C. Maurer, "φυλή," *TDNT* 9:245–50. James B. Mayor (*The Epistle of James* [repr., Grand Rapids: Kregel, 1990],

judgment and justice play large,[27] as they certainly play in James's conception of "the faith of our glorious Lord Jesus Christ" and "the kingdom promised to those who love him [God]" (2:1, 5, respectively).[28]

Considering δόξα ("glory" or "reputation") as a rhetorical trope, we find that it is regarded as an external good and that it is closely related to "honor" (τιμή), another external good that is defined as "a sign of the reputation [δόξα] for doing good [εὐεργετικῆς]" (Aristotle, *Rhet.* 1.5.4, 9). Both "glory" and "honor," then, are advantageous goods, desirable, and "are generally accompanied by the possession of those things for which men are honored" (Aristotle, *Rhet.* 1.6.13; Cicero, *Inv.* 2.55.166). Moreover, "glory" and "honor" are regarded as component parts of "happiness" (εὐδαιμονία), and the latter is very often a fundamental subject in deliberative discourse (Aristotle, *Rhet.* 1.5.4; 1.5.2). Though the term εὐδαιμονία does not occur in the New Testament, the closely related terms χαρά ("joy") and μακάριος ("blessed, supremely blissful") are frequent, and they are vital topics in James. We observe that "joy" is invoked in the prescript (χαίρειν, 1:1), is prominent in the first admonition of the letter (1:2), and enhances a call to repentance (4:9). Likewise, "supreme happiness" (μακάριος) appears in both the central proposition of the letter (1:12) and in the first reference to "the perfect law, the law of liberty" (1:25); the cognate verb μακαρίζω occurs in the first section of the *peroratio* (5:11), where the rhetorical exigence of the letter, namely, "the steadfast endurance of various trials" (1:12), is recalled and emphasized in the light of "the *parousia* of the Lord" (5:7, 8).[29] From a rhetorical perspective, then, James's use of δόξα puts forth the honor and reputation of Jesus Messiah.[30]

---

30) says the "chosen people are still regarded as constituting twelve tribes." Further, there is evidence to suggest that Jesus understood his own mission as part of "a task which would include the restoration of Israel" (E. P. Sanders, *Jesus and Judaism* (Philadelphia: Fortress, 1985), 106, see also 91–119.

[27] Richard A. Horsley, *Jesus and the Spiral of Violence: Popular Jewish Resistance in Roman Palestine* (San Francisco: Harper & Row, 1987); Sanders, *Jesus and Judaism;* Dale C. Allison, *Jesus of Nazareth: Millenarian Prophet* (Minneapolis: Fortress, 1998).

[28] See particularly James's use of: κριτής ("judge," 2:4; 4:11, 12; 5:9); κριτήριον ("court," 2:6); κρίνειν ("to judge," 2:12; 4:11 [3x], 12; 5:9); and κρίσις ("judgment," 2:13; "condemnation," 5:12). Likewise, δίκαιος ("righteous, just," 5:6, 16); δικαιοσύνη ("righteousness," 1:20; 2:23; 3:18); and δικαιόω ("to make just," 2:21, 24, 25).

[29] On the relation of χαίρειν and μακάριος, see Aristotle, *Eth. nic.* 7.11.2; and for the relation of μακάριος and εὐδαιμονία, see *Eth. nic.* 1.7.16; 1.12.4.

[30] Wachob, *Voice of Jesus,* 69–70; for the topic of the "praiseworthy," which is generally defined as "what produces an honorable remembrance, at the time of the event and afterwards" (*Rhet. Her.* 3.4.7). We may safely assume that "the faith of

"Messiah" ("anointed one") refers in the Old Testament to a variety of persons who are appointed for a specific task that affects Israel. For example, the priest is an "anointed one" (Lev 4:3, 4), and Cyrus of Persia is "one anointed" as God's agent for the redemption of God's people (Isa 45:1). Typically, however, the term "messiah" is connected with the Davidic king (2 Sam 7:8–16; see also 1 Sam 10:1; 12:3; Ps 18:50; 20:6). Even after there was no longer a Davidide on the throne, the term played in the prophetic hope for an "anointed" Davidide as the future king (Isa 9:2–7; 11:1–9; Jer 33:15; Ezek 37:23–24). That "the earthly king from the line of David had become a type of God's Messiah" is also evident in some of the royal psalms (e.g., Pss 2; 45; 72; 89; 132).[31] In the book of Daniel, there are two references to an "anointed one": 9:25 refers to a future "anointed prince" coming to Jerusalem (probably Zerubbabel or Joshua); and 9:26 refers to the murder of "an anointed one" (probably Onias III). Thus the messiah, particularly in these traditions, is associated with the "rule of God," and that is apparently what is celebrated.

There are various references to a "messiah" or "anointed one" in apocalyptic literature (e.g., *Sib. Or.* 3:652–656; *Pss. Sol.* 17–18; *1 En.* 37–71; *T. Sim.* 7:2; *T. Jud.* 24; *T. Levi* 18:1–11; CD XX, 1; 1QS IX, 11; *2 Bar.* 29–30; 39–42; 72–74; *4 Ezra* 7; 11:37–12:34; 13:3–14:9; *3 Ezra* 45:5; 48:10 [A]). For our present purpose, however, the most significant of these are found in *Psalms of Solomon* (from the mid-first century B.C.E.) and in *1 Enoch* (the Similitudes; probably from the first-half of the first century C.E.). In the *Psalms of Solomon* 17–18, the "Lord Messiah" (17:32; 18:5), who is also "the son of David" (17:21), is the future (apocalyptic) judge and righteous king of Israel (17:26, 29). The Gentiles shall be under his "yoke," and the nations from the ends of the earth shall bring him gifts and come "to see his glory" (17:30–31). "Under the rod of the Lord Messiah's discipline [παιδείς]" there will be direction for everyone "in works of righteousness in the fear of God" (18:7, 8). Yet, it is clear that though the Lord Messiah represents God as God's king, God alone is *the* king (17:1, 34, 46; 18:1, 7–8, 10–12). Accordingly the messianic rule is summarized "in the phrase βασιλεία τοῦ θεοῦ (17:3)" and its "purpose" is "to glorify God" (17:30–31).[32]

---

our glorious Lord Jesus Christ" (Jas 2:1) is considered "praiseworthy." Further, while the "praiseworthy" was understood to have its source in the "right," both of the latter were understood as components of the larger topic "honor." The latter and its corollary category "security" were subsumed under the topic of "advantage," which is the aim of a deliberative speech. For a general discussion, see *Rhet. Her.* book 3.

[31] Brevard Childs, *Biblical Theology of the Old and New Testaments: Theological Reflection on the Christian Bible* (Minneapolis: Fortress, 1992), 193–94.

[32] Reiser, *Jesus and Judgment*, 50.

According to R. B. Wright, this is the first Jewish text in which an "anointed one" is designated "Son of David" (ὁ υἱὸς Δαυιδ) and the only Jewish text in which he is the "Lord Messiah" (χριστὸς κύριος).[33] Furthermore, the "Lord Messiah" of the *Psalms of Solomon* is quite similar to God's eschatological judge in *1 En.* 37–71. Among his various designations ("the Elect One of righteousness and of faith," 39:6; "the Elect One," 45:3; "the Righteous and Elect One," 53:6; "the Son of Man," 46:3; "the Chosen One," 48:5), he is twice referred to as the "messiah" (48:10; 52:4).[34]

While these uses of "messiah" indicate that the term had no settled, technical meaning in the time of Jesus, they do show that in some Jewish circles "it denoted a political or priestly agent sent from God as part of the triumphant establishment of God's power."[35] We underscore the often observed facts that "Son of David," "Lord Messiah," "the Son of Man," "the Righteous One," and "Messiah"—all of which could serve as designations for various representatives of God in the eschatological judgment—are also used of Jesus Christ in the New Testament. Two of them, "Lord (Jesus) Messiah" (1:1; 2:1) and "the righteous one" (5:6, 16), occur in James.

The possibility that "the Righteous One" in the Similitudes of *1 Enoch* "was a conventional messianic designation in early Christianity, specifically in Jewish Christian circles,"[36] becomes rather intriguing when we note that in the immediate context of James's references to the *parousia* of the Lord (5:7, 8), there is also a reference to "the righteous one." Addressing the rich outsiders, James says: "You have condemned, you have killed the righteous one; he does not resist you" (5:6). This, of course, has no explicit connection to Jesus. Nevertheless, observing (in Acts 3:13–15; 7:51–53) that the ascription of "heavenly *glory*" to Jesus, the Righteous One, is "fused with his death as a martyr," Richard B. Hays has again raised the possibility that "the righteous one" in Jas 5:6 "is an oblique reference to Jesus and that the motif of nonresistance derives from the traditions about Jesus' passion"; not that James uses "the Righteous One" titularly, but that for James "Jesus is the prototype who provides its material content."[37] In any case, the "Lord Messiah," "glory," "honor," "the righteous one," and "justice" are apocalyptic topics that play large in the theocentric rhetoric of James.

---

[33] R. B. Wright, "The Psalms of Solomon," *OTP* 2:646.

[34] See John J. Collins, *The Apocalyptic Imagination: An Introduction to the Jewish Matrix of Christianity* (New York: Crossroad, 1984), 147.

[35] Pheme Perkins, "Messiah," *HBD*, 630.

[36] Hays, "The Righteous One," 200–201.

[37] Ibid., 194–95, 201, 204.

While James's conceptions of the *parousia* and judgment of the Lord appear to join with other motifs in suggesting a concern for the restoration of Israel, his references to eschatological judgment, which buttress his concern for justice, indicate that the law (νόμος) is the criterion by which justice is measured (4:12; 2:12).[38] The term νόμος is the law of Moses, the law of God (4:12; 2:8, 11; see also Exod 20:13, 15; Lev. 19:18).[39] The term νόμος occurs ten times in James, and each case presupposes the law in its unity and entirety (see 2:10). The logic of the rhetoric in Jas 2:1–13 subsumes the references to God's action, law, and judgment (2:5, 8–13) under a reference to Jesus' faith and argues that holding Jesus' faith and fulfillment of God's law are counterparts (2:1, 12–13). We shall discuss this further below; here, we simply note that it is probable that James ("a servant of God and the Lord Jesus Christ," 1:1) appropriates "*all* of Torah" in relation to the teachings of Jesus.[40] In other words, for James, "the followers of Jesus belong to law-abiding Israel and the fulfillment of the law, though without any emphasis upon circumcision and ritual law, is the appropriate interpretation of the teachings of Jesus."[41] James stresses the ethical dimensions of the law.

Thus the law, as Jesus taught it, serves as the criterion for justice in the judicial proceedings of the community (2:1–13; 1:25).[42] For example, in

---

[38] The "lawful/unlawful" is a topic of "justice," and both of the latter are subtopics of "honor" (Cicero, *Inv.* 2.53.160). The noun παραβάτης ("transgressor," Jas 2:9, 11) is infrequent in the New Testament, occurring only five times (Paul uses it 3x: Rom 2:25, 27; Gal 2:18; see Johannes. Schneider, "παραβαίνω, παράβασις, παραβάτης, ἀπαράβατος, ὑπερβαίνω," *TDNT* 5:740–42). Like the terms ἁμαρτία ("sin," 2:9; 1:15 [2x]; 4:17; 5:15, 16, 20) and ἐλέγχειν ("to rebuke," "to convict") with which James associates it, "a transgressor" evokes the topics "shame" and "dishonor" (Aristotle, *Rhet.* 6; 2.6.14). Compare also the typically forensic ἐλέγχειν ("to rebuke," "to convict") in Ps 49:8–23 LXX, where the Lord testifies against and "convicts" Israel (vv. 7, 8, 21); see *Pss. Sol.* 17:25–26; Wis 1:8; 4:20; and in 1:9 (ἔλεγχος). See Reiser, *Jesus and Judgment,* 44, 49.

[39] O. J. F. Seitz, "James and the Law," *SE* 2 (1964): 485.

[40] Johnson, "Friendship with the World," 457; Davids, *James,* 114.

[41] Helmut Koester, *Ancient Christian Gospels: Their History and Development* (Philadelphia: Trinity Press International, 1990), 171. Whatever the author may or may not have thought about the so-called cultic ordinances of the law, matters such as circumcision and dietary ordinances, we do not know: "He simply passes over them in silence" (Seitz, "James and the Law," 485). To put it differently but fairly, he mentions the cross, the resurrection, and the gospel just as frequently as he does circumcision, that is, not at all.

[42] See Roy Ward, "The Communal Concern of the Epistle of James" (Ph.D. diss., Harvard University, 1966); idem, "The Works of Abraham: James 2:14–26," *HTR* 61 (1969): 283–90; idem, "Partiality in the Assembly, James 2:2–4," *HTR* 62 (1969): 87–97.

James's concern for speech-ethics, which runs throughout the discourse (1:19–21, 26; 3:1–12), the law is the standard for judgment (4:11–12). Speech-ethics, therefore, are intrinsic to the practice of justice.[43] Consider James's prohibition of swearing (5:12): he appears to draw on a saying of Jesus that must have been something like the one found in the pre-Matthean Sermon on the Mount (Q^Matt 5:34–37), but James recontextualizes it without attribution as an argument for telling the truth. Note that he undergirds this argument with a reference to judgment.[44] In similar fashion, James's understanding of the law is the basis upon which the world, as a system of values, is judged inimical to God.[45]

The law is an issue of importance in apocalyptic literature as well (CD XV, 5–11; 1QS V, 8–9; 4 Ezra 9:36; 2 Bar. 17:4; 32:1; 38:1–2; 44:7; 46:3; 48:22; 51:3, 4–7; 54:5, 15). Particularly significant for James are the intertextual connections with the Testaments of the Twelve Patriarchs, which stress the ethical dimensions "rather than the specific legal statutes of the Torah."[46] Compare, for example: Jas 4:11–12 and T. Benj. 10:8–10; T. Levi 13:1–2; Jas 2:10 and T. Ash. 2:2–10; Jas 2:12–13 and T. Iss. 5:1–2; 7:6–7; T. Zeb. 5:1; Jas 2:8 and T. Dan 6:3; Jas 2:5 and T. Jos. 11:1. These comparisons with James, however, cannot conclusively show dependence one way or the other. Luke Johnson correctly assesses the situation: "What is clear is that they share a remarkably similar dualistic appropriation of Greco-Roman ethics within the symbolic world of Torah."[47]

3. Topic: The Trials of Faith

The rhetorical situation envisioned in the letter of James is developed in the theme of "various trials" (πειρασμοῖς ποικίλοις).[48] Thus, according to the exordium (Jas 1:2–12), the rhetorical exigence or problem that James addresses is "the testing of the community's faith" (τὸ δοκίμιον ὑμῶν

---

[43] William R. Baker, Personal Speech-Ethics in the Epistle of James (WUNT 2/68; Tübingen: Mohr Siebeck, 1995).

[44] See Wachob and Johnson, "Sayings of Jesus."

[45] Johnson, "Friendship with the World."

[46] Howard C. Kee, "The Testaments of the Twelve Patriarchs," OTP 1:779.

[47] Luke T. Johnson, The Letter of James (AB 37A; Garden City, N.Y.: Doubleday, 1995), 46.

[48] See Davids, James, 35–38; E. Fry, "The Testing of Faith: A Study of the Structure of the Book of James," BT 29 (1978): 427–35; Hartin, James and the Q Sayings of Jesus, 26–34; Hoppe, Der theologische Hintergrund des Jakobusbriefes, 1–43, 119–48; Ulrich Luck, "Weisheit und Leiden: Zum Problem Paulus und Jakobus," TLZ 92 (1967): 253–58; idem, "Der Jakobusbrief und die Theologie des Paulus," TGl 61 (1971): 163–64.

τῆς πίστεως, 1:2–4) in "various trials." In other words, the trials that concern James do not appear to be those of a particular persecution, as in 1 Peter, nor do they have the heightened "connotations of eschatological tribulation," as in Paul. Instead, they are "the perennial experience of life in God's service," similar to Ben Sira and other of the wisdom tradition (e.g., Sir 2:1; Wis 3:4–5; Prov 27:21; *Pss. Sol.* 16:14–15; *T. Jos.* 2:7).[49] Though the text does not precisely define these various afflictions, it clearly suggests that in them the community experiences the trial of its faith (1:2).[50] Accordingly, as the letter unfolds, then, "the trial of faith" lends a thematic structure to the discourse. Moreover, the particular trials that are addressed are always handled with respect to the overriding concern of "communal relations."[51]

For example, the *exordium* (1:2–12) and *narratio* (1:13–27) rehearse both the positive and negative dimensions of the trial of faith. The positive aspects and results are stated in the *exordium* (1:3–4, 12); the negative dimension—the temptation with evil—is opened in the *narratio*. For James God is not the source of temptation with evil (1:13, 17–18); this temptation arises out of human desires for pleasure (1:14). Thus the text stresses the necessity of an undivided heart, a complete commitment to God and God's purposes (see 1:8; 4:8; 5:11; *1 En.* 91:3–4, 18–19).[52] This view is further embellished in the *confirmatio* (2:1–5:6), where the topics of the world and wisdom are opened with respect to the human desires that produce sin: the inward desires are informed by a wisdom that is "earthly, unspiritual, and devilish" (3:15). This wisdom belongs to "the world" (4:4) and "the devil" (4:7) and is opposed to "the wisdom from

---

[49] Laws, *James*, 51, 52; see also B. R. Halson, "The Epistle of James: 'Christian Wisdom'?" *SE* 4 (1968): 308–14; and especially Hoppe, *Der theologische Hintergrund des Jakobusbriefes*.

[50] The similarities between Jas 1:2–4 and 1 Peter 1:6–7; Rom 5:2–4 should not be allowed to hide the particular argument that James is making here: "that *you* [plural] may be perfect and complete, lacking in nothing" (Jas 2:4) is at issue with regard to "*your* faith," that is, "the community's faith" (ἀδελφοί μου). James is concerned with the beloved community's faithfulness to God: that they should be "rich in faith" (2:5; see below). The "various trials" are the means of testing faithfulness; πίστις occurs sixteen times: Jas 1:3, 6; 2:1, 5, 14 (2x), 17, 18 (3x), 20, 22 (2x) 24, 26; 5:15.

[51] Ward, "Partiality in the Assembly"; J. B. Soucek, "Zu den Problemen des Jakobusbriefes," *EvT* 18 (1958): 460–69. James uses the term "brother/brothers," ἀδελφός, nineteen times: 1:2, 9, 16, 19; 2:1, 5, 14, 15; 3:1, 10, 12; 4:11 (3x); 5:7, 9, 10, 12, 19; "sister," ἀδελφή, occurs in 2:15.

[52] See O. J. F. Seitz, "Antecedents and Significance of the Term *DIPHYCHOS*," *JBL* 66 (1947): 211–19; idem, "Afterthoughts on the term 'Dipsychos,'" *NTS* 4 (1957): 327–34.

above," God's wisdom (3:17; 1:2). For James, then, the temptation toward evil comes from within (4:2–3) and from without (3:14–16). The argumentative dimensions of James's development of the topics of "desire" and "pleasure" clearly imply the need for God's wisdom, a wisdom that can promote and secure the well-being of the community.[53] The wisdom from below brings disorder, wickedness of every kind, and death (3:16); its harvest is neither righteousness nor life (1:19–27; 5:20).

Observe that James never suggests that the various trials in which the community's faith is tested can be removed. It does maintain, however, that this exigence can be modified. Given the quality of trials of faith, the fundamental rhetorical stasis in the letter of James is one of fact: "What shall we do?"[54] James answers this question by seeking to persuade its hearers to endure their various trials of faith (1:2–5), to resist evil and honor God (4:7–10). From a rhetorical perspective, the whole letter turns on the central *propositio* (1:12): those who faithfully endure trials of faith are those who really love God, and it is they who will receive the promised reward and supreme joy (1:12, 25; 2:5, 26; 3:13, 18; 5:11, 19–20).[55]

Trials and tribulations are indigenous to apocalyptic literature (e.g., *2 Bar.* 25:1–2; 48:20; 52:6–7; *Sib. Or.* 5:269–270; *T. Mos.* 8:1; *4 Ezra* 13:16–19; cf. Zeph 1:15; Hab 3:16; Dan 12:10), and some of the motifs and themes associated with them are also found in James. In my opinion, however, the numerous references to testing in the wisdom tradition are particularly important (e.g., Sir 2:1–18; 6:12–9:18; 33:1–2, 12–13; Wis 1–5). James's immediate association of "various trials" (1:2–4) with "wisdom" (1:5) warrants this inference. The wisdom in view here, of course, is the wisdom that comes only from God (3:15, 17–18; cf. 1:17) and is the means by which to understand and endure "the various trials" into which the community may fall. Observing that James intimately associates God's wisdom with "the word of truth" (1:18) and that the "prayer for wisdom" marks both the opening (1:6–8) and the closing of the letter (5:13–20), it is difficult to miss the connection in James between "the trials of faith," "wisdom,"

---

[53] On the topic of advantage or benefit, i.e., well-being, in deliberative rhetoric, see Aristotle, *Rhet.* 1.3.5; Cicero, *Inv.* 2.51.159–56.169; *Rhet. Her.* 3.2.3.

[54] See R. Nadeau, "Hermogenes' On Stases: A Translation with an Introduction and Notes," *Speech Monographs* 31 (1964): 361–424. In judicial rhetoric, which refers to past time, the issue would be: "What was done?" In deliberative rhetoric, which refers to future action, the issue is: "What shall be done?" See George Kennedy, *New Testament Interpretation through Rhetorical Criticism* (Chapel Hill: University of North Carolina Press, 1984), 18–19, 46–47.

[55] See Wachob, *Voice of Jesus,* 158–60.

"prayer," and "the righteous one" (5:6, 16; cf. *1 En.* 37:1; 48; Wis 1–5; Ps 36:30 LXX; *Pss. Sol.* 17:23, 29; 18:7).

According to James, "faith" is obedience to God that comprises thoughts, words, and deeds.[56] Consequently, the exhortations to "patience" in no sense imply a *passive* "waiting" for the "the coming of the Lord" (5:7–11, 13–20). For James the trials of faith are to be endured by courageous actions that cohere with the compassion and mercy of "the faith of the Lord Jesus Christ" (2:1): "I by my works will show you my faith" (2:18).[57] Thus the topic of the trials of faith opens up the topic of rewards and punishments.

4. Topics: The Rich, the Poor, and the Kingdom of God

The principal trial that besets the community to which James writes appears to be the conflict between the rich and the poor and the accompanying opposition to the world as a system of values opposed to God.[58] More than one-fourth of the letter is concerned with this problem (1:9–11; 2:1–13, 15–16; 4:13–5:6), and it is a prominent moral issue in the Jesus tradition and in much of early Christian literature. The first argument in the *probatio* (2:1–13) deals with this conflict and is pivotal for the entire discourse. Within this argumentative unit, 2:5 stands as one of James's most important parallels to a Jesus logion.

In previous investigations I have offered lengthy discussions of Jas 2:5; here, I simply note the following facts. There are four other performances of this saying (Matt 5:3; Luke 6:20b; *Gos. Thom.* 54, and Pol. *Phil.* 3.2). All five performances share two key terms ("the poor" and "the kingdom"), which they exploit to produce sentences that feature a single, common denominator—"God's kingdom is promised to the poor." Of the five performances, Jas 2:5 is conspicuously different. For instance, the four other performances are beatitudes attributed to Jesus. They are also enthymemes: each consists of a conclusion (a macarism) and a premise (a ὅτι clause), with one premise unstated and tacitly assumed. Because of the differences,

---

[56] Ibid., 70.

[57] "Endurance" is one of the subtopics of "courage" (*Rhet. Her.* 3.2.3; 3.3.6; 4.25.35). On patience, perseverance, confidence, and high-mindedness, see especially Cicero, *Inv.* 2.54.163. On the topic of perseverance or endurance, see also Aristotle, *Virtue and Vices* 4.4. In James the topic of "endurance" is presupposed in connection with the "trials of faith." Connected with "endurance" and "patience" are the uses of τελεῖν (2:8) and τηρεῖν (2:10; 1:27). Both of the latter concern "the law" (and see παραμένειν in connection with "the perfect law, the law of liberty," 1:25).

[58] Dibelius, *James,* 48.

some scholars separate Jas 2:5 from its argumentative context and argue that it simply states a "principle of the traditional piety of the poor."[59]

The notion that God has a special concern for the poor is clearly present in both the Old Testament and Jewish literature, and there is little doubt that Jas 2:5 evokes that tradition. But, as Dean Deppe reminds us, "there are no references in the OT, intertestamental literature, or the Talmud specifically saying that God is giving the kingdom to the poor."[60] The most likely source for Jas 2:5 is not the traditional piety of the poor but the teaching of Jesus.

This conclusion finds strong support in the following facts. First, the term "kingdom" appears only here in James and is enhanced by the immediate occurrence of βασιλικός in 2:8. Second, this term, which is so distinctive in the language of Jesus, appears in a statement about God that is marked by, subsumed under, and intimately connected to Jesus' own faith (2:1).[61] Third, the historical example in 2:5 achieves its rhetorical meaning and function by recalling Jesus' own faith as the measure for the elect community's faith.[62] Fourth, Jas 2:5 presupposes that the saying of Jesus to which it alludes is, like the faith of Jesus that it recalls, already known to James's addressees. Moreover, recent studies on the development of the Jesus tradition suggest that the Jesus logion alluded to in Jas 2:5 is an early, widely known, and exploited saying of Jesus.[63] In sum, 2:5 is a statement—about God's action with reference to "the poor"—that recalls Jesus' own faith (2:1) in language that resonates with the texture of a well-known wisdom saying of Jesus in which the poor are promised God's kingdom.[64]

There are, however, remarkable differences in the perspectives of the various performances of this saying. While Q[Matt] 5:3 and Jas 2:5 address "the poor of God" as those who in their actions love God by obeying God's law, in neither of the latter are the socially and economically impoverished

---

[59] Koester, *Ancient Christian Gospels,* 74.

[60] Dean R. Deppe, "The Sayings of Jesus in the Epistle of James" (Ph.D. diss., University of Amsterdam, 1989; Chelsea, Mich.: Bookcrafters, 1989), 90.

[61] For the suggestion that the reference to Jesus' faith in 2:1 functions as a "global allusion" that evokes the whole of what our author perceives Jesus to have believed, said, and done, see Wachob, *Voice of Jesus,* 122. For the term "global allusion," see Robert Alter, *The Pleasures of Reading in an Ideological Age* (New York: Simon & Schuster, 1989), 124.

[62] Wachob, *Voice of Jesus,* 78–113.

[63] John Kloppenborg, *The Formation of Q: Trajectories in Ancient Wisdom Collection* (SAC; Philadelphia: Fortress, 1987); Koester, *Ancient Christian Gospels.*

[64] Wachob, *Voice of Jesus,* 114–53.

promised the kingdom on the basis of their situation, as they are in in Q[Luke] 6:20b and *Gos. Thom.* 54. In Q[Matt] 5:3 and Jas 2:5 the kingdom is the incentive or reward of those whose actions conform to the Torah as interpreted by Jesus and summarized in the love command, as it is not in Q[Luke] 6:20b; *Gos. Thom.* 54; and Pol. *Phil.* 2.3. The grammar and logic of Jas 2:5 very clearly say that the poor are chosen by God, for God, that they might be rich in faith now in obedience to God and therefore receive the promised reward—God's kingdom. In my opinion, it is beyond dispute that in Jas 2:5 the author is reciting a saying of Jesus very much like that in the pre-Matthean Sermon on the Mount, so that "the poor in spirit" of Q[Matt] 5:3 are synonymous with "the rich in faith" of Jas 2:5.[65] Put differently, the rhetoric in the pre-Matthean Sermon on the Mount argues that God's law is ratified in the words of Jesus and in the obedience of his followers, while the rhetoric in James argues that God's law is ratified in the faith of Jesus and—as the allusion to the saying of Jesus makes clear—also in the faith of his servants.

In broaching the topics—the rich and the poor and the kingdom of God—James has some striking parallels with apocalyptic literature. For example, in James the terms "the poor" and "the rich" are technical terms, the latter referring to the wealthy outsiders who oppress "the poor" insiders, the beloved community. This reminds us of *1 En.* 92–105 (see 94:6–7; 99:3; cf. Ps 36:14 LXX; *Pss. Sol.* 10:6; 15:1; Wis 1–5; 1QpHab XII, 3, 10; 4QpPs37 II, 9; III, 10), in which the poor are identified with God's pious poor, who obey the Torah: "those who love God" (cf. *Pss. Sol.* 14:1).[66]

That "rich" and "poor" are technical terms for James does not mean that there are no wealthy persons in James's community.[67] On the contrary, the grammar and logic of 2:1–13 presuppose that there are wealthy members of the beloved community; so, also, the language of "the reversal of fortune" (1:12–13) and the prophetic indictments of the arrogant merchants and the wealthy (4:13–5:6). While the latter are outsiders, the argument is directed to the community, which is replicating in itself the behavior of those who live by the wisdom of the world.[68]

It follows that there are indeed this-worldly benefits and rewards to be obtained for both the poor and the wealthy members of James's community,

---

[65] See ibid., 138–53; Wachob and Johnson, "Sayings of Jesus," 442–46.

[66] See George W. E. Nickelsburg, "Riches, the Rich, and God's Judgment in 1 Enoch 92–105 and the Gospel according to Luke," *NTS* 25 (1978): 324–44; Simon Légasse, "Les pauvres en Esprit et les 'Volontaires' de Qumran," *NTS* 8 (1962): 336–45.

[67] Ward, "Communal Concern of the Epistle of James," 78–98.

[68] Wachob, *Voice of Jesus,* 182–93.

if the "royal law" is obeyed.[69] The rhetorical example of Jas 2:5 discloses the author's basis for differentiating the elect poor from the rich outsiders ("Has not God chosen...?"). It functions sociorhetorically to set forth in one sentence the social identity, the way of life, and the goal of God's chosen poor. In other words, it calls for the community to remember its God-honored identity and status. Thus it not only promotes the collective honor of the elect poor over against the rich and powerful outsiders and the way of life they exemplify, but—coupled with the social comparison in 2:2–4, which demands justice for community members without regard for worldly advantage—2:5 also calls the beloved community to honor its impoverished members.

Recognizing that the concepts "poor" and "rich" are not mere economic terms and that the elect poor is comprised of some members who are materially wealthy, James's rhetoric opens the door for those with plenty to assume an even more honorable status within the elect community. Apparently, the benefit offered to the wealthy community members is that they, like God, the giver of "every good and perfect gift" (1:17), are to become the honored patrons of their more impoverished community members.[70] Those with wealth and possessions are expected to employ their "goods" with respect to the needs of their fellow community members, just as God employs good gifts with respect to them. Likewise, the reminder concerning traditional Jewish covenantal obligations toward the widows and orphans (1:27) and the exhortation concerning the suffering and the sick (5:13) seem to indicate that if the rhetoric of James is successful, those community members who have material needs could expect material benefits from those who possess them.

That James views the world as a system of values opposed to God (4:4) does not mean that the community members are to withdraw from life in the world. The text not only reflects a community whose members are busily involved with making a living in the world; it suggests that some in the community are doing this quite successfully (hence the invectives in 4:13–5:6). James never condemns this involvement. Instead, the text advocates that the community wisely live out its peculiar, God-given identity in the world but without being contaminated by the world's God-less values and wisdom (4:4). In other words, the beloved community is expected to live in association with "the rich," but it must not live as "the rich" live.

---

[69] Ibid., 196–201.

[70] Within a patron-client system the "sharing of wealth in order to gain status is a way to solve the problem of inequality within a society with high demands for solidarity" (Halvor Moxnes, *The Economy of the Kingdom: Social Conflict and Economic Relations in Luke's Gospel* [Philadelphia: Fortress, 1988], 78, 79).

The rhetoric of James clearly envisions a reversal of the powers and values that dominate the world, but never does it offer even the slightest suggestion that the beloved community should act violently toward the world. To the contrary, the advice to endure worldly trials (1:12, 25), wisely (1:5–11; 3:13–18) avoiding wrath (1:19–20) and patiently waiting for the Lord (5:7–12), suggests that God's elect community must faithfully and humbly wait on God to reverse the worldly system. It is equally clear, however, that the community does not wait for God to reform its own behavior. The rhetoric calls for an immediate correction of the community's interpersonal relations in thoughts, words, and deeds in the light of God's truth, "the perfect law of liberty" (1:21, 25; 2:8–13; 5:19–20).

That there are future rewards—to receive the crown of life (1:12; *T. Benj.* 4:1) and the kingdom that God promised to those who love him (2:5; *Pss. Sol.* 17:3)—"James, a servant of God and of the Lord Jesus Christ" (1:1) presupposes throughout his discourse. And he exploits these apocalyptic topics in exhorting his community to live in the certainty that the *parousia* and judgment of the Lord is imminent (5:7–9). Because the diety that they serve is "a compassionate and merciful Lord" (5:11), he exhorts his community to reclaim the "sinner from the error of his way" (5:19–20); since the deity they serve is a righteous judge (4:12), James lovingly warns his listeners that "judgment is without mercy to one who has shown no mercy; yet mercy triumphs over judgment" (2:13).

5. Conclusions and Comments

The Epistle of James is not an apocalypse; indeed, one searches in vain to find within it numerous elements that are frequently found in many so-called apocalypses. For example, there are no visions, no seers, no angels, no apocalyptic scenarios, and no otherworldly journeys. However, as we have seen there are several topics within James that are typically associated with apocalyptic literature. From a rhetorical perspective, James's choice of these topics is an important aspect of the inventional theory that stands behind the the text as we have it; their configuration and function within this thoroughly deliberative discourse are constituitive elements in an effort to persuade a community (or communites) of Christian Jews to think and act in particular ways. James is hardly interested in merely inculcating values; inculcate values he does, but always in the deliberative effort to persuade his hearers to particular ways of thinking and acting.

Our brief excursion into the apocalyptic intertextuality of James suggests that the use of such well-known cultural topics in early Christianity as (1) the *parousia* and (2) judgment of the Lord, (3) justice, (4) the trials of faith, (5) the poor and the rich, and (6) the kingdom of God presumes "insider knowledge" for both James and his addressees. Accordingly, this

interaction with the cultural intertexture of early Christianity suggests that
the letter of James belongs to "a particular culture or to people who have
learned about that culture through some kind of interaction with it."[71]

The rhetorical environment from which James speaks reflects two
basic cultures: Hellenistic-Roman culture and Jewish culture.[72] The dominant culture is Hellenistic-Roman, and as an encyclical to Christian Jews
in the dispersion (1:1), the letter of James clearly reflects the "system of
attitudes, values, dispositions, and norms" of that culture.[73] James also
draws from Jewish culture, adopts a subcultural position to Jewish tradition, and uses it counterculturally against Hellenistic-Roman culture. In
other words, the rhetoric of James affirms "the fundamental value orientation" of Jewish tradition while rejecting "the norms and values which
unite the dominant culture."[74]

Most scholars recognize the thoroughly Jewish-Christian character of
the letter of James.[75] Nothing in the text reflects hostility to Jewish tradition. Moreover, the fundamental significance of the Torah, as "the perfect
law of freedom" (1:25), has for James a strong testimony for its close relation to Jewish religion. That James holds Jesus to be Messiah and Lord (1:1;
2:1) is best understood as an intramural conflict within a Jewish subculture.
Thus James's rhetoric is Jewish-Christian rhetoric. While it is true that James
easily exploits and plays common topics in the Hellenistic-Roman culture,
much in the fashion of the moralists and some philosophers, it does so in
a way that is informed by Jewish culture. For James, Israel's God is the only
God, and the Torah of God is the one law (4:12; 2:10–11); and honor is
the reputation of those who humbly and faithfully depend on the one God
and fulfull the whole law (2:8, 10; 1:25).

That which makes James's rhetoric subcultural to Jewish cultural rhetoric and differentiates it from a thoroughgoing Jewish cultural rhetoric is

---

[71] Robbins, *Exploring the Texture of Texts,* 58.

[72] Wachob, *Voice of Jesus,* 189–93.

[73] Vernon K. Robbins, "Rhetoric and Culture: Exploring Types of Cultural
Rhetoric in a Text," in *Rhetoric and the New Testament: Essays from the 1992 Hei-
delberg Conference* (ed. Stanley E. Porter and Thomas H. Olbricht; JSNTSup 90;
Sheffield: Sheffield Academic Press, 1993), 447.

[74] Ibid., 455. In my opinion, "the value conflict" that James has with Hellenistic-
Roman culture is "one which is central, uncompromising, and wrenching to the
fabric of the culture." Thus "the concept of counterculture also implies a differen-
tiation *between* the two cultures which are more distinct than the areas of *overlap*"
(ibid., quoting K. A. Roberts, "Toward a Generic Concept of Counter-Culture," *Sociological Focus* 11 [1978]: 112–13, 121).

[75] Wachob, *Voice of Jesus,* 163–70, 190.

the fact that James is a Christian version of a Jewish value system.[76] James apparently appropriates all of the Torah through the teachings of Jesus, and because Jesus summarized the fulfillment of the Torah in the love-command, the rhetoric of James subsumes this interpretation under Jesus' own faith. For James, then, holding Jesus' faith (2:1) and fulfilling the Torah (2:10) are synonymous. Both find their essence in loving one's neighbor as oneself (2:8). In the countercultural rhetoric of James the only wealth that God honors is being "rich in faith" (2:5).

The general worldview of James and the conceptual language within which it is disclosed suggest that life in this world receives its significance from the eschatological future, but the eschatological future of those who hold Jesus' faith is determined by their present behavior.[77] "Present behavior"—this is the chief concern of James. "I by my works will show you my faith" (2:18). Thus James uses so-called apocalyptic topics to support his argument that the beloved community, a countercultural community, should live (in this world) the same faith-obedience to God that Jesus lived. Apocalyptic topics, just like wisdom and prophetic topics, are configured by James for this argumentative purpose.[78] The eschatological horizon informs James's rhetoric. The judgment and the kingdom are certain: "So speak and act as those who are to be judged under the law of liberty; for judgment is without mercy to one who has shown no mercy; yet mercy triumphs over judgment" (2:12–13).

---

[76] Ibid., 191.

[77] See Hans Dieter Betz, "Eschatology in the Sermon on the Mount and the Sermon on the Plain," *SBL Seminar Papers, 1985* (SBLSP 22; Atlanta: Scholars Press, 1985), 343–50.

[78] E. Baasland, "Der Jakobusbrief als neutestamentliche Weisheitsschrift," *ST* 36 (1982): 119–39; idem, "Literarische Form, Thematik und geschichtliche Einordnung des Jakobusbriefes," *ANRW* 25.5:3646–84.

The Oral-Scribal and Cultural Intertexture of Apocalyptic Discourse in Jude and 2 Peter

Duane F. Watson

Intertextuality can be defined as "the ways a new text is created from the metaphors, images, and symbolic world of an earlier text or tradition."[1] In my analysis of the intertextuality of Jude and 2 Peter I will utilize the discussion of intertextuality formulated by Vernon Robbins in his two recent works.[2] More specifically I will concentrate on two of the types of intertexture that he describes, namely, oral-scribal and cultural. Oral-scribal intertexture involves a text's recitation, recontextualization, and reconfiguration of other texts, both oral and written.[3] Cultural intertexture is a text's interaction with knowledge of a particular people or culture, knowledge that is not generally known by other peoples or cultures. "Cultural intertexture appears in word and concept patterns and configurations; values, scripts, codes, or systems ... and myths.... Cultural intertexture appears in a text either through reference or allusion and echo."[4]

Both Jude and 2 Peter lend themselves well to the analysis of oral-scribal intertexture because of their heavy reliance upon other texts, traditions, images, and symbols. Second Peter even has a literary reliance upon Jude that can be examined for oral-scribal intertexture. Both letters lend themselves to analysis of cultural intertexture because they are written to early Christians trying to define themselves against Mediterranean culture as well as Judaism from which they emerged and whose traditions, values, and myths they inherited. These early Christians are in the process of adopting and adapting, as well as creating, their own cultural knowledge.

---

[1] Gail R. O'Day, "Jeremiah 9:22–23 and 1 Corinthians 1:26–31: A Study in Intertextuality," *JBL* 109 (1990): 259.

[2] *Exploring the Texture of Texts: A Guide to Socio-Rhetorical Interpretation* (Valley Forge, Pa.: Trinity Press International, 1996) and *The Tapestry of Early Christian Discourse: Rhetoric, Society and Ideology* (New York: Routledge, 1996).

[3] Robbins, *Exploring the Texture of Texts,* 40–58; idem, *Tapestry of Early Christian Discourse,* 96–115.

[4] Robbins, *Exploring the Texture of Texts,* 58. For full discussion, see 58–62 and idem, *Tapestry of Early Christian Discourse,* 108–15.

In the following essay I will focus particularly upon the apocalyptic discourse in these two letters and its oral-scribal and cultural intertextural connections with Jewish and early Christian texts and traditions, both apocalyptic and nonapocalyptic.[5]

1. The Intertexture of Apocalyptic Discourse in the Epistle of Jude

The Epistle of Jude exhibits an imminent eschatology. The very presence of the false teachers in the church is a sign that the *parousia* is near (vv. 14–15). The argumentation in the entire body of the letter supports Jude's main proposition that the false teachers in the church are notorious sinners whose appearance was prophesied and who will be judged at the impending *parousia* (v. 4). They will experience a swift and sudden destruction, as have other notorious sinners of the past (vv. 5–19). The argumentation of Jude is apocalyptic discourse with strong intertextural connections to apocalyptic and nonapocalyptic Jewish traditions and texts that provide assumptions, examples, emotive images, and warrants for its proofs.[6]

In his argumentation Jude uses a mix of oral tradition and written texts.[7] As expected in an early Christian source, the oral tradition used is both Jewish and emerging early Christian. Oral tradition in Jude includes the traditional scheme of three examples of divine judgment on sinners in verses 5–7 (the wilderness generation, the Watchers, and Sodom and Gomorrah) and a Jewish paraenetic and haggadic tradition in verse 11 within the context of an early Christian prophecy (Cain, Balaam, and Korah).[8] In addition, in verses 17–18 there is the summary of apostolic, apocalyptic warnings from the preaching and teaching of the early church.

Written texts upon which Jude draws include the Hebrew Old Testament and the two Jewish pseudepigraphical and apocalyptic works of *1 Enoch* and the *Testament of Moses*. Regarding the Old Testament, Jude

---

[5] Anders Gerdmar (*Rethinking the Judaism-Hellenism Dichotomy: A Historiographical Case Study of Second Peter and Jude* [ConBNT 36; Stockholm: Almqvist & Wiksell, 2001]) thoroughly investigates the apocalyptic nature of Jude and 2 Peter and their reliance upon Jewish apocalypticism.

[6] For detailed study of the argumentation of Jude, see Duane F. Watson, *Invention, Arrangement, and Style: Rhetorical Criticism of Jude and 2 Peter* (SBLDS 104; Atlanta: Scholars Press, 1988), 29–79.

[7] For discussion of Jude's use of oral and written traditions and texts, see J. Daryl Charles, *Literary Strategy in the Epistle of Jude* (Scranton, Pa.: University of Scranton Press, 1993), 91–166.

[8] This paraenetic and haggadic tradition is found in written sources (see discussion of this verse below), but Jude's use of it cannot be identified with any one written source. I am treating it as an oral source.

uses it frequently (v. 11, Num 26:9; v. 12, Prov 25:14 and Ezek 34:2; v. 13, Isa 57:20; v. 23, Amos 4:11 and Zech 3:3). He was familiar with the Hebrew Bible and makes his own Greek translation. He is unfamiliar with the LXX, for "at no point where he alludes to specific verses of the OT does he echo the language of the LXX."[9] Jude relies heavily upon *1 Enoch* (vv. 6, 12–16), with his only formal quotation from a written source being *1 En.* 1:9 (vv. 14–15). He is familiar with *1 En.* 1–36 (vv. 6, 12–13, 14–16; cf. v. 8), *1 En.* 80 (vv. 12–13), and perhaps *1 En.* 83–90 (v. 13). He is familiar with the Aramaic text (vv. 6, 14) but probably the Greek text as well (v. 15). Jude also knows the *Testament of Moses,* both its extant portion (v. 16) and its lost ending (v. 9, quoting Zech 3:2).[10]

1.1. First Proof That the False Teachers Are Ungodly and Subject to Judgment (vv. 5–10)

Jude's first proof of his proposition (v. 4) is from comparison of examples. Verses 5–7 provide the examples of notorious sinners judged by God, and verses 8–10 provide the comparison with the false teachers. The resulting proof is that the false teachers are comparable notorious sinners and thus also subject to judgment. Verses 5–7 provide the traditional Jewish paraenetic schema of three examples of divine judgment of sinners. Each example is an oral-scribal intertextural recitation of the type in which the author summarizes a span of text (or oral tradition) that includes various episodes.[11] Jude is giving a brief rendering of the account of the exodus and the wilderness wanderings from Exodus and Num 14 and 26:64–65 (v. 5), the fall of the Watchers from Gen 6:1–4 and *1 En.* 6–19 (especially ch. 10) (v. 6), and the judgment of Sodom and Gomorrah from Gen 18:16–19:29 (v. 7). This threefold schema is found also in Sir 16:7–10; CD II, 17–III, 12; 3 Macc 2:4–7; *T. Naph.* 3:4–5; *m. Sanh.* 10:3; and 2 Pet 2:4–8. It is found in paraenetic contexts after maxims that God punishes sin, and serves as a warning not to follow the examples of the sinners cited.[12]

Since Jude assumes that the audience has knowledge of these sinners, he is probably using recitation that has come down in early Christian tradition. However, his recitation is geared to meet the needs of

---

[9] Richard Bauckham, *Jude, 2 Peter* (WBC 50; Waco, Tex.: Word, 1983), 7. For more on Jude's use of the Old Testament, see idem, "James, 1 and 2 Peter, Jude," in *It is Written: Scripture Citing Scripture* (ed. D. A. Carson and H. G. M. Williamson; Cambridge: Cambridge University Press, 1988), 303–6.

[10] Bauckham, *Jude, 2 Peter,* 7.

[11] Robbins, *Exploring the Texture of Texts,* 43–44; idem, *Tapestry of Early Christian Discourse,* 106.

[12] Bauckham, *Jude, 2 Peter,* 46–47.

his argumentation and moves beyond the usual use of this schema to provide warning examples. Jude's recitation is part of his proof of verses 5–10 supporting his proposition in verse 4 that the false teachers among his audience are ungodly and subject to judgment. His recitation emphasizes the sin and judgment described in the biblical and extrabiblical narratives. In accordance with his apocalyptic outlook, Jude uses the schema to show that God judges sinners within history and will once more act within history to judge the ungodly false teachers corrupting his community. "In Jude the examples are not given as warnings to his readers, but as prophetic types of which the false teachers ... are the antitypes."[13] The examples of the schema are prophetic types supporting the argument from comparison of examples.

Verses 8–10 draw the comparison between the prophetic types of sinners and their judgment and the false teachers and their judgment. Like the Watchers and the inhabitants of Sodom and Gomorrah, the false teachers defile the flesh; like the Israelites, Watchers, and Sodomites, they reject authority; and like the Sodomites, they revile angels (v. 8). Verses 9–10 amplify the comparison. Verse 9 is an oral-scribal recitation of the now-lost ending of the *Testament of Moses*.[14] Jude's recitation is one that recites a narrative in one's own words but also incorporates recitation of a text with exact words.[15] He uses the example of the faithful archangel Michael, who, even with all his authority, did not judge the devil, the accusing angel, for his slander of Moses for the murder of the Egyptian. Rather, Michael let the Lord be the judge. Michael rebuked the devil by quoting Zech 3:2, "The Lord rebuke you." The quotation comes from the fourth vision of Zechariah (3:1–10) that is set in the heavenly court. There God rebukes Satan for attempting to accuse Joshua the high priest. Thus Michael is portrayed in the *Testament of Moses* (and subsequently Jude as well) as appealing to God to rebuke Satan with divine authority, authority that God has already exercised toward Satan using the exact same reprimand. Michael realizes that this authority to rebuke Satan is God's alone. Michael's example of a powerful being acting humbly before God strongly contrasts the foolishness of the false teachers in Jude's community, who, even as mere mortals, dare to slander the good angels upholding the law of Moses,[16] arrogance that

---

[13] Ibid., 47.

[14] Ibid., 7, 47–48. See his reconstruction of the story of the lost ending of the *Testament of Moses* on which this analysis relies (pp. 65–76).

[15] For this type of recitation, see Robbins, *Exploring the Texture of Texts,* 42–43; and idem, *Tapestry of Early Christian Discourse,* 104–5.

[16] "Slander the glorious ones" probably refers to slandering the angels who gave the Mosaic law, uphold the order of creation, and condemn the behavior of the false teachers. For this exegesis, see Bauckham, *Jude, 2 Peter,* 58–59, 62–63.

subjects them to impending judgment (v. 10). Jude's proof from example is that if the false teachers sin like notorious sinners of the past—including their foolish slander of good angels—then their fate will be the same destruction experienced by those sinners.

1.2. Second Proof That the False Teachers Are Ungodly and Subject to Judgment (vv. 11–13)

Jude 11–13 is another proof from example. Here the examples are provided by a supernatural oracle, a prophecy. Verse 11 is a prophetic woe oracle of an early Christian prophet, perhaps Jude himself.[17] It incorporates three examples of ungodly men from the Old Testament who were judged for their sins. Cultural intertexture plays a large role in the construction of the prophecy, particularly by reference or allusion. "A *reference* is a word or phrase that points to a personage or tradition known to people on the basis of tradition.... An *allusion* is a statement that presupposes a tradition that exists in textual form, but the text being interpreted is not attempting to 'recite' the text."[18] Only those familiar with Jewish and early Christian tradition would recognize the three personages and the texts and traditions referenced. Whereas in the last proof recitation was used to create a comparison with the false teachers, here reference is used to describe the false teachers in terms of the ungodly of the Old Testament and Jewish tradition and to pronounce judgment upon them.

Unlike the first proof, in which the figures from the Old Testament were ungodly, these three examples were also known as false teachers and thus more closely relate to the exigence of Jude's congregation. In Jewish tradition Cain was not only the first murderer (which cannot be the reference here), but also the archetypal sinner and teacher of others about sin,[19] a teacher who denied divine judgment.[20] Although in the Old Testament Balaam refused to curse Israel for money (Num 22:18; 24:13), in Jewish tradition Balaam's advice to Balak to parade beautiful women before the Israelites was responsible for the immorality and apostasy of Israel (Num 25:1–3).[21] Balaam's involvement was thought to be confirmed by his presence with the Midianite kings when they were all killed by the Israelites (Num 31:8; Josh 13:21–22), his presence being interpreted as his return for payment.[22]

---

[17] Ibid., 77–79.

[18] Robbins, *Exploring the Texture of Texts*, 58. For full discussion, see 58–60; idem, *Tapestry of Early Christian Discourse*, 110.

[19] 1 John 3:11; *T. Benj.* 7:5; Philo, *Post.* 38–39; *1 Clem.* 4.7.

[20] *Tg. Ps.-J.* and *Tg. Neof.*, on Gen 4:8.

[21] *L.A.B.* 18:13; Philo, *Mos.* 1.295–300; Josephus, *Ant.* 4.126–130; *y. Sanh.* 10.28d.

[22] *b. Sanh.* 106a.

Korah, who led a rebellion against Moses and Aaron (Num 16:1–35; 26:9–10), was portrayed in Jewish tradition as an antinomian heretic who denied the authority of the law as given by Moses.[23]

Verses 12–13 apply the woe oracle of verse 11 to the false teachers of Jude's congregation. They use a combination of cultural intertextural references to the Old Testament and oral-scribal recontextualization of biblical and extrabiblical Jewish texts so that negative images and metaphors from nature and tradition can be used as succinct descriptors of the false teachers. This application is composed of six metaphors. The second metaphor, "shepherding themselves," is a cultural intertextural reference or allusion to Ezek 34:2b: "Ah, you shepherds of Israel who have been feeding yourselves! Should not shepherds feed the sheep?" In Ezek 31 God chastises the leadership of Israel for misusing the people of Israel whose lives were in their care and who supplied their needs. He promises judgment for the fat, well-fed shepherds.

Central in the application of the prophecy is an extensive use of oral-scribal intertexture—recontextualization involving the last four metaphors. Recontextualization "presents wording from biblical texts without explicit statement or implication that the words 'stand written' anywhere else."[24] The last four of these metaphors derive from *1 En.* 2:1–5:4 (a comment on *1 En.* 1:9, a passage that Jude quotes immediately following in vv. 14–15) and 80:2–8 (with the exception of the metaphor of the sea). They represent the four regions of the universe: clouds in the sky, trees on dry ground, waves in the sea, and stars in the heavens. In *1 En.* 2:1–5:4 these four regions are used to affirm that nature conforms to the laws that God established for it. These images of the obedience of nature are contrasted with the disobedience of the false teachers. In *1 En.* 80:2–8 three of these regions describe nature not abiding by these laws in the last days. Jude recontextualizes these images of nature in the last days as it transgresses the laws laid down for it. He creates metaphors to describe the behavior of the false teachers in his congregation, behavior befitting the disobedient in the days before the *parousia*.[25] Recontextualization amplifies the rebellion of the false teachers against the order established by God, as well as their corrupting influence.

This oral-scribal recontextualization from *1 Enoch* employs four examples of intertexture. Two of these examples are oral-scribal recitations of the Old Testament. Jude's "They are waterless clouds carried along by the

---

[23] *L.A.B.* 16:1; *Tg. Ps.-J.* on Num 16:1–2; *Num. Rab.* 18:3, 12.

[24] Robbins, *Exploring the Texture of Texts,* 48. For full discussion, see 48–50; idem, *Tapestry of Early Christian Discourse,* 107.

[25] Bauckham, *Jude, 2 Peter,* 90–91.

winds" (v. 12) is a recitation of Prov 25:14: "Like clouds and wind without rain is one who boasts of a gift never given." Jude's "wild waves of the sea, casting up the foam of their own shame" (v. 13) is a recitation of Isa 57:20 in just slightly different words: "But the wicked are like the tossing sea that cannot keep still; its waters toss up mire and mud." In Isaiah the wicked are compared to the tossing sea and its mire and mud, but in Jude the sea and its mire are used as metaphors for the false teachers.

The other two examples from nature are cultural intertextural references or allusions to Jewish and early Christian tradition. One is "autumn trees without fruit, twice dead, uprooted" (v. 12), a metaphor drawn from the traditional image of a tree and its fruit that was often associated with judgment (Ps 52:5; Prov 2:22; Wis 4:4; Matt 3:10 par. Luke 3:9; Matt 7:19; 15:13; Luke 13:9). Here the metaphor is associated with the second death of the wicked after the judgment of the last day (Rev 2:11; 20:6, 14; 21:8). The other cultural reference is "wandering stars, for whom the deepest darkness has been reserved forever" (v. 13), a reference to the Watchers of Gen 4:1–6 as transmitted in tradition, especially *1 En.* 18:13–16; 83–90. The Watchers were represented as wandering stars that disobeyed God, were cast from heaven in a dark abyss, and were bound there until the last judgment when they are to be cast into a fiery abyss.

These oral-scribal recitations and recontextualizations as well as the cultural intertextural references and allusions allow Jude to claim that the false teachers are dangerous leaders concerned only for themselves: promising benefit but never delivering, producing corruption and shame, leading others astray, and heading for judgment on all counts. Rhetorically it serves to vilify the false teachers and lessen their *ethos* by association with negative images and traditions.

1.3. Third Proof That the False Teachers Are Ungodly and Subject to Judgment (vv. 14–16)

Jude 14–16 provides a third proof from example, this time using oral-scribal recitation of a supernatural oracle. The proof is that the teachers in the community are the ungodly of prophecy and are subject to the judgment described. In verses 14–15 Jude quotes *1 En.* 1:9: "See, the Lord is coming with ten thousands of his holy ones, to execute judgment on all, and to convict everyone of all the deeds of ungodliness that they have committed in such an ungodly way, and of all the harsh things that ungodly sinners have spoken against him." He seems to have known the Greek version but made his own translation from the Aramaic version.[26] Jude's recitation of this written text is of the type that

---

[26] For detailed analysis, see ibid., 93–96.

changes a few words.[27] Compare *1 En.* 1:9: "Behold, he will arrive with ten million of the holy ones in order to execute judgment upon all. He will destroy the wicked ones and censure all flesh on account of everything that they have done, that which the sinners and the wicked ones committed against him." Jude changes "he" into "the Lord," referring to the Lord Jesus. This transforms the prophecy, making it a reference to the *parousia* and judgment of Jesus rather than the Day of God.[28] It is an example of early Christian christological interpretation of the Old Testament that often understands Jesus rather than God as the referent of "Lord." Old Testament theophanic texts about the coming of God were applied to the *parousia*.[29] Another change is that in *1 Enoch* the focus is "all flesh," but in verse 16, Jude's application of the prophecy, the focus of judgment is more narrowly the false teachers in the community. It is they, as ungodly sinners, who are singled out to experience the judgment of the *parousia*.

1.4. Fourth Proof That the Teachers Are Ungodly and Subject to
        Judgment (vv. 17–19)

In verses 17–19 Jude provides a proof from example based on an authoritative judgment—here a supernatural oracle or prophecy. It is an apocalyptic prophecy of the apostles received by the community at its founding (vv. 17–18) that is applied to the false teachers (v. 19). The apocalyptic prophecy is probably not an exact quotation but a summary oral-scribal recitation of the general content of many apostolic prophecies concerning the *parousia*. Jude's recitation of these prophecies could have many forms, but he summarizes them to emphasize the topics of scoffing and ungodly lusts to befit the false teachers.[30] Here oral-scribal intertexture helps argumentation not only by developing topics but also by lending to it the authority of apostolic prophecy.

---

[27] Robbins, *Exploring the Texture of Texts,* 41; idem, *Tapestry of Early Christian Discourse,* 104.

[28] Matthew Black, "The Maranatha Invocation and Jude 14, 15 (I Enoch 1:9)," in *Christ and Spirit in the New Testament: In Honour of Charles Francis Digby Moule* (ed. Barnabas Lindars and Stephen S. Smalley; Cambridge: Cambridge University Press, 1973), 189–96; C. D. Osborn, "The Christological Use of 1 Enoch i.9 in Jude 14, 15," *NTS* 23 (1976–77): 334–41.

[29] Isa 40:10 (Rev 22:12); Isa 63:1–6 (Rev 19:13, 15); Isa 66:15 (2 Thess 1:7); Zech 14:5 (1 Thess 3:13; *Did.* 16.7). See Bauckham, *Jude, 2 Peter,* 96–97.

[30] Similar prophecies of immoral believers in the last days include 2 Tim 3:1–9; *Ascen. Isa.* 3:21, 25–28.

1.5. Concluding Exhortation (vv. 20–23)

Jude 20–23 is exhortation to the faithful to contend for the faith in light of the infiltration of the false teachers into the community, teachers he has now clearly identified as false and the subject to judgment. To contend for the faith was a major purpose of his letter (v. 3). In verse 23 there is an oral-scribal reconfiguration of Zech 3:2–4. Zechariah 3:2 is already found in the quotation of *Testament of Moses* in verse 9. Now Jude instructs the faithful to "save others by snatching them out of the fire." In Zech 3:2 Joshua the high priest is described by God as a "brand plucked from the fire." The passage is set in the context of a vision of the purification of the high priest and a promise of the purification of the people that will save them from the fire of divine wrath. Jude reconfigures the imagery so that the faithful in the community now function in God's capacity of saving the unfaithful from the fire of judgment at the impending *parousia*. Although not as apparent, there may also be a reconfiguration of Amos 4:11, where God describes Israel after judgment and in light of mercy as "a brand snatched from the fire." Again, in Jude this reconfiguration places the faithful of the community in God's role of saving the unfaithful from destruction.

In the process the faithful are to be "hating even the tunic defiled by their [the unfaithfuls'] bodies." In Zech 3:3–4 Joshua the high priest is "dressed with filthy clothes" symbolizing his ritual impurity and sin. Those around Joshua are ordered by the angel to take off his filthy clothes. Jude reconfigures the imagery in light of the Christ event. The faithful cannot take off the filthy clothes (i.e., cleanse the unfaithful of their sins), but they do need to be careful not to be corrupted by those clothes (i.e., sins) in the process of extending mercy. In Jude the images from Zechariah are reconfigured in moral exhortation grounded in the reality of the Christ event and the impending *parousia* judgment.

1.6. Conclusions

Jude's use of intertexture is colored by his apocalyptic outlook and influenced by the rhetorical approach suggested by his exigence. He uses various forms of oral-scribal and cultural intertexture in his *logos* or argumentation to create proofs that the false teachers of his community are ungodly and subject to the approaching judgment of the *parousia*. In his first proof from comparison of examples (vv. 5–10) Jude uses oral-scribal recitation that summarizes spans of biblical and extrabiblical texts and oral tradition. He creates prophetic types of sinners who were judged with which to compare the false teachers (vv. 5–8). He uses oral-scribal recitation that summarizes a pseudepigraphical text, with a quotation of the Old Testament included, in order to amplify the comparison (vv. 9–10). In his second proof (vv. 11–13), Jude uses a prophecy based on cultural references and allusions to notorious sinners of the Old Testament and Jewish tradition, their false teaching, and their judgment to portray the false teachers (v. 11). In the application of the prophecy, negative images and metaphors from nature provide descriptors of the false teachers and associate them with sin and judgment (vv. 12–13). These descriptors are drawn from cultural intertextural references and allusions to the Old Testament and Jewish and early Christian tradition, along with oral-scribal recitation of the Old Testament and recontextualization of *1 Enoch*. In his third proof (vv. 14–15) Jude uses oral-scribal recitation of a pseudepigraphical text with slight alterations to make a prophecy of the Day of God refer to the *parousia* of Jesus Christ. In his fourth proof (vv. 17–19) Jude uses an oral-scribal recitation of apostolic prophecy in his own words to emphasize the scoffing and lust of the false teachers. In his concluding exhortation (vv. 20–23) Jude appropriates oral-scribal intertexture and reconfigures an Old Testament passage so as to ground his exhortation in the reality of the Christ event and the imminent *parousia*.

Jude's use of intertexture is guided not only by the needs of logical proof or *logos* but also by the needs of *ethos* and *pathos*. Intertextural connections to the Old Testament and Jewish tradition, both oral and written, and emerging Christian tradition lend Jude's argumentation the authority associated with these texts and traditions. Jude does not push his own authority in this letter. To give his letter authority he relies heavily upon oral-scribal and cultural interconnections to traditions and texts that have their own authority. The material recited and recontextualized is primarily prophetic in nature, coming from Isaiah, Ezekiel, and *1 Enoch*. Jude's confident application of these prophecies and prophetic material to the false teachers strongly indicates that he has his own prophetic insight and is functioning as a prophet in his leadership of the community.

The negative emotions associated with the intertextural connections help Jude elicit negative emotions from his community that can be directed to the false teachers and their program. It is particularly important to have elicited these negative emotions before his ending exhortation to better ensure that the congregation will do as he desires.

Jude's use of written sources is revealing, both for placing the letter and its audience in the landscape of early Christianity and for discovering the hermeneutic of its author. Jude makes use of the apocalyptic works of *1 Enoch* and the *Testament of Moses*. *First Enoch* seems to have circulated only in Palestine in Aramaic in the first century and did not receive widespread use in Christian circles until it was translated into Greek.[31] The *Testament of Moses* is also placed in first-century Palestine.[32] These Jewish

---

[31] Bauckham, *Jude, 2 Peter,* 139–40.
[32] J. Priest, "Testament of Moses," *OTP* 1:920–22.

apocalyptic works situate Jude within Palestine among Jewish-Christian circles that were highly apocalyptic in outlook. "To say that Jude belongs to apocalyptic Jewish Christianity is not a very precise statement, but the dominance of the apocalyptic outlook in Jude and his use of the Jewish apocalypses at any rate locates him in circles where apocalyptic was not just one influence, but the dominant vehicle through which faith in Jesus found expression."[33]

In this environment Jewish apocalyptic texts were interpreted in light of Jesus. Jude can interpret the Jewish apocalyptic texts in light of Jesus inaugurating the last days. "Its [Jude's] hermeneutical principle is the apocalyptic principle that inspired Scripture speaks of the last days in which the interpreter is living."[34] Jude can interpret the authoritative Jewish texts, which at that time included *1 Enoch* and the *Testament of Moses*, in light of his own time and the *parousia*. He can recite, recontextualize, reconfigure, reference, and allude to these materials as eschatological typology and apocalyptic prophecy in order to create argumentation to prove that the false teachers in the churches are the fulfillment of prophecy about the *parousia* and subject to its judgment. The same hermeneutic of applying Scripture to contemporary events affecting the community was used by the Essenes at Qumran, another apocalyptic Palestinian community. For example, in 1QpHab the Essenes were able to interpret portions of Habbakkuk as referring to the Romans in their own day and in turn the presence of the Romans as a sign of the approach of the Day of the Lord.

2. The Intertexture of Apocalyptic Discourse in 2 Peter

The exigence of 2 Peter is eschatological skepticism arising from the delay of the *parousia* (3:4, 9). The skeptics deny the reality of the *parousia*, claiming that it is a cleverly devised myth and fabrication of the apostles and their misinterpretation of Old Testament prophecy (1:16–21). The author of 2 Peter shares the imminent eschatology of the early church. He assumes that he and his audience will witness the *parousia* (1:19; 3:14) and the skeptics will experience its judgment (2:1, 12). This approach to eschatological delay is similar to that of Jewish apocalyptic in acknowledging the delay of divine intervention while at the same time reaffirming its imminence.[35] In fact our author uses Jewish apocalyptic and Jewish-Christian apocalyptic tradition and sources to create his polemic, including

---

[33] Bauckham, *Jude, 2 Peter,* 10.

[34] Ibid.

[35] Richard J. Bauckham, "The Delay of the Parousia," *TynBul* 31 (1980): 3–36.

an apocalyptic interpretation of the transfiguration (1:16–18), apocalyptic portions of Jude, and a Jewish apocalypse underlying 3:4–13.

Second Peter uses a variety of intertextural connections in the creation of his proofs, refutation, and vilification.[36] These include connections with the Old Testament, Jewish apocalyptic and Jewish-Christian apocalyptic sources, extrabiblical Jewish haggadic traditions, Gospel tradition, and the Epistle of Jude. Noticeably lacking are connections to Jewish pseudepigraphical works. This is somewhat surprising since these works are often apocalyptic and make a ready resource for debate about eschatological skepticism.

The following are certain or highly probable oral-scribal and cultural intertextural connections with the Old Testament. These include: 1:17–18 (Ps 2:6–7 from Gospel tradition; Isa 42:1), 1:19 (Num 24:17); 2:4 (Gen 6:1–4); 2:5 (Gen 6:5–8:19, esp. v. 17); 2:6 (Gen 19:1–23, esp. v. 29); 2:8–9 (Gen 19:1–23); 2:15–16 (Num 22:21–35); 2:22 (Prov 26:11); 3:5 (Gen 1:1–10); 3:6 (Gen 7); 3:8 (Ps 90 [LXX 89]:4); 3:9 (Hab 2:3); 3:10 (Mal 3:19; Isa 34:4); 3:12 (Isa 34:4; 60:22); 3:12–14 (Hab 2:3); and 3:13 (Isa 65:17; 66:22). Many of these intertextural connections are taken from the sources our author used, including 1:17–18 (oral Gospel tradition); 2:22 (a proverb); and 3:4–13 (a Jewish apocalyptic source). Our author often utilizes the Septuagint: 1:19 (Num 24:17); 2:2 (Isa 52:5); 2:5 (Gen 6:17); 2:6 (Gen 19:29); 3:12 (Isa 34:4); and 3:13 (Isa 65:17). Many connections to the Old Testament do not come from the LXX and were already made in the sources that our author used: 2:22 (Prov 26:11); 3:9, 12–14 (Hab 2:3); and 3:12 (Isa 60:22).[37]

Our author uses both Jewish apocalyptic and Jewish-Christian apocalyptic sources. A Jewish apocalyptic source underlies 3:4–13. Jewish-Christian apocalyptic sources used include the interpretation of the transfiguration from oral tradition (1:16–18) and the Epistle of Jude (2:1–18; 3:1–3). The latter provided extrabiblical Jewish haggadic traditions (2:4–5, 7–8, 15–16). Gospel tradition, oral or written, and independent of the canonical Gospels is also a source. There is an allusion in 1:14 to Peter knowing of his own death (tradition also appearing in John 21:18–19) and the tradition of the transfiguration (1:16–18). These are used as part of the pseudonymous ruse that the author is actually Peter. There are also recontextualizations of a saying of Jesus about unrepentance (2:20; Matt 12:45 par. Luke 11:26) and of a prophecy of Jesus that the Day of the Lord would come as a thief (3:10; Matt 24:43 par. Luke 12:39).

---

[36] For detailed study of the argumentation of 2 Peter, see Watson, *Invention, Arrangement, and Style*, 81–146.

[37] Bauckham, *Jude, 2 Peter*, 138. For more on the use of the Old Testament in 2 Peter, see Bauckham, "James, 1 and 2 Peter, Jude," 313–15.

2.1. Defense of the *Parousia* Using Proof of Eyewitness Testimony and Documents (1:16–19)

In 1:16–19 our author constructs two proofs that the apostolic preaching of the *parousia* is trustworthy. One is a proof from eyewitness testimony (vv. 16–18) and the other a proof from documents (v. 19). Regarding the first, the transfiguration is used as a proof from eyewitness testimony that the apostolic proclamation of the *parousia* is based on experience. One element of the testament genre, of which 2 Peter is an example, is an apocalyptic revelation given to the testator, a revelation that forms the basis for predictions made in the testament.[38] This is how the transfiguration most broadly functions in 1:16–18. More narrowly the transfiguration account functions to refute the claims of the false teachers that the apostolic proclamation of the power and coming (παρουσία) of Jesus is a "cleverly devised myth" (v. 16). In the guise of the apostle Peter our author uses the transfiguration as a proleptic vision of the exalted Christ who receives honor and glory from God to carry out God's eschatological judgment and rule. It is a promise of the future manifestation of his glory at the *parousia*.

The voice is conveyed to Jesus by the "Majestic Glory" from heaven. This is an element of apocalyptic discourse that the voice of revelation be from heaven, yet not be identified explicitly as the voice of God.[39] Psalm 2:7 provides the content of the heavenly voice and conveys considerable meaning. Psalm 2 is a royal psalm composed for the coronation of a king. It describes the nations as ready to rebel against the new king (vv. 1–3), the installation of the new king (vv. 4–7), and God's promise to the new king of universal dominion (vv. 8–11). Psalm 2:7 is a formula of adoption whereby the new king is adopted as God's son: "You are my son; today I have begotten you." The formula is uttered in the context of God promising: "I have set my king on Zion, my holy hill" (v. 6). The psalm was understood messianically in Judaism to describe the Messiah's rule over the nations.

Our author reconfigures Ps. 2:7. "Reconfiguration is recounting a situation in a manner that makes the later event 'new' in relation to a previous event. Because the new event is similar to a previous event, the new event replaces or 'outshines' the previous event, making the previous event a 'foreshadowing' of the more recent one."[40] Our author uses Ps 2:7 as the content of the voice "This is my Son" (2 Pet 1:17) within the stated context of the

---

[38] *1 En.* 93; *2 Bar.* 81:4; *T. Levi* 2–5; 8; *Adam and Eve* 25–29; *2 En.* 39:2; *L.A.B.* 28:4; Bauckham, *Jude, 2 Peter,* 205.

[39] Dan 4:31; *1 En.* 13:8; 65:4; *2 Bar.* 13:1; 22:1; Rev 4:4, 8; 10:4; 11:12; 14:13; 16:1.

[40] Robbins, *Exploring the Texture of Texts,* 50; idem, *Tapestry of Early Christian Discourse,* 107–8.

"holy mountain" (1:18), a designation for Mount Zion in the Old Testament. God is appointing Jesus as eschatological king over the nations. Revelation 2:26–28 portrays Jesus using Ps 2:8–9 to claim that the authority to rule the nations was given him by the Father. In addition, "with whom I am well pleased" is a reconfiguration of Isa 42:1, the first Servant Song (Isa 42:1–4) and ties Jesus to the servant who will bring justice to the nations.[41]

Our author's account of the transfiguration from the Gospel tradition appears to be independent of the Synoptic Gospel accounts (Mark 9:2–8; Matt 17:1–8; Luke 9:28–36). Guided by his polemical needs, he understands the transfiguration as God's appointment of Jesus as eschatological king and judge. Anything from the Gospel tradition that does not promote the advancement of his polemic is dismissed. For example, he makes no use of the transfiguration to portray Jesus as a prophet like Moses or portray the transfiguration in terms of the theophany at Sinai. The words of God are different from those in the Synoptic Gospels, especially the omission of the command "listen to him." The latter derives from Deut 18:15 and would portray Jesus as a prophet like Moses. Our author "is presenting Jesus as eschatological divine vicegerent, not as eschatological prophet."[42]

Verse 19 offers a second proof that the proclamation of the *parousia* is not a cleverly devised myth. The proclamation is true because it relies on very firm Old Testament messianic prophecy. The audience is urged to heed this prophecy "until the day dawns and the morning star rises in your hearts" (1:19). The "day" to dawn is the eschatological age to be inaugurated by the *parousia* (cf. 3:10: "Day of the Lord"). It will be an age of light in contrast to the age of darkness in which our author and his audience are living (cf. 3:18: "day of eternity"; cf. Rom 13:12). The imagery is based on the apocalyptic dualism of light and darkness, with prophecy introducing some light into the present darkness until the full light of the coming age materializes. This coming age is inaugurated when "the morning star rises in your hearts." "The morning star rises" (φωσφόρος ἀνατείλῃ) is a recitation with modification of Num 24:17: "a star shall come out of Jacob" (ανατελεῖ ἄστρον ἐξ Ἰακὼβ). Numbers 24:17 was interpreted messianically in Judaism.[43] Here it refers to the *parousia* of Christ. Our author substitutes "morning star" (φωσφόρος) for "star" (ἄστρον) and refers to Venus, the

---

[41] Bauckham (*Jude, 2 Peter,* 220) argues that our author probably sees no further connection with Isa 42:1 than the election of Jesus, but authority over all the nations is implicit in the election of Jesus and suits the needs of the argumentation at this juncture.

[42] Ibid., 219.

[43] *T. Levi* 18:3; *T. Jud.* 24:1; 1QM XI, 6–7; CD VII, 18–20; *y. Ta'an.* 68d.

morning star, as the star that inaugurates the dawn of a new day (cf. Rev 22:16). The *parousia* inaugurates the coming age of light, and Christians will perceive it with their hearts.

2.2. Counteraccusation (2:1–3a)

In 2:1–3a our author moves from defending the apostolic preaching of the *parousia* to attacking the false teachers. There were many early Christian prophecies of the coming of false prophets in the last days.[44] It is typical of a testament for the testator to prophesy about the future, and false teachers are often mentioned in the testaments of the New Testament.[45] Our author is using cultural intertexture—early Christian prophecies of the coming of false prophets and teachers in the end times—to create his apostolic prophecy about false teachers in the last days. In the guise of Peter he creates a prophecy of false teachers, but it is tailored to meet the specifics of his own exigence and time. These false teachers bring "destructive opinions," and eschatological destruction is swiftly coming upon them (2:1, 3b; 3:7, 16). Their very appearance is a sign that the end has come.

2.3. Defense of God's Judgment As Not Idle or Asleep Using a Proof from Example (2:3b–10a)

In 2:3b–10a our author moves to refute the false teachers' claim that divine judgment is idle and asleep (2:3b). He uses an elaborate proof of comparison of example. He uses three examples of judgment against sinners. Two of the three examples are recited from Jude 6–8 with modifications—the Watchers and the cities of Sodom and Gomorrah. Our author has substituted the generation of Noah for Jude's wilderness generation, I surmise, because the judgment of letting a generation die of natural causes over forty years in the wilderness did not serve well as a type of sudden and cataclysmic eschatological judgment. In Jude the two examples are used as prophetic types of sinners who were judged to which false teachers are compared. In 2 Peter all three examples are examples of judgment used in proof, as prototypes of eschatological judgment.

The first example, the Watchers (Gen 6:1–4), are kept in deepest darkness until the eschatological judgment (2 Pet 2:4). Verbal echoes of *1 Enoch* in Jude 6 disappear, especially a reference to the sexual sin of the angels in taking human wives. The Watchers was a widespread tradition in Judaism beyond *1 Enoch,* which may explain our author's retention of it. When he mentions that the angels were cast into Tartarus he is adding

---

[44] Matt 7:15–20; 24:11, 14; Mark 13:22; 1 John 4:1; Rev 16:13; 19:20; 20:10; *Did.* 16.3; Hegesippus, ap. Eusebius, *Hist. eccl.* 4.22.6.

[45] Acts 20:29–30; 2 Tim 3:1–9; 4:3–4.

vocabulary that ties the Watchers to the myth of the Greek Titans. The second example, Noah's generation (Gen 6:17), was destroyed by water (2 Pet 2:5). Their destruction was considered by Jewish and early Christian tradition as a prototype of eschatological judgment.[46] This may explain why our author has added it to his recitation of Jude. The third example is Sodom and Gomorrah, which were destroyed by fire (Gen 19:29). It serves as a prototype of the fiery judgment awaiting the unrighteous at the *parousia* (2 Pet 3:7, 10, 12). Often the judgment of the flood and Sodom and Gomorrah were linked as two prototypes of eschatological judgment (e.g., Luke 17:26–30).

In addition to Jude 6–8, in 2:5–8 our author has added two examples of the righteous and their fate in opposition to the unrighteous and their fate (Noah and his family, Abraham and Lot). The suffering of the righteous in a wicked world is an apocalyptic theme, and these examples of the righteous among the wicked allow our author indirectly to portray his audience as the righteous suffering under the wicked false teachers and sharing separate fates on the day of judgment. Our author uses oral-scribal recitation of a span of text to present God's salvation of Noah and his family (Gen 6:5–8:19) and the struggles of Lot in Sodom and Gomorrah (Gen 19:1–23). The righteousness of Lot is a cultural allusion to a Jewish exegetical tradition.[47] The conclusion is that while the righteous and unrighteous live together now, the unrighteous are kept for judgment and the righteous will be rescued from trial (πειρασμός). The trial may be that of the righteous in a wicked world and/or the trial of the last days.

2.4. Vilification of the False Teachers (2:10b–22)

Second Peter 2:10b–22 is a digression that vilifies the false teachers and tries to elicit negative *pathos* from the audience. This vilification includes some apocalyptic discourse. Hardly anything of *1 Enoch* in Jude 12–13 remains in our author's description of the false teachers in 2:17. Jude's "they are waterless clouds carried along by the winds" is the only one of Jude's four nature metaphors from *1 Enoch* remaining. Our author has recast this single nature metaphor as two: "waterless springs and mists driven by a storm." Jude's nature metaphor is derived from the Hebrew text of Prov 25:14, for the LXX does not have this translation. Our author, being dependent upon the LXX, would see no reason to maintain the metaphor in its exact form. The division and modification of the metaphor provides him with more emphatic dual negative metaphors for the emptiness of the false teachers' teaching. In contrast, our author does retain verbatim Jude's reference to

---

[46] *1 En.* 1–16; 1QH X, 35–36; Matt 24:37–39; 2 Pet 3:5–7.

[47] Wis 10:6; *Gen. Rab.* 49:13; Gerdmar, *Rethinking the Judaism-Hellenism Dichotomy*, 141–43.

the wandering stars (Watchers)—"for them the deepest darkness has been reserved." It is retained to refer to the eschatological fate of the wicked that Jewish tradition often cast as darkness.[48] This retention of judgment language puts the previous nature metaphors in an apocalyptic framework.

There is a nearly verbatim use of a saying of Jesus in 2:20. It regards the state of the person into whom an unclean spirit returns and the state of the evil generation of his time: "the last state has become worse for them than the first" (Matt 12:45 par. Luke 11:26). Our author recontextualizes the words from oral tradition, Q, or a written Gospel to describe the fate of the apostate. A similar recontextualization is made by Herm. *Mand.* 5.2.7 and 12.5.4. This may be a familiar application of the saying of Jesus within the church of Rome from which 2 Peter and the *Shepherd of Hermas* derive.[49] Being in a worse state is in terms of one's standing before Jesus as eschatological judge about to bring swift destruction upon the world.

2.5. An Apology for the Delay of the *Parousia* and Divine Judgment (3:1–13)

Our author now offers a refutation of the false teachers' eschatological skepticism, an apology for the *parousia*. Richard Bauckham argues that 2 Pet 3:4–13 relies upon a written Jewish apocalypse that also appears in *1 Clem.* 23.3–4; *2 Clem.* 11.2–4; 16:3; and perhaps *1 Clem.* 23.5 and 27.4.[50] First Clement 23–27 is also a defense of traditional eschatology. The most noted correspondences are (1) 2 Pet 3:4 and *1 Clem.* 23.3 and *2 Clem.* 11.2; (2) 2 Pet 3:5–7 and *1 Clem.* 27.4; and (3) 2 Pet 3:10, 12 and *2 Clem.* 16.3. Let us look at these:

(1) 2 Pet 3:4 and *1 Clem.* 23.3; *2 Clem.* 11.2

Where is the promise of his coming? For ever since our ancestors died, all things continue as they were from the beginning of creation! (2 Pet 3:4)

Let this Scripture be far from us in which he says, "Wretched are the double-minded, who doubt in their soul and say, "We have heard these things even in the days of our fathers, and behold we have grown old, and none of these things has happened to us." (*1 Clem.* 23.3)

For the prophetic word also says:—"Miserable are the double-minded that doubt in their heart, who say, These things we heard long ago and in the

---

[48] Tob 14:10; *1 En.* 46:6; 63:6; *Pss. Sol.* 14:9; 15:10.

[49] Bauckham, *Jude, 2 Peter,* 277.

[50] Ibid., 283–85. See D. von Allmen ("L'apocalyptique juive et le retard de la parousie en II Pierre 3:1–13," *RTP* 16 [1966]: 256–64), who tries to determine what material the author borrows from the apocalyptic source and what is peculiar to him.

time of our fathers, but we have waited from day to day, and have seen none of them." (*2 Clem.* 11.2)

(2) 2 Pet 3:5–7 and *1 Clem.* 27.4

They deliberately ignore this fact, that by the word of God heavens existed long ago and an earth was formed out of water and by means of water, through which the world of that time was deluged with water and perished. But by the same word the present heavens and earth have been reserved for fire, being kept until the day of judgment and destruction of the godless. (2 Pet 3:5–7)

By the word of his majesty did he establish all things, and by his word can he destroy them. (*1 Clem.* 27.4)

(3) 2 Pet 3:10, 12 and *2 Clem.* 16.3

But the day of the Lord will come like a thief, and then the heavens will pass away with a loud noise, and the elements will be dissolved with fire, and the earth and everything that is done on it will be disclosed … waiting for and hastening the coming of the day of God, because of which the heavens will be set ablaze and dissolved, and the elements will melt with fire? (2 Pet 3:10, 12)

But you know that "the day" of judgment is already "approaching as a burning oven, and some of the heavens shall melt," and the whole earth shall be as lead melting in the fire, and then shall be made manifest the secret and open deeds of men. (*2 Clem.* 16.3)

This Jewish apocalyptic source explained eschatological delay and has been surmised to be the lost book of *Eldad and Modad* quoted in Herm. *Vis.* 2.3.4. Based in part upon the shared vocabulary of *1 Clement, 2 Clement,* and 2 Peter, Bauckham makes the point that this apocalyptic source was respected in the Roman church of the late first and early second century from which these three works emerged.[51]

Whether or not there is a Jewish apocalyptic source underlying 2 Pet 3:4–13 is a matter of speculation. In the analysis of the apocalyptic intertexture of the apology of 2 Pet 3:4–13 to follow, I am assuming that some of the intertextural connections probably preceded our author in tradition (oral and/or written) while other connections he made himself. Except for passages just cited where a source is indicated most clearly, it is nearly impossible to distinguish what may be original to an oral or written source

---

[51] Bauckham, *Jude, 2 Peter,* 140, 283–85; idem, "Delay of the Parousia," 3–36.

from what changes and additions our author may have made in its use. I will examine the intertextural connections and their implications without concern for their origin—our author or a source—unless there is enough evidence to do so.

In the opening of his apology in 3:2–3 our author recites Jude 17–18:

> But you, beloved, must remember the predictions of the apostles of our Lord Jesus Christ; for they said to you, "In the last time there will be scoffers, indulging their own ungodly lusts." (Jude 17–18)

> that you should remember the words spoken in the past by the holy prophets, and the commandment of the Lord and Savior spoken through your apostles. First of all you must understand this, that in the last days scoffers will come, scoffing and indulging their own lusts. (2 Pet 3:2–3)

Our author has made two notable additions to his recitation of Jude. First, the prophecy is no longer cited as an element of proof or as a quotation of the apostles. Central now is the creation of *ethos* for the prophecy of the appearance of scoffers in the last days that follows in 3:4. Through the guise of pseudonymity, the prophecy now originates in Peter himself as the spokesman for the apostles. Peter is portrayed as prophesying the appearance of the scoffers current in the time of our author. Peter experienced the transfiguration and witnessed God's elevation of Jesus as his eschatological vice-regent (1:16–18). He saw this heavenly mystery and can now affirm the *parousia* with confidence. He adds to his authority by duplicity with the prophets of the Old Testament (cf. 1:19–21) and the commandment of the Lord spoken through the apostles who founded the community (cf. 1:16–18). Now Peter, the Old Testament prophets, the Lord, and the apostles of the community all speak in one voice on the coming of false teachers in the last days.

Second, the content of the scoffers' scoff has been added to Jude: "Where is the promise of his coming? For ever since our ancestors died, all things continue as they were from the beginning of creation!" (3:4). Whereas in Jude the problem is denial of authority and subsequent immorality, now these are more specifically grounded in the denial of the promise of the *parousia* as given by Christ, a promise that seemed to be limited temporally to the lifetime of those to whom Jesus gave it.[52] Through cultural intertexture, the taunt of the scoffers is given negative connotations. It is framed in the form of a rhetorical question molded upon the Old Testament (LXX). "Where is?" (ποῦ ἐστιν), the opening formula of the question, has many

---

[52] Matt 16:28 par. Mark 9:1 par. Luke 9:27; Matt 24:34 par. Mark 13:30 par. Luke 21:32; John 21:22–23.

intertextural connections with the Old Testament. When God does not intervene on behalf of the psalmist, the psalmist's enemies question, "Where is
your God" (lxx Ps 41:4, 11). A similar taunt is given by the enemies of Israel
when God does not intervene for Israel (lxx Pss 78:10; 113:10; Joel 2:17; Mic
7:10), by those in Israel when God does not punish the wicked and reward
the righteous (Mal. 2:17), and by Jeremiah's enemies at the nonfulfillment of
his prophecies (Jer 17:15). The taunt in 2 Peter encapsulates the frustration
over God's delay in executing justice on earth and vindicating God's people.

The content of the false teachers' taunt may derive from the Jewish
apocalyptic source where the basis for the taunt is the lack of fulfillment of
the Old Testament prophecies of the Day of Lord, fulfillment lacking since
the days of the fathers, that is, of Israel. If so, the taunt is here recontextualized to refer to the lack of fulfillment of the prophecy of the *parousia* as
given by Christ. There had been no fulfillment since the days of "the
fathers," that is, the first generation of Christians who heard the promises
and in whose lifetime the promises were to have been fulfilled. In the pseudonymous ploy of 2 Peter these words of eschatological skepticism become
part of Peter's prophecy and quote the very opponents faced by our author.

In 2 Pet 3:5–7 our author uses an enthymeme to refute the opponents'
claim that God's judgment has not been enacted on the world stage since
creation. He employs two oral-scribal recitations that summarize a span of
text as his premise, showing that God has enacted judgment through his
word on the world stage in the past. In 3:5–6 he recites the account of the
creation of the world out of the waters of chaos (Gen 1:1–10) and the flood
account in which the destructive force of those waters was released (Gen
7). These are also cultural intertextural allusions to the broader perspective
of shared ancient Near Eastern myth that described a primeval sea from
which earth and sky emerged.[53] There are also more narrow cultural intertextural allusions because the emergence of earth and sky by the word of
God is from the Jewish-Christian adaptation of that myth.[54]

These recitations/allusions form a premise that supports our author's
conclusion that God will use the same word to destroy the world by fire
at the *parousia* that God used to separate the waters of chaos and send
the flood (3:7). The conclusion is supported by cultural intertexture. The
idea of a judgment by fire is found in Jewish eschatology, especially the
destruction of the wicked by fire.[55] The correlation of the flood and

---

[53] Gen 1:1–10; Pss 33:7; 136:6; Prov 8:27–29; Sir 39:17; Herm. *Vis.* 1.3.4.

[54] Gen 1:3–30; Pss 33:6; 148:5; Wis 9:1; *4 Ezra* 6:38, 43; *Sib. Or.* 3:30; Heb 11:3;
1 Clem. 27.4; Herm. *Vis.* 1.3.4.

[55] 1QH III, 19–36; *Sib. Or.* 3:54–87; 4:173–181; 5:211–213, 531; *Adam and Eve*
49:3; Josephus, *Ant.* 1.70.

eschatological conflagration is common to Jewish apocalyptic literature.[56] The shorter parallel in *1 Clement* is informative: "By the word of his majesty did he establish all things, and by his word can he destroy them" (*1 Clem.* 27.4). It indicates that our author probably used an apocalyptic source and may have elaborated it to tie together the word of God, the flood, and the *parousia*.[57]

In 2 Pet 3:8–13 our author refutes that part of the claim of the false teachers that the promise of the *parousia* is invalidated by its delay. He begins in verse 8 with a proof from a document by reciting Ps 90:4 (LXX 89:4) with modifications for rhetorical amplification. "For a thousand years in your sight are like yesterday when it is past, or like a watch in the night" is recited as "with the Lord one day is like a thousand years, and a thousand years are like one day." This modified recitation may have been made already in the apocalyptic source our author is using. Psalm 90:4 provides a reason for the delay of the *parousia*—God's different perception of time. Jewish apocalyptic sources argued that the period before the end may seem long, but it was short in God's eyes.[58]

In 3:9 our author uses cultural intertexture to create a proof from traditions rooted in Hab 2:3 (LXX, Aquila). Habakkuk 2:3 is part of God's response to Habakkuk's complaint that the righteous suffer at the hands of the wicked. God responds, "For there is still a vision for the appointed time; it speaks of the end, and does not lie. If it seems to tarry, wait for it; it will surely come, it will not delay." Habakkuk 2:3 was commonly used in Judaism in discussions of God's delay in fulfilling promises.[59] The association of repentance and the eschaton was traditional in apocalyptic thought as well.[60] This apocalyptic material is made part of our author's proof from enthymeme that the delay of the fulfillment of the promise of the *parousia* does not make the promise a lie because it is in God's plan and mercy to allow people to repent beforehand.

---

[56] *1 En.* 10:11–11:2; *Sib. Or.* 1:195; 7:11.

[57] Whereas the idea of the world being created by God's word is common in Jewish and Christian literature, only in 2 Pet 3:5–7 and *1 Clem.* 27.4 do we find a reference to the world being destroyed by God's word. This is further indication that an apocalyptic source underlies both books. Bauckham, *Jude, 2 Peter*, 296–97.

[58] Sir 18:9–11; *2 Bar.* 48:12–13; *L.A.B.* 19:13a. See Bauckham, *Jude, 2 Peter*, 308–9.

[59] Sir 32:22 [Hebrew]; 35:19 LXX; 1QpHab VII, 5–12; Heb 10:37; *2 Bar.* 20:6; 48:39; *b. Sanh.* 97b. A. Strobel, *Untersuchungen zum eschatologischen Verzögesungsproblem auf Grund der spätjüdisch-urchristlichen Geschichte vom Habakuk 2,2ff* (NovTSup 2; Leiden: Brill, 1961), chs. 2–3.

[60] *2 Bar.* 89:12; *4 Ezra* 7:33–34, 82; 9:11.

Regarding 3:10, the apocalyptic source that our author may be relying upon for 3:4–13 seems to have combined LXX Mal 3:19 and LXX Isa 34:4. The combination is found both here in 3:12 and the parallel in *2 Clem.* 16.3 that is also suspected of being from this apocalyptic source.[61] In addition, our author again relies upon LXX Isa 34:4 in 3:12.

Διότι ἰδοὺ ἡμέρα κυρίου ἔρχεται καιομένη ὡς κλίβανος
For, behold, the day of the Lord is coming, burning like an oven. (LXX Mal 3:19)

καὶ τακήσονται πᾶσαι αἱ δυνάμεις τῶν οὐρανῶν
and all the powers of the heavens will melt. (LXX Isa 34:4, B, Lucian)

ἔρχεται ἤδη ἡ ἡμέρα τῆς κρίσεως ὡς κλίβανος καιόμενος, καὶ τακήσονται τινες τῶν οὐρανῶν, καὶ πᾶσα ἡ γῆ ὡς μόλιβος ἐπὶ πυρὶ τηκόμενος, καὶ τότε φανήσεται τὰ κρύφια καὶ φανερὰ ἔργα τῶν ἀνθρώπων.
But you know that "the day" of judgment is already "approaching as a burning oven, and some of the heavens shall melt," and the whole earth shall be as lead melting in the fire, and then shall be made manifest the secret and open deeds of men. (*2 Clem.* 16.3).

῞Ηξει δὲ ἡμέρα κυρίου ὡς κλέπτης, ἐν ᾗ οἱ οὐρανοὶ ῥοιζηδὸν παρελεύσονται, στοιχεῖα δὲ καυσούμενα λυθήσεται, καὶ γῆ καὶ τὰ ἐν αὐτῇ ἔργα εὑρεθήσε-ται ... οὐρανοὶ πυρούμενοι λυθήσονται καὶ στοιχεῖα καυσούμενα τήκεται.
But the day of the Lord will come like a thief, and then the heavens will pass away with a loud noise, and the elements will be dissolved with fire, and the earth and everything that is done on it will be disclosed ... the coming day of God, because of which the heavens will be set ablaze and dissolved, and the elements will melt with fire? (2 Pet 3:10, 12).

In light of the prophecy of Jesus that the day of the Lord will come like a thief in the night,[62] our author modifies the recitation of LXX Mal 3:19 from his source. The addition of "as a thief" (ὡς κλέπτης) helps him reaffirm the apostolic proclamation of the *parousia* in terms of the Old Testament prophetic proclamation of the Day of the Lord, thus reconfiguring the proclamation. This reconfiguration may be facilitated by a possible reference to Hab 2:3 continued from 3:9. Aquila's version of Hab 2:3 reads,

---

[61] Our author's reliance upon a source is further indicated by the quotation of Mal 3:1 in *1 Clem.* 23.5 directly after the quotation of the scoffers that *1 Clement* shares with 2 Pet 3:4. Also, *2 Clem.* 16.1 is similar to 2 Pet 3:9. For full discussion, see Bauckham, *Jude, 2 Peter*, 304–6.

[62] Matt 24:43–44 par. Luke 12:39–40; 1 Thess 5:2; Rev 3:3; 16:15.

ἐρχόμενος ἥξει καὶ οὐ βραδυνεῖ, "he will surely come and will not be slow," and 2 Pet 3:10 begins with the verb ἥξει, "he will come."

Our author modifies the recitation of LXX Isa 34:4 from the apocalyptic source where it describes the judgment accompanying the Day of the Lord. His modification is indicated by a comparison of the use of LXX Isa 34:4 in *2 Clem.* 16.3, which is also probably from this source. Our author substitutes the verb παρέρχεσθαι ("pass away") for "melt" (τήκεσθαι). Παρέρχεσθαι is used in the Gospel tradition to describe the fate of the heavens and earth at the *parousia*.[63] Our author also adds the description "with a roar." A roar (ῥοιζηδόν) is part of the apocalyptic tradition of sounds describing the eschatological conflagration.[64] God's voice announcing his coming as a warrior is often associated with thunder and roaring.[65] The warning here is that, despite the mercy of God, repentance should not be postponed because judgment is pending. The inherent threat is that once all the planets are dissolved God will have direct view of the earth and all its habitants and their deeds.

2.6. Concluding Exhortation

Second Peter 3:11–13 is the exhortation that often concludes letters and testaments. Apocalyptic intertexture here serves to provide eschatological warrants for the behavior prescribed. The exhortation probably derives from the apocalyptic source.[66] Since the heavens and earth will be destroyed by fire and replaced by a new heaven and earth where righteousness dwells, the audience needs to be righteous in order to dwell there. The reference to Hab 2:3 from verse 9 is continued in the verb προσ-δοκῶντας ("waiting for," v. 12). In the Habakkuk text the action commanded in light of the eschatological delay is "wait for it/him."[67] Here hastening is added to the concept of waiting—if more people repent, then God does not have to delay the *parousia* out of God's grace (cf. 3:9).

The audience is commanded to wait until "the elements will melt with fire." This is another recitation of LXX Isa 34:4 (B, Lucian). Whereas in verse 10 this text was used in an affirmation of the *parousia* as part of the refutation of the false teachers, here it is used as eschatological warrant for

---

[63] Matt 5:18; 24:35; Mark 13:31; Luke 16:17; 21:33.

[64] *Sib. Or.* 4:175; 1QH III, 32–36; *Apoc. El.* (C) 3:82.

[65] Pss 18:13–15 (LXX 17:14–16); 77:18 (LXX 76:19); 104:7 (LXX 103:7); Amos 1:2; Joel 4:16 (Eng. 3:16).

[66] The verb προσδοκᾶν, "to wait for" (vv. 12, 13, 14), is also found in the quotation of the scoffers in *1 Clem.* 23.5, which in turn is also suspected to derive from this apocalyptic source.

[67] LXX: ὑπόμεινον αὐτόν; Aquila: προσδέχου αὐτόν.

ethical behavior. The promise of a new heavens and earth is a cultural intertextural connection with examples of the promise as reflected in Isa 65:17 and 66:22 and Jewish apocalyptic and early Christianity.[68]

2.7. Conclusions

In the apocalyptic discourse of 2 Peter our author utilizes a variety of oral-scribal and cultural intertextural connections to mold Jewish and early Christian traditions and texts to create argumentation or *logos* and meet the needs of his exigence. In the refutation of the claim that the apostolic preaching of the *parousia* was a cleverly devised myth (1:16), he creates two proofs. One is a proof from eyewitness testimony from independent Gospel tradition of the transfiguration account (1:16–18). It incorporates reconfiguration of Ps 2:6–7 and Isa 42:1 to show that the transfiguration was God's appointment of Jesus as eschatological vice-regent—an authority that Jesus will exercise at the *parousia*. The other is a proof of document or supernatural oracle that messianic prophecies support the *parousia* proclamation (1:19). A recitation of Num 24:17 amplifies the proof. Cultural intertexture plays a role in our author's counteraccusation (2:1–3a). In the guise of the apostle Peter he uses early Christian prophecy of false teachers and prophets to create Peter's prophecy of false teachers (2:1–3a). In defense of God's judgment he creates a proof from comparison of example using Old Testament examples of judgment as prototypes of eschatological judgment (2:3b–10a). He recites Jude without its references to *1 Enoch,* and, out of apocalyptic tradition, he adds recitation of the righteous saved from among the wicked who are judged (Gen 6:5–8:19; 19:1–23). In his vilification of the false teachers (2:10b–22) our author recites and modifies a metaphor from Jude 12–13 in order to portray the false teachers as wicked and headed for judgment (2:17). He also reconfigures a saying of Jesus from early tradition, Q, or a written Gospel to portray how precarious is the false teachers' spiritual status as slaves to corruption when judgment approaches (2:19).

In 2 Pet 3:2–3 our author recites Jude 17–18 with modification to establish the *ethos* of his apology for the delay of the *parousia*. The taunt of 3:4 has many oral-scribal intertextural connections with the Old Testament taunts from Israel and her enemies. It gives our author's opponents

---

[68] *Jub.* 1:29; *1 En.* 45:4–5; 72:1; 91:6; *Sib. Or.* 5:212; *2 Bar.* 32:6; 44:12; 57:2; *4 Ezra* 7:75; *L.A.B.* 3:10; *Apoc. El.* (C) 3:98; Matt 19:28; Rom 8:21; Rev 21:1. Gerdmar (*Rethinking the Judaism-Hellenism Dichotomy,* 128, 157) argues that the opening of 3:13, "In accordance with his promise," indicates that the verse is a quotation of Isa 65:17 (MT). However, that promise can just as well be part of cultural intertexture.

a negative voice for their dismay about the delay of the *parousia*. In 3:5–7 he constructs an enthymeme from oral-scribal recitation of and cultural allusion to God's word in creation and the judgment of the flood. These provide a premise for his conclusion that God will use that same word to destroy the world by fire. In 3:8 he recites Ps 90:4 with modification to create a proof from document to demonstrate that the delay of the *parousia* is not necessarily delay from God's perspective. In 3:9 he relies on cultural intertexture dependent upon Hab 2:3 to create an enthymene to prove that delay is really God's forbearance, not neglect of God's promise. In 3:10 he recites Mal 3:19 and Isa 34:4 from his apocalyptic source and modifies them with Christian tradition to serve, not as an affirmation of the Day of the Lord, but as an affirmation of the *parousia*. Concluding paraenesis in 3:11–13 receives its ethical warrant from recitation of Isa 34:4 and cultural intertextural references to the expectation of a new heaven and new earth.

The intertexture of apocalyptic discourse in 2 Peter uses early Christian tradition that incorporates Old Testament messianic texts pertaining to the Day of the Lord and its judgment. These are applied to Jesus as ruler of the nations and as judge at the *parousia*. These texts include Ps 2:6–7 and Isa 42:1 within the context of the transfiguration account (1:16–18), Num 24:17 within a proof of the reliability of messianic prophecy about the *parousia* (1:19), and Mal 3:19 and Isa 34:4 in a description of the judgment of the *parousia* (3:10). The latter comes from our author's apocalyptic source and indicates that the Roman church had already tied messianic prophecy to *parousia* expectation. His emphasis upon the reliability of Old Testament prophecy (1:19; 3:1–2) probably refers to the prophecy of the Day of the Lord. Now that Jesus is interpreted as the Lord of those prophecies they are the bedrock support for the proclamation of the *parousia*.

Like Jude our author's use of intertexture is guided by the need to increase the *ethos* of his argumentation. Whether recitation of written sources or cultural references and allusions to Jewish and early Christian traditions, the authority of these sources and their images, metaphors, expectations, and warrants lend authority to his argumentation. Like Jude our author does not push his own authority but rather relies heavily on the *ethos* of his sources. However, above and beyond traditions our author relies ultimately upon the *ethos* of the apostle Peter through the use of pseudonymity. Jude uses prophetic tradition to present himself as a prophet. Our author relies less on prophetic intertexture and more upon the prophetic nature of the testament genre to present Peter as a prophet. Our author uses early Christian prophecy of false teachers and prophets to create prophecies of false teachers in Peter's own words that align with the current experience of his church (2:1–3a; 3:3–4).

Like Jude our author's use of apocalyptic intertexture is guided by the need to elicit *pathos* from his audience. Jude relies on apocalyptic intertextural connections with negative images and characters of tradition to vilify his opponents, but our author uses these more as examples within argumentation without explicit comparison with the false teachers (2:4b–10a). He vilifies his opponents some by association with these examples, but much more as subjects of the fulfillment of early Christian prophecy of apostates and end-time scoffers (2:1–3a; 3:3–4). In his digression denouncing the false teachers (2:10b–22), in that portion that is apocalyptic discourse (2:17–21), the degrading metaphor in 2:17 is drawn from Jude's prophecy of judgment (vv. 12–13), and the statement of negative spiritual status is reconfigured from a saying of Jesus from early tradition, Q, or a written Gospel (2:19). Our author uses apocalyptic discourse to describe the negative state of the false teachers in relation to judgment and thus to vilify them.

What is ostensibly lacking in 2 Peter are intertextural connections to Jewish pseudepigraphical works utilized by Jude (*Testament of Moses* and *1 Enoch*). These are entirely absent from 2 Peter, even where 2 Peter utilizes Jude (discussed above). Verbal echoes of *1 Enoch* in Jude 6 disappear from 2 Pet 2:4, especially the reference to the sexual sin of the angels in taking human wives, which is not in the biblical account of Gen 6:1–4. Hardly anything of *1 Enoch* in Jude 12–13 remains in 2 Pet 2:17, except one of Jude's four nature metaphors. The quote of *1 En.* 1:9 in Jude 14–15 is absent from 2 Peter. The recitation of the *Testament of Moses* in Jude 9 is generalized in 2 Pet 2:11 to eliminate reference to Michael and the devil.[69] Since the *Testament of Moses* was not widely known in early Christianity and *1 Enoch* was widely used in the second century, it is unlikely that the author of 2 Peter disapproved of Jewish apocalyptic works. He probably uses one in 3:4–13! It is more likely that these works were known in Palestinian Christianity from which Jude emerged and our author was unfamiliar with them within the context of the Roman church from which he writes.[70]

Our author's heavy reliance upon early Christian tradition of the transfiguration (1:16–19), Jude (2:1–18; 3:1–3), and an apocalyptic source (3:4–13) for his apocalyptic discourse indicates that he was not immersed in a context with a strong apocalyptic fervor (as indicated as well by the nature of his exigence!). He borrows his apocalyptic material to prove that the *parousia* will occur rather than freely construct his argumentation with apocalyptic images and traditions. Unlike Jude the dominant vehicle

---

[69] The claim that 2 Pet 2:3 is dependent on *T. Mos.* 7:6 and 2 Pet 2:13 on *T. Mos.* 7:4, 8 is rightly rejected by E. M. Laperrousaz, "*Le Testament de Moïses*," *Sem* 19 (1970): 63–66.

[70] Bauckham, *Jude, 2 Peter,* 139–40.

expressing faith in Jesus is not apocalyptic (e.g., 1:3–15). Apocalyptic materials are used as a resource to reaffirm the *parousia* and Jesus as God's vice-regent within a context in which the church expected to be waiting for some time for their manifestation. Unlike Jude he does not interpret texts and traditions as if they spoke to his time, but rather as they spoke to the reality of the *parousia*.

Final Topics: The Rhetorical Functions of Intertexture in Revelation 14:14–16:21

David A. deSilva

The ways in which the Revelation to John converses with and incorporates the Jewish Scriptures have consistently commanded the attention of interpreters.[1] What is perhaps the most creative text in the Bible is also in many respects the least original at the level of "invention," since many of the images, phrases, and actions in Revelation have identifiable antecedents in the Jewish Scriptures. Revelation is frequently understood to pursue intertextual conversations not only with Jewish Scriptures and intertestamental literature but also with local phenomena in the cities of the addressees[2] and with the Roman imperial ideology articulated in coins, inscriptions, and, most prominently, the architectural representations and performance of the ruler cult.[3] John certainly plays on "the

---

[1] See J. Cambier, "Les images de l'Ancient Testament dans l'Apocalypse de Saint Jean, *NRT* 77 (1955): 113–22; Eduard Lohse, "Die Alttestamentliche Sprache des Sehers Johannes," *ZNW* 52 (1961): 122–26; G. K. Beale, *The Use of Daniel in Jewish Apocalyptic Literature and in the Revelation of St. John* (Lanham, Md.: University Press of America, 1984); J. P. Ruiz, *Ezekiel in the Apocalypse: The Transformation of Prophetic Language in Revelation 16:17–19:10* (Frankfurt: Lang, 1989); J. Fekkes, *Isaiah and Prophetic Traditions in the Book of Revelation: Visionary Antecedents and their Developments* (JSNTSup 93; Sheffield: JSOT Press, 1994); Steve Moyise, *The Old Testament in Revelation* (JSNTSup 115; Sheffield: Sheffield Academic Press, 1995); G. K. Beale, *John's Use of the Old Testament in Revelation* (JSNTSup 166; Sheffield: Sheffield Academic Press, 1998).

[2] This is an especially prominent feature of Colin J. Hemer, *The Letters to the Seven Churches of Asia in Their Local Setting* (JSNTSup 11; Sheffield: JSOT Press, 1986); William M. Ramsey, *The Letters to the Seven Churches of Asia and Their Place in the Plan of the Apocalypse* (London: Hodder & Stoughton, 1904); C. H. H. Scobie, "Local References in the Letters to the Seven Churches," *NTS* 39 (1993): 606–24.

[3] Dominique Cuss, *Imperial Cult and Honorary Terms in the New Testament* (Fribourg: University Press, 1974); Ethelbert Stauffer, *Christ and the Caesars* (trans. K. and Ronald Gregor Smith; Philadelphia: Westminster, 1955); Leonard L. Thompson, *The Book of Revelation: Apocalypse and Empire* (New York: Oxford University Press, 1990); David A. deSilva, "The 'Image of the Beast' and the Christians in Asia

'evocative power' of shared experiences" in addition to "the 'evocative power' of texts."[4]

Alongside interest in Revelation's intertexture has arisen a strong interest in the rhetoric of Revelation (and apocalyptic literature more broadly).[5] Revelation certainly resists analysis in terms of the parts of an oration and even defies being classified strictly as either a deliberative or epideictic work. However, John does seek to have an effect on the audiences that will hear Revelation, to move them to remain in or adopt certain courses of action and to continue to embody certain values. Revelation is John's instrument of persuasion offered in an attempt to win over the hearers to (or confirm them in) John's view of the world and his assessment of a correct response to that world.

It is possible to study how John creates and destroys *ethos,* promoting the credibility of his interpretation of the hearers' situation and undermining

---

Minor," *TJ* 12 NS (1991): 185–208; Steven Friesen, *Twice Neokoros: Ephesus, Asia, and the Cult of the Flavian Imperial Family* (Leiden: Brill, 1993).

[4] Moyise, *Old Testament in Revelation,* 125. J. W. Mealy (*After the Thousand Years: Resurrection and Judgement in Revelation 20* [JSNTSup 70; Sheffield: JSOT Press, 1992], 13) also draws attention to the repetitions within Revelation as an important aspect of how Revelation conveys meaning: "context in Revelation consists of a system of references that progressively build up hermeneutical precedents in the text, precedents that precondition the meaning of each new passage in highly significant ways." What Moyise would call "intratexture" (*Old Testament in Revelation,* 126) Robbins would call repetitive texture (Vernon K. Robbins, *Exploring the Texture of Texts: A Guide to Socio-Rhetorical Interpretation* [Valley Forge, Pa.: Trinity Press International, 1996], 8–9; idem, *The Tapestry of Early Christian Discourse: Rhetoric, Society and Ideology* [New York: Routledge, 1996], 46–50), an important aspect of inner texture distinct, however, from intertexture and therefore falling outside the scope of the present investigation.

[5] Several papers presented at the 1998 meeting of the Rhetoric and the New Testament Section of the Society of Biblical Literature (and published in the *SBL Seminar Papers, 1998* [2 vols.; SBLSP 37; Atlanta: Scholars Press, 1998]) attest to this phenomenon: see Greg Carey, "Apocalyptic Ethos," 2:731–61; Loren L. Johns, "The Lamb in the Rhetorical Program of the Apocalypse of John," 2:762–84; David A. deSilva, "The Persuasive Strategy of the Apocalypse: A Socio-Rhetorical Investigation of Revelation 14:6–13," 2:785–806. See also John T. Kirby, "The Rhetorical Situations of Revelation 1–3," *NTS* 34 (1988): 197–207; Robert M. Royalty Jr., "The Rhetoric of Revelation," *SBL Seminar Papers, 1997* (SBLSP 36; Atlanta: Scholars Press, 1997), 596–617; David A. deSilva, "Honor Discourse and the Rhetorical Strategy of the Apocalypse," *JSNT* 71 (1998): 79–100. A collection of essays edited by L. Gregory Bloomquist and Gregory Carey (*Vision and Persuasion: Rhetorical Dimensions of Apocalyptic Discourse* [St. Louis: Chalice, 1999]) also bears witness to the growing interest and level of scholarly collaboration in the area of the rhetoric of apocalyptic literature.

that of rival voices like those of "Jezebel" and the "Nicolaitans." One may readily discern when John is using topics of the just, expedient, and honorable or when he is depicting one behavior or commitment as right or safe and another as dishonorable or dangerous.[6] One may identify pieces of argumentation, as in the rationales of angelic hymns, or describe the vivid appeals to *pathos* throughout Revelation. John frequently employs praise and censure in his presentation of many of his *dramatis personae.* Nevertheless, it is also apparent that one must move beyond the modes of classical rhetorical criticism if one hopes to treat John's rhetoric adequately, where persuasion is more allusive and associative than argumentative, more experiential than didactic.[7]

The present study examines the intersection of these two areas of investigation. It seeks to offer a full investigation neither of the intertexture of Rev 14:14–16:21 (for there are many details of intertexture that will not be considered, since they are not germane to the rhetorical strategy of the passage) nor of the rhetoric of Rev 14:14–16:21 (since there are many rhetorical and argumentative strategies at work in this passage that are not intertextual). Rather, the focus remains much more narrowly the rhetorical contributions of intertexture in these chapters.[8]

Many scholars have attempted to classify the ways in which John refers to older traditions.[9] Vernon Robbins's discussion of intertexture makes a

---

[6] See Anaximenes, *Rhet. Alex.* 1421b.21–1423a.13; *Rhet. Her.* 3.2.3–3.4.8.

[7] Sociorhetorical interpretation is very promising in this regard, opening up the model of "rhetorical" analysis to include repetitive patterns, intertextual associations, social and cultural topics, and ideological analysis. For a preliminary attempt to probe how this mode of analysis can display John's persuasive techniques more fully than classical rhetorical criticism, see David A. deSilva, "A Socio-Rhetorical Investigation of Revelation 14:6–13: A Call to Act Justly toward the Just and Judging God," *BBR* 9 (1999): 65–117.

[8] A study of intertexture in Rev 14:6–13 can be found in ibid., 85–103.

[9] The critical editions of the Greek New Testament, for example, have identified "allusions and citations" or "allusions and verbal parallels." Several scholars have attempted to refine these categories, making meaningful distinctions within the broad category of "allusions." See, on this question, A. Vanhoye, "L'utilisation du livre d' Ezékiel dans l'Apocalypse," *Bib* 43 (1962): 436–76, esp. 473–76; Fekkes, *Isaiah and Prophetic Traditions,* passim; G. K. Beale, "A Reconsideration of the Text of Daniel in the Apocalypse," *Bib* 67 (1986): 536–43; Jon Paulien, "Elusive Allusions: The Problematic Use of the Old Testament in Revelation," *BR* 23 (1988): 37–53, esp. 39–43. Paulien's article, for example, distinguishes between "direct allusions" and "echoes." The former indicates intertexture that John intended for the attentive hearer to catch, while the latter indicates a connection between Revelation and some other text that the hearer could have made, but without being consciously

very important contribution to this conversation.[10] He provides a sophisticated taxonomy commensurate with the complexities of John's use of Jewish Scriptures and intertestamental literature, raising the level of precision possible in this discussion. Robbins's model also calls us to be more attentive to conversations between the New Testament and Greco-Roman texts, as well as to expand the definition of "text" to include oral and written texts, texts on paper, metal, and stone, as well as "scripts" of a nonverbal but nonetheless commonly shared sort—texts written on human hearts and on shared perceptions and experiences of the world, as it were. This allows the interpreter to hold together the many different kinds of intertexture that have been proposed by scholars, from the Jewish Scriptures to local references to anti-imperialist propaganda. The present study will utilize Robbins's model as a means for uncovering and analyzing the kinds of intertexture the hearer encounters in Rev 14:14–16:21 (focusing mainly on oral-scribal and cultural intertexture), with a view always to suggesting ways in which hearing Revelation's text in light of these other subtexts enhances its rhetorical impact.

1. The Rhetorical Situations and General Strategy of Revelation

In order to evaluate the contributions of intertexture to the rhetorical strategy of John's Apocalypse, it is helpful to have in mind a sense of the challenges and choices facing his audience with regard to which he seeks to effect persuasion. This is itself an area of considerable debate; in the interest of brevity I will simply present a succinct encapsulation of the position I have presented at length elsewhere.[11]

---

employed by John as such. Direct allusions would include verbal parallels (shared strings of words), thematic parallels (shared concepts using different words), and structural parallels (modeling a passage on an Old Testament antecedent without using the same words). This last category is very much in keeping with the breadth of what literary critics would consider under the heading of intertexture. John Hollander, for example, is willing to contemplate intertextual echo in "pieces of voices as small as single words, and as elusive as particular cadences" (*The Figure of Echo: A Mode of Allusion in Milton and After* [Berkeley and Los Angeles: University of California Press, 1981], 88), by which he means poetical rhythms sharing no actual lexical terms in common, but a mere "tuneful correspondence" (Moyise, *Old Testament in Revelation,* 109) rather than shared words. "Structural" allusions are thus as potentially informing and evocative as lexical correspondence.

[10] Robbins, *Exploring the Texture of Texts,* 40–68; idem, *Tapestry of Early Christian Discourse,* 96–143.

[11] For a more detailed description of the "rhetorical situations" of Revelation's audiences, see David A. deSilva, "The Revelation to John: A Case Study in Apocalyptic

John writes to seven different Christian communities, each facing distinctive challenges. Part of the genius of Revelation is its ability to speak to each of these different situations while also articulating what John hopes will be adopted as the universal *ethos* for the Christian culture. Chapters 2–3 present seven oracles spoken by the glorified Christ to each of the seven churches, praising certain commitments and behaviors, censuring others, and calling the audiences to adopt certain courses of action for their future well-being. The language is overtly deliberative, urging particular courses of action for the sake of gaining advantages (the rewards) and avoiding disadvantages (the threatened punishments or consequences), supported by epideictic topics concerning what is praiseworthy and what is dishonorable within each congregation. These oracles give us the clearest picture of the rhetorical situations addressed by Revelation.

Some believers in Smyrna and Philadelphia have chosen loyalty to the values of the Christian group even at the cost of ongoing and escalated hostility from the dominant culture or other, more powerful groups (such as the Jewish community). Many in Pergamum and Thyatira, and a few in Sardis, have also shown exceptional loyalty to God and Jesus (2:13, 24–25) or have maintained an adequate distance from the dominant culture (3:4). As the way to eternal advantage, such Christians are encouraged to persevere in their commitment to their current course of action. For them, Revelation will act in line more with the goals of epideictic rhetoric in affirming values already held than with deliberative rhetoric in persuading to affirm values not already held.

The congregations at Ephesus, Pergamum, and Thyatira have been exposed to the influence of an alternative interpretation of Christian values and behavior. The "Nicolaitans" and "Jezebel" represent an interpretation of the group's central values that would make room for participation in activities that represent values central to the dominant culture, for example, idol worship. They contend that worship of God and participation in the rites that assure their non-Christian neighbors of their goodwill, reliability, and solidarity are not contradictory.[12] They represent a voice that calls for

---

Propaganda and the Maintenance of Sectarian Identity," *Sociological Analysis* 53 (1992): 375–439; idem, "Socio-Rhetorical Interpretation of Revelation 14:6–13," 67–73. My reconstruction is deeply indebted to Adela Yarbro Collins, *Crisis and Catharsis: The Power of the Apocalypse* (Philadelphia: Westminster, 1984); D. E. Aune, "The Social Matrix of the Apocalypse of John," *BR* 26 (1981): 16–32; Thompson, *Book of Revelation*.

[12] On the social and economic dangers facing those who abstained from all idolatrous expressions of worship, see J. M. Ford, *Revelation* (AB 38; Garden City, N.Y.: Doubleday, 1975), 406; David A. deSilva, *Despising Shame: Honor Discourse and Community Maintenance in the Epistle to the Hebrews* (SBLDS 152; Atlanta: Scholars Press, 1995), 146–51.

lessening tension between the Christian group and the dominant culture, seeking the security of the group through peaceful coexistence.[13] John wants to demonstrate that the worship of God and the worship of idols is fundamentally incompatible and that the person who engages in the latter cannot escape punishment for sharing God's honor with God's enemies. He regards these other voices as especially great dangers to the churches and dedicates much of his vision to rendering their position untenable.

Still other congregations, like the majority of believers at Sardis or the church at Laodicea, labor under such self-deception that John sees his task to be to "wake them up" to the dangers of their position. Laodicean Christians profit along with their non-Christian neighbors, drinking in the wealth that the "peace of Rome" makes possible, without knowing their poverty or the nature of the partner with whom they are cavorting! By their attitudes toward wealth and the present time as an opportunity to become enriched, they show themselves to have accepted the ideology of Rome itself. John seeks to topple this ideology through his visions, showing believers the "true" nature of Rome and her emperors and warning them against accepting any share in or partnership with a system built on the violence, injustice, and arrogance that calls down God's vengeance.

The visions of chapters 4–22 support the rhetorical goals of these oracles in a most innovative manner. Rather than arguing directly that the courses urged in the oracles are "advantageous" or that alliances with the objects of censure or warning are "disadvantageous,"[14] John presents a narrative of the "things that must shortly come to pass." In other words, he narrates the future. Aristotle, who had assigned an important place to narration in forensic and epideictic speeches, never considered this as an available rhetorical strategy, since it was impossible: "in deliberative oratory narrative is very rare, because no one can narrate things to come" (*Rhet.* 3.16.11). The genre of apocalypse allows John to overcome this obstacle. His fundamental claim to be able to declare with certainty what will happen in the future ("what must shortly take place," 1:1, 19; 4:1; 22:6) allows him to "narrate" God's judgments being in fact poured out upon all who refuse to "fear God" and "give God glory" (e.g., 16:1–11).

---

[13] Thus Charles H. Talbert, *The Apocalypse: A Reading of the Revelation of John* (Louisville: Westminster John Knox, 1994), 19; Ford, *Revelation,* 291; Robert H. Mounce, *The Book of Revelation* (rev. ed.; NICNT; Grand Rapids: Eerdmans, 1998), 81; A. LeGrys, "Conflict and Vengeance in the Book of Revelation," *Exp-Tim* 104 (1992): 76–80; G. B. Caird, *The Revelation of St. John* (London: Black, 1966), 39.

[14] Revelation 4:1–22:5 is, in effect, neither deliberation, nor epideixis, nor forensics. Deliberative, epideictic, and forensic topics can be found throughout the vision, but it would be forcing the categories to fit Revelation into any one of them.

The primary rhetorical mode of Revelation, then, is a "narrative demonstration,"[15] tracing out various possible courses of action (e.g., compliance with the demands of the ruler cult and partnership with Rome in her sins versus nonparticipation in idolatry and in the polluted prosperity of the imperial system) and graphically depicting the incentives and disincentives to either course, as well as the ultimate consequences that attend one's choice. Within this narrative demonstration, John is quite clear about what characters, actions, and partnerships are honorable and what are dishonorable, who should be emulated and who not. The hearers can "see," as it were, what will be the end of the course they have chosen or are contemplating choosing. As they engage the vision, they will examine their current location and commitments in light of the topics of advantage (honor and security), the consideration of the consequences, the weighing of relative expediency, and the like. They will also find their emotions aroused at many points, leading them further in the direction that John promotes.

John rarely "intrudes" in the visionary chapters to give instructions or exhortations to the hearers. He relies on the persuasiveness of the future he presents—the impression of plausibility and even certainty that the narrative creates—to engage the hearers and nurture in them the commitment to respond as he would have them respond to innovation within the group, intimidation outside the group, and potential partnership with those outside the group. This makes for a rhetorical strategy that is sufficiently flexible to address every element within John's diverse audience. Some members of his audience are already wholly committed to preserving the distinctive contours of the Christian group no matter what the cost in terms of society's hostility. Some members are looking for innovative ways in which to negotiate commitment to this group and peaceful (even profitable) coexistence with the larger society. It is a picture that engages the hearers and asks them to engage it from their particular vantage point in the world. Each different audience—indeed, each person or family within each audience—will continue to deepen its reading of its own situation and options in light of those visions.

---

[15] A term used by the author of 4 Maccabees (3:19), for whom the stories of the nine martyrs provide proof in narrative form of the proposition he had previously been demonstrating by more deductive means. In his narration, the author includes deliberative speeches, both protreptic and apotreptic, but these are placed on the lips of the characters spoken in the ears of other characters (e.g., Antiochus to Eleazar). They are not spoken directly to the audience, but the audience nevertheless hears the speeches and will ponder its own situation and life choices in light of those speeches.

The success of this "narrative demonstration" depends on the persuasiveness of the future John narrates. What strategies does he use to impress upon the hearers that the facts of what he depicts as happening "shortly" are in reality what he alleges them to be?[16] For if the hearers accept this future as the plausible or, in the best case, certain future, they will regulate their actions, choices, and associations in the present in such a way as to achieve "advantage" and avoid "disadvantage" in that future. Hence it is critical to the success of John's strategy that the hearers desire to "keep the words of this book" (22:7; cf. 1:3; 22:9): it is a vision of the outcome that will guide the hearers' steps now.

Intertexture, particularly oral-scribal and cultural intertexture, is a primary resource for John as he seeks to establish the credibility of this future he narrates. We might thus observe at the outset that intertexture serves in general to establish the *ethos* of John and the authority (persuasiveness) of his message. By recontextualizing the content of authoritative "prophecy," John subtly invites these Scriptures to lend their considerable authority to his own visions. If the words of the prophets and psalms were inspired in their original contexts, they remain recognizable as "inspired" in the new context. John's vision comes across as authentic revelation from the divine realm already to the extent that it is infused directly with older revelations previously accepted by the addressees as authentic divine revelations. John gives the texts new shape, referents, and direction, but the older texts lend their power to that new shape. The biblical word becomes John's word. His frequent weaving in of small phrases and descriptions known from Daniel or other prophetic and apocalyptic literature enhances the hearers' impression that they are hearing another authoritative vision—another species of the same genre, as it were. John does not cite his Old Testament sources, however, because for John to say "as it is written in the prophet Isaiah" would detract from the immediacy of the hearers' experience of John's vision and would call attention to its derivative or secondary character. Although such citations lend authority to other New Testament arguments, here they would actually diminish the authority that John claims for the apocalypse, which he has consistently presented as a primary revelation from God.

There are many other, more specific ways in which intertexture serves both to render John's narration of the future plausible and to guide the

---

[16] The pressing need facing John here is not very different from the primary challenge facing the deliberative orator, who must "prove ... that the facts are what the supporter of a measure maintains they are" (Aristotle, *Rhet.* 1.1.10). See also Anaximenes, *Rhet. Alex.* 1428b.12–17: "in exhortations and dissuasions it has to be proved about the matter under consideration that the line of action which we are urging or opposing itself has the effect that we assert it has; or if not, that actions resembling this line of action generally or invariably turn out in the way we assert."

hearers to act "advantageously" with regard to that future. These will be displayed as this essay turns to Rev 14:14–16:21 in the form of a commentary on the principal rhetorical contributions of intertexture.

2. Revelation 14:14–20: Defining the Main Point of Deliberation

Revelation 14:14–20 serves chiefly to reinforce the "hour of judgment" as the principal challenge facing the hearers, requiring judicious action and preparation in the present. John recontextualizes Dan 7:13 to present the first character in this episode:

Ἐπὶ τὴν νεφέλην ... ὅμοιον υἱὸν ἀνθρώπου (Rev 14:14)
Ἐπὶ τῶν νεφελῶν ... ὡς υἱὸς ἀνθρώπου (Dan 7:13).

In Daniel, the "one like a son of man" comes to receive the kingdom and represents the "holy ones" of God. John continues to connect God's coming to claim the kingdom with the execution of judgment (as in Rev 11:17–18). The description of this judgment consists of three scenes: the harvesting of the earth, the gathering in of the vineyard, and the trampling of the winepress.

The whole appears to be a narrative amplification of Joel 3:13 (4:13 MT/LXX): "put in the sickle, for the harvest is ripe. Come, tread, for the winepress is full.... Multitudes, multitudes in the valley of decision! For the Day of the Lord is near in the valley of decision."[17] John heightens the drama of Joel's scene by first drawing attention to the "sharp sickle" in the hand of the "one like a son of man" (14:14). He then recontextualizes the first part of Joel 3:13 in the angel's invitation to that figure: "*Send out your sickle* and reap, because the hour to reap came, *because the harvest* of the earth *ripened*." Following up on this invitation, John adds the narration of the harvest being carried out (14:16).[18] John then creates a logically intervening

---

[17] The Hebrew word translated "decision" actually provides a clever pun, since it can also signify a sharp threshing instrument.

[18] There is some debate concerning whether or not this first harvest should be heard as a positive ingathering of the elect or as simply a doublet for the punitive judgment expressed by the winepress scene. Although Jesus' sayings feature the image of harvesting to describe both the ingathering of the righteous and the burning of the wicked (see Matt 13:24–30, 37–43), it seems more likely that John intended both harvests to be heard as two expressions of a single, punitive judgment. First, there is an obvious parallelism between 14:7, ὅτι ἦλθεν ἡ ὥρα τῆς κρίσεως αὐτοῦ, and 14:15, ὅτι ἦλθεν ἡ ὥρα θερίσαι. Moreover, Jer 28:33 LXX, a text that John clearly knew, had already used the image of a grain harvest to speak of the judgment of Babylon (thus strengthening the link between 14:7–8 and 14:15): "yet a short while and the time of her harvest will come." It would be impossible, however, to

scene between the grain harvest and the treading of the winepress, namely, the harvesting of the vineyard.[19] This scene parallels the first quite closely: an angelic figure appears already holding a "sharp sickle" (14:17); another angel gives a similar command with a similar rationale ("send out your sharp sickle and harvest the clusters of the vineyard of the earth, for her grapes are ripe," 14:18–19); and the action is then carried out (14:19a).

Finally, John moves to the treading of the winepress. First the "grapes" are "thrown into the great winepress of the wrath of God" (14:19). John's description of the nature of this winepress as "wrath [τοῦ θυμοῦ] of God" comes from another prominent text in which the treading of the winepress provides an image for judgment:

> "Why are your garments as of one coming from trampling the winepress [ἀπὸ πατητοῦ ληνοῦ]?" ... "I have trampled them in wrath [κατεπάτησα αὐτοὺς ἐν θυμῷ], ... and I have poured out their blood upon the ground [τὸ αἷμα αὐτῶν εἰς γῆν]. For the day of payback came for them, ... and my wrath arose [ὁ θυμός μου ἐπέστη], and I trampled them in my wrath and poured out their blood upon the ground." (Isa 63:2–6)

As a final detail, John adds that the winepress was trampled "outside the city" (ἔξωθεν τῆς πόλεως), which recontextualizes the pentateuchal phrase "outside the camp" or, in references to laws holding after the Israelites take possession of Canaan, "outside the city." While this is sometimes a reference to a "clean place" (Lev 6:11; Num 19:3, 9) or even a holy place where God's tabernacle is pitched (Exod 33:7), it is most often an unclean place where sin offerings are burned (Exod 29:14; Lev 4:12, 21; 8:17; 9:11; 10:4; 16:27), where all things leprous are cast (whether people or building materials; Lev 13:46; 14:40–41, 45), and, most poignantly here, where sinners are executed (blasphemers, Lev 24:14, 23; adulterers, Num 5:3–4; Sabbath violators, Num 15:35–36).

Isaiah's connection of the pouring out of blood with the treading of this winepress leads John to include this detail as well. In describing the quantity of blood exuding from the treading of the winepress ("blood went out ... as high as the horses' bridles"), John alludes to another description

---

demonstrate that the hearers would all take the vision this way, especially since there are contemporary references to a dual harvest (Jesus' parable being a prominent example). For a detailed review of arguments, see David E. Aune, *Revelation 6–16* (WBC 52b; Nashville: Nelson, 1998), 800–803; and G. K. Beale, *Revelation* (NIGTC; Grand Rapids: Eerdmans, 1998), 773–79.

[19] The LXX translators had already taken this step in Joel 4:13, translating the more neutral Hebrew word for harvest (*qāṣîr*) with a word distinctly associated with fruit harvesting, namely, τρύγητος.

of God's execution of judgment, namely, *1 En.* 100:3–4: "The horse shall walk through the blood of sinners up to his chest; and the chariot shall sink down up to its top. In those days, the angels shall descend into the secret places. They shall gather together into one place all those who gave aid to sin. And the Most High will arise on that day of judgment in order to execute a great judgment upon all the sinners."[20]

John's extensive use of oral-scribal intertexture in 14:14–20 weaves together Old Testament images of judgment as a means of reminding the hearers of God's thoroughgoing commitment to tread down the ungodly. It expands those images in order to impress upon the hearers all the more the danger and horror of that judgment and thus the paramount importance of providing for themselves a strategy for meeting that challenge in safety. This certain judgment posits an impending crisis, indeed, identifies the real crisis facing each audience, and calls for a strategy to encounter and survive that crisis (rather than the less-threatening crises of temporal hardship or deprivation).

3. Revelation 15:2–4; 16:5–7: Reinforcement of Major Premises

John employs recontextualization extensively in two poetic passages celebrating God's justice, namely, 15:2–4 and 16:5–7. The rhetorical purpose of these hymns is to reinforce major premises learned from the Jewish cultural heritage concerning God's justice, premises that in turn reinforce the necessity of the consequences John posits and thus the plausibility of the future he narrates. Rome, guilty of the same crimes as Babylon in the eyes of John (as also in the eyes of the authors of *4 Ezra* and *2 Baruch*), will most assuredly fall under the judgment of the same God whose values and opposition to injustice, greed, and self-glorification never changes.

Chapters 15 and 16 interact to a large extent with Exod 1–15, far more extensively than can be displayed here.[21] "Conquerors" singing the "Song of Moses and of the Lamb" while standing "beside the Sea" (15:1–2) recalls in a rather obvious way the Exodus setting,[22] even though the content of the "Song of Moses" in Deut 32 appears to be more in view here. Those

---

[20] The quotation is from *OTP* 1:81.

[21] Beale (*Revelation,* 787) aptly notes the tendency to view God's eschatological deliverance in terms of God's prototypical deliverance in Exodus. The *Apocalypse of Abraham* also speaks of God preparing ten plagues (as in Egypt) against the heathen (29:15; 30:1–8).

[22] Beale (ibid., 791–92) finds rabbinic texts that speak of the Red Sea becoming "a crystallized ... kind of glass" (*Midr. Pss.* 136:7; see also *Mek. de Rabbi Ishmael,* Beshallah 5:15), a tradition drawn out from the detail in Exod 15:8, "the deeps were congealed."

who "overcome" the beast and its image by virtue of enduring the cost of nonparticipation in the cult now celebrate the Lord's deliverance of the faithful ones as a second and grander exodus. As the Nestle-Aland text leads the reader to believe, almost every line of the song they sing is a recontextualization of an earlier declaration about God and God's dealings with humanity:

> 15:3b Great and wonderful are your works, Lord God Almighty,
> μεγάλα καὶ θαυμαστὰ τὰ ἔργα σου, κύριε ὁ θεὸς ὁ παντοκράτωρ·
> 15:3c Just and true are your ways, O King of the nations:
> δίκαιαι καὶ ἀληθιναὶ αἱ ὁδοί σου, ὁ βασιλεὺς τῶν ἐθνῶν·
> 15:4a Who will not fear, Lord, and glorify your name?
> τίς οὐ μὴ φοβηθῇ, κύριε, καὶ δοξάσει τὸ ὄνομά σου;
> 15:4b For you alone are holy,
> ὅτι μόνος ὅσιος,
> 15:4c for all the nations will come and worship before you,
> ὅτι πάντα τὰ ἔθνη ἥξουσιν καὶ προσκυνήσουσιν ἐνώπιόν σου,
> 15:4d for your just decrees have been made manifest.
> ὅτι τὰ δικαιώματά σου ἐφανερώθησαν.

Perhaps the single most informative subtext for John in this hymn is Ps 85:9–10 LXX, which lauds God as "great," "doing wonders" (μέγας ... καὶ ποιῶν θαυμάσια, cf. Rev 15:3b) and God "alone" (θεὸς μόνος, cf. Rev 15:4c), as well as predicts that "all the nations that you made will come and worship before you and glorify your name" (πάντα τὰ ἔθνη ... ἥξουσιν καὶ προσκυνήσουσιν ἐνώπιόν σου ... καὶ δοξάσουσιν τὸ ὄνομά σου, which Rev 15:4a and 4c recontextualize in a slightly abbreviated but otherwise verbatim manner). Nevertheless, several other passages have been used in the invention of this hymn. Revelation 15:3b resonates with a number of texts confessing the "great and wonderful works of the Lord":

> Ἐξωμολογοῦντο τὰ ἔργα τὰ μεγάλα καὶ θαυμαστὰ τοῦ θεοῦ, Tob 12:22
> Μεγάλα τὰ ἔργα κυρίου, Ps 110:2 LXX
> Θαυμάσια τὰ ἔργα σου, Ps 138:14 LXX

While it is difficult to decide with certainty, Rev 15:3b may well represent a combined recontextualization of Pss 110:2 and 138:14. In light of the fact that John had just described the sight of the seven angels with the seven last "plagues" (πληγάς) as a "great and wondrous (μέγα καὶ θαυμαστόν) sign" (15:1), it is likely that he understood these "works" to be enactments of judgment, akin to the "great and wondrous plagues" (πληγὰς μεγάλας καὶ θαυμαστάς, Deut 28:59) that God promised to bring upon disobedient Israel. The divine title "Lord God Almighty" recontextualizes Amos 3:13 LXX and 4:13 LXX exactly: κύριε ὁ θεὸς ὁ παντοκράτωρ.

A similar situation appertains to Rev 15:3c, which alludes to several Jewish scriptural texts concerning the "truth" and "justice" of God's ways and works:

His works are true and all his ways are judgments [ἀληθινὰ τὰ ἔργα αὐτοῦ καὶ πᾶσαι αἱ ὁδοὶ αὐτοῦ κρίσεις]. (Deut 32:4)
You are just ... all your works are true and your ways straight and all your judgments are true [δίκαιος εἶ ... πάντα τὰ ἔργα σου ἀληθινά, καὶ αἱ ὁδοί σου εὐθεῖαι καὶ πᾶσαι αἱ κρίσεις σου ἀληθιναί]. (Dan 3:27 LXX)
The Lord is just in all his ways [δίκαιος κύριος ἐν πάσαις ταῖς ὁδοῖς αὐτοῦ]. (Ps 144:17 LXX)

The divine title here is a translated recontextualization of Jer 10:7 MT: "King of the nations."

Revelation 15:4a continues to recontextualize Jer 10:7 MT, which also asks "who would not fear you?"[23] and, as seen above, Ps 85:9 LXX. Revelation 15:4b, which declares that God "alone is holy" (ὅτι μόνος ὅσιος), alludes to two epithets of God celebrated frequently in Jewish hymns, but never together (see, for example, Deut 32:4: δίκαιος καὶ ὅσιος κύριος; Neh 9:6: σὺ εἶ αὐτὸς κύριος μόνος; Isa 37:16: σὺ θεὸς μόνος). While Rev 15:4c is most clearly a verbatim recontextualization of Ps 85:9 LXX, it also resonates with other texts articulating the same hope (e.g., Isa 66:23: "all flesh will come before me to worship," ἥξει μᾶσα σὰρξ ἐνώπιόν μου προσκυνῆσαι; Zech 14:16: "the nations coming ... to worship the Lord, the King," τῶν ἐθνῶν τῶν ἐλθόντων ... τοῦ προσκυνῆσαι). The final element of Rev 15:4 does not recontextualize any identifiable passage. Rather, it refers with new words to a conviction expressed in Ezekiel and the *Psalms of Solomon* to the effect that the righteous judgments of God will be made known to the earth (*Pss. Sol.* 2:10: καὶ γνώσεται ἡ γῆ τὰ κρίματά σου πάντα τὰ δίκαια; cf. 8:8; Ps 97:2 LXX) with the result that the nations of the earth will at last acknowledge the one God (see Ezek 38:22–23, which includes blood, fire, and hail amongst the punishments, as will John).

The old songs about God—God's power, justice, and truth manifesting themselves in God's judicial actions on behalf of God's people and against God's adversaries—will be renewed in the future. John's narration of the future celebrations of those who will emerge victorious from the present contest carries with it the implicit claim that the unfolding future will demonstrate the ongoing validity and reliability of the

---

[23] The LXX lacks Jer 10:5–8, as do several MSS of Jeremiah found at Qumran, which has suggested to text critics that these verses are a later interpolation into Jeremiah's denunciation of the folly of idolatry.

premises articulated in those ancient songs. God's justice and power will consistently result in God's actions against the unjust and on behalf of those who do justice (i.e., "keep God's commandments and faith with Jesus," 14:13). All nations will come to recognize the constant truth in the cosmos that they currently suppress in their idolatries, violence, economic rapine, and false ideologies. John reaffirms the future articulated by the ancient witnesses (e.g. Ps 85:9–10 LXX; Isa 66:23) in which those outside the Christian group—those who act according to values different from those espoused within Christian culture and even seek to pressure Christians to conform to non-Christian values—will recognize which set of values was really in line with the ultimate values of God. These are foundational premises that John hopes will guide the hearers' deliberations in the present.

The second passage, Rev 16:5–7, is likewise concerned with affirming God's commitment to bring justice to human affairs as a core premise for the hearers' use in interpreting and evaluating their times and their choices. After the waters are turned into blood, the "angel of the waters"[24] exclaims:

16:5b Just are you, the One who is and who was, the Holy One, because you judged these things,
δίκαιος εἶ, ὁ ὢν καὶ ὁ ἦν, ὁ ὅσιος, ὅτι ταῦτα ἔκρινας,
16:6a because they poured out the blood of the holy ones and prophets,
ὅτι αἷμα ἁγίων καὶ προφητῶν ἐξέχεαν
16:6b and you have given to them blood to drink, for they deserve it.
καὶ αἷμα αὐτοῖς δέδωκας πιεῖν· ἄξιοί εἰσιν.

The voices from below the altar, previously identified as those "slaughtered on account of the word of God and the testimony they bore" (Rev 6:9), speak a second time, this time to affirm that God has avenged their blood and brought the vindication for which they had cried out in 6:10: "Yes, Lord God Almighty, true and just are your judgments" (ναί, κύριε ὁ θεὸς ὁ παντοκράτωρ, ἀληθιναὶ καὶ δίκαιαι αἱ κρίσεις σου, 16:7b).

The angel opens his declaration with words familiar from Ps 118:137 LXX and Dan 3:27 LXX: "Just are you" (δίκαιος εἶ). Significantly, both of those subtexts go on to declare the reliability or constancy of God's judgments. The *Psalms of Solomon,* moreover, make frequent declarations concerning God's justice being demonstrated in the judgments

---

[24] This is probably not one of the angels responsible for pouring out the plagues, all the more as two of them were involved in this plague of blood, but rather the angel whose sphere of authority is "water," similar to the "angel having authority over fire" introduced in 14:18.

God brings upon both Gentiles and Jerusalem (*Pss. Sol.* 2:15: ἐν τοῖς κρίμασίν σου ἡ δικαιοσύνη σου; see also 17:10). Here John makes a reference, then, to Jewish cultural knowledge about God's character and commitment to bring justice to the earth. The divine title used here expands on God's self-designation in Exod 3:14 as "the one who is" (ἐγώ εἰμι ὁ ὤν).

The angel's description of the crime of the inhabitants of the earth (αἷμα ἁγίων καὶ προφητῶν ἐξέχεαν) recontextualizes the complaint of Ps 78:3 LXX: "they poured out their blood [ἐξέχεαν τὸ αἷμα αὐτῶν] like water around Jerusalem," a text that goes on to ask God to "make known among the nations … the vindication of the spilled blood of your slaves" (ἡ ἐκδίκησις τοῦ αἵματος τῶν δούλων σου τοῦ ἐκκεχυμένου, 78:10). The Song of Moses in Deuteronomy has also affirmed that God "avenges the blood of his children" (τὸ αἷμα τῶν υἱῶν αὐτοῦ ἐκδικᾶται, Deut 32:43). The angel's description of the punishment decreed by God alludes to Isa 49:26, where those who afflicted God's people "will drink as new wine their own blood" (πίονται … τὸ αἷμα αὐτῶν). The way in which the angel has framed crime and punishment (blood for blood) and underscored the fitting way in which the punishment fits the crime may allude to Gen 9:6.[25] This increases the likelihood of the "plague of blood" referring not merely to a transformation of natural elements but to the widespread slaughter of the wicked. It is worth comparing this text with *Sib. Or.* 3:311–313: "then you [Rome] will be surfeited with blood, as formerly you yourself did spill the blood of good and just people, whose blood even now cries to the farthest heaven."[26]

The martyrs themselves provide the antiphon to this verse, and it is most fitting that those who had cried out for justice should now be seen to affirm firsthand the premise articulated earlier in 15:3, with the significant specification of "ways" now as "judgments":

"Lord God Almighty, true and just are your judgments."
κύριε ὁ θεὸς ὁ παντοκράτωρ, ἀληθιναὶ καὶ δίκαιαι αἱ κρίσεις σου (Rev 16:7)
"Lord God Almighty, just and true are your ways."
κύριε ὁ θεὸς ὁ παντοκράτωρ· δίκαιαι καὶ ἀληθιναὶ αἱ ὁδοί σου (Rev 15:3)

While this antiphon, then, is on the one hand a variant on the earlier hymn of the conquerors, it also exhibits a closer recontextualization of Dan 3:27 LXX than its predecessor ("true are your judgments," αἱ κρίσεις σου ἀληιναί) as well as offers a paraphrase of Ps 18:10 LXX: "the judgments

---

25 Beale, *Revelation,* 820.
26 Ibid.

of the Lord are true, altogether justified" (τὰ κρίματα κυρίου ἀληθινά δεδικαιωμένα).

John's narration of the victory of God over Babylon, the pouring out of the plagues upon the beast and his kingdom, and the celebration of the conquerors in heaven all provide a narrative confirmation of the truth of these basic Jewish/Christian convictions about God's power, justice, and manifestation of these attributes to the unbelievers. The result is that the faithful will be vindicated in the sight of those who now live without heeding the decrees of the one God. In John's vision of the future, the victims of human injustice themselves speak as witnesses (almost in a forensic sense here) to God's unfailing commitment to bring justice. The many texts within the Jewish tradition that speak of God's justice and are brought into John's narrative in very direct ways (the intertexture is here at its most transparent in chs. 14–16) focus the hearers on the major enthymeme implicitly at work in John's narration of future events: since God is just, God intervenes to punish the unjust and oppressor and to deliver God's faithful clients.

This premise, furthermore, combines with John's bridging of the horizons between Babylon and Rome to provide further support for the future he posits for the Roman imperial system. Aristotle had advised studying one's own city's past wars and other cities' wars when advising about war, since "similar causes are likely to have similar results" (*Rhet.* 1.4.9).[27] John clearly has done a similar investigation as he pondered the fall of pagan empires in the past, as interpreted by Israel's prophets, and then considered what must be the outcome of Rome's excesses and sins. Oral-scribal intertexture, then, elevates God's justice almost as a necessary sign of Rome's demise:[28] Rome's arrogance, violence, idolatries, and economic rapine cry out for the inevitable intervention and judgment of a just God (for which Babylon and her fate serve as a remarkable precedent).

---

[27] This becomes a commonplace for enthymemes in *Rhet.* 2.23.25: when the cause exists, the effect exists.

[28] On necessary signs, see *Rhet.* 1.2.18: "if one were to say that it is a sign that a man is ill, because he has a fever, or that a woman has had a child because she has milk, this is a necessary sign. This alone among signs is a *tekmerion* (an evidence); for only in this case, if the fact is true, is the argument irrefutable." In John's cosmos, governed by a just God who acts consistently to bring down the ungodly empires, the fact that Rome has committed idolatry, violence, and the like can be offered as a necessary sign that it will come under God's judgment. The historical precedents appealed to (always indirectly) by John will support this argument, should there be any among the congregations who have their doubts about the necessity of this sign.

4. Revelation 16: Historical Precedents and the Plausible Future

Revelation 16 narrates the "pouring out"[29] of the bowls of God's wrath on the kingdom of the Beast, culminating in the destruction of "the great city" Babylon and the cities of the nations.[30] As in *Apoc. Ab.* 29–30 and several rabbinic texts,[31] John looks to Exodus, the narration of God's first great deliverance of God's holy people, for language by which to describe God's final deliverance of God's people. Where John describes the "plagues" (significantly) that God will unleash upon the godless Roman world, intertexture with Exodus is at its thickest, as the following comparisons show:

And there came a sore … upon the people.
καὶ ἐγένετο ἕκλος … ἐπὶ τοὺς ἀθρώπους (Rev 16:2)
And there came sores … among the people.
καὶ ἐγένετο ἕλκη … ἐν τοῖς ἀνθρώποις (Exod 9:10)

And [the sea] became blood … and every living soul in the sea died.
καὶ [τὴν θάλασσαν] ἐγένετο αἷμα … καὶ πᾶσα ψυχὴ ζωῆς ἀπέθανεν τὰ ἐν τῇ θαλάσσῃ (Rev 16:3)
And all the water in the river turned into blood, and the fish in the river died.
καὶ μετέβαλεν πᾶν τὸ ὕδωρ τὸ ἐν τῷ ποταμῷ εἰς αἷμα καὶ οἱ ἰχθύες οἱ ἐν τῷ ποταμῷ ἐτελεύτησαν (Exod 7:20–21)

---

[29] The command to "pour out the seven vials of the wrath of God upon the earth" (ἐκχέετε τὰς ἑπτὰ φιάλας τοῦ θυμοῦ τοῦ θεοῦ εἰς τὴν γῆν) refers to Jewish cultural intertexture about God's interaction with the ungodly, in which God is frequently said to "pour out wrath" upon the nations. Noteworthy among these texts is Jer 10:25 (ἔκχεον τὸν θυμόν σου ἐπὶ ἔθνη τὰ μὴ εἰδότα σε … ὅτι κατέφαγον τὸν Ιακωβ), which offers as the motivation for God's pouring out wrath the nations' ravaging of God's people. John preserves this as the motivation behind the plagues, explicating this connection in 16:5–7. See also Ps 68:24 LXX: ἔκχεον ἐπ᾽ αὐτοὺς τὴν ὀργήν σου; Zeph 3:8: τοῦ ἐκχέαι ἐπ᾽ αὐτοὺς πᾶσαν ὀργὴν θυμοῦ μου.

[30] George Wesley Buchanan (*The Book of Revelation* [Lewiston, N.Y.: Mellen, 1993], 428–31) argues that "the great city" refers to Jerusalem, which was in fact divided in three parts during the civil strife of 68–70 C.E. (*War* 5.1.1–5); the reference to Babylon would not, then, be resumptive but add "Rome" to the list of casualties after Jerusalem and all the cities of the nations. The main problem with this reading is that John himself identifies "the great city" with "Babylon" immediately following (Rev 17:18, where the "woman" named "Babylon" in 17:3–6 is interpreted by the angel as "the great city that has dominion over the kings of the earth"). Additionally, those who lament over Babylon lament her as "the great city" (18:10, where the identification is made explicit; see also 18:15, 19).

[31] Beale (*Revelation*, 825) cites several rabbinic texts positing that the Egyptian plagues will befall Rome in the end time (for example, *Lev. Rab.* 6:6; *Exod. Rab.* 14:3; *Midr. Pss.* 22:3; 27:1).

The third poured his bowl into the rivers ... and it became blood.
ὁ τρίτος ἐξέχεεν τὴν φιάλην αὐτοῦ εἰς τοὺς ποταμοὺς ... καὶ ἐγένετο
αἷμα (Rev 16:4)
He struck the water in the river ... and all the water in the river turned
into blood.
Ἐπάτεξεν τὸ ὕδωρ τὸ ἐν τῷ ποταμῷ ... μετέβαλεν πᾶν τὸ ὕδωρ τὸ ἐν τῷ
ποταμῷ εἰς αἷμα (Exod 7:20–21)[32]

And his kingdom became darkened.
καὶ ἐγένετο ἡ βασιλεία αὐτοῦ ἐσκοτωμένη (Rev 16:10)
And let darkness be upon the land of Egypt.
καὶ γενηθήτω σκότος ἐπὶ γῆν Αἰγύπτου (Exod 10:21)

three unclean spirits like frogs
τρία ἀκάθαρτα ὡς βάτραχοι (Rev 16:13)
he drew out the frogs, and the frog came up and covered the land of Egypt.
ἀνήγαγε τοὺς βατράχους· καὶ ἀνεβιβάσθη ὁ βάτραχος καὶ ἐκάλυψεν τὴν
γῆν Αἰγύπτου (Exod 8:2 LXX)[33]

And great hailstones ... came down from heaven upon people ... exceedingly great.
καὶ χάλαζα μεγάλη ... καταβαίνει ἐκ τοῦ οὐρανοῦ ἐπὶ τοὺς ἀνθρώπους ...
σφόδρα (Rev 16:21)[34]
many exceedingly great hailstones
χάλαζα πολλὴ σφόδρα (Exod 9:24)

At three other points, John's seven last plagues intersect with the Exodus
plagues. First, John preserves by means of a structural parallel the sense of
purposeful action behind these plagues. That Moses (or Aaron) must first
stretch out his hand, or that an angel first pours out a bowl, to initiate a
plague conveys the same impression: they happen not merely "on their
own" but by God's direction. Second, John chooses to express the ampli-
tude of an earthquake that forms part of the seventh plague by
recontextualizing an expression found in Exod 9:18:

---

[32] See also Ps 77:44 LXX: καὶ μετέστρεψεν εἰς αἷμα τοὺς ποταμοὺς αὐτῶν.

[33] Noteworthy in Exod 8:2–3 LXX is the ability of the pagan priest, like the false
prophet, to command the frogs. The uncleanness of the frog (Lev 11:9–12, 41–47;
Beale, Revelation, 832) may also be alluded to here in the identification of the frogs
and "unclean" spirits.

[34] It is possible that the fourth plague (the sun being made to burn the beast and
his people "with fire" (ἐν πυρί) harkens back to Exod 9:23 as well, where the hail
was accompanied by fire, which "ran down to the earth."

such as had not occurred since people were upon the earth
οἷος οὐκ ἐγένετο ἀφ᾽ οὗ ἄνθρωπος ἐγένετο ἐπὶ τῆς γῆς (Rev 16:18)
that has ever fallen in Egypt from the day it was founded until now
τοιαύτη οὐ γέγονεν ἐν Αἰγύπτῳ ἀφ᾽ ἧς ἡμέρας ἔκτισται (Exod 9:18; cf.
10:6; 11:6)

This expression had already been taken into the Jewish apocalyptic tradition,[35] another sign of the influence of exodus traditions on Jewish
speculation about God's future acts of deliverance. Finally, the response of
the beast and his subjects to these plagues, who "slander" the name of God
and do not repent of their deeds to give God honor (16:9, 11, 21), recalls
the response of Pharaoh and his subjects, who were similarly hardened
rather than won over by these visitations of judgment (Exod 7:22; 8:15, 19,
32; 9:7, 12, 34–35; etc.). The recalcitrance of God's enemies thus also binds
the episodes together.

Oral-scribal intertexture serves two principal rhetorical purposes
here. First, it contributes to the plausibility of John's narration of the
future. Aristotle and Anaximenes both observe that the use of "examples"
(historical precedents rather than fables or analogies) assist deliberative
orators in their primary task, namely, demonstrating that matters will turn
out as they allege:[36]

> Examples are most suitable for deliberative speakers, for *it is by exam-
> ination of the past that we divine and judge the future*. (Aristotle, *Rhet.*
> 1.9.40)
> While the lessons conveyed by fables are easier to provide, those derived
> from facts are more useful for deliberative oratory, because *as a rule the
> future resembles the past*. (Aristotle, *Rhet.* 2.20.8)

The fact that God was indeed able to work great and wondrous plagues
upon Egypt (and chose to act in this rather colorful manner, punishing by
degrees and by diverse phenomena) so as to bring justice and deliverance
to God's people lends plausibility to John's narration of a future in which

---

[35] Notably, Dan 12:1 (ἔσται … θλῖψις οἷα οὐ γέγονεν ἀφ᾽ οὗ γεγένηται ἔθνος ἐπὶ
τῆς γῆς) and Mark 13:19 (ἔσονται … θλῖψις οἷα οὐ γέγονεν ποιαύτη ἀπ᾽ ἀρχῆς
κτίσεως).

[36] Anaximenes refers to judicial situations when he advises that examples be
used "in order that your audience may be more ready to believe your statements
when they realize that another action resembling the one you allege has been
committed in the way in which you say that it occurred" (*Rhet. Alex.* 1429a.25–28).
If known actions that occurred prior to the case concerning which the forensic orator is making allegations renders his reconstruction of the case more plausible, then
the same should still hold true for deliberative causes.

God does this again. The scale may now be grander, but the action is no different. John is also able to capitalize on the tendency within Scripture and within Jewish culture to portray God's future interventions in terms of God's prior ones, itself perhaps another sign that people were willing to embrace a vision of the future as plausible more readily when it resembles the past.

Second, it continues to evoke historical precedents in the minds of the hearers that support John's forecast of the future and guide the hearers in their deliberations about the present in light now both of past and future. Immersing the hearers' situation (namely, Roman imperial rule) in the scriptural situation of God's visitations upon Egypt guides them to see their present situation in light of the exodus. Given God's ability and commitment to pour out God's wrath upon injustice, identifying with God's holy ones will always be more secure and advantageous than identifying with God's enemies. Although temporarily afflicted, when the "hour of God's judgment came" it was far more advantageous to be found among the Hebrews than the Egyptians.

The details of the sixth bowl plague point to a second area of intertexture in which historical references and recontextualizations of older texts contribute to the plausibility of John's future by means of presenting a future that both resembles the past and is supported by historical precedents. The "great river Euphrates"[37] figured prominently in prophetic announcements of the disasters that would befall Judah. The powers east of the Euphrates ("north" of Israel) threatened to sweep over not only Israel[38] but all the Gentile nations in the area as well (Jer 46:6–10). The associations of the forces beyond "the great river" and bloody destruction are quite strong.

The drying up of the Euphrates ("and its water was dried up," Rev 16:12), while possibly evoking images of the drying up of the Red Sea ("he made the sea dry," Exod 14:21), provides a notable reference to military

---

[37] The Euphrates is an important feature of Jewish and Roman cultural maps. It is the boundary of Israel's inheritance, a boundary used in the promises given to Abraham and to the exodus generation (Gen 15:18; Exod 23:31; Deut 11:24; Josh 1:4) and appearing in the descriptions of Solomon's kingdom (1 Kgs 4:21, 24; 2 Chr 9:26), when Israel's boundaries were at their greatest, not to be achieved again until the Hasmonean dynasty. Although the boundary of the Roman Empire was sometimes east, sometimes west of the Euphrates, that river still served as an approximate ideological boundary of the Roman map until Trajan's victory over the Parthians in 114–116 C.E. (Caird, *Revelation,* 122).

[38] Isaiah 8:7–8 and Jer 47:2 both use the image of the Euphrates overflowing and flooding Israel as a metaphor for the Assyrian and Babylonian armies invading. See also Jer 1:14–16; 6:22–26; and 24:9–11.

history, since Cyrus, coming from Persia in the East, was in fact able to capture Babylon because the Euphrates was dried up (either because Cyrus's armies diverted the river from its bed [as in Herodotus, *Hist.* 1.189–191] or because it was the naturally low time for the river). This event is also known from the Jewish Scriptures, especially Isa 44:24–45:6 ("I will dry up your rivers," 44:27).[39] That the river is dried up so as to allow the "kings from the east" to cross over and enter into a battle continues to reconfigure this historical precedent, particularly as it is scripted in Isaiah. Isaiah 42:2, 25, for example, had spoken of God arousing "one from the east," namely Cyrus, to crush Babylon and bring release to captive Israel. John reconfigures this scene, as many kings "from the east" are roused to move against "Babylon."[40]

The site chosen for the battle is also rich with historical reminiscences preserved in the Jewish Scriptures. Ἀρμαγεδών transliterates the Hebrew for "Mount of Megiddo,"[41] a reference to the mountain nearest to the city of Megiddo (just like the "waters of Megiddo" in Judg 5:19 refers to the Wadi Kishon, the torrent close by Megiddo), probably Mount Carmel.[42] This city was a strategically critical stronghold between west and east, and the plain stretching before it is rich in military history—particularly in international battles for domination. This history includes the defeat of Sisera (Judg 4:5), Gideon's defeat of the Midianites (Judg 7:1), the deaths of Saul and Jonathan (1 Sam 31:1–6) in a battle against the Philistines, the death of King Ahaziah (2 Kgs 9:27–28) after being shot by Jehu's forces, and the death of King Josiah as he attempted to stop Pharoah Neco from crossing through Palestine to wage war on the king of Babylon (2 Kgs 23:29). If there was a single spot in Israel's geography where one could "sit upon the ground and tell sad stories of the death of kings," Megiddo was it. Shea adds that the battle between Ahab and Elijah, between Baal and Yahweh

---

[39] W. H. Shea, "The Location and Significance of Armageddon in Rev 16:16," *AUSS* 18 (1980): 157–62, esp. 157–58.

[40] Buchanan posits that this is a reference to the Jewish hope that the Parthians would join forces with them and overthrow Rome (*Revelation,* 417, 419). The antagonism of the Parthians toward Rome and their consequent predilection for assisting Jews against Roman-imposed rule in the late Hasmonean/early Herodian period (See Josephus, *War* 1.248–270) provide support for this theory. These eastern kings should not, in his view, be seen as the beast's allies but as his adversaries (Buchanan, *Revelation,* 425, 427). The fact that *1 En.* 56:5–7 speaks of Parthian kings laying siege to Jerusalem (and being defeated) should not preclude, however, the possibility that they are hostile not only to Rome.

[41] Possibly, but less likely, "City of Megiddo," if the first syllable represents Hebrew *'îr* rather than *har.*

[42] Shea, "Location and Significance of Armageddon," 159–60.

on Carmel, should also be heard as a resonance here (he says "the" resonance, but there is neither need nor warrant for arguing for any single
referent).[43] The unholy trio summons all nations to this place, just as Ahab
and Elijah had summoned all Israel; the victory is won the same way,
namely, with fire descending from heaven.[44]

Patterning the final battle in which God defeats "Babylon" and brings
relief to God's people after a prominent precedent in which God did the
same to end the Babylonian exile renders this future more plausible, since
it resembles what has already become historical fact. John also achieves
this, however, by laying out at some length God's "strategy" for accom-
plishing this end—the ways and means by which God will position God's
enemies for defeat. Rather than speak vaguely about God's victory, John
uses specificity and detail to make that victory appear more feasible and
real. God has chosen a location known for its strategic importance,[45] one
where large hostile forces could be routed (as in the defeat of Sisera's
army), and now will add to the historic wailing of that space with the
defeat of "the kings of the earth."

Chapter 16 closes with the announcement of the fall of Babylon, to
whom God remembered "to give to her the cup of the wine of the violent
passion of his anger" (Rev 16:19; cf. 14:10). Identifying Rome with "Babylon" allows John to bring together many pieces of "authoritative" texts from
authoritative denunciations of Babylon and other pagan seats of empire in
Isaiah, Jeremiah, and Ezekiel into a deconstruction of Roman imperial ideology in Rev 17 and 18. The label affords an unusual but strikingly effective
way of considering a historical precedent to predict the outcome of a new
venture. John's virtual identification of Babylon and Rome achieves the
same end as the example in deliberative rhetoric (Aristotle, *Rhet.* 1.2.8;
1.4.9; 1.9.40; 2.20.8; Anaximenes, *Rhet. Alex.* 1428b.12–17; 1429a.25–28).
Deliberative orators use historical examples as a means of convincing the

---

[43] Ibid., 160–61.

[44] Shea (ibid., 161) and Beale (*Revelation,* 835) regard 16:12–16 as merely the
preparation for the battle that is actually fought and won in Rev 19:11–21, a reading that has much to commend it since no other battle is recounted after all these
preparations in 16:12–16, and no preparations are narrated other than these prior
to the battle in Rev 19:11–21. (I would not identify the battle in 20:6–8 with
19:11–21, however, as does Beale.)

[45] Buchanan (*Revelation,* 422) suggests that "if Parthians had come to rescue
Palestine from the Romans during the war between Vitellius and Vespasian, there
would have been Jewish volunteers to meet them at Mount Carmel, just as there
were at the beginning of Herod's rule, because Megiddo was one of the most
strategic fortresses in Palestine, and it was the first one the Parthians would have
reached as they came to Palestine from the north ([Josephus,] *War* 1.250)."

hearers that the outcome of the course they promoted (or from which they sought to dissuade the audience) would indeed be as they predicted.[46] The ability to predict outcomes from comparison with other, known situations is important since "similar results naturally arise from similar causes" (*Rhet.* 1.4.9). The judgment of Rome, John posits, is an absolute certainty since the same causes for judgment are present in Rome as were present in Babylon (as well as other cities similarly judged by God, as, for example, Tyre in Ezek 26). The example also thus becomes a "previous verdict" (*Rhet.* 2.23.12) that has already guided the divine court in pronouncing its sentence upon Babylon's new manifestation.

The mode by which John presents this, however, is rhetorically far more effective than an "argument from example." Aristotle was aware that deliberative proofs worked on probabilities. Analogies and examples were used to establish the probability that the consequences would be as the orator predicted, but they could never establish their certainty. John is able to suppress the element of analogy, never saying that the fate of Rome will be "like" that of Babylon. Rather, he completely closes the distance between the historical precedent that informs his language and the present case under consideration by identifying the two, thus also closing the distance between probability and certainty. The element of "certainty" is reinforced as John continues to "narrate" the reasons for Rome's downfall using the very oracles of God from Isaiah, Jeremiah, and Ezekiel and finally singing of the execution of this judgment in Rev 17–18. By embroidering portions of the Old Testament prophets into his denunciation of Rome, John again causes the hearers to set their present situation and world in the interpretive context of authoritative Scriptures. Throughout Revelation this is a central mode of persuasion in John's visionary rhetoric. In effect, he causes them to inhabit the world of everyday experience and the world of the Scriptures simultaneously, knowing that this will lead them both to see the world and to respond to it in ways that John considers faithful to the Christian tradition. Without John ever having to exhort the hearer directly on this point (18:4 will come very close to this, of course), John's addressees will nevertheless be able to discern that any course favoring partnership with Rome—an enemy of God certain to be judged and toppled—will be less expedient than a course favoring exclusive allegiance to the one God.

5. Other Rhetorical Functions of Intertexture in Revelation 16

Chapter 16 does not use intertexture solely to render more plausible a future in which God intervenes to punish and destroy the ungodly, though

---

[46] "Examples are most suitable for deliberative speakers, for it is by examination of the past that we divine and judge the future" (Aristotle, *Rhet.* 1.9.40).

this appears to be a major rhetorical contribution of intertexture in this chapter. At least two other rhetorical objectives are also promoted by intertexture. First, when John arrives in the sequence of plagues at "the Great Day of God Almighty" (τῆς ἡμέρας τῆς μεγάλης τοῦ θεοῦ τοῦ παντοκράτορος)—which recalls the foundational Jewish and Christian expectation of the "Day of the Lord," the day when God's wrath is released and the destruction of the ungodly ensues—this becomes an opportunity to interact with Christian cultural intertexture. The voice of Jesus interjects a warning and elevates a certain posture for emulation as advantageous in light of that warning: "Behold I come as a thief ['Ιδοὺ ἔρχομαι ὡς κλέπτης]: blessed are those who watch and keep their garments, lest they walk about naked and people see their shame [μακάριος ὁ γρηγορῶν καὶ τηρῶν τὰ ἱμάτια αὐτοῦ, ἵνα μὴ γυμνὸς περιπατῇ καὶ βλέπωσιν τὴν ἀσχημοσύνην αὐτοῦ]" (Rev 16:15).

Jesus' warning here refers to Christian traditions that declare that the "Day of the Lord" (cf. "the Great Day of God Almighty," Rev 16:14) "comes as a thief." Especially worthy of comparison are 1 Thess 5:2–4 and 2 Pet 3:10:

> As a thief in the night, so comes the Day of the Lord [ὡς κλέπτης ... ἔρχεται].... But you, brothers and sisters, are not in the dark, so that the Day overtakes you as a thief [ὡς κλέπτης]. (1 Thess 5:2–4)
> The Day of the Lord will come as a thief ["Ηξει ... ὡς κλέπτης]. (2 Pet 3:10)

Hearers might also recall the saying, recorded in Matt 24:42–44, in which Jesus uses the image of the thief coming at an unknown hour to illustrate his own return. The makarism continues to refer to these traditions, particularly to an instruction of Jesus connected directly with the similitude of the thief coming at an unknown hour:

> Watch [γρηγορεῖτε], therefore, because you do not know in what hour your Lord comes [ὁ κύριος ὑμῶν ἔρχεται]. (Matt 24:42; cf. Mark 13:35)
> Watch [γρηγορεῖτε], therefore, because you do not know the day [τὴν ἡμέραν, cf. Rev 16:14] nor the hour. (Matt 25:13)
> What I say to you I say to all: Watch [γρηγορεῖτε]. (Mark 13:37)

The exhortation to "watch" becomes a common exhortation in Christian culture, although not always in an eschatological context (e.g., 1 Pet 5:8, which cautions against falling into the snares of the devil; or Acts 20:31, which admonishes against accepting perversions of the message Paul preached). Revelation 16:15 and 1 Thess 5:6 ("not sleeping as do the rest, let us be watchful [γρηγορῶμεν]," namely, for the Day of the Lord) both recontextualize the admonition in a manner in keeping with Jesus' saying.

The warning serves to underscore, as did the first angel's announcement (14:7) and the descriptions of judgment (14:14–20), the future crisis
that the hearers must now keep foremost in their minds as they consider
what actions are truly expedient. As they cast their eyes to their everyday
circumstances, soft-pedaling their testimony to Jesus and even pouring a
libation or two to their neighbor's gods as a token of goodwill and civic
unity might indeed seem advantageous. For this reason, John must throw
ever before their eyes that coming crisis of divine judgment and visitation,
so that the hearers may choose their present actions with a view to safety
and avoidance of dishonor on the "Great Day of God Almighty." The passages that focus on this coming crisis use both oral-scribal and cultural
intertexture as a means of giving expression to that event and its consequences, reminding the hearers of that larger tradition that must shape
their worldview and their lives. The makarism proposes for emulation a
posture that makes for security on that Day, namely, remaining vigilant and
alert for Jesus' return and doing those things that are in keeping with that
expectation. Those people, for example, who heed the first angel's summons (14:7) and avoid the course of action the consequences of which
were laid out by the third angel (14:9–11) are "watching" for that Day.
Those who chose an idolatrous peace with Rome have put aside their garments and gotten in bed with the Whore.

A recontextualization of Ezek 16:36–39 provides the rationale for this
makarism, offering an abbreviated argument from the contrary ("for those
who fail to watch and keep their garments will walk about naked and have
their shame seen by people"). Ezekiel had spoken of the punishment that
would befall Israel for her idolatries and defiling alliances thus: in the presence of all Israel's former lovers, "they shall see your shame [ὄψονται
πᾶσαν τὴν αἰσχύνην σου] ... and they shall strip you of your garments
[ἐκδύσουσίν σε τὸν ἱματισμόν σου] ... and leave you naked and bare
[γυμνὴν καὶ ἀσχημονοῦσαν]." John uses Ezekiel's language in order to posit
the negative consequences of failing to deliberate wisely with regard to
meeting the forthcoming challenge of Jesus' return. People who act so as
to gain peace with, and temporal reward in, the idolatrous dominant culture will find themselves disgraced on the "Great Day of God Almighty."
Ezekiel thus provides the language for an appeal to a topic of disadvantage (i.e., dishonor) frequently used in apotreptic discourse. As John's
discourse progresses, these same images are reused to describe the fate of
Babylon itself, linking more closely the fate of those who fail to "watch"
for the Day of the Lord to the fate of God's enemies.

The second objective is accomplished more subtly, elevating the value
of "keeping God's commandments" and underscoring the danger of choosing a path contrary to that value. The seventh plague presents in summary
fashion the destruction of Rome and the other "cities of the nations," the

former of which will be developed at length in Rev 17:1–19:8. John has chosen to color this plague with shades of the Sinai theophany when God gave the law to Israel: the commandments the violation of which was cited as the cause for the driving out of the Canaanites from the land (especially the pollution of idols). The phenomena accompanying the fall of the pagan cities are "lightnings and voices and thunders and a great earthquake" (ἐγένοντο ἀστραπαὶ καὶ φωναὶ καὶ βρονταί καὶ σεισμὸς ἐγένετο μέγας, Rev 16:18), each of which was also connected with the Sinai theophany: "there were lightnings and voices" (ἐγίνοντο φωναὶ καὶ ἀστραπαι, Exod 19:16); "the land shook … the mountains were shaken" (γῆ ἐσείσθη … ὄρη ἐσαλεύθησαν, Judg 5:4–5). Psalm 76:19 LXX merges Sinai with the Red Sea, describing "the voice of your thunder [φωνὴ τῆς βροντῆς σου] … your lightnings [αἱ ἀστραπαί σου]" and the "shaking" and "trembling" of the earth (ἐσαλεύθη καὶ ἔντρομος ἐγενήθη ἡ γῆ). At the conclusion of God's judgments, therefore, there is a literal "echo" of the rumblings that accompanied the giving of the law. This echo sets God's eschatological judgments in the interpretive light of the giving of the law, suggesting that the "unlawful" way of life (e.g., any course of action contrary to God's law, among which returning to participation in idolatrous cults would be a pressing issue for Gentile Christians) will lead to ruin in the end, even if it brings temporary relief or prosperity.

6. Conclusion

John's creative use of older texts and cultural traditions (oral-scribal and cultural intertexture) contributes greatly to his rhetorical strategy and the persuasiveness of his narration of the future. What was impossible for Aristotle becomes possible for John, as he depicts a future the plausibility of which is reinforced by numerous historical precedents and examples. The addressees are confronted thus not with a vision that has the appearance of a flight of fancy, but one in which the future very much resembles the past and in which the same relationships of cause and consequence are observable that have been at work throughout God's dealings with humanity. At critical junctures in this narrative demonstration, the older texts about God's character and commitment to do justice upon the earth are affirmed and reinvigorated, reminding the hearers of the principal, unchanging premises that guide the unfolding of history and thus provide a reliable basis for divining the future.

Within this narration of the future, John continues to use the language of the Jewish Scriptures and the traditions of both Jewish and Christian cultures to align the hearers with certain values and courses of action. He uses topics familiar from deliberative oratory (showing a course of action to be just, honorable, lawful, expedient, and leading to safety) as well as argumentative strategies familiar from the same (arguments from the consequence, relative expediency, and the like). Epideictic topics are also enhanced by intertexture, particularly through labeling and by depicting certain figures as "honorable" or "blessed," hence holding them up for emulation. Perhaps most central to the success of John's cause, cultural intertexture (supported by instances of oral-scribal intertexture) is employed to remind the hearers of that forthcoming crisis of the "Day of the Lord" concerning which they must now deliberate wisely. This Day is prominently featured and dramatically depicted so that safety on that Day will displace any contrary agenda that threatens total commitment to the Christian group and its distinctive values.

Bibliography

1. Primary Sources

Aristotle. *The "Art" of Rhetoric.* Translated by J. H. Freese. LCL. Cambridge: Harvard University Press, 1926.

———. *Nicomachean Ethics.* Translated by H. Rackham. LCL. Cambridge: Harvard University Press, 1932.

[Aristotle] *Rhetorica ad Alexandrum.* Translated by W. S. Hett and H. Rackham. LCL. Cambridge: Harvard University Press, 1983.

Butts, J. R. (1986). "The Progymnasmata of Theon: A New Text with Translation and Commentary." Ph.D. diss., Claremont Graduate School, 1986.

Cicero. *De Inventione, De Optimo Genere Oratorum, Topica.* Translated by H. M. Hubbell. LCL. Cambridge: Harvard University Press, 1949.

[Cicero] *Rhetorica ad Herennium.* Translated by Harry Caplan. LCL. Cambridge: Harvard University Press, 1981.

Charlesworth, James H., ed. *The Old Testament Pseudepigrapha.* 2 vols. Garden City, N.Y.: Doubleday, 1983–85.

Elliott, J. K., ed. *The Apocryphal New Testament: A Collection of Apocryphal Christian Literature in an English Translation Based on M. R. James.* Oxford: Clarendon, 1993.

Hennecke, Edgar, ed. *New Testament Apocrypha.* Edited by Wilhelm Schneemelcher. Translated and edited by McL. Wilson. Rev. ed. 2 vols. Louisville: Westminster John Knox, 1991–92.

Hock, Ronald F., and Edward N. O'Neil. *The Progymnasmata.* Vol. 1 of *The Chreia in Ancient Rhetoric.* Atlanta: Scholars Press, 1986.

Laperrousaz, E. M. *Le Testament de Moïse. Sem* 19 (1970): 1–140.

Nadeau, R. "Hermogenes' On Stases: A Translation with an Introduction and Notes." *Speech Monographs* 31 (1964): 361–424.

Priest, J. *Testament of Moses.* OTP 1:919–34.

2. General Reference

Achtemeier, Paul, et al., eds., *HarperCollins Bible Dictionary.* 2d ed. San Francisco: HarperSanFrancisco, 1996.

Hawthorne, Gerald F., Ralph P. Martin, and Daniel G. Reid, eds. *Dictionary of Paul and His Letters.* Downers Grove, Ill.: InterVarsity, 1993.

3. Studies in Intertextuality

Aichele, George, and Gary A. Phillips, eds. *Intertextuality and the Bible.* *Semeia* 69/70 (1995).

Clayton, Jay, and Eric Rothstein. *Influence and Intertextuality in Literary History.* Madison: University of Wisconsin Press, 1991.

Evans, Craig A., and James A. Sanders, eds. *Paul and the Scriptures of Israel.* SSEJC 1. JSNTSup 83. Sheffield: Sheffield Academic Press, 1993.

Fishbane, Michael. *Biblical Interpretation in Ancient Israel.* Oxford: Clarendon, 1985.

————. "Inner Biblical Exegesis: Types and Strategies of Interpretation in Ancient Israel." Pages 19–37 in *Midrash and Literature.* Edited by Geoffrey H. Hartmann and Sandord Budick. New Haven: Yale University Press, 1986.

Hollander, John. *The Figure of Echo: A Mode of Allusion in Milton and After.* Berkeley and Los Angeles: University of California Press, 1981.

O'Day, Gail R. "Intertextuality." Pages 546–48 in *Dictionary of Biblical Interpretation.* Edited by John H. Hayes. 2 vols. Nashville: Abingdon, 1999.

————. "Jeremiah 9:22–23 and 1 Corinthians 1:26–31: A Study in Intertextuality." *JBL* 109 (1990): 259–67.

Robbins, Vernon K. *Exploring the Texture of Texts: A Guide to Socio-Rhetorical Criticism.* Valley Forge, Pa.: Trinity Press International, 1996.

————. *The Tapestry of Early Christian Discourse: Rhetoric, Society and Ideology.* New York: Routledge, 1996.

Worton, Michael, and Judith Still, eds. *Intertextuality: Theories and Practices.* Manchester: Manchester University Press, 1990.

4. Studies in Apocalyptic Discourse and Literature

Aune, David E. "Early Christian Eschatology." *ABD* 2:594–609.

Betz, Hans Dieter. "Eschatology in the Sermon on the Mount and the Sermon on the Plain." Pages 343–50 in *SBL Seminar Papers, 1985.* SBLSP 24. Atlanta: Scholars Press, 1985.

————. "On the Problem of the Religio-Historical Understanding of Apocalypticism." *JTC* 6 (1969): 134–56.

Boomershine, Thomas E. "Epistemology at the Turn of the Ages in Paul, Jesus, and Mark: Rhetoric and Dialectic in Apocalyptic and the New Testament." Pages 147–67 in *Apocalyptic and the New Testament: Essays in Honor of J. Louis Martyn.* Edited by Joel Marcus and Marion L. Soards. JSNTSup 24. Sheffield: Sheffield Academic Press, 1989.

Carey, Greg. "Apocalyptic Ethos." Pages 731–61 in vol. 2 of *SBL Seminar Papers, 1998.* 2 vols. SBLSP 37. Atlanta: Scholars Press, 1998.

————. "Introduction: Apocalyptic Discourse, Apocalyptic Rhetoric." Pages 1–17 in *Vision and Persuasion: Rhetorical Dimensions of Apocalyptic Discourse*. Edited by Greg Carey and L. Gregory Bloomquist; St. Louis: Chalice, 1999.

Carey, Greg, and L. Gregory Bloomquist. *Vision and Persuasion: Rhetorical Dimensions of Apocalyptic Discourse*. St. Louis: Chalice, 1999.

Collins, Adela Yarbro. *Cosmology and Eschatology in Jewish and Christian Apocalypticism*. JSJSup 50. Leiden: Brill, 1996.

————. *Crises and Catharsis: The Power of the Apocalypse*. Philadelphia: Westminster, 1984.

————. "Early Christian Apocalyptic Literature." *ANRW* 25.6:4665–4711.

Collins, John J., ed. *Apocalypse: The Morphology of a Genre. Semeia* 14 (1979).

————. *The Apocalyptic Imagination: An Introduction to the Jewish Matrix of Christianity*. New York: Crossroad, 1987.

————. "Introduction: Towards the Morphology of a Genre." *Semeia* 14 (1979): 1–20.

Gammie, John. "From Prudentialism to Apocalypticism: The Houses of the Sages amid the Varying Forms of Wisdom." Pages 479–97 in *The Sage in Israel and the Ancient Near East*. Edited by John Gammie and Leo Perdue. Winona Lake, Ind.: Eisenbrauns, 1990.

Hanson, Paul D. *The Dawn of Apocalyptic: The Historical and Sociological Roots of Jewish Apocalyptic Eschatology*. Rev. ed. Philadelphia: Fortress, 1979.

Humphrey, Edith. *The Ladies and the Cities: Transformation and Apocalyptic Identity in Joseph and Aseneth, 4 Ezra, the Apocalypse and the Shepherd of Hermas*. JSPSup 18. Sheffield: JSOT Press, 1995.

Käsemann, Ernst. "Zum Thema der urchristlichen Apokalyptic." *ZTK* 59 (1962): 257–84.

Murphy, Frederick J. "Introduction to Apocalyptic Literature." *NIB* 7:1–16.

Reiser, Marius. *Jesus and Judgment: The Eschatological Proclamation in Its Jewish Context*. Minneapolis: Fortress, 1997.

Russell, D. S. *The Method and Message of Apocalyptic: 200 BC–AD 100*. OTL. London: SCM, 1964.

Silberman, Lou H. "The Human Deed in a Time of Despair: The Ethics of Apocalyptic." Pages 191–202 in *Essays in Old Testament Ethics (J. Philip Hyatt, In Memoriam)*. Edited by James L. Crenshaw and John T. Willis. New York: Ktav, 1974.

5. Rhetorical and Literary Studies

5.1. General Studies

Alter, Robert. *The Pleasures of Reading in an Ideological Age*. New York: Simon & Schuster, 1989.

Barilli, Renato. *Rhetoric*. Minneapolis: University of Minnesota Press, 1989.

Bormann, Ernest G. "Colloquy: I. Fantasy and Rhetorical Vision Ten Years Later." *QJS* 68 (1982): 288–305.

———, "Fantasy and Rhetorical Vision: The Rhetorical Criticism of Social Reality." *QJS* 58 (1972): 396–407.

———. *The Force of Fantasy: Restoring the American Dream*. Carbondale: Southern Illinois University Press, 1985.

———. *Small Group Communication: Theory and Practice*. 3d ed. New York: Harper and Row, 1990.

Bormann, Ernest G., John F. Cragan, and Donald C. Shields. "In Defense of Symbolic Convergence Theory: A Look at the Theory and its Criticisms after Two Decades." *Communications Theory* 4 (1994): 259–94.

———. "An Expansion of the Rhetorical Vision Component of the Symbolic Convergence Theory: The Cold War Paradigm Case." *Communication Monographs* 63 (1996): 1–28.

Bové, Paul A. "Discourse." Pages 50–65 in *Critical Terms for Literary Study*. Edited by F. Lentricchia and T. McLaughlin. Chicago, University of Chicago Press, 1990.

Cragan, John F., and Donald C. Shields. *Applied Communication Research: A Dramatistic Approach*. Prospect Heights, Ill.: Waveland, 1981.

Farrell, Thomas B. "Aristotle's Enthymeme As Tacit Reference." Pages 93–106 in *Rereading Aristotle's Rhetoric*. Edited by Alan G. Gross and Arthur E. Walzer. Carbondale and Edwardsville: Southern Illinois University Press, 2000.

Fish, Stanley E. *Self-Consuming Artifacts: The Experience of Seventeenth-Century Literature*. Berkeley and Los Angeles: University of California Press, 1972.

Foss, Sonja K., compiler. *Rhetorical Criticism: Exploration and Practice*. Prospect Heights, Ill.: Waveland, 1989.

Foss, Sonja K., Karen A. Foss, and Robert Trapp. *Contemporary Perspectives on Rhetoric*. Prospect Heights, Ill.: Waveland, 1985.

Hester, James D. "Speaker, Audience and Situations: A Modified Interactional Model." *Neot* 32 (1998): 251–71.

Hollander, John. *The Figure of Echo: A Mode of Allusion in Milton and After*. Berkeley and Los Angeles: University of California Press, 1981.

Kennedy, George. *The Art of Rhetoric in the Graeco-Roman World*. Princeton, N.J.: Princeton University Press, 1972.

———. *New Testament Interpretation through Rhetorical Criticism*. Chapel Hill: University of North Carolina Press, 1984.

Lanigan, Richard L. "From Enthymeme to Abduction: The Classical Law of Logic and the Postmodern Rule of Rhetoric." Pages 49–70 in *Recovering Pragmatism's Voice: The Classical Tradition, Rorty, and the Philosophy of Communication*. Edited by Lenore Langsdorf and Andrew R. Smith. Albany: State University of New York Press, 1995.

Miller, A. B., and J. D. Bee, "Enthymemes: Body and Soul," *Philosophy and Rhetoric* 5 (1972): 201–14.

Miller, Carolyn R. "The Aristotelean Topos: Hunting for Novelty." Pages 130-46 in *Rereading Aristotle's Rhetoric*. Edited by Alan G. Gross and Arthur E. Walzer. Carbondale and Edwardsville: Southern Illinois University Press, 2000.

Ong, Walter J. Introduction to "A Fuller Course in the Art of Logic (1672)," Pages 144-205 in *Complete Prose Works of John Milton*. Volume 8: *1666–1682*. Edited by Maurice Kelley. New Haven: Yale University Press, 1982.

———. *Orality and Literacy: The Technologizing of the Word*. New York: Routledge, 1982.

Perelman, Chaim, and Lucie Olbrects-Tyteca. *The New Rhetoric: A Treatise on Argumentation*. Translated by John Wilkinson and Purcell Weaver. Notre Dame, Ind.: University of Notre Dame Press, 1969.

Ricour, Paul. "The Hermeneutic Function of Distanciation." *Philosophy Today* 17 (1973): 129–41.

Thom, Johan C. "'The Mind Is Its Own Place': Towards a Definition of Topos." In *Early Christianity and Classical Culture: Essays in Honor of Abraham J. Malherbe*. Edited by John T. Fitzgerald et al. Valley Forge, Pa.: Trinity Press International, 2002 (forthcoming).

Toulmin, Stephen E. *The Uses of Argument*. Cambridge: Cambridge University Press, 1964.

Warnick, Barbara. "Two Systems of Invention: The Topics in Rhetoric and The New Rhetoric." Pages 107–29 in *Rereading Aristotle's Rhetoric*. Edited by Alan G. Gross and Arthur E. Walzer. Carbondale and Edwardsville: Southern Illinois University Press, 2000.

Zulick, Margaret D. "Generative Rhetoric and Public Argument: A Classical Approach." *Argument and Advocacy* 33 (1997): 109–19.

5.2. In Biblical Studies

Bloomquist, L. Gregory, "Methodological Criteria for Apocalyptic Rhetoric: A Suggestion for the Expanded Use of Sociorhetorical Analysis." Pages 181–203 in *In Vision and Persuasion: Rhetorical Dimensions of Apocalyptic Discourse*. Edited by Greg Carey and L. Gregory Bloomquist. St. Louis: Chalice, 1999.

———. "Refining Ideological Texture." Paper presented at the Rhetoric and Early Christian Discourse Panel, Canadian Society of Biblical Studies and Canadian Society for the Study of Rhetoric, Edmonton, Alberta, May 27, 2000.

Gitay, Yehoshua. *Prophecy and Persuasion: A Study of Isaiah 40–48*. ForTLing 14. Bonn: Linguistica Biblica, 1981.

———. "Rhetorical Criticism and the Prophetic Discourse." Pages 13–24 in *Persuasive Artistry: Studies in New Testament Rhetoric in Honor of George A. Kennedy*. Edited by Duane F. Watson. JSNTSup 50. Sheffield: Sheffield Academic Press, 1991.

Robbins, Vernon K. "Argumentative Textures in Socio-Rhetorical Interpretation." Pages 27–65 in *Argumentation in Biblical Texts*. Edited by Anders Eriksson, Thomas H. Olbricht, and Walter Übelacker. Emory Studies in Early Christianity. Harrisburg, Pa.: Trinity Press International, 2002.

———. "The Dialectical Nature of Early Christian Discourse." *Scriptura* 59 (1996): 353–62.

———. *Exploring the Texture of Texts: A Guide to Socio-Rhetorical Criticism*. Valley Forge, Pa.: Trinity Press International, 1996.

———. "The Present and Future of Rhetorical Analysis." Pages 24–52 in *The Rhetorical Analysis of Scripture: Essays from the 1995 London Conference*. Edited by Stanley E. Porter and Thomas H. Olbricht. JSNTSup 146. Sheffield: Sheffield Academic Press, 1997.

———. "Rhetoric and Culture: Exploring Types of Cultural Rhetoric in a Text." Pages 443–63 in *Rhetoric and the New Testament: Essays from the 1992 Heidelberg Conference*. Edited by Stanley E. Porter and Thomas H. Olbricht. JSNTSup 90. Sheffield: Sheffield Academic Press, 1993.

———. "Socio-Rhetorical Hermeneutics and Commentary." Pages 284–97 in *EPI TO AUTO*. Edited by J. Mrazek et al. Praha-Trebenice: Mlyn, 1998.

———. *The Tapestry of Christian Early Discourse: Rhetoric, Society and Ideology*. New York: Routledge, 1996.

Roberts, K. A. "Toward a Generic Concept of Counter-Culture." *Sociological Focus* 11 (1978): 111–26.

Watson, Duane F. "Rhetorical Criticism of the Pauline Epistles Since 1975." *CurBS* 3 (1995): 219–48.

Wuellner, Wilhelm H. "Toposforschung und Torahinterpretation bei Paulus und Jesus." *NTS* 24 (1978): 463–83.

6. The Old Testament

Anderson, Bernhard W. "Exodus and Covenant in Second Isaiah and Prophetic Tradition." Pages 339–60 in *Magnalia Dei: The Mighty Acts of God: Essays on the Bible and Archaeology in Memory of G. Ernest Wright*. Edited by Frank Moore Cross et al. Garden City, N.Y.: Doubleday, 1976.

———. "Exodus Typology in Second Isaiah." Pages 177–95 in *Israel's Prophetic Heritage: Essays in Honor of James Muilenburg*. Edited by Bernhard W. Anderson and Walter Harrelson. London: SCM, 1962.

Barstad, Hans M. *A Way in the Wilderness: The Second Exodus in the Message of Second Isaiah.* Journal of Semitic Studies Monograph 12. Manchester: University of Manchester, 1989.

Barthel, Jörg. *Prophetenwort und Geschichte: Die Jesajaüberlieferung in Jes 6–8 and 28–31.* FAT 19. Tübingen: Mohr Siebeck, 1997.

Ceresko, Anthony R. "The Rhetorical Strategy of the Fourth Servant Song (Isaiah 52:13–53:12): Poetry and the Exodus-New Exodus." *CBQ* 56 (1994): 42–55.

Daube, David. *The Exodus Pattern in the Bible.* All Souls Studies 2. London: Faber & Faber, 1963.

Durham, John I. "Isaiah 40–55: A New Creation, A New Exodus, A New Messiah." Pages 47–56 in *The Yahweh/Baal Confrontation and Other Studies in Biblical Literature and Archaeology: Essays in Honour of Emmett Willard Hamrick.* Edited by Julia M. O'Brien and Fred L. Horton Jr. Lewiston, N.Y.: Mellen, 1995.

Fichtner, Johannes. "Isaiah among the Wise." Pages 429–38 in *Studies in Ancient Israelite Wisdom.* Edited by James L. Crenshaw. New York: Ktav, 1976.

Fishbane, Michael. "The 'Exodus' Motif: The Paradigm of Historical Renewal." Pages 121–40 in *Text and Texture: Close Readings of Selected Biblical Texts.* New York: Schocken, 1979.

Fisher, Fred L. "The New and Greater Exodus: The Exodus Pattern in the New Testament." *SWJT* 20 (1977): 69–79.

Fohrer, George. *Das Buch Jesaja.* 2 vols. ZBK. Zürich and Stuttgart: Zwingli, 1962, 1966.

Hartmann, Louis F., and Alexander A. Di Lella. *The Book of Daniel.* AB 23. New York: Doubleday, 1978.

Hungenberger, G. P. "The Servant of the Lord in the 'Servant Songs' of Isaiah: A Second Moses Figure." Pages 105–40 in *The Lord's Anointed: Interpretation of Old Testament Messianic Texts.* Edited by Philip E. Satterthwaite et al. Grand Rapids: Baker, 1995.

Jensen, Joseph. *The Use of tôrâ by Isaiah: His Debate with the Wisdom Tradition.* CBQMS 3. Washington, D.C.: Catholic Biblical Association of America, 1973.

Kim, Sungsoo, "A Study of the Exodus Motif in Isaiah." Thesis, Calvin Theological Seminary, 1983.

Landy, Francis. Review of Jörg Barthel, *Prophetenwort und Geschichte: Die Jesajaüberlieferung in Jes 6–8 and 28–31. JBL* 118 (1999): 543–45.

Lindbloom, J. *Prophecy in Ancient Israel.* Philadelphia: Fortress, 1962.

Loewenstamm, Samuel E. *The Evolution of the Exodus Tradition.* Translated by Baruch J. Schwartz. Jerusalem: Magnes, 1992.

Marbock, Johannes. "Exodus zum Zion: Zum Glaubensweg der Gemeinde nach einigen Testen des Jesajabuches." Pages 163–79 in *Die Alttestamentliche Botschaft als Wegweisung: Festschrift für Heinz Reinelt*. Edited by Josef Zmijewski. Stuttgart: Katholisches Bibelwerk, 1990.

Martin-Achard, Robert. "Sagesse de Dieu et sagesse humaine chez Ésaie." Pages 137–44 in *Maqqēl Shâqēdh: La Branche D'Amandier: Hommage à Wilhelm Vischer*. Montellier: Causse, Graille & Castelnau, 1960.

McKenzie, John L. *Second Isaiah*. AB 20. Garden City, N.Y.: Doubleday, 1968.

Meeks, Wayne A. "Moses As God and King." Pages 354–71 in *Religions of Antiquity: Essays in Memory of Erwin Ramsdell Goodenough*. Edited by Jacob Neusner. SHR 14. Leiden: Brill, 1970.

Nixon, R. E. *The Exodus in the New Testament*. The Tyndale New Testament Lecture, 1962. London: Tyndale, 1963.

North, C. R. "The 'Former Things' and the 'New Things' in Deutero-Isaiah." Pages 111–26 in *Studies in Old Testament Prophecy: Presented to Theodore H. Robinson*. Edited by H. H. Rowley. Edinburgh: T&T Clark, 1957.

Ogden, Graham S. "Moses and Cyrus: Literary Affinities between the Priestly Presentation of Moses in Exodus vi–viii and the Cyrus Song in Isaiah xliv 24–xlv 13." *VT* 28 (1978): 195–203.

Pagels, Elaine. *The Origin of Satan*. New York: Random House, 1995.

Perdue, Leo. *Wisdom and Creation: The Theology of Wisdom Literature*. Nashville: Abingdon, 1994.

Piper, Otto A. "Unchanging Promises: Exodus in the New Testament." *Int* 11 (1957): 3–22.

Rendtorff, Rolf. "The Book of Isaiah: A Complex Unity. Synchronic and Diachronic Reading." Pages 32–49 in *New Visions of Isaiah*. Edited by Roy F. Melgin and Marvin A. Sweeney. JSOTSup 214. Sheffield: Sheffield Academic Press, 1996.

———. "Zur Komposition des Buches Jesaja." *VT* 34 (1984): 295–320.

Schoors, Antoon. "Les choses antérieures et les choses novelles dans les oracles Deutéro-Isaïens." *ETL* 40 (1964): 19–47.

Seitz, Christopher R. *Isaiah 1–39*. IBC. Louisville: Knox, 1993.

Stansell, Gary. "Isaiah 28–33: Blest Be the Tie That Binds (Isaiah Together)." Pages 68–103 in *New Visions of Isaiah*. Edited by Roy F. Melugin and Marvin A. Sweeney. JSOTSup 214. Sheffield: Sheffield Academic Press, 1996.

Steinmann, Jean. *Le Prophète Isaïe: Sa Vie, Son Oevre et Son Temps*. 2d ed. Paris: Cerf, 1955.

Stuhlmueller, Carroll. *Creative Redemption in Deutero-Isaiah*. AnBib 43. Rome: Biblical Institute Press, 1970.

Watts, John D. W. *Isaiah*. 2 vols. WBC 24, 25. Waco, Tex.: Word, 1985, 1987.

Watts, Rikki E. "Consolation or Confrontation? Isaiah 40–55 and the Delay of the New Exodus." *TynBul* 41 (1990): 31–59.

———. *Isaiah's New Exodus and Mark*. WUNT 2/88. Tübingen: Mohr Siebeck, 1997.

Whedbee, J. William. *Isaiah and Wisdom*. Nashville: Abingdon, 1971.

Wildberger, Hans. *Jesaja*. 3 vols. BKAT. Neukirchen-Vluyn: Neukirchener Verlag, 1974–82.

Wilk, Florian. *Die Bedeutung des Jesajabuch für Paulus*. FRLANT. Göttingen: Vanderhoeck & Ruprecht, 1998.

Zimmerli, Walther. "Le nouvel 'exode' dans le message des deux grandes prophètes de l'exil." Pages 216–27 in *Maqqél Shâqédh: La Branche d'Amandier: Hommage à Wilhelm Vischer*. Montpelier: Causse, Graille & Castelnau, 1960.

7. The New Testament

7.1. General Studies

Aune, David E. *Prophecy in Early Christianity and the Ancient Mediterranean World*. Grand Rapids: Eerdmans, 1983.

Balz, Horst, and Gerhard Schneider, eds. *Exegetical Dictionary of the New Testament*. 3 vols. Grand Rapids: Eerdmans, 1978–83.

Bultmann, Rudolf. *Theology of the New Testament*. Translated by Kendrick Grobel. 2 vols. New York: Scribner's, 1957.

Childs, Brevard S. *Biblical Theology of the Old and New Testaments: Theological Reflection on the Christian Bible*. Minneapolis: Fortress, 1992.

Hübner, Hans. *Corpus Paulinum*. Vol. 2 of *Vetus Testamentum in Novo*. Göttingen: Vanderhoeck & Ruprecht, 1997.

Koch, P. Robert. "Der Gottesgeist und der Messias." *Bib* 27 (1946): 241–68.

Langton, Edward. *Essentials of Demonology*. London: Epworth, 1949

Meade, David G. *Pseudonymity and Canon: An Investigation into the Relationship of Authorship and Authority in Jewish and Earliest Christian Tradition*. Grand Rapids: Eerdmans, 1987.

Perrin, Norman. *The New Testament: An Introduction. Proclamation and Parenesis, Myth and History*. New York: Harcourt Brace Jovanovich, 1974.

Petersen, Norman R. *Literary Criticism for New Testament Critics*. GBS. Philadelphia: Fortress, 1978.

von Rad, Gerhard. *Old Testament Theology*. Translated by D. M. G. Stalker. 2 vols. New York: Harper & Row, 1962, 1965.

Strobel, A. *Untersuchungen zum eschatologischen Verzögesungsproblem auf Grund der spätjüdisch-urchristlichen Geschichte vom Habakuk 2,2ff*. NovTSup 2. Leiden: Brill, 1961.

7.2. Q, the *Gospel of Thomas,* and Gospel Tradition

Horsley, Richard. "Social Conflict in the Synoptic Sayings Source Q." Pages 37–52 in *Conflict and Invention: Literary, Rhetorical, and Social Studies on the Sayings Gospel Q.* Edited by John Kloppenborg. Valley Forge, Pa.: Trinity Press International, 1995.

————. *Whoever Hears You Hears Me: Prophets, Performance, and Tradition in Q.* Harrisburg, Pa.: Trinity Press International, 1999.

————. "Wisdom Justified by Her Children: Examining Allegedly Disparate Traditions in Q." Pages 733–51 in *SBL Seminar Papers, 1994.* SBLSP 33. Atlanta: Scholars Press, 1994.

Jacobson, Arland. *The First Gospel: An Introduction to Q.* Sonoma, Calif.: Polebridge, 1992.

Kloppenborg, John. *The Formation of Q: Trajectories in Ancient Wisdom Collection.* Studies in Antiquity and Christianity. Philadelphia: Fortress, 1987.

————. Review of P. J. Hartin, *James and the Q Sayings of Jesus. CBQ* 54 (1992): 567–68.

————. "The Sayings Gospel Q and the Quest of the Historical Jesus." *HTR* 89 (1996): 307-44.

————. "Symbolic Eschatology and the Apocalypticism of Q." *HTR* 80 (1987): 287–306.

Kloppenborg Verbin, John S. *Excavating Q: The History and Setting of the Sayings Gospel.* Minneapolis: Fortress, 2000.

Koester, Helmut. *Ancient Christian Gospels: Their History and Development.* London: SCM; Philadelphia: Trinity Press International, 1990.

Lührmann, Dieter. *Die Redaktion der Logienquelle.* WMANT 33. Neukirchen Vkuyn: Neukirchener Verlag, 1969.

Michel, Hans-Joachim. *Die Abschiedsrede des Paulus an die Kirche Apg 20, 17–38.* SANT 35. Munich: Kösel, 1973.

Reed, Jonathan. "The Social Map of Q." Pages 17–36 in *Conflict and Invention: Literary, Rhetorical, and Social Studies on the Sayings Gospel Q.* Edited by John Kloppenborg. Valley Forge, Pa.: Trinity Press International, 1995.

Robbins, Vernon K. "Enthymemic Texture in the Gospel of Thomas." Pages 343–66 in *SBL Seminar Papers, 1998.* SBLSP 37. Atlanta: Scholars Press, 1998.

————. "Progymnastic Rhetorical Composition and Pre-Gospel Traditions: A New Approach." Pages 111–47 in *The Synoptic Gospels: Source Criticism and the New Literary Criticism.* Edited by Camille Focant. BETL 110. Leuven: Leuven University Press, 1993.

Robinson, James. "LOGOI SOPHON: On the Gattung of Q." Pages 71–113 in *Trajectories through Early Christianity.* Edited by James M. Robinson and Helmut Koester. Philadelphia: Fortress, 1971.

Schulz, Siegfried. *Q: Die Spruchquelle der Evangelisten*. Zürich: Theologischer Verlag, 1972.

Tödt, Heinz. *Der Menschensohn in der synoptischen Überlieferung*. Gütersloh: Mohn, 1959.

Tuckett, Christopher. *Q and the History of Early Christianity*. Edinburgh: T&T Clark, 1996.

7.3. The Gospels and the Acts of the Apostles

Allison, Dale C. *Jesus of Nazareth: Millenarian Prophet*. Minneapolis: Fortress, 1998.

————. *The New Moses: A Matthean Typology*. Edinburgh: T&T Clark, 1993.

Best, Ernest Best. *The Temptation and The Passion: The Markan Soteriology*. 2d ed. SNTSMS 2. Cambridge: Cambridge University Press, 1990.

Betz, Hans Dieter. *The Sermon on the Mount: A Commentary on the Sermon on the Mount, including the Sermon on the Plain (Matthew 5:3–7:27 and Luke 6:20–49)*. Hermeneia. Minneapolis: Fortress, 1995.

Bloomquist, L. Gregory. "The Rhetoric of the Historical Jesus?" Pages 98–117 in *Whose Historical Jesus?* Edited by M. Desjardins and W. Arnal. Studies in Christianity and Judaism 7. Waterloo: Wilfrid Laurier Press, 1997.

————, "Rhetorical Argumentation and the Culture of Apocalyptic: A Socio-Rhetorical Analysis of Luke 21." Pages 173–209 in *The Rhetorical Interpretation of Scripture: Essays from the 1996 Malibu Conference*. Edited by Stanley E. Porter and Dennis L. Stamps. JSNTSup 180. Sheffield: Sheffield Academic Press, 1999.

Boring, Eugene. *Sayings of the Risen Jesus*. SNTSMS 46. Cambridge: Cambridge University Press, 1982.

Bousset, Wilhelm. *Kyrios Christos*. Translated by John E. Steely. Nashville: Abingdon, 1970.

Brandenburger, Egon. *Markus 13 und die Apokalyptik*. Göttingen: Vandenhoeck & Ruprecht, 1984.

Collins, Adela Yarbro. *The Beginnings of the Gospel: Probings of Mark in Context*. Minneapolis: Fortress, 1992.

Conzelmann, Hans. *The Theology of Luke*. Translated by G. Buswell. New York: Harper & Row, 1961.

Crossan, John Dominic. *In Parables: The Challenge of the Historical Jesus*. New York: Harper & Row, 1973.

Fitzmyer, Joseph A. *The Gospel according to Luke*. 2 vols. AB 28–28A. Garden City, N.Y.: Doubleday, 1981.

Guelich, Robert A. *Mark 1–8:26*. WBC 34A. Dallas: Word, 1989.

Gundry, Robert H. *Mark: A Commentary on His Apology for the Cross*. Grand Rapids: Eerdmans, 1993.

Horsley, Richard. *Jesus and the Spiral of Violence: Popular Jewish Resistance in Roman Palestine.* San Francisco: Harper & Row, 1987.

———. "Wisdom and Apocalypticism in Mark." Pages 223–44 in *In Search of Wisdom: Essays in Memory of John G. Gammie.* Edited by L. G. Perdue et al. Louisville: Westminster John Knox, 1993.

Keck, Leander E. "The Spirit and the Dove." *NTS* 17 (1970–71): 41–67.

Koester, Helmut. "Apocryphal and Canonical Gospels." *HTR* 73 (1980): 105–30.

Lambrecht, Jan. *Once More Astonished: The Parables of Jesus.* New York: Crossroad, 1981.

Lohmeyer, Ernst. *Das Evangelium des Markus.* 16th ed. KEK 2. Göttingen: Vandenhoeck & Ruprecht, 1963.

Mack, Burton L. "Teaching in Parables: Elaboration in Mark 4:1–34." Pages 143–60 in *Patterns of Persuasion in the Gospels.* Edited by Burton Mack and Vernon K. Robbins. Sonoma, Calif: Polebridge, 1989.

Mack, Burton L., and Vernon K. Robbins, *Patterns of Persuasion in the Gospels.* Sonoma, Calif.: Polebridge, 1989.

Malherbe, Abraham J. "The Christianization of a Topos (Luke 12:13–34)." *NovT* 38 (1996): 123–35.

Mauser, Ulrich. *Christ in the Wilderness: The Wilderness Theme in the Second Gospel and Its Basis in the Biblical Tradition.* London: SCM, 1963.

Meynet, Roland. "Qui donc est 'le plus fort'? Analyse rhétorique de Mc 3,22–30; Mt 12,22–37; Luc 11,14–26." *RB* 90 (1983): 334–50.

Moxnes, Halvor. *The Economy of the Kingdom: Social Conflict and Economic Relations in Luke's Gospel.* Philadelphia: Fortress, 1988.

Nickelsburg, George W. E. "Riches, the Rich, and God's Judgment in *1 Enoch* 92–105 and the Gospel According to Luke." *NTS* 25 (1978): 324–44.

Robbins, Vernon K. "From Enthymeme to Theology in Luke 11:1–13." Pages 191–214 in *Literary Studies in Luke-Acts: A Collection of Essays in Honor of Joseph B. Tyson.* Edited by R. P. Thompson and T. E. Phillips. Macon, Ga.: Mercer University Press, 1998.

———. *Jesus the Teacher: A Socio-Rhetorical Interpretation of Mark.* Minneapolis: Fortress, 1992.

———. "Mark 1.14–20: An Interpretation at the Intersection of Jewish and Graeco-Roman Traditions." *NTS* 28 (1982): 220–36.

———. "Rhetorical Composition and the Beelzebul Controversy." Pages 161–93 in *Patterns of Persuasion in the Gospels.* Edited by Burton L. Mack and Vernon K. Robbins. Sonoma, Calif.: Polebridge, 1989.

———. "Rhetorical Ritual: Apocalyptic Discourse in Mark 13." Pages 95–121 in *Vision and Persuasion: Rhetorical Dimensions of Apocalyptic Discourse.* Edited by Gregory Carey and L. Gregory Bloomquist. St. Louis: Chalice, 1999.

————. "Summons and Outline in Mark: The Three-Step Progression." *NovT* 23 (1981): 97–114. Repr., Pages 103–20 in *The Composition of Mark's Gospel: Selected Studies from Novum Testamentum*. Edited by David E. Orton. Brill's Readers in Biblical Studies 3. Leiden: Brill, 1999.

Roth, Wolfgang Roth. *Hebrew Gospel: Cracking the Code of Mark*. Oak Park, Ill.: Meyer-Stone, 1988.

Sanders, E. P. *Jesus and Judaism*. Philadelphia: Fortress, 1985.

Stauffer, Ethelbert. *Christ and the Caesars: Historical Sketches*. Translated by K. and Ronald Gregor Smith. Philadelphia: Westminster, 1955.

Taylor, Vincent. *The Gospel According to St. Mark*. London: Macmillan, 1952.

Tolbert, Mary Ann. *Sowing the Gospel: Mark's World in Literary-Historical Perspective*. Minneapolis: Fortress, 1989.

Tuñi Vancells, J. O. "El cuarto evangelio y el tiempo: Notas para un estudio de la concepción del tiempo en el cuarto Evangelio." *Estudios eclesiásticos* 57 (1982): 129–54.

7.4. Paul, Eschatology/Apocalyptic, and the Use of the Old Testament

Baird, William. "Pauline Eschatology in Hermeneutical Perspective." *NTS* 17 (1971): 314–27.

Baumgarten, Jörg. *Paulus und die Apokalyptik: Die Auslegung apokalyptischer Überlieferungen in den echten Paulusbriefen*. WMANT 44. Neukirchen-Vluyn: Neukirchener Verlag, 1975.

Beker, J. Christiaan. *Paul the Apostle: The Triumph of God in Life and Thought*. Philadelphia: Fortress, 1980.

Court, John M. "Paul and the Apocalyptic Pattern." Pages 57–66 in *Paul and Paulinism: Essays in Honour of C. K. Barrett*. Edited by M. D. Hooker and S. G. Wilson. London: SPCK, 1982.

DeBoer, Martinus C. "Paul and Apocalyptic Eschatology." Pages 345–83 in *The Origins of Apocalypticism in Judaism and Christianity*. Vol. 1 of *The Encyclopedia of Apocalypticism*. Edited by J. J. Collins. New York: Continuum, 1998.

Delling, Gerhard. "Zur eschatologischen Bestimmtheit der Paulinischen Theologie." Pages 57–101 in *Zeit und Endzeit: Zwei Vorlesungen zur Theologie des Neuen Testaments*. BibS(N) 58. Neukirchen-Vluyn: Neukirchener Verlag, 1970.

Donfried, Karl Paul. "The Kingdom of God in Paul." Pages 175–90 in *The Kingdom of God in Twentieth Century Interpretation*. Edited by Wendell Willis. Peabody, Mass.: Hendrickson, 1987.

Dunn, James D. G. *The Theology of Paul the Apostle*. Grand Rapids: Eerdmans, 1998.

Ellis, E. Earle. *Paul's Use of the Old Testament*. Edinburgh and London: Oliver & Boyd, 1957.

Gager, John G. "Functional Diversity in Paul's Use of End-Time Language." *JBL* 89 (1970): 325–37.

Hall, Robert G. "Arguing Like an Apocalypse: Galatians and an Ancient Topos outside the Greco-Roman Rhetorical Tradition." *NTS* 42 (1996): 434–53.

Hays, Richard B. *Echoes of Scripture in the Letters of Paul.* New Haven: Yale University Press, 1989.

————. " 'The Righteous One' As Eschatological Deliverer: A Case Study in Paul's Apocalyptic Hermeneutics." Pages 191–215 in *Apocalyptic and the New Testament: Essays in Honor of J. Louis Martyn.* Edited by Joel Marcus and Marion L. Soards. JSNTSup 24. Sheffield: JSOT Press, 1989.

Howell, Don N. "Pauline Eschatological Dualism and its Resulting Tensions." *TJ* 14 (1993): 3–24.

Keck, Leander E. "Paul and Apocalyptic Theology." *Int* 38 (1984): 229–41.

Koch, Dietrich-Alex. *Die Schrift als Zeuge des Evangeliums: Untersuchungen zur Verwendung und zum Verständnis der Schrift bei Paulus.* Tübingen: Mohr Siebeck, 1986.

Longenecker, Richard N. "The Nature of Paul's Early Eschatology." *NTS* 31 (1985): 85–95.

Martyn, J. L. *Galatians.* AB 33A. New York: Doubleday, 1997.

Matlock, R. Barry. *Unveiling the Apocalyptic Paul: Paul's Interpreters and the Rhetoric of Criticism.* JSNTSup 127. Sheffield: Sheffield Academic Press, 1996.

Meeks, Wayne A. "Social Functions of Apocalyptic Language in Pauline Christianity." Pages 687–705 in *Apocalypticism in the Mediterranean World and the Near East.* Edited by David Hellholm. Tübingen: Mohr Seibeck, 1983.

O'Day, Gail R. "Jeremiah 9:22–23 and 1 Corinthians 1:26–31: A Study in Intertextuality." *JBL* 109 (1990): 259–67.

Roetzel, Calvin. "Paul As Organic Intellectual: The Shaper of Apocalyptic Myths." Pages in 221–43 in *Common Life in the Early Church.* Edited by Julian Hills. Harrisburg, Pa.: Trinity Press International, 1998.

Sahlin, Harald. "The New Exodus of Salvation according to Paul." Pages 81–95 in *The Root of the Vine: Essays in Biblical Theology.* Edited by Anton Friedrich et al. London: Dacre, 1953.

Schweitzer, Albert. *The Mysticism of Paul the Apostle.* Translated by William Montgomery. New York: Henry Holt, 1931.

Segal, Alan F. *Paul the Convert: The Apostolate and Apostasy of Saul the Pharisee.* New Haven: Yale University Press, 1990.

————. "Paul's Thinking about Resurrection in Its Jewish Context." *NTS* 44 (1998): 400–419.

Silva, Moisés. "Old Testament in Paul." Pages 630–42 in *Dictionary of Paul and His Letters.* Edited by Gerald F. Hawthorne et al. Downers Grove, Ill.: InterVarsity, 1993.

Soards, Marion L. "Paul: Apostle and Apocalyptic Visionary." *BTB* 16 (1986): 148–50.

Tabor, James D. *Things Unutterable: Paul's Ascent to Paradise in its Greco-Roman, Judaic, and Early Christian Contexts.* Lanham, Md.: University Press of America, 1986.

Wiefel, Wolfgang. "Die Hauptrichtung des Wandels im eschatalogischen Denken des Paulus." TZ 30 (1974): 65–81.

7.5. The Pauline Epistles

Barclay, John M. G. "Conflict in Thessalonica." *CBQ* 55 (1993): 512–30.

Belleville, Linda L. "A Letter of Apologetic Self-commendation." *NovT* 31 (1989): 142–63.

Betz, Hans Dieter. *Der Apostel Paulus und die sokratische Tradition. Eine exegetische Untersuchung zu seiner "Apologie" 2 Korinther 10–13.* Tübingen: Mohr Siebeck, 1972.

Bruce, F. F. *1 and 2 Thessalonians.* WBC 45. Waco, Tex.: Word, 1982.

Chevallier, Max-Alain. "L'argumentation de Paul dans II Corinthiens 10 à 13." *RHPR* 70 (1990): 3–15.

De Boer, Martinus C. *The Defeat of Death: Apocalyptic Eschatology in 1 Corinthians 15 and Romans 5.* JSNTSup 22. Sheffield: JSOT Press, 1988.

deSilva, David A. "'Worthy of His Honor': Honor Discourse and Social Engineering in 1 Thessalonians." *JSNT* 64 (1996): 49–79

Donfried, Karl P. "The Cults of Thessalonica and the Thessalonian Correspondence." *NTS* 31 (1985): 336–56.

Doughty, Darrell J. "The Presence and Future of Salvation in Corinth." *ZNW* 66 (1975): 61–90.

Eriksson, Anders. *Traditions As Rhetorical Proof: Pauline Argumentation in 1 Corinthians.* ConBNT 29. Stockholm: Almqvist & Wiksell, 1998.

Fee, Gordon D. *The First Epistle to the Corinthians.* NICNT. Grand Rapids: Eerdmans, 1987.

Fitzmyer, Joseph A. "Glory Reflected on the Face of Christ (2 Cor 3:7–4:6) and a Palestinian Jewish Motif." *TS* 42 (1981): 630–44.

Gillman, John. "Signals of Transformation in 1 Thessalonians 4:13–18." *CBQ* 47 (1985): 263–81.

Hellholm, David. "Enthymemic Argumentation in Paul: The Case of Romans 6." Pages 119–79 in *Paul and His Hellenistic Context.* Edited by Troels Engberg-Pedersen. Minneapolis: Fortress, 1995.

Hester, James D. "A Fantasy Theme Analysis of 1 Thessalonians." In *Rhetorical Analyses of Scripture: Papers at the Florence Conference, 1998.* Edited by Dennis Stamps. Sheffield: Sheffield Academic Press, forthcoming.

————. "The Invention of 1 Thessalonians: A Proposal." Pages 251–79 in *Rhetoric, Theology and Scripture*. Edited by Stanley Porter and Tom Olbricht. JSNTSup 131. Sheffield: Sheffield Academic Press, 1996.

Hill, C. E. "Paul's Understanding of Christ's Kingdom in 1 Corinthians 15:20–28." *NovT* 30 (1988): 297–320.

Howard, J. K. "'Christ our Passover': A Study of the Passover-Exodus Theme in 1 Corinthians." *EvQ* 41 (1969): 97–108.

Johnson, Elizabeth. *The Function of Apocalyptic and Wisdom Traditions in Romans 9–11*. SBLDS 109. Atlanta: Scholars Press, 1989.

Lindemann, Andreas. "Paulus und die Korinthische Eschatologie: Zur These von einer 'Entwicklung' im Paulinischen Denken." *NTS* 37 (1991): 373–99.

Malan, F. S. "The Use of the Old Testament in 1 Corinthians." *Neot* 14 (1981): 134–70.

McCant, Jerry W. "Paul's Thorn of Rejected Apostleship." *NTS* 34 (1988): 550–72.

Mearns, Christopher L. "Early Eschatological Development in Paul: The Evidence of 1 Corinthians." *JSNT* 22 (1984): 19–35.

————. "Early Eschatological Development in Paul: The Evidence of I and II Thessalonians." *NTS* 27 (1981): 137–57.

Mitchell, Margaret M. *Paul and the Rhetoric of Reconciliation: An Exegetical Investigation of the Language and Composition of 1 Corinthians*. HUT 28. Tübingen: Mohr Siebeck; Louisville: Westminster John Knox, 1991.

Oropeza, B. J. "Apostasy in the Wilderness: Paul's Message to the Corinthians in a State of Eschatological Liminality." *JSNT* 75 (1999): 69–86.

————. "Laying to Rest the Midrash: Paul's Message on Meat Sacrificed to Idols in Light of the Deuteronomic Tradition." *Bib* 79 (1998): 57–68.

————. *Paul and Apostasy: Eschatology, Perseverance and Falling Away in the Corinthian Congregation*. WUNT. Tübingen: Mohr Siebeck, 2000.

Plank, Karl. *Paul and the Irony of Affliction*. Atlanta: Scholars Press, 1987.

Pogoloff, Stephen M. *Logos and Sophia: The Rhetorical Situation of 1 Corinthians*. SBLDS 134. Atlanta: Scholars Press, 1992.

Probst, Hermann. *Paulus und der Brief: Die Rhetorik des antiken Briefes als Form der paulinischen Korintherkorrsepondenz (1 Kor 8–10)*. WUNT 2/45. Tübingen: Mohr Siebeck, 1991.

Ramsaran, Rollin A. *Liberating Words: Paul's Use of Rhetorical Maxims in 1 Corinthians 1–10*. Valley Forge, Pa.: Trinity Press International, 1996.

Schüssler Fiorenza, Elisabeth. "Rhetorical Situation and Historical Reconstruction in 1 Corinthians." *NTS* 33 (1987): 386–403.

Scott, James M. "The Triumph of God in 2 Cor 2:14." *NTS* 42 (1996): 260–81.

Söding, Thomas. "Der Erste Thessalonicherbreif und die frühepaulinische Evangeliumsverkündigung. Zur Frage einer Entwicklung der paulinischen Theologie." *BZ* 35 (1991): 180–203.

Thiselton, Anthony C. "Realized Eschatology at Corinth." *NTS* 24 (1977–78): 510–26.

Wanamaker, Charles A. *The Epistles to the Thessalonians.* NIGTC. Grand Rapids: Eerdmans, 1990.

Watson, Duane F. "Paul's Appropriation of Apocalyptic Discourse: The Rhetorical Strategy of 1 Thessalonians." Pages 61–80 in *Vision and Persuasion.* Edited by Greg Carey and L. Gregory Bloomquist. St. Louis: Chalice, 1999.

Webb, W. J. *Returning Home: New Covenant and Second Exodus as the Context for 2 Corinthians 6:14–7:1.* JSNTSup 85. Sheffield: JSOT Press, 1993.

Welborn, L. L. *Politics and Rhetoric in the Corinthian Epistles.* Macon, Ga.: Mercer University Press, 1997.

Witherington, Ben. *Conflict and Community in Corinth: A Socio-Rhetorical Commentary on 1 and 2 Corinthians.* Grand Rapids: Eerdmans, 1995.

Yeo, Khiok-Khng. *Rhetorical Interaction in 1 Corinthians 8 and 10: A Formal Analysis with Preliminary Suggestions for a Chinese, Cross-Cultural Hermeneutic.* BibInt 9. Leiden: Brill, 1995.

Young, Frances, and David F. Ford. *Meaning and Truth in 2 Corinthians.* Cambridge: SPCK, 1987.

7.6. Hebrews and the Catholic Epistles

Baasland, E. "Der Jakobusbrief als neutestamentliche Weisheitsschrift." *ST* 36 (1982): 119–39.

———. "Literarische Form, Thematik und geschichtliche Einordunung des Jakobusbriefes." *ANRW* 25.5:3646–84.

Baker, William R. *Personal Speech-Ethics in the Epistle of James.* WUNT 2/68. Tübingen: Mohr Siebeck, 1995.

Bauckham, Richard. "The Delay of the Parousia." *TynBul* 31 (1980): 3–36.

———. "James, 1 and 2 Peter, Jude." Pages 303–17 in *It is Written: Scripture Citing Scripture.* Edited by D. A. Carson and H. G. M. Williamson. Cambridge: Cambridge University Press, 1988.

———. James: *Wisdom of James, Disciple of Jesus the Sage.* New York: Routledge, 1999.

———. *Jude, 2 Peter.* WBC 50. Waco, Tex.: Word, 1983.

Black, Matthew. "The Maranatha Invocation and Jude 14, 15 (I Enoch 1:9)." Pages 189–96 in *Christ and Spirit in the New Testament: In Honour of Charles Francis Digby Moule.* Edited by Barnabas Lindars and Stephen S. Smalley. Cambridge: Cambridge University Press, 1973.

Cantinat, Jean C. M. *Les Épitres de Saint Jacques et de Saint Jude.* SB. Paris: Gabalda, 1973.

Charles, J. Daryl. *Literary Strategy in the Epistle of Jude.* Scranton, Pa.: University of Scranton Press, 1993.

Davids, Peter H. *The Epistle of James. A Commentary on the Greet Text.* NIGTC. Grand Rapids: Eerdmans, 1982.

Deppe, Dean B. "The Sayings of Jesus in the Epistle of James." Diss., University of Amsterdam. Chelsea, Mich.: Bookcrafters, 1989.

deSilva, David. *Despising Shame: Honor Discourse and Community Maintenance in the Epistle to the Hebrews.* SBLDS 152. Atlanta: Scholars Press, 1995.

Dibelius, Martin. *James: A Commentary on the Epistle of James.* Revised by H. Greeven. Translated by M. A. Williams. Hermeneia. Philadelphia: Fortress, 1975.

Fry, E. "The Testing of Faith: A Study of the Structure of the Book of James." *BT* 29 (1978): 427–35.

Gerdmar, Anders. *Rethinking the Judaism-Hellenism Dichotomy: A Historiographical Case Study of Second Peter and Jude.* ConBNT 36. Stockholm: Almqvist & Wiksell, 2001.

Halson, B. R. "The Epistle of James: 'Christian Wisdom'?" *SE* 4 (1968): 308–14.

Hartin, Patrick J. *James and the Q Sayings of Jesus.* JSNTSup 47. Sheffield: JSOT Press, 1991.

Hoppe, Rudolf. *Der theologische Hintergrund des Jakobusbriefes.* FB 28. Würzburg: Echter Verlag, 1977.

Johnson, Luke Timothy. "Friendship with the World/Friendship with God: A Study of Discipleship in James." Pages 166–83 in *Discipleship in the New Testament.* Edited by F. Segovia. Philadelphia: Fortress, 1985.

———. *The Letter of James.* AB 37A. Garden City, N.Y.: Doubleday, 1995.

Laws, Sophie. *The Epistle of James.* HNTC. San Francisco: Harper & Row, 1980.

Légasse, Simon. "Les pauvres en Esprit et les 'Volontaires' de Qumran." *NTS* 8 (1962): 336–45.

Luck, Ulrich. "Der Jakobusbrief und die Theologie des Paulus." *TGl* 61 (1971): 161–79.

———. "Weisheit und Leiden: Zum Problem Paulus und Jakobus." *TLZ* 92 (1967): 253–58.

Martin, Ralph P. "The Life-Setting of the Epistle of James in the Light of Jewish History." Pages 97–103 in *Biblical and Near Eastern Studies: Essays in Honor of William Sanford LaSor.* Edited by G. Tuttle. Grand Rapids: Eerdmans, 1978.

Mayor, James B. *The Epistle of James.* London: Macmillan, 1892. Repr. of 3d edition. Grand Rapids: Kregel, 1990.

Osborn, C. D. "The Christological Use of 1 Enoch i.9 in Jude 14, 15," *NTS* 23 (1976–77): 334–41.

Penner, Todd C. *The Epistle of James and Eschatology: Re-reading an Ancient Christian Letter.* JSNTSup 121. Sheffield: JSOT Press, 1996.

Ropes, James H. *A Critical and Exegetical Commentary on the Epistle of St. James*. ICC. Edinburgh: T&T Clark, 1916.

Seitz, O. J. F. "Afterthoughts on the Term 'Dipsychos.'" *NTS* 4 (1957): 327–34.

———. "Antecedents and Significance of the Term 'DIPSYCHOS.'" *JBL* 66 (1947): 211–19.

———. "James and the Law." *SE* 2 (1964): 472–86.

Soucek, J. B. "Zu den Problemen des Jakobusbriefes." *EvT* 18 (1958): 460–69.

von Allmen, D. "L'apocalyptique juive et le retard de la parousie en II Pierre 3:1–13." *RTP* 16 (1966): 256–64.

Wachob, Wesley H. "'The Rich in Faith' and 'the Poor in Spirit': The Socio-Rhetorical Function of a Saying of Jesus in the Epistle of James." Ph.D.diss., Emory University, 1993.

———. The Voice of Jesus in the Social Rhetoric of James. SNTSMS 106. Cambridge: Cambridge University Press, 2000.

Wachob, Wesley H. and Luke Timothy Johnson. "The Sayings of Jesus in the Letter of James." Pages 430–50 in *Authenticating the Words of Jesus*. Edited by Bruce Chilton and Craig A. Evans. Leiden: Brill, 1999.

Ward, Roy B. "The Communal Concern of the Epistle of James." Ph.D. diss., Harvard University, 1966.

———. "James, Letter of." *IDBSup*, 469–70.

———. "Partiality in the Assembly, James 2:2–4." *HTR* 62 (1969): 87–97.

———. "The Works of Abraham: James 2:14–26." *HTR* 61 (1968): 283–90.

Watson, Duane F. *Invention, Arrangement, and Style: Rhetorical Criticism of Jude and 2 Peter*. SBLDS 104. Atlanta: Scholars Press, 1988.

7.7. The Book of Revelation

Aune, David E. *Revelation*. 3 vols. WBC 52. Dallas: Word, 1997–98.

———. "The Social Matrix of the Apocalypse of John." *BR* 26 (1981): 16–32.

Beale, G. K. *John's Use of the Old Testament in Revelation*. JSNTSup 116. Sheffield: Sheffield Academic Press, 1998.

———. "A Reconsideration of the Text of Daniel in the Apocalypse." *Bib* 67 (1986): 536–43.

———. *Revelation*. NIGTC. Grand Rapids: Eerdmans, 1998

———. *The Use of Daniel in Jewish Apocalyptic Literature and in the Revelation of St. John*. Lanham, Md.: University Press of America, 1984.

Buchanan, George Wesley. *The Book of Revelation*. Lewiston, N.Y.: Mellen, 1993.

Caird, G. B. *The Revelation of St. John*. London: Black, 1966.

Cambier, J. "Les images de l'Ancient Testament dans l'Apocalypse de Saint Jean." *NRT* 77 (1955): 113–22.

deSilva, David A. "Honor Discourse and the Rhetorical Strategy of the Apocalypse." *JSNT* 71 (1998): 79–100.

——. "The 'Image of the Beast' and the Christians in Asia Minor." *TJ* 12 ns (1991): 185–208.

——. "The Persuasive Strategy of the Apocalypse: A Socio-Rhetorical Investigation of Revelation 14:6–13." Pages 785–806 in volume 2 of the *SBL Seminar Papers, 1998*. 2 vols. SBLSP 37. Atlanta: Scholars Press, 1998.

——. "The Revelation to John: A Case Study in Apocalyptic Propaganda and the Maintenance of Sectarian Identity." *Sociological Analysis* 53 (1992): 375–439.

——. "A Socio-Rhetorical Investigation of Revelation 14:6–13: A Call to Act Justly toward the Just and Judging God." *BBR* 9 (1999): 65–117.

Fekkes, J. *Isaiah and Prophetic Traditions in the Book of Revelation: Visionary Antecedents and their Developments*. JSNTSup 93. Sheffield: JSOT Press, 1994.

Ford, J. M. *Revelation*. AB 38. Garden City, N.Y.: Doubleday, 1975.

Hemer, Colin J. *The Letters to the Seven Churches of Asia in their Local Setting*. JSNTSup 11. Sheffield: JSOT Press, 1986.

Johns, Loren L. "The Lamb in the Rhetorical Program of the Apocalypse of John." Pages 762–84 in volume 2 of the *SBL Seminar Papers, 1998*. 2 vols. SBLSP 37. Atlanta: Scholars Press, 1998.

Kirby, John T. "The Rhetorical Situations of Revelation 1–3." *NTS* 34 (1988): 197–207.

LeGrys, A. "Conflict and Vengeance in the Book of Revelation." *ExpTim* 104 (1992): 76–80.

Lohse, Eduard. "Die Alttestamentliche Sprache des Sehers Johannes." *ZNW* 52 (1961): 122–26.

Mealy, J. W. *After the Thousand Years: Resurrection and Judgement in Revelation 20*. JSNTSup 70. Sheffield: JSOT Press, 1992.

Mounce, Robert H. *The Book of Revelation*. Rev. ed. NICNT. Grand Rapids: Eerdmans, 1998.

Moyise, Steve. *The Old Testament in Revelation*. JSNTSup 115. Sheffield: Sheffield Academic Press, 1995.

Paulien, John. "Elusive Allusions: The Problematic Use of the Old Testament in Revelation." *BR* 23 (1988): 37–53.

Ramsey, William M. *The Letters to the Seven Churches of Asia and their Place in the Plan of the Apocalypse*. London: Hodder & Stoughton, 1904.

Royality, Robert M. "The Rhetoric of Revelation." Pages 596–617 in volume 2 of the *SBL Seminar Papers, 1997*. 2 vols. SBLSP 36. Atlanta: Scholars Press, 1997.

Ruiz, J. P. *Ezekiel in the Apocalypse: The Transformation of Prophetic Language in Revelation 16:17–19:10*. Frankfurt: Peter Lang, 1989.

Scobie, C. H. H. "Local References in the Letters to the Seven Churches." *NTS* 39 (1993): 606–24.

Shea W. H. "The Location and Significance of Armageddon in Rev 16:16." *AUSS* 18 (1980): 157–62.

Talbert, Charles H. *The Apocalypse: A Reading of the Revelation of John.* Louisville: Westminster John Knox, 1994.

Thompson, Leonard L. *The Book of Revelation: Apocalypse and Empire.* New York: Oxford University Press, 1990.

Vanhoye, A. "L'utilisation du livre d'Ezékiel dans l'Apocalypse." *Bib* 43 (1962): 436–76.

8. The Social and Cultural World of the New Testament

Cotter, Wendy. *Miracles in Greco-Roman Antiquity: A Sourcebook for the Study of New Testament Miracle Stories.* London: Routledge, 1999.

Cuss, Dominique. *Imperial Cult and Honorary Terms in the New Testament.* Fribourg: Universitätsverlag, 1974.

Elliott, John H. *What Is Social-Scientific Criticism?* Minneapolis: Fortress, 1993.

Ferguson, Everett. *Demonology of the Early Christian World.* Symposium 12. Lewiston, N.Y.: Mellen, 1984.

Friesen, Steven. *Twice Neokoros: Ephesus, Asia, and the Cult of the Flavian Imperial Family.* Leiden: Brill, 1993.

Malherbe, Abraham J. "Hellenistic Moralists and the New Testament." *ANRW* 26.1:267–333.

———. *Moral Exhortation, A Greco-Roman Sourcebook.* LEC. Philadelphia: Westminster, 1986.

Malina, Bruce J. *The New Testament World: Insights from Cultural Anthropology.* Rev. ed. Atlanta: Knox, 1993.

Moxnes, Halvor. "Honor and Shame." Pages 19–40 in *The Social Sciences and New Testament Interpretation.* Edited by Richard L. Rohrbaugh. Peabody, Mass.: Hendrickson, 1996.

Peacock, James L. *The Anthropological Lens: Harsh Light, Soft Focus.* Cambridge: Cambridge University Press, 1986.

Pilch, John J. *The Cultural Dictionary of the Bible.* Collegeville, Minn.; Liturgical Press, 1999.

Pilch, John J., and Bruce J. Malina, eds. *Biblical Social Values and Their Meaning: A Handbook.* Peabody, Mass.: Hendrickson, 1993.

Schürer, E. *The History of the Jewish People in the Age of Jesus Christ (175 B.C.–A.D. 135).* Revised and edited by G. Vermes et al. Vols. 1–3.2. Edinburgh: T&T Clark, 1973–87.

Index of Primary Sources

Hebrew Scriptures

[1] Scholarly convention uses the Gospel of Luke's versification to refer to Q texts.

Ancient Jewish and Christian Sources

Greek and Latin Authors

Index of Modern Authors